Healing Centers & Retreats

Healthy Getaways for Every Body and Budget

By Jenifer Miller

John Muir Publications

John Muir Publications, P.O. Box 613, Santa Fe, New Mexico 87504

Printed in the United States of America.
First edition. First printing August 1998.

Library of Congress Cataloging-in-Publication Data
Miller, Jenifer, 1968–
    Healing centers and retreats: healthy getaways for every body and budget / by Jenifer Miller.
    p.   cm.
    Includes index.
    ISBN 1-56261-404-5 (pbk.)
1. Health resorts—United States—Directories. 2. Health resorts—Canada—Directories.
3. Alternative medicine—United States—Directories. 4. Alternative medicine—Canada—
Directories.
I. Title.
RA805.M59   1998
613'.122'02573—dc21   98-25847
                                                                        CIP

Editors: Sarah Baldwin, Bruce Owens
Production: Mladen Baudrand, Nikki Rooker
Cover Design: Marie J.T. Vigil
Typesetting: Diane Rigoli
Printer: Banta

Cover photos: *large*—Courtesy of the Association for Research and Enlightenment (A.R.E)
                small (2)—Courtesy of Canyon Ranch Health Resorts

Foreword by Burton Goldberg. In addition to publishing *Alternative Medicine, The Definitive Guide*,
Burton Goldberg is publisher of *Alternative Medicine Guide to Cancer, Alternative Medicine Guide to
Heart Disease, Alternative Medicine Guide to Chronic Fatigue, Fibromyalgia and Environmental Illness,
Alternative Medicine Guide to Women's Health*, and *Alternative Medicine* magazine.

Distributed to the book trade by
Publishers Group West
Berkeley, California

Table of Contents

Healing Centers and Retreats in the United States

Healing Centers and Retreats in Canada

Other Healing Centers

Foreword

This is a book we all could use. These days, so many of us work too hard and too long, we rush to get the kids to after-school and weekend activities, we worry about finances and the future, and, in the process, we often neglect ourselves. This book gives you the opportunity to stop neglecting yourself and start taking care of both your mental and your physical health. The choices listed here—healing centers and retreats throughout the United States and Canada—can give you a jump-start on a healthier way of living. The approaches range from natural food therapies to massage therapy, from shiatsu to shamanism.

As publisher of *Alternative Medicine* magazine, I've seen how more and more people are willing to take responsibility for their health and well-being. They know they can do something about those nagging illnesses and problems. They know help is out there, in both conventional and alternative forms. Over the years, so-called "alternative" therapies have become so widely used and accepted that they're not so alternative anymore. In fact, according to the *New England Journal of Medicine*, in recent years Americans made more visits to alternative practitioners than to primary care physicians. Over 40 percent of the population has tried some form of alternative healing.

One of the biggest obstacles to good health today is stress. Untreated, stress can cause serious problems. Chronic stress hurts our immune systems and causes illnesses such as heart disease, high blood pressure, and other afflictions, as well as less serious problems like anxiety and headaches. The National Institutes of Health actually recommends alternative healing therapies over conventional medicine for treating stress. The healing centers and retreats in this book can help you reverse stress-related health problems and prevent them, too.

This book invites you to doctor yourself in a truly enjoyable way. Whether you choose to have structural body work done, to detoxify and cleanse, or to improve your nutrition, you will see a change for the better. Our bodies are not designed to become ill—they are designed to heal and become healthy. It is up to us to walk that road and to honor our whole being. A healthy being is a healthy body, mind, and spirit.

Here's hoping you'll choose to use this book to create the health you're meant to have.

Burton Goldberg
"The Voice of Alternative Medicine"
Publisher and creator of *Alternative
Medicine: The Definitive Guide*

Acknowledgments

This book would not be possible without the loving help and constant support of my entire family, especially my phenomenal mother and father. Not only did they go far beyond the call of parental duty to help me gather information for this book, but they were always, always there for me. No one has parents like I do.

I am also grateful to the hundreds of people I spoke with while compiling this book. Many of you went far beyond providing information and thanked me wholeheartedly for taking on this project. I will repeat now, as I did then, that this book exists because of your efforts, and it is you who are to thank. In particular, I would like to thank Dr. Roger Jahnke of Health Action for his many referrals, including the one to the remarkable Dr. Ernest Shearer. I would also like to thank Tara Grace of Maui Visions Vacations, who was especially helpful in providing referrals to those remote Hawaiian centers I otherwise could not have listed. Thanks also to Anne Harding, who provided priceless support and creative feedback. Dr. Ann McCombs of the Center for Optimal Health managed to carve an hour out of her busy schedule to explain to me the dynamics of treating patients from a holistic perspective. As she is a board member of the American Holistic Medical Association, I am grateful that she could share her knowledge and experience with me.

The editorial team at John Muir Publications stands to be lauded for their decision to pursue this book project, and I thank them for choosing me as the author. And special thanks go out to my associates Karen Hill, Andrea Lundblad, and Deborah Wong, who were absolutely invaluable in helping me gather information and in providing the kind of support that can't be squeezed into a small sentence.

It would be criminal to forget Priscilla and Eulie for all the hair on my keyboard and the warm, sleepy looks. I would also like to send love and gratitude to my dear friend Megan Burke for the delicious linguini and encouragement, and to Deborah Kuznitz for making that call. Thanks also go out to Laura Winters, who still encourages me to achieve my dreams, and to Linda Jimenez, Kay Rynerson, and Penny Parker for supporting me in the darker days. I would also like to thank my mentor, Daisaku Ikeda, for showing me the way to a healthy, happy life.

About This Book

If you're like most people, you rarely carve out the time to focus on yourself and your health. Your life is filled with responsibilities—career, home, family, community—and it's hard to put your own well-being ahead of all those obligations. Even if you do make time for yourself, you may not have the knowledge or the practical experience to change years of bad habits. So you remind yourself to eat healthier, but you hardly ever do. You chide yourself for not starting an exercise program as the weeks pass by. You ignore the creaks and twinges and, sometimes, even the pain, thinking or hoping that eventually they'll just go away. Or maybe you do exercise and eat right, but still you feel fatigued, worn down by the stresses of everyday life.

This book is about taking the time to learn how to live a healthier life. It's about getting away from the daily grind, resting, and recovering from whatever ails you. It's about reconnecting with the healer within you and learning valuable skills for lifelong vitality. When you choose one of the getaways described in this book, you're taking the first step toward reclaiming your health. Whether you spend three days or a month at a retreat, even if you start out physically exhausted or spiritually depleted, you'll come home energized and committed to making positive changes in your life. And you'll learn through direct experience that total health encompasses body, mind, and spirit.

Healing Centers and Retreats Included in This Book

As a former editor for *Spa* magazine, I have had the opportunity to learn about the latest advances in health and healing. In selecting the centers for inclusion in this book, I talked to spa owners about their philosophies and compiled information from a variety of sources. I learned what it takes for a center to offer a healing experience: inviting surroundings, a dedicated and well-trained staff, and a commitment to helping people. I avoided centers that offered quick fixes and cure-alls.

I chose places offering a wide variety of programs that transcend the traditional spa experience. While many of the centers do offer familiar spa services, they also specialize in "alternative" treatments ranging from yoga, acupuncture, and various food therapies to wilderness survival training, Native American ceremonies, and sound therapy. Many of these treatments are not, in fact, new and experimental, as the word "alternative" suggests, but come from the ancient healing traditions of China, India, Europe, Latin America, and elsewhere. Though the centers and retreats in this book represent a broad range of approaches, all of them aim to help you rediscover your body's natural rhythms to gain greater control of your health.

The places in this book have been chosen for one overriding reason: to help you begin your journey to well-being.

How to Use This Book

The book provides 170 full-page listings, organized alphabetically first by state and then by center name. Canadian listings follow state listings. Each listing has as narrative section describing the center and its programs. This section is followed by practical information on various topics, including days and hours of operation, accommodations, rates, credit cards, meal plans, services, recreational activities, facilities, staff, special notes, nearby attractions, and directions. Prices listed throughout the book reflect American dollars, except for centers based in Canada, in which case the "$" symbol refers to Canadian dollars.

Following these 170 listings, about 60 additional healing centers and retreats are listed in Other Healing Centers. This section includes two types of places: residential centers and retreats that address serious medical conditions, such as cancer or AIDS, and outpatient centers with an alternative approach. The latter category includes some of the country's best holistic health care centers.

At the back of the book you'll find a resource guide and a glossary. The resource guide lists alternative health associations, educational facilities, and health benefit services. The glossary defines most services and treatments mentioned in the book—refer to it as you read through the listings so you understand exactly what each center is offering. Finally, three indices will help you navigate the book and find a center in an area or with an approach that appeals to you.

How to Choose the Healing Center That's Right for You

Your trip is for and about you—it's not about "shoulds" and "ought tos." This book includes more than 230 healing centers and retreats, and choosing the best one for you means asking lots of questions. First, think about what you want for the time you'll be away as well as your longterm goals for healthy living. Pick a center or retreat that offers programs you are excited about and can imagine fitting into your life after you return home.

Are you adventurous? Try ecotourism. At Angel's Nest of Mother Maui, for example, you can hike past remote Hawaiian lagoons and rare wild orchids, kayak amidst sea turtles, and take a helicopter ride to the top of a volcano—all while learning yogic breathwork and eating a vegetarian diet of local fruits and vegetables. If your idea of healing includes relaxing under the hands of an experienced masseuse at one of the world's most luxurious spas, try a place like The Peaks at Telluride or Tucson's Canyon Ranch, where the staff-to-guest ratio is three to one. Is your diet of french fries, coffee, and ice cream taking its toll? Try cleansing your system at a detoxifying center such as the We Care Holistic Health Center, where guests do juice fasts, or the Optimum Health Institute, which serves live organic vegan meals and offers classes on stress reduction and positive thinking.

As you are thinking about what kind of experience you want, take your physical needs and limitations into account. Are you able to hike every day? Can you handle a juice fast? At many centers, the meal plan is an essential part of the healing program, so make sure it appeals to you. If the brochure doesn't describe meals, ask for a copy of the menu. What about your geographic preferences—do you want to stay close to home or travel to a distant locale? Consider your need for personal space. Are you comfortable with group situations? Or do you need the seclusion and privacy of, say, the Hydeout, where only a few guests visit at any one time?

Your budget will also play a role in your decision. The fees for programs in this book range from under a hundred dollars up to thousands, depending on the program, location, length of stay, and season. If you are hoping that insurance will cover the costs, be sure to investigate beforehand. Most policies allow only a limited number of alternative health treatments, and then only when they address a specific ailment. In addition to these policy restrictions, most of the centers in this book don't accept insurance cards. Canada has a more open policy, and some of the Canadian centers do accept insurance. Inquire about your insurance policies as well as the policies of the centers before booking your stay.

Once you have narrowed your choices, call to request a brochure and discuss the programs offered. In some cases, the owner of the center may speak with you personally. See if you can establish a rapport with this person. Are your questions being answered? Do you feel confident enough to spend a week receiving meals, massage, or counseling from this person and his or her staff members? If you are contacting a larger spa or center, request the name of someone you can call with detailed questions. And ask for the names of guests or patients who have gone through the program.

Whatever your choice of getaway, you can count on discovering more about your health and on learning practical steps toward a better quality of life. The changes you make will have far-reaching effects on both you and your loved ones. As Charla Hermann of Hawkwind says of that center's philosophy, "First we heal ourselves, then our family, then the planet."

Healing Centers & Retreats

in the
United States

Hawkwind Earth Renewal Cooperative

P.O. Box 11
Valley Head, AL 35989
(205) 635-6304; fax (423) 629-9848

Set in the foothills of the Appalachians in northeast Alabama, Hawkwind Cooperative is a retreat and teaching center dedicated to the Earth's renewal. Primarily an interfaith circle, Hawkwind honors and encourages the individual path of personal and planetary healing through various alternative techniques, including those drawn from the ancient wisdom of indigenous peoples, hands-on energy, holotropic breathwork, harmonics, and sound therapy. The cooperative's 77 acres include Native American ceremonial grounds, campgrounds, gardens, and a sweat lodge.

Hawkwind directors Reverend Tarwater and Reverend Charla Hermann welcome guests to share in the healing experience enjoyed by the hundreds of friends and spiritual family that come together each month throughout the year. Tarwater, a craftsman, drum maker, and ceremonial leader of Lakota/Scottish heritage, also leads workshops. Hermann, a Wyoming native and former broadcasting industry veteran, directs Hawkwind's outreach and crisis services. Of Hawkwind's philosophy, Hermann comments, "First we heal ourselves, then our family, then the planet. Our work must grow corn for generations to come."

Hawkwind functions as a membership organization comprised of several co-ops (artist, food, and barter) and Will's Creek Trading Post, among other organizations. Family workshops and programs address topics like holistic health based on Native American earth practices, ceremonial healing skills, earth skills and herbs, rites of passage, a crisis support circle, drumming, and dancing. Monthly activities include a spirit healing dance, potluck dinners, and sweat lodge gatherings, including a moon lodge for women during their sacred time. Non-co-op members are welcome at most retreats, gatherings, and workshops, some of which are led by well-known teachers of Native American medicine, personal healing, and spiritual ecology.

In addition to workshops, Hawkwind offers a Teaching and Healing Circles video series in which Native American elders explain the principles of change and discuss solutions for personal and planetary healing. Grandfather Wallace Black Elk narrates *Return to the Sacred Hoop*, in which he shares his philosophy of ceremony and healing. Black Elk is an internationally renowned Lakota Sioux Elder.

Hours and Days of Operation: Weekend gatherings and workshops offered year-round. Some events require registration 90 days in advance.

Accommodations: 60 acres of campgrounds; bunkhouse for 12.

Rates: Vary according to services. Tuition for weekend programs $12–$150. No charge for participating in Native American ceremonies.

Credit Cards: AE, D, MC, V.

Meal Plans: Guests contribute to potluck meals.

Services: Rite-of-passage ceremonies, bodywork, massage, spiritual healing, dance, spiritual counseling, day care.

Facilities: 77-acre estate with Trading Post, barter co-op, artists' co-op, food co-op, Moon Lodge, community kitchen, outhouses, solar shower, organic garden, tepee circle with fire pits.

Staff: In addition to co-op staff, 15 volunteer healers.

Special Notes: Hawkwind is not a commune; reservations required for all visits.

Nearby Attractions: Caverns, parks, aquariums, museums.

Getting There: Central to Birmingham, Alabama; Atlanta, Georgia; and Chattanooga, Tennessee. Take Highway 285 from Atlanta's Hartsfield International Airport.

Uchee Pines Institute

30 Uchee Pines Road
Seale, AL 36875-5702
(334) 855-4764; fax (334) 855-4780

For 25 years, the Uchee Pines Institute has offered retreats to help people achieve and maintain total health in body, mind, and soul. Uchee is also known as Anvwodi, the Cherokee word for "get well place," and that is exactly what Calvin and Agatha Thrash envisioned when they founded Uchee Pines. Both Calvin and Agatha are medical doctors who have co-authored several books on natural remedies and preventive medicine.

Uchee is staffed by a team of Seventh-Day Adventists who specialize in natural methods of healing and want to help guests gain control of their health. Retreats provide a score of noninvasive remedies and educational seminars on preventive medicine. Participants learn what they can do naturally, for themselves and others, to combat disease. They are encouraged to rediscover the natural rhythms of their bodies through rest, a healthy diet, sunlight, fresh air, and community service, such as chopping wood or tending the orchard.

The 21-day retreats begin on Mondays. After meeting the staff and settling into a room, guests meet with a Lifestyle Counselor, who remains with them throughout the program. The counselor serves as both therapist and cheerleader, working closely with each guest to ensure that the natural healing can occur as quickly and thoroughly as possible. During the program, guests have a complete physical exam, two blood profiles, regular consultations with a physician, hydrotherapy and thermal treatments, exercise, and massage. Participants attend lectures and take classes on health, natural remedies, gardening, and cooking. They are also encouraged to get as much fresh air, sun, and water as they can tolerate. The program is enhanced by the peaceful rural setting, the simple vegetarian meals, and the chance to rest from the daily 9-to-5 grind. Though the seminars can be intense, there is plenty of time to relax, establish new friendships, and develop a more meaningful relationship with God.

Hours and Days of Operation: 2- to 21-day programs offered year-round.

Accommodations: 7 rooms with twin beds, modern furnishings, semi-private baths. Campsites and trailer hookups available for seminar guests.

Rates: 21-day program $3,300; inquire about rates for spouses or other accompanying people. 4-day seminars $250 per person, $425 for married couples, $75 extra per child. All rates include housing, meals, workshops.

Credit Cards: D, MC, V.

Meal Plans: 3 vegetarian meals daily.

Services: Massage, water therapy, physical exam, blood work, physiotherapy, health lectures, natural remedies, morning church services, classes.

Facilities: 200-acre wooded retreat center with farm, main lodge, walking trails, and orchard.

Staff: Lifestyle Center staff includes 4 medical doctors and 10 counselors trained in various types of therapies.

Special Notes: Smoking not allowed.

Nearby Attractions: Callaway Gardens features a Butterfly House and azalea show; Roosevelt State Park; Little White House in Warm Spring, Georgia; Canyon State Park.

Getting There: 15 miles from Columbus, Georgia, in east-central Alabama. If arriving in Columbus by plane or bus, pickup available for an extra $15.

Association for Research and Enlightenment (A.R.E.)

4017 North 40th Street
Phoenix, AZ 85018
(602) 955-0551; fax (602) 956-8269

"The mind is the builder, the physical is the result." This statement, from a "reading" by the famous psychic and healer Edgar Cayce, summarizes the philosophy of the medical clinic at the Association for Research and Enlightenment (A.R.E.), which adheres to the general rules of Cayce medicine. Born in the Bible Belt in 1910 and possessing only minimal education, Cayce awakened to his psychic gifts after a visit from what some describe as an angel. After healing his own loss of physical speech by following the angel's instructions, he was able to diagnose health problems in others with remarkable success. When Cayce died in 1945, he left behind a legacy of over 14,000 psychic readings, 9,000 of which were health oriented.

The clinic addresses all forms of illness, from emphysema, arthritis, and diabetes to emotional imbalances, stress, and lack of vitality. It draws on many healing treatments and applies them according to the unique needs of each patient. Through diet, herbs, castor oil packs, chiropractic, biofeedback, visualization, and other mind-body techniques, the body begins to coordinate itself in a healthful manner. The intent is to get patients to examine their condition and understand how closely emotional, spiritual, and psychological well-being is connected with physical well-being.

An 11-day holistic residential program known as the Temple Beautiful embodies the Cayce experience. Designed and administered by a physician, the program includes massage, acupressure, reflexology, steam baths, whirlpools, colonic therapy, biofeedback instruction and monitored autogenic exercise to teach relaxation skills, and pain- and stress-reducing energy therapies. The staff works with each participant to design a program to be followed at home.

Hours and Days of Operation: Mon–Fri, 8:30–5. Residential programs, varying in length, offered year-round.

Accommodations: Up to 17 people in the clinic's spacious Oak House. Private rooms may be available.

Rates: 11-day residential program $4,900. Rates for office visits vary.

Credit Cards: MC, V.

Meal Plans: 3 meals daily, with an emphasis on fruits and vegetables. Some guests may be placed on special diets by the clinic physician.

Services: Daily morning exercise, osteopathy, homeopathy, hydrotherapy, chiropractic, craniosacral therapy, massage, acupressure, reflexology, colonic therapy, energy medicine, biofeedback instruction, group and inner-process work, dream interpretation, relaxation skills, movement techniques, lectures on meditation and prayer.

Facilities: Desert clinic established at Cayce's request, including treatment rooms, whirlpool, steam cabinet.

Staff: About 25 staff members, including doctors and massage therapists. All trained and licensed in their respective fields.

Special Notes: A.R.E. is a nonprofit organization; all funding is received through donations. Facilities are wheelchair accessible; however, nonambulatory guests must be accompanied by an attendant.

Nearby Attractions: Grand Canyon, Sedona, painted desert, petrified forest, museums.

Getting There: Complimentary transportation provided to and from Skyharbor Airport in Phoenix. Clinic located 4 miles north of the airport.

Canyon Ranch

8600 East Rockcliff Road
Tucson, AZ 85750
(800) 742-9000 or (520) 749-9000; fax (520) 749-7755
Web site: www.canyonranch.com

Cacti, mesquite, acacia, and palo verde trees make up the desert landscape surrounding the 70 acres of Canyon Ranch. Built around a spacious hacienda in the foothills of the Santa Catalina Mountains, this renowned health spa was voted the world's best by readers of *Condé Nast Traveler* magazine. The staff, which outnumbers guests three to one, consists of physicians, psychologists, registered dietitians, exercise physiologists, and certified health educators and bodyworkers.

Since its founding in 1979, Canyon Ranch has developed many lifestyle programs emphasizing the relationship between body, mind, and spirit. The one-week Life Enhancement Program, offered year-round, is designed to address health objectives. Elements of the package include nutrition and diet management consultations, behavioral health classes, exercise physiology consultations, and movement therapy. From time to time, Canyon Ranch also offers weeklong programs that address specific health issues, such as arthritis, heart disease, asthma, and women's health.

Guests are allowed to select their own schedule of activities from the wide array of options: tai chi, yoga, chi kung, meditation and breathing, tennis, basketball, mountain biking, golf, horseback riding, spa treatments, and seven gyms containing ultramodern fitness equipment. Sign up for activities in advance. Evening talks are given by noted psychologists, authors, naturalists, and other specialists.

Hours and Days of Operation: 4-, 7-, and 10-night packages offered year-round.
Accommodations: 180 casitas and suites. Modern southwestern furnishings and desert colors decorate all rooms. The Life Enhancement Center has special quarters for 25 people. All rooms are air-conditioned.
Rates: Vary according to room, season, and package. 7-night packages begin at $3,640 per person during the high season for double-occupancy room, meals, and use of spa, resort facilities, and some services.
Credit Cards: AE, D, MC, V.
Meal Plans: 3 healthy gourmet meals daily, plus snacks. Vegetarian option.
Services: More than 40 fitness classes a day, movement therapy, exercise physiology, medical and behavioral health services, consultation on nutrition and diet, holistic health and body composition, biofeedback, 15 types of massage, herbal and aroma wraps, hydromassage, salon services, private sports lessons, handwriting and tarot card reading.
Recreational Activities: Hiking, swimming, mountain biking, horseback riding, basketball, golf, tennis.
Facilities: 70-acre desert retreat with adobe-style cottages, demonstration kitchen, creative arts center, health and healing center, 62,000-square-foot spa complex including lounge, 7 gymnasiums, aerobic and strength training rooms, squash and racquetball courts, 8 tennis courts, basketball court, 4 pools, yoga/meditation dome, sauna, steam and inhalation rooms, whirlpools, private sunbathing areas, walking trails, cactus gardens, streams, pools, fountains.
Staff: About 800 total staff, all licensed and certified. Staff to guest ratio 3 to 1.
Special Notes: Minimum age of guests is 14. Alcoholic beverages not permitted in public areas; smoking not allowed indoors or in public areas. All facilities provide access for people with disabilities.
Nearby Attractions: Santa Catalina Mountains; Arizona–Sonora Desert Museum; Biosphere 2; Nogales, Mexico; jeep rides; Sabino Canyon; Mount Lemmon.
Getting There: About 30 minutes by car from Tucson. Complimentary shuttle service is provided to and from Tucson Airport.

Centre for Well-Being at the Phoenician

6000 East Camelback Road
Scottsdale, AZ 85251
(800) 888-8234 or (602) 423-2405; fax (602) 947-4311

Make no mistake, this Mobil Five-Star resort is a luxury destination. Yet *Town and Country*, just one of many magazines to comment on the Centre for Well-Being at the Phoenician, has called it "one of the most healing and nurturing spots on the planet." How does a member of the prestigious ITT Sheraton Luxury Collection manage to offer healing modalities? Through detoxification and Ayurvedic rituals, through the use of herbs and mud long prized by Native Americans in the Southwest for their therapeutic properties, through classes in herbology and nutrition, and through a lifestyle consultation that focuses on mind-body connections. Specialized one-, four-, and eight-day programs focus on the principles of well-being and creating balance in everyday life.

The center is located on 250 acres of pools, fountains, and lawn and a 2-acre cactus garden containing 350 varieties of cactus and succulents. Although this world-class resort would never describe itself as a healing center alone, many profoundly therapeutic treatments are available on the spa menu, for example, neuromuscular therapy, lymphatic massage, and the centuries-old practices of jin shin jyutsu, reflexology, and shiatsu. Neuromuscular therapy is recommended for those who have chronic pain, headaches, or injuries such as whiplash and tennis elbow; lymphatic massage helps to remove toxins and activates the body's natural immune system. Jin shin jyutsu, reflexology, and shiatsu are all said to reduce fatigue, release muscular aches, and restore well-being.

Hours and Days of Operation: Open daily, 6 a.m.–8 p.m. Packages averaging 1 week offered year-round.
Accommodations: 581 guest rooms, 69 luxury suites, 4 presidential suites. Rooms include Berber carpeting and authentic McGuire furniture with Philippine leather strapping. Every piece of art and decor hand-selected.
Rates: Vary according to lodging, program, and season. A standard single guest room $180 in summer, $355 in fall, $410 in winter.
Credit Cards: AE, D, MC, V.
Meal Plans: "Choices" cuisine breakfast included in some programs.
Services: Massage and body therapies from various traditions, health consultations, neuromuscular therapy, craniosacral therapy, jin shin jyutsu, reflexology, reiki, body wraps, body scrubs, facials, tai chi, salon services, personal training, astrology, tarot readings, meditation.
Recreational Activities: Hiking.
Facilities: 250-acre resort with museum-quality fine art and antiques, business center, ballroom, multimedia theater, 3 boardrooms, 23 breakout rooms, 9 dining facilities, fitness room, Swiss shower, whirlpools, sauna, steam room, 24 treatment rooms, meditation atrium, golf course, croquet lawn, oversize chess board, basketball half-court, lawn bowling, billiards, 9 swimming pools, tennis garden, water slide, necklace lake, lagoons, waterfalls, cactus garden.
Staff: 1,757 total staff, with 108 health center employees. Health center staff comprises a fitness director, treatment coordinator, 40 massage therapists, 10 aestheticians, tai chi and meditation instructor, 5 yoga instructors, 10 aerobics instructors. All licensed, experienced, and certified.
Special Notes: Facilities accessible for people with disabilities. The Japanese Assistance Network (JAN) offers assistance to Japanese-speaking guests through a bilingual operator.
Nearby Attractions: Camelback Mountain, Desert Botanical Garden, Frank Lloyd Wright's Taliesin West, Heard Museum, Phoenix Art Museum, Sedona arts and spiritual community.
Getting There: About 20 minutes by car from downtown Phoenix.

Merritt Center

Merritt Lodge of Payson
P.O. Box 2087
Payson, AZ 85547
(800) 414-9880 or (520) 474-4268; fax (520) 474-8588

With her radiant smile and long silver braid running down her back, Betty Merritt looks like everyone's dream grandmother. Merritt is a bodywork therapist and self-renewal consultant who founded the Merritt Center and Lodge with her husband, Al, 10 years ago to provide a secluded, natural setting for people to find rejuvenation and self-empowerment. The center, 90 miles north of Phoenix within the Tonto National Forest, hosts year-round classes, workshops, and experiential programs for groups and individuals seeking personal growth. The programs also provide free time for lazily rocking in a wicker chair, taking a guided hike through tall desert pines, or relaxing in a whirlpool under the stars.

The Heart Renewal Program is especially beneficial for people who want to evaluate their lifestyles and learn methods and strategies for improving health. Because it focuses on changing long-lived and sometimes detrimental habits, the program asks guests to bring a spouse or close friend to support the process. Program facilitators include a board-certified cardiologist, a registered dietitian, a nurse with over 20 years of experience, and Betty Merritt. The program is designed to complement an existing health routine and is not meant to be a substitute for medical treatment.

Over the course of a weekend, guests learn how the heart and related systems work together as well as lifesaving tips on how to handle an emergency situation. Other discussion topics include how to cope with stress, the benefit of alternative therapies in healing, how exercise can strengthen the heart, how emotions and beliefs affect health, and how to create a support system of family and friends. Guests also take home a plan to help them continue implementing positive lifestyle changes.

Hours and Days of Operation: Weekend workshops and personal retreats averaging 1–2 weeks offered year-round.

Accommodations: Lodge with 12 rooms containing twin- or king-size beds.

Rates: Lodging and meals, single occupancy, $75 per day; room for 2, including lodging and meals, $110 per day.

Credit Cards: MC, V.

Meal Plans: 3 buffet-style meals a day. Special diets accommodated with advance notice.

Services: Personal growth seminars and workshops, Swedish massage, forest hiking, kiatsu bodywork, craniosacral therapy, drumming, Native American healing ceremonies, dream work, hatha yoga, tai chi, meditation.

Facilities: Small meeting room, multipurpose meeting room, veranda, dining room and kitchen, library, sleeping porch, outdoor hot tub on deck, hammocks, organic garden, meditation garden, sweat lodge, exercise room.

Staff: In addition to Betty Merritt, guest seminar facilitators include experienced health professionals such as Gail Turner, a board-certified cardiologist and head of the Golden Rainbow Valley HeartCare and Healing Center. A medical doctor, counselor, licensed massage therapist, reiki practitioner, and craniosacral therapist are on call.

Special Notes: Merritt recommends bringing all-terrain shoes, swimsuit, seasonal clothing, books, tapes, and cassette player.

Nearby Attractions: Tonto National Forest, Mogollon Rim, Grand Canyon.

Getting There: 90 miles north of Phoenix. Call for directions.

Miraval, Life in Balance Resort and Spa

5000 East Via Estancia Miraval
Catalina, AZ 85737
(800) 825-4000 or (520) 825-4000; fax (520) 825-5199
E-mail: miravalaz@aol.com   Web site: www.miravalresort.com

Set amid the Santa Catalina Mountains, just 30 miles north of Tucson, lies Miraval, a three-year-old spa/holistic lifestyle resort. Though traditional and luxurious spa treatments are available, Miraval promotes a philosophy of well-being through harmony among the body, mind, and spirit. The resort is operated by Next Health, which also manages the Sierra Tucson Hospital, renowned for developing the Sierra Model of treatment for mental, emotional, and behavioral disorders.

Personal guides assist guests in choosing a program combining stress management, self-discovery, and luxury resort recreational activities that complement one another and promote balanced well-being. Packages include lodging, meals, airport transfer, one personal service or fitness consultation per night, all resort programs and activities, and 24-hour room service. Over 120 activities are offered, ranging from aerobic exercise to Zen meditation. A common theme running throughout virtually all the curricula is the philosophy of "Mindfulness." An introductory class is offered to lay the foundation for this awareness-promoting principle.

A day at Miraval can begin with a morning meditation timed to greet the rising sun. A buffet breakfast of fresh fruit, juices, cereal, and yogurt might precede a class in Desert Mandala, where guests learn traditional and contemporary techniques of sandpainting. Music and storytelling accompany the process to relay an understanding of how nature reflects the many facets of human experience. A hot-stone massage might follow, using smooth, warm basalt stones. After lunch there is time for chi nei tsang, the oriental abdominal massage. For the ambitious, zero balancing and acupuncture can be squeezed in before dinner. Guests might choose to end the day with a marine hydrotherapy bath and body wrap.

Hours and Days of Operation: Day visits and various packages available year-round.
Accommodations: Single and double rooms in luxury, casita-style rooms and suites with southwestern decor. Some suites have whirlpools and fireplaces.
Rates: $300–$1,050 per person, per night.
Credit Cards: AE, D, DC, MC, V.
Meal Plans: 3 gourmet spa meals a day, including complimentary in-room snacks and beverages. A variety of dietary needs and tastes are accommodated.
Services: Massage, hydrotherapy, body wraps, scalp treatments, facials, manicures, pedicures, over 120 activities including tai chi, yoga, sandpainting, meditation.
Recreational Activities: Mountain biking, horseback riding, aerobics, cooking classes.
Facilities: 135-acre desert resort with 106 adobe buildings, spa, 2 restaurants, exercise equipment, 2 aerobics studios, 4 tennis courts, meditation gardens, croquet lawn, 5 swimming pools, challenge course.
Staff: About 200 total staff, including massage therapists, yoga and tai chi instructors, nutritional counselors, aestheticians, fitness trainers.
Special Notes: Minimum age of spa guest is 17. Six rooms are specially designed to accommodate people with disabilities. Tipping not allowed. Pets not allowed.
Nearby Attractions: Biosphere 2, Sonoran Desert Museum, Tombstone, Sabino Canyon, Mission San Xavier del Bac.
Getting There: 30 miles north of Tucson. Round-trip transportation provided in luxury vans from Tucson Airport.

Phoenix Program

c/o Scottsdale Holistic Medical Group
7350 East Stetson Drive, Suite 128
Scottsdale, AZ 85251
(602) 961-4733; fax (602) 496-8476

This group of health professionals in Scottsdale, Arizona, takes an approach to wellness similar to that of the Edgar Cayce philosophy: "the spirit is the life, the mind is the builder, and the physical is the result." Holistic medicine, as defined by the Scottsdale Holistic Medical Group, is not limited to a particular treatment but reflects the working partnership created with each patient to facilitate the healing process. The ultimate goal is to bring out the internal physician in each patient.

Part of what makes this health care clinic slightly different from the alternative answer to a doctor's office is the seven-day Phoenix Program. This program is based on the belief that insight into the body, mind, and spirit is the first step toward lasting health and happiness. Guests are encouraged to strengthen their own "tap roots," based on the habit of a desert tree. As the tree matures, it eventually encounters a thick caliche layer below the desert sand. It will then either avoid the obstacle and spread roots to the side or concentrate all its growth energy into bursting through the layer. Regardless of species, the trees that break through the caliche survive all inclement weather because they have tapped nourishment far below the surface. This metaphor underlies this residential retreat, which is designed to teach guests how to break through their own obstacles and attain lasting well-being.

The program is scheduled around the requests of participants, and only five are allowed at a time. After an initial physical evaluation, guests receive an individualized program of treatments and therapies. In the pleasant resort-style home, guests eat healthy meals designed to aid their particular healing process. Four hours each morning are spent receiving medical services and treatments, such as energy balancing, osteopathic manipulation, guided imagery, and psychological counseling.

At the end of the week, guests will have a personal wellness program to take home and continue the journey to total health.

Hours and Days of Operation: 1-week retreats scheduled around participant's request.
Accommodations: 5 private rooms in resort-style home.
Rates: $4,000 includes room, board, workshops.
Credit Cards: None accepted for the Phoenix Program.
Meal Plans: All meals included and planned for each specific retreat on the basis of the medical needs of participants.
Services: Biofeedback, daily medical counseling, massage therapy, electro-acuscope, nutritional and psychological counseling, energy balancing, osteopathic manipulation, jin shin jyutsu, workshops in dream interpretation, meditation, balancing the spiritual center, diet and exercise, visualization, interpersonal relationships, guided imagery, stress management, spiritual growth.
Facilities: Resort setting with outdoor pool and gardens.
Staff: Full medical staff. Size of staff varies according to size of group. Inquire for details.
Special Notes: Workshops included in program cost, but services are not.
Nearby Attractions: Frank Lloyd Wright home, Cosanti Foundation sculpture garden, Desert Botanical Gardens, Sedona spiritual energy tour, Phoenix Art Museum, the Heard Museum, Buckhorn hot mineral water baths.
Getting There: Shuttle service provided to and from Skyharbor Airport in Phoenix.

Reevis Mountain School and Sanctuary

HC 2, Box 1534
Roosevelt, AZ 85545
(520) 467-2675

Reconnection, self-reliance, and service to humanity—all are facets of the Reevis Mountain School experience. The school began as a New Age community in 1980, built around a homestead, an organic farm, a creek, and two underground springs. An altitude of 3,300 feet in Arizona's Superstition Mountains is not only conducive to an orchard of some 100 fruit and nut trees, it relieves the sting of hot summers.

Reevis has grown to include a greenhouse, a community house, a stone masonry shower house, tepees, cabins, and yurts. It provides a unique wilderness experience for those seeking everything from a personal health retreat to outdoor survival skills. Plant study seminars, workshops, and retreats are offered throughout the year, such as the Fasting Meditation Retreat, which provides guests with three days of guided meditation, fasting, and a serene wilderness environment.

Peter Bigfoot, program facilitator at Reevis, is an adjunct professor at the Southwest College of Naturopathic Medicine. Bigfoot founded Reevis in 1979 as a nonprofit educational institute dedicated to fostering personal health, harmonious relationships and a reverence for the planet. A recognized authority on Southwest plant life and desert survival, Bigfoot walked into the Sonoran Desert with no food or water in July 1976 and trekked 85 miles in 15 days. Today, Bigfoot draws on his knowledge and experience to teach self-reliance skills and natural healing. Guests can receive health consultations with Bigfoot, which may result in some herbal and dietary recommendations. Jin shin jyutsu touch-healing treatments are also available.

The Reevis country store sells a line of handcrafted herbal remedies. All herbs are either hand-picked from the organic garden or found growing wild in the surrounding area.

Hours and Days of Operation: Workshops and classes ranging from 1½–8 days, as well as personal retreats, offered year-round.
Accommodations: 2 cabins, 4 yurts, 1 tepee, camping space.
Rates: $50 per day, per person. Includes meals. Work-exchange discounts available through negotiation.
Credit Cards: None accepted.
Meal Plans: 2 full meals a day consisting of whole grains and vegetables from the Reevis garden and seasonal fruits and nuts from the orchard. All foods are organic, whenever possible, and homemade.
Services: Workshops, classes, jin shin jyutsu touch healing, meditation, natural medicine, Southwestern herbology, natural foods preparation, survival skills, navigation skills, guided hikes to nearby Indian ruins.
Facilities: Community house, stone masonry shower house, greenhouse, organic garden, vineyard, orchard, 2 underground springs, country store, small poultry farm, perennial creek.
Staff: Peter Bigfoot and Jutta Morris, nutritional counselor and cook, plus residential volunteer staff.
Special Notes: Reevis recommends guests bring a sleeping bag and pad, tent, 1-quart plastic bottle, seasonal clothing, day pack, flashlight, and towel. Visitors not allowed without prior notice.
Nearby Attractions: Cliff dwellings in nearby Tonto National Monument, Theodore Roosevelt Lake and Dam, Superstition Wilderness.
Getting There: 3 hours by car from Phoenix. Four-wheel-drive vehicle recommended. Shuttle service available through prior arrangement.

Sound Listening and Learning Center

2701 East Camelback Road #205
Phoenix, AZ 85016
(602) 381-0086; fax (602) 957-6741
E-mail: drbthmpsn@aol.com   Web site: www.soundlistening.com

In his newsletter *Self Healing*, Dr. Andrew Weil lists the Tomatis Method, the primary program of the Sound Listening and Learning Center, as a noninvasive, safe alternative to Ritalin in adults and children suffering from attention-deficit and hyperactivity disorders. The method was developed by Alfred A. Tomatis, a French physician who believed that the ear plays an essential role in healthy brain functioning. Tomatis had impressive results in the 1970s, when he consulted on a case of depression and fatigue among an order of Benedictine monks that had frustrated medical experts. Learning that the monks had recently taken the daily Gregorian chants out of their schedule, he recommended they resume, and their symptoms soon lifted.

Since its opening in 1987, the goal of the Sound Listening and Learning Center has been to help individuals and families achieve positive change despite a history of failure. The listening and voice training work is relatively quick and effective for a range of problems, including lost or delayed speech, attention-deficit and hyperactivity disorders, dyslexia, and learning disabilities. The work has also proven successful for people who want to develop more of a musical ear or to pick up a second language faster—or even to open a few creative channels. Founding director Dr. Billie Thompson believes that by improving listening ability and related vocal expression, a person's body becomes more balanced, the ear achieves better precision, learning becomes easier, motivation to succeed in life increases, and personal interactions are more effective.

To learn which program is best, each person receives an initial assessment. First is a listening test and then a consultation to recommend the appropriate program. Participants then enroll in the 60-hour listening program, which normally includes three segments of 15 days and two eight-day sessions. Each intensive consists of daily two-hour audio-vocal sessions, two reassessments, and two half-hour consultations. Guests (listeners) hear filtered Mozart, Gregorian chants, or their own mother's voice while enjoying art, puzzles, games, or social interaction.

Hours and Days of Operation: Open 7 days a week for services, with scheduling available until 8 p.m.

Accommodations: The center provides a list of several hotels and apartments in the area.

Rates: Complete 60-hour individual program, including assessment $3,330. Group programs slightly less, outreach programs to different locations slightly more.

Credit Cards: MC, V.

Meal Plans: Guests provide their own meals. Many area restaurants offer regional foods.

Services: The primary program is the Tomatis Method of auditory and listening integration training, which is supported by other innovative methods that use the body, mind, and emotions. The Rubenfeld Synergy Method combines Feldenkrais, Alexander posture work, Gestalt therapy, Ericksonian hypnosis.

Facilities: Listening Lab with testing facility and consultation rooms.

Staff: No medical doctors, but staff have clinical and educational certification.

Special Notes: For further research, see *The Ear and Language*, by Alfred A. Tomatis, and *The Mozart Effect*, by Don Campbell. A Sound Listening and Learning Center opened in Pasadena, California, in 1994. Every month, the center holds free information presentations.

Nearby Attractions: Grand Canyon, Heard Museum of the Southwest, botanical gardens, golf courses.

Getting There: About 8 miles north of Skyharbor Airport in Phoenix.

Tree of Life Rejuvenation Center

P.O. Box 1080
Patagonia, AZ 85624
(602) 394-2060; fax (602) 394-2099

The Tree of Life Rejuvenation Center is located high in Arizona's spectacular Patagonia Mountains. Dr. Gabriel and Nora Cousens, co-directors of the center, have been teaching rejuvenation courses for eight years. Gabriel Cousens, the internationally acclaimed author of *Spiritual Nutrition and the Rainbow Diet, Sevenfold Peace,* and *Conscious Eating* and the health editor for *Frontier Magazine,* has practiced holistic medicine and psychiatry for 24 years. His disciplines include nutrition, naturopathy, homeopathy, acupuncture, and individual, couples, and family therapy.

There is a lot happening at Tree of Life: seminars, training programs, a nonsectarian health ministry, zero-point process training, and the Healthy Lifestyle Center. Health ministry training is a three-day affair, and topics include a living-foods program; how to fast, cleanse, purify, and detoxify; juicing; and learning about the synergy of physical, mental, emotional, spiritual, and ecological health, among others. The panchakarma experience lasts one week. It begins with a special diet, along with specific herbs and essential oils to help stimulate the liver and digestive organs and allow them to dislodge toxins more easily. After the cleansing treatments, massage is given to remove toxins from tissues and discover where energy blockages are occurring. An herbal sauna follows the massage, and in some cases special Ayurvedic poultices and herbal masks may be used to enhance the cleansing process. Zero-point process training teaches participants, over a four-day period, how to dissolve limiting beliefs, fears, and resistance.

Dr. Cousens also maintains a health practice at the center. Services include guided fasting, brain biochemistry balancing, and the testing of body fluids and "blood life." A list of costs and services can be obtained by request.

Hours and Days of Operation: Health practice: Sun–Thu, 8:30–5; individualized health programs varying in length offered year-round.
Accommodations: 2 guest houses with comfortable private and semiprivate rooms.
Rates: Vary according to program and services. $45 per day average.
Credit Cards: AE, MC, V.
Meal Plans: 3 meals a day included in some programs. Meals designed to complement the healing regimen.
Services: Acupuncture, detoxification programs, massage, reiki, reflexology, individualized health programs, guided fasting, panchakarma, nutritional counseling, health training, zero-point process training, neutral aromatic baths, free newsletter.
Facilities: Clinic, spa facilities, hydrotherapy pools. Plans being made for a future Rejuvenation Center.
Staff: 11 health professionals, including Dr. Gabrielle Cousens.
Special Notes: Smoking not allowed. For panchakarma, wear comfortable clothes that you don't mind getting oily.
Nearby Attractions: Patagonia Mountains; Nogales, Mexico; bird sanctuary; Parker Canyon; Saguaro National Park; Tombstone; Colossal Cave.
Getting There: About 1 hour by car southeast of Tucson.

Ancestral Voice—Center for Indigenous Lifeways

108D Oliva Court
Novato, CA 94947
(415) 897-7991 (phone/fax)
E-mail: Ancestor@gte.net

The buffalo skin tepees and medicine rattles may only be museum displays to some, but the spirit of traditional Indian medicine remains alive—as does its capacity to heal. Phillip Scott, founder of Ancestral Voice—Center for Indigenous Lifeways, continues the native traditions through actively teaching and applying the ancient methods in experiential workshops. Scott, a board member of the American Medical Holistic Association, has more than 16 years of experience as a practitioner of native medicine and shamanism. His experience also includes 15 years as a tai chi practitioner and Vietnamese acupuncturist, and he is a certified massage therapist.

Trained by native medicine teachers and elders, Scott draws on their healing techniques for workshops and healing intensives. The goal of the five-year-old center, located in the coastal rolling hills of the San Francisco Bay Area, is to disseminate and preserve the shamanic and indigenous way of life. As a healing center, workshop participants learn to discover, cultivate, and maintain balance in all aspects of their lives.

A typical day does not exist at the center, but a few common elements can be found. A morning sun-greeting ceremony is followed by instruction in tai chi. Breakfast follows, and a counseling session occurs midmorning. Lunch and leisure time fill the day until therapies, treatments, and healings in the afternoon. An evening sun ceremony is followed by dinner and leisure time. Entertainment or an experiential workshop might be squeezed in before bed. Wild-crafted herbal preparations are prescribed during the intensive for all manner of physical, psychological, emotional, and spiritual imbalances.

Hours and Days of Operation: Office hours: Mon–Fri, 8–6. Evenings, weekends, and holidays by appointment. Residential programs are available by appointment year-round. Crisis intervention is available 24 hours a day, 7 days a week.

Accommodations: Available at the center, in the homes of local community members, or at nearby hotels and motels.

Rates: Vary according to recommendations. Hourly therapy and treatments $60–$85. Weekend workshops $265, weeklong workshops $950. Ceremonies are a respectful donation.

Credit Cards: None accepted.

Meal Plans: Consist of either outings to nearby restaurants or 3 nutritionally balanced organic meals per day (included in weeklong workshops only).

Services: Prayer, healing circles, bodywork, native healing, tai chi, rites of passage, pilgrimages to sacred sites, Vietnamese acupuncture, herbal medicine, indigenous ceremonies and rituals.

Facilities: Swimming pool, hiking and biking trails, archery range, tennis courts, golf course.

Staff: In addition to Phillip Scott, 6 volunteer administrative and ceremonial assistants.

Special Notes: Apprenticeships in shamanism and energy medicine are available.

Nearby Attractions: Miwok Park, Museum of the American Indian, Mission San Rafael, Bay Area Discovery Museum, Terwilliger Nature Center, China Camp State Park, Mount Tamalpais, Point Reyes National Seashore, Muir Woods, Marin Headlands, the Marine Mammal Center, Stinson Beach, Bolinas Lagoon, Tomales Bay, Samuel B. Taylor Park, Napa wine country, Monterey Bay Aquarium, zoo, aquarium, seasonal whale watching.

Getting There: Easy access from either the San Francisco or Oakland Airport. Shuttle service available for a fee. Car not necessary but recommended.

Chopra Center for Well-Being

7630 Fay Avenue
La Jolla, CA 92037
(619) 551-7788; fax (619) 551-9570
Web site: www.chopra.com

It's hard not to have heard of Deepak Chopra. Being the only author ever to land simultaneously on both the *New York Times* best-seller lists, for fiction and nonfiction, is just one of his numerous achievements. Chopra's message, that unconditional health is within everyone's reach, can be found in books, videos, lectures, and television appearances. Because of his enormous appeal, PBS uses his video lectures during its pledge week. Chopra has helped bring Ayurveda into the mainstream and, with the opening of the Chopra Center for Well-Being, is now offering its benefits to the public.

The center is divided into three main elements. The first is patient care, which extends to anyone with immediate health concerns as well as to those who want to feel rejuvenated. The anti-aging program is also an element of patient care. The second is the development of educational programs. One such course, The Magic of Healing, lasts eight weeks and includes classes on nutrition, body types, meditation, psychophysiological techniques, eliminative procedures, herbal remedies, and looking at the human being in the context of environment, body, mind, and spirit. The third element is research, which benefits patients through the comfort of knowing that the most up-to-date technology is behind every service offered at the center.

As for the extended-stay programs, at this time there are only two: Creating Health, which is offered in both three- and seven-day programs, and Ayurvedic Purification, which lasts for seven days. Creating Health begins with an orientation and includes natural cooking and wellness classes, primordial sound meditation, Ayurvedic therapy, yoga and breathing techniques, gourmet vegetarian meals, discussions on Chopra's Seven Laws of Spiritual Success, and personal empowerment sessions. Ayurvedic Purification includes a home preparation program, a mind-body medical consultation, an educational session with a nurse, traditional panchakarma, Ayurvedic meals, extended meditation practices, and yoga and breathing techniques.

Hours and Days of Operation: Daily, 7–7.
Accommodations: Overnight accommodations are not available, but a concierge service arranges any lodging needs. Some hotels within walking distance of the center.
Rates: Multiday programs $1,250–$2,750.
Credit Cards: MC, V.
Meal Plans: 3 organic, vegetarian meals per day with residential program.
Services: Panchakarma treatments, Ayurvedic therapies, massage, body scrubs, facials, primordial sound meditation, mind-body medicine consultations, children's programs.
Facilities: Spacious modern health center with classrooms, treatment rooms, sauna, steam room, restaurant, music/bookstore.
Staff: About 60 staff members, including 3 medical doctors, instructors, chefs, therapists trained in traditional massage with at least 500 hours of experience.
Special Notes: Smoking not allowed. Facilities accessible for people with disabilities, but guests with disabilities must bring an attendant to help massage therapists assist them on and off the tables.
Nearby Attractions: San Diego Zoo, Wild Animal Park, beaches, parks.
Getting There: About 20 minutes by car from the San Diego Airport. Transportation available to and from the airport.

Esalen Institute

Highway 1
Big Sur, CA 93920-9616
(408) 667-3000; fax (408) 667-2724
E-mail: catguy@esalen.org; Web site: www.esalen.org

On a 27-acre stretch of land between the Pacific Ocean and the coastal ridge of the Santa Lucia Mountains lies the Esalen Institute. The word Esalen comes from the Native American tribe known as the Esselen, who once made these breathtaking seaside grounds and natural hot springs their home. Since its founding in 1962, the institute's programs have revolved around the exploration of unrealized human capacity.

Over the years, the center has gained renown for its blend of East/West philosophies and its experimental workshops. Philosophers, psychologists, artists, and religious thinkers have all made the winding coastal drive to Esalen, and some are still in residence today. Visit the occasional forums where they share ideas with the community.

With such diverse programs as "Maps of the Jungle: Negotiating the Primitive Dimensions of the Workplace," "The Home Within the Heart: Ojibwe Tribal Healings," and "Core Holoenergetics: The Art and Science of Conscious Healing," the question is, How does one experience Esalen? For those who can't decide on one of the hundred or so programs, the program "Experiencing Esalen" is a good choice. It offers an introduction to therapeutic bodywork and healing practices such as Gestalt, massage, sensory awareness, and meditation. Visits generally range from a weekend to five- or seven-day workshops. Longer stays are available with the Ongoing Residence program, as a seminarian, or through the work-study program.

Hours and Days of Operation: Programs averaging a week in length offered year-round. Residential and volunteer programs available.
Accommodations: Shared housing with 2 or 3 persons per room and, in some cases, shared bathrooms. Couples will be housed together. Bunk-bed rooms available on a limited basis;

meeting rooms sometimes used as shared sleeping-bag space and may be available for workshop participants with limited financial means.
Rates: Vary according to length of stay, lodging, and program. 7-day rate per person with standard accommodations $1,220, 5-day rate $795, weekend rate $425. Scholarship assistance available.
Credit Cards: AE, MC, V.
Meal Plans: 3 meals a day, served buffet style and using fresh organic vegetables. Vegetarian options available.
Services: Personal growth and holistic health workshops including shamanic healing, Gestalt therapy, neurolinguistics; craniosacral therapy, Rolfing, Feldenkrais, Heller, Esalen and deep-tissue massage, hiking, yoga, tai chi, children's program.
Recreational Activities: Concerts, hiking, nature walks, swimming, work-study programs.
Facilities: A 27-acre ocean-side campus with meeting rooms, educational resources information center, treatment rooms, rustic lodges, heated outdoor pool, natural rock pools with hot mineral springs, bookstore, hiking trails.
Staff: About 50 staff members who work on a long-term basis, including licensed massage therapist and counselors. Support staff include work-study students and guest facilitators.
Special Notes: Smoking is not allowed in any accommodations or meeting rooms. A recently purchased vehicle now provides a means of transportation to the baths for those with physical limitations. Flashlight recommended.
Nearby Attractions: Ventana Wilderness, Tassajara Zen Monastery, Los Padres National Forest, Big Sur State Park, Hearst Castle in San Simeon.
Getting There: 3½ hours by car south of San Francisco and 45 minutes by car south of Monterey.

George Ohsawa Macrobiotic Foundation

P.O. Box 426
Oroville, CA 95965
(530) 533-7702; fax (530) 533-7908

Imagine campfires, mountain swims, meals prepared over open wood fires, and waterfall hikes—with the added benefit of healing workshops, discussions on health and high performance, how to relax under pressure, or self-healing through food. This is the George Ohsawa Macrobiotic Foundation yearly summer camp, set in California's Tahoe National Forest. Although macrobiotics, which can be described as the study of the natural laws of change, is based on philosophies that are thousands of years old, George Ohsawa is the father of the modern-day practice. The nonprofit foundation, chartered in 1971, educates the general public through publications, a mail-order catalog, a database of resource connections, and its yearly summer retreats. Ohsawa's teachings promote nutrition and healing based on the fundamental belief that humans are designed to be healthy. Through eating and living in as natural a way as possible, wellness is obtained and maintained. "Natural" includes a diet based on grains and fresh vegetables that is free of overprocessed foods.

The retreat is a great way for anyone interested in macrobiotics to truly immerse oneself in its principles and to actually live those principles for one week to ten days. A typical day starts with a polar bear swim, meditation, or gentle exercise before breakfast. Afterward, campers attend a midmorning lecture by one of several guest speakers. They may then take a box lunch to the shore of the American River and walk it off afterward by trekking to Mildred Lake. Volleyball and more free time follows dinner; from 8 to 10 p.m., campfires, music, dancing, or a variety show might be the evening's headliner.

Hours and Days of Operation: Summer camps last 7–10 days. Call for dates.

Accommodations: There are no enclosed accommodations. Only tent sites are available. Guests provide their own sleeping bags, tents, and ground cover. Campers, RVs, and motor homes are welcome and must be parked in the lots provided.

Rates: $50 discount available for members of the George Ohsawa Macrobiotic Foundation. Membership $25 within the United States and includes a discount on books and supplies as well as a subscription to *Macrobiotics Today*. Family Camp fees with pre-registration $500 for G.O.M.F. members, $550 for nonmembers, $300 for kids 3–16. For kids under 3, call before registering. Activities Camp fees $425 for G.O.M.F. members, $475 for nonmembers. Prices go up $50 for late registration.

Credit Cards: AE, MC, V.

Meal Plans: 3 daily macrobiotic meals.

Services: Healing workshops, massage, dietary consultations, hiking, bicycling, volleyball, swimming, optional rafting, storytelling, dancing.

Facilities: Campgrounds, hiking trails, streams.

Staff: Noted speakers, including top macrobiotic teachers; experienced cooks; and children's program leaders. Average length of professional experience 15–20 years.

Special Notes: Smoking not allowed within the camp boundaries. No dogs allowed.

Nearby Attractions: Tahoe National Forest, Lake Tahoe, Reno.

Getting There: About 2 hours by car from the Sacramento Airport. Shuttle service available for a fee.

Harbin Hot Springs

P.O. Box 782
Middletown, CA 95461
(707) 982-2477
Web site: www.harbin.org

In the 1880s, a stagecoach brought people suffering from gout, dyspepsia, and rheumatism to the Harbin Hot Springs Health and Pleasure Resort for the cure of "taking the waters." Hundreds of years before them, indigenous people had named Harbin *eetawyomi,* or "the hot place." More than 36,000 gallons of mineral water flow up to the Earth's surface a day from seven natural springs on the 1,160 acres of Harbin property, in a secluded mountain valley in northern California. Heated by volcanic action, two hot springs feed the Hot and Warm Pool complex while cold springs feed the remaining pools and the resort's "tap water" tanks.

For 25 years, the Heart Consciousness Church has owned and operated Harbin Hot Springs, and the resort's operations are handled by a community of residents. Preferring to present itself as a retreat rather than a resort because of its homey, laid-back atmosphere and clothing-optional policy, Harbin now offers workshops, seasonal packages, community living, or the opportunity to simply bathe in the hot, warm, and cold pools. The School of Shiatsu and Massage, also located at Harbin, brings students from Europe, Japan, and throughout the United States to study bodywork either for professional requirements or to expand their personal growth. The school's director, Harold Dull, is responsible for inventing Watsu (the in-water form of shiatsu), which has proven to have profound rehabilitative results in treating emotional trauma, sleep disorders, and cerebral palsy.

For those interested in retreat packages, they are offered during weekdays throughout the winter months and include lodging, a daily massage, and breakfast.

Hours and Days of Operation: 24 hours a day, 7 days a week.

Accommodations: Private rooms, each with a unique design and either private or European-style bathrooms, cabins, dormitories, and campsites.

Rates: $75–$185, double occupancy; $30–$90 single. Camping $165 per week, $115 for children under 18. Day visit passes $15–$20, $10–$15 for children under 18.

Credit Cards: MC, V.

Meal Plans: Breakfast provided with off-season package. On-grounds cafés and restaurants serve fresh organic food from the Harbin Hot Springs garden.

Services: Holistic health and personal growth workshops, rebirthing, rebalancing, hypnotherapy, chiropractic treatments, and various types of massage, including Esalen, deep tissue, reflexology, shiatsu, and Watsu; yoga, meditation, dance, 12-step meetings, full- and new-moon celebrations.

Facilities: 1,160-acre foothill estate including the School of Shiatsu and Massage, rustic cabins, conference facilities, vegetarian kitchen, restaurant, poolside café, 2 warm pools, hot pool, cold plunge, dry sauna, swimming pool, redwood sundeck, garden, forest trails.

Staff: About 150 resident staff. All bodyworkers certified and insured.

Special Notes: Bring a towel, flashlight, sandals, and footwear appropriate for rocky terrain. Pool area clothing optional; the dressing facilities co-ed. Open fires, candles, and camp stoves forbidden; smoking allowed only in a designated area next to parking lot. Inquire about pool maintenance schedule.

Nearby Attractions: Wine country, galleries, Clearlake recreational area.

Getting There: About 2½ hours by car north of San Francisco.

Health Action—Institute for Self-Initiated Healing at the Maes Center for Natural Health Care

19 East Mission Street, Santa Barbara, California 93101
(805) 563-8660; fax (805) 563-8662
E-mail: doctor@maescenter.com   Web sites: www.maescenter.com; www.HealerWithin.com

Dr. Roger Jahnke, author of *The Healer Within* and founder of Health Action in Santa Barbara, believes that the most profound medicine is produced within the human body and that everyone can learn to tap into it. Dr. Jahnke and his colleague Dr. Luc Maes, a renowned physician of both naturopathic and chiropractic medicine, and their associates in numerous fields of natural healing have created an innovative spa, retreat, and healing program. Each client has a healing and rejuvenation program specifically tailored to their needs.

The center focuses on maximizing health to eliminate disease. Rejuvenation, education, and inspiration complement natural healing methodologies to accelerate one's personal journey towards health and transformation. Clients are encouraged to explore the area's magnificent mountains and beaches and are educated about food and lifestyle choices as they learn the self-healing philosophies of natural medicine. The program integrates the benefits of oriental and naturopathic medicine, including acupuncture, homeopathy, herbal medicine, chiropractic, massage, clinical nutrition, and diet modification. Four essential methods are taught in the self-healing process: (1) gentle movement of the body, (2) self-applied massage, (3) breath practice, and (4) deep relaxation or meditation.

In 1983 a powerful program called PHASES was developed with the idea that people improve in "phases" rather than in one swift stroke. This program, also known as the Circle of Life, helps people view their attitudes and lifestyles holistically. The goal is to help people master stress, make better choices, and achieve a higher state of wellness. The PHASES program uses qigong, tai chi, yoga, and the methods from *The Healer Within*. Each participant leaves with tools to help them continue to heal and to sustain their health gains at home.

Although the treatments are gentle and noninvasive, Dr. Jahnke, Dr. Maes, and their associates have had remarkable success treating chronic ailments including fibromyalgia, cancer, multiple sclerosis, arthritis, chronic fatigue, and stress-related disorders. Their work is recognized throughout the country.

Hours and Days of Operation: Mon–Fri, 10–5. Nonclinical services by appointment on weekends.
Accommodations: Out-of-town visitors encouraged to contact the Santa Barbara Chamber of Commerce for information about the many unique and affordable hotels in the area.
Rates: Vary according to services. Inquire for details.
Credit Cards: MC, V.
Meal Plans: No meals provided, but many restaurants serving healthy and gourmet foods are within minutes of the center.
Facilities: Spanish style setting. Center includes multiple treatment rooms, group meeting space, and naturopathic pharmacy.
Staff: In addition to Dr. Jahnke, OMD, and Dr. Luc Maes, ND, DC, staff includes a health and lifestyle counselor and coach, an herbalist, massage and acupressure therapists.
Services: Instruction in self-healing methods, qigong, tai chi, acupuncture, homeopathy, chiro-practic, herbal medicine, clinical nutrition, massage, and detoxification. Medical diagnostic services available when needed.
Special Notes: For more information, review the book *The Healer Within*, the video *Awaken the Medicine Within*, and the above Web sites.
Nearby Attractions: Pacific Ocean, Coastal Mountain Range, museums, theater, lectures, regional spa services, golf, tennis, shopping, Santa Barbara's gardens.
Getting There: About 1½ hours by car north of Los Angeles International Airport and 10 minutes from the Santa Barbara Airport.

Health Classic

P.O. Box 30254
Santa Barbara, CA 93130-0254
(805) 898-0089; fax (805) 898-1428

Founded eight years ago, Health Classic offers retreats several times throughout the year that revolve around the philosophy that the way people eat affects the environment. Retreats are dedicated to the promotion of individual and societal health and the explanation of the interrelatedness between the two. A strong connection between individual lifestyle and overall societal health is emphasized. For five days, guests live a healthy lifestyle in a natural setting at various centers and spas throughout the country.

White Sulphur Springs Resort and Spa was the site of the 1997 Fall Retreat, located in the heart of California's Napa Valley on 300 acres of redwood, oak, fir, and madrone forests with spring-fed creeks and year-round waterfalls. The week's program included over 60 natural health workshops and classes, including understanding nutrition, stress reduction, men's and women's health issues, the macrobiotic way of life, Ayurvedic studies, oriental medicine, herbology, and environmental and lifestyle issues. Among the eight keynote speakers were world-renowned Michio Kushi, founder of the Kushi Institute; Dr. John McDougal, author of four national best-sellers and host of both a talk-radio and a weekly television show; and Dr. Susan Lark, author of *The Women's Self-Help Library*. It was also possible to book a private consultation with any one of the speakers as well as with a counselor or therapist.

In addition to classes, days included the use of hot springs, spa, pool, and hiking trails. Hands-on, participatory massage workshops introduced some to the benefits of massage and bodywork while others spent time with Health Classic's golf professional, Les Boland, learning how to improve their swings. A typical evening could wind up with guests country line dancing after a delicious nondairy, nonsugar dessert prepared by Health Classic's dessert chefs.

Hours and Days of Operation: Mon–Fri, 9–6. 5-day workshops offered in the fall.
Accommodations: Range from standard singles and doubles to private cottages.
Rates: $315–$1,045 per person, including lodging, meals, program.
Credit Cards: MC, V.
Meal Plans: 3 gourmet, organic, vegetarian meals a day.
Services: Workshops on macrobiotic lifestyle, cooking classes, personal health consultations, stress management techniques, Ayurvedic sound healing, Do-In, health lectures, group discussion, yoga, tai chi, qigong, Tibetan rites, energy therapies.
Recreational Activities: Dancercise, Swingolf, country line dancing.
Facilities: Most facilities include hiking rails, hot tub, and swimming pool.
Staff: Doctors, nurses, well-known authors, state-certified acupuncturists. Other workshop facilitators not mentioned above include Lino Stanchich, author of *Power Eating Program: You Are What You Eat*; David Briscoe, general manager of the Vega Institute and author of *A Personal Peace: Macrobiotic Reflections on Mental and Emotional Recovery*; Meredith McCarty, author of several books and videos, including *Fresh from a Vegetarian Kitchen*; Bill Tara, author of *The Magic Mirror* and a forceful advocate for natural health care and a healthy environment; and Kaare Bursell, a former veterinary surgeon in England and now a full-time counselor and lecturer.
Special Notes: Child care available at an additional cost. Call the Health Classic office for reservations. Health Classic also has a catalog of health supplies and operates a bookstore.
Nearby Attractions: Depends on location. Inquire for details.
Getting There: Depends on location. Inquire for details.

Heartwood Institute

220 Harmony Lane
Garberville, CA 95542
(707) 923-5004; fax (707) 923-5010

On a 240-acre campus surrounded by rolling meadows, forests of Douglas fir, oak, madrone, manzanita, and California bay laurel—replete with red tail hawks, wild turkeys, owls, bobtail cats, and foxes—lies the educational community of Heartwood. It is devoted to serving as a catalyst for planetary healing through helping people achieve physical, psychological, and spiritual well-being. "We believe that every personal healing is a step toward the healing of all," reads the institute's course catalog.

Several times throughout the year, Group Wellness Retreats are offered at this 20-year-old institute. Retreats can revolve around spirituality, such as the Zen and Pure Land Meditation Retreat, or around physical health, like the Polarity Cleansing Diet, intended for people who are ready to break dietary habits and commit to a healthier lifestyle. Personalized Wellness Retreats can be arranged at any time throughout the year with advance notice. Guests can create their own schedule of private sessions in a wide variety of body therapies, oriental healing arts, and hypnotherapies with Heartwood's professionally trained and experienced staff.

As a school, Heartwood is recognized by many professional alternative health organizations nationwide, including the American Massage Therapy Association and the American Oriental Bodywork Therapy Association. In addition to the retreats, the general public is invited to join Heartwood's one- to three-week intensives designed for holistic health professionals to study bodywork and massage, oriental healing arts, hypnotherapy, and addiction counseling. Each quarter Heartwood also offers an 11-week program known as Life Exploration. This 200-hour course is designed as an opportunity to take time away from one's work and lifestyle to reflect on life and acquire the skills necessary for healing, wholeness, and self-actualization. Life Exploration is intended for refreshing mind, body, and spirit, not career training.

Hours and Days of Operation: 1-, 2-, and 3-week intensives offered year-round.
Accommodations: Private and shared preferred rooms with sheets, pillows, comforters, and bath towels. Standard dormitory-style shared rooms with communal bath. Campsites available.
Rates: Weekend retreat $240, preferred rooms with all linens furnished $80 (single) and $130 (double). Camping retreat fee $55 per day and includes meals.
Credit Cards: MC, V.
Meal Plans: 3 meals a daily, mostly organic vegetarian. Guests may use the snack kitchen.
Services: Classes and workshops on bodywork and massage, including deep-tissue massage, shiatsu, Swedish and Esalen, breathwork and jin shin jyutsu, transformational therapy and hypnotherapy, nutritional counseling, lectures.
Recreational Activities: Dances.
Facilities: 240-acre hillside campus with log community lodge, spacious deck, dining room with piano, outdoor heated swimming pool, hot tub, wood-fired sauna,
Staff: About 40 teaching staff, 40 work-study volunteers, 50 students, and 10 licensed massage therapists.
Special Notes: Pets not allowed. Guest are advised to bring a sleeping bag, bed linens, towels, toiletries, flashlight, snack foods, a day pack, rain gear, seasonal clothing; massage students should bring oil, loose clothing, 2 or more sheets for classroom use.
Nearby Attractions: Sinkyone Wilderness State Preserve; Humboldt Redwoods; Victorian architecture; museums, restaurants, and galleries in Arcata and Eureka.
Getting There: 1 hour by car east of Garberville. Shuttle service available for local Greyhound station and Eureka/Arcata Airport for an additional fee.

Hellerwork International, LLC

406 Berry Street
Mount Shasta, CA 96067
(800) 392-3900 or (530) 926-2500; fax (530) 926-6839
E-mail: hellerwork@hellerwork.com   Web site: www.hellerwork.com

To understand what would motivate a person to travel from anywhere in the country for 11 90-minute Hellerwork sessions with founder, Joseph Heller, just imagine having the opportunity to take a self-confidence seminar from Dale Carnegie. In the late 1960s, Heller—then an aerospace engineer studying the effects of gravity on rockets and other aeronautic structures—attended several human potential workshops and encounter groups at Kairos, a human development center in Los Angeles. While at Kairos, Heller met Ida Rolf, the founding mother of Structural Integration, also known as Rolfing. Heller's interest in gravity's effects aligned, so to speak, perfectly with the philosophies of Structural Integration. In 1972, Heller became a certified Rolfer and three years later was appointed director of the Rolf Institute. His belief that simply restructuring the body was not enough spurred him on to create the field of bodywork, which now carries his name.

Referring to his work, Heller often uses the term "bodymind." Based on the idea that the body has an emotional, physical, and psychological "memory," 11 sessions cover different areas of the body. The purpose is not only to restructure and align but also to teach the individual how to use his or her body in normal activities. After the actual bodywork, lessons are given in standing, sitting, walking, and even shaking hands. For those planning a visit to the Mount Shasta educational center, a minimum stay of five to six days is recommended for the series of 11 sessions with Heller. During the stay, two sessions lasting about 1½ hours each are scheduled each day. Heller travels frequently, so it is important to call the office with plenty of advance notice.

Hours and Days of Operation: Office hours: Tue–Fri, 9–5. Sessions scheduled over a period of 5–6 days offered year-round. Joseph Heller will arrange to see clients at their convenience, as his schedule allows.

Accommodations: None. Guests referred to a number of local hotels and bed-and-breakfasts.

Rates: $90 per session.

Credit Cards: D, MC, V.

Meal Plans: No meals provided, but several area restaurants have unique regional flavors.

Services: A series of Hellerwork sessions and educational instruction.

Facilities: Private office with treatment rooms.

Staff: In addition to Joseph Heller, a support staff and a certified Hellerwork practitioner with 14 years of experience.

Special Notes: Hellerwork International will provide a geographical directory of Hellerwork practitioners on request.

Nearby Attractions: Art galleries and live theater in Mount Shasta, Blackberry Bluegrass Festival, Old Fashioned 4th of July, Box Canyon Dam, Castle Lake, Sisson Museum, Lake Siskiyou, Stewart Mineral Springs, recreational climbing, volcanic exhibit, mountain biking, scenic chairlift rides, snowmobiling, swimming, cross-country and downhill skiing, snowboarding, waterskiing, windsurfing, tennis.

Getting There: Nearest airports are in Redding, 60 miles south, and Medford, 80 miles north.

Hydeout Health and Growth Associates

28195 Fairview Avenue
Hemet, CA 92544
(909) 927-1768; fax (909) 927-1548

In 1957, Evart Loomis, a homeopathic physician and surgeon, founded one of the first holistic health retreats in America, known as Meadowlark. Since then, Evart and wife, Fay, a counselor, author, and lecturer, have formed Hydeout, a quiet healing retreat resting on a 580-acre ranch in the desertlike terrain of southeastern California. The stars are brilliant at night in this wide open dry-brush region. Rabbits, coyotes, and owls are common sights and sounds when hiking some of the several miles of trails. No telephones or television disturb the process of growth and healing during individualized retreats.

Hydeout provides a quiet retreat house equipped with two bedrooms, a living and dining area with a fireplace, and a fully equipped kitchen complete with a juicer. Inspirational art, books, and audio- and videotapes are available to encourage a contemplative experience. Only three people can be accommodated at one time, which adds to the sense of seclusion. One does not come to Hydeout to socialize but to focus on an inward journey to wellness. Before arriving at Hydeout, guests are asked to examine where they are in life and where they would like to be. An optional consultation on arrival can help guests with this highly personal assessment. The initial consultation is multifaceted, reviewing the individual's physical, mental, emotional, and spiritual status and needs. In designing a program best suited to the needs of each person, the Loomises consider diet, exercise, stress, trauma, chronic illness, chemical toxicity, genetic influences, belief systems, and personal relationships. Daily consultations are also available with the purpose of providing the guest with insights that will lead to total wellness.

Hours and Days of Operation: Personal retreats varying in length offered year-round.

Accommodations: One single and one double bedroom.
Rates: Per day $75 single, $100 double, $125 triple; last day is free for a weekly stay. Initial consultation $150, follow-up $75.
Credit Cards: None accepted.
Meal Plans: Guests are responsible for buying and preparing their own food in a fully equipped kitchen.
Services: Medical consultations, guided fasting, educational material, homeopathy, kinesiology, dream analysis, journaling.
Facilities: 580-acre ranch with hiking trails and labyrinth. Hydeout, which includes bedrooms, kitchen, and livingroom with fireplace, is decorated with fine art.
Staff: Dr. Evart Loomis and Fay Loomis, intuitive counselor.
Special Notes: Consultations recommended with the fasting program. Telephones and television not available.
Nearby Attractions: Scenic Idylwild, Desert Hot Springs, Palm Desert, outdoor recreation, theater, shopping, dining, museums in San Diego and Los Angeles.
Getting There: Located halfway between Los Angeles and San Diego.

Kumar Frantzis Summer Retreats

P.O. Box 99
Fairfax, CA 94978-0099
(415) 454-5243; fax (415) 454-0907

B. K. Frantzis has over 35 years of experience in oriental healing practices, martial arts, and meditation. He holds black belts in judo, jujitsu, karate, and aikido and spent two years in India studying advanced yoga and Tantric practices. After practicing chi kung and tui na bodywork in hospitals and clinics in Chinese hospitals, Frantzis became the first westerner to receive certification as a teacher of tai chi by the People's Republic of China. For ten years, Frantzis studied in Hong Kong, Taiwan, and mainland China with some of China's greatest martial arts masters. The late Chinese Taoist sage Liu Hung Chieh accepted Frantzis as his disciple in 1981 and later officially adopted him as his son in a traditional ceremony. Frantzis also holds an advanced degree in acupuncture and is a doctor of health sciences with an emphasis on body-mind therapies.

Each summer, Frantzis hosts several retreats during July and August at Anvil Ranch, a 12,000-acre wilderness only two hours north of San Francisco. The retreats demonstrate various methods of chi kung, the benefits of which include stress relief, the prevention of illness, increased personal health, and vitality. The Wu style is recommended for people healing from injuries or who suffer from back problems. Bend-the-bow-and-shoot-the-arrow spinal chi kung helps people consciously control the movement of vertebrae, enabling them to correct left and right imbalances in the body. Students spend five hours each day learning tai chi, and every other day they have the option of participating in an early morning hour-long additional class. When not learning chi kung, guests can hike along ridge trails, relax in the outdoor hot tub, and soak in the five-mile views or enjoy a swim in a natural lake.

Frantzis also hosts a similar retreat in Corfu, Greece. Guests stay in a seventeenth-century restored Venetian villa or in private bungalows surrounded by gardens of bougainvilleas, hibiscus, almond, and olive groves.

Hours and Days of Operation: 3 weeks in July and August.
Accommodations: Double rooms and indoor dormitory-style rooms available on a first-come, first-served basis. Some campsites available; campers must bring their own equipment.
Rates: Classes, accommodations, food $759.
Credit Cards: MC, V.
Meal Plans: 3 gourmet meals a day, both vegetarian and nonvegetarian. Guests with dietary restrictions may have to bring their own food. Inquire for details.
Services: Daily workshops on chi kung, tai chi, meditation.
Facilities: 12,000-acre natural wilderness setting, ranch house, hot tub, deck with 5-mile views, ridge trails, natural lake, beaches.
Staff: B. K. Frantzis and assistant.
Special Notes: People with medical, emotional, or mental imbalances should consult a physician or psychotherapist before embarking on the retreat. Training retreats for instructors also available. Some classes provide continuing education credits for California licensed acupuncturists.
Nearby Attractions: Sonoma County wineries, beaches.
Getting There: From the San Francisco Airport, take the Airport Express to Santa Rosa. At 2 p.m., a free shuttle transports guests to Anvil ranch. Shuttle reservations must be made in advance.

Land of Medicine Buddha

5800 Prescott Road
Soquel, CA 95073
(408) 462-8383; fax (408) 462-8380

Land of Medicine Buddha rests on 55 acres of forest and meadowland in the foothills of the Santa Cruz Mountains. The late Lama Thubten Yeshe and Lama Zopa Rinpoche were inspired to found the center as a place to make available the essence of the Buddha's teachings of wisdom and compassion in an atmosphere that transcends national and cultural barriers. The center is designed to be a place of healing where the qualities of love and compassion can be awakened in each individual. Groups are welcome to rent out all or part of the facilities for workshops and conferences.

Programs are dedicated to healing the body, mind, and environment. During a five-day retreat, guests might either learn about the Chinese healing arts or explore Tibetan Buddhist spiritual and wellness practices. A typical day can include a morning class on the healing traditions of chi kung, meditation, Tibetan Buddhism, nutritional therapy, visualization techniques, or purification practices. Afternoons are usually open for exploring the wild herbs and flowers of the adjacent state park or taking a therapeutic mineral soak. Workshop participants are asked to volunteer one or two hours of work, which usually involves kitchen duty or groundskeeping. Other activities include a monthly "Medicine Buddha Practice" meeting and special evening classes hosted by guest teachers.

Land of Medicine Buddha is part of the Foundation for the Preservation of the Mahayana Tradition, an international network of individuals devoted to the transmission of Mahayana Buddhism as a living tradition and practice. A network of retreat centers, monasteries, hospices, publishing house, and healing centers is found in more than 20 countries.

Hours and Days of Operation: 2- to 5-day programs offered year-round. Personal retreats available when scheduled programs are not in session. Office hours: Daily, 10:30 a.m.–12:30 p.m. and 1:30 p.m. – 4:30 p.m.

Accommodations: Single, double, or triple rooms, each with private bath. Campsites available.

Rates: Individuals $40 per day; groups $30 per day per person.

Credit Cards: MC, V.

Meal Plans: 3 organic, vegetarian meals a day for groups, 2 meals a day for individuals.

Services: Programs focusing on spiritual and healing practices, meditation, massage, hiking, qigong.

Facilities: A 55-acre forested retreat center with main lodge, kitchen, meeting rooms, bookstore, sauna, camping facilities.

Staff: Massage therapists and bodyworkers available by reservation.

Special Notes: Smoking, alcohol, and nonprescription drugs not allowed. Some facilities accessible for people with disabilities.

Nearby Attractions: Capitola Village, Monterey, Santa Cruz beach boardwalk, redwood forests, beaches.

Getting There: 45 minutes by car from the San Jose Airport, 1½ hours by car from the San Francisco Airport. Greyhound bus service and Airporter shuttle available from either location.

Maharishi Ayur-Veda Medical Center

17308 Sunset Boulevard
Pacific Palisades, CA 90272
(310) 454-5531; fax (310) 454-7841
Web sites: www.maharishi-medical.com; www.vedic-health.com

The Maharishi Ayur-Veda approach to health maintains the belief that a balance exists between the body and its own "inner intelligence," an intelligence that is tapped through Vedic knowledge. Through restoring and maintaining this balance, thought, behavior, and everyday tendencies harmonize with the "Natural Law." This harmony is the basis of good health.

The Maharishi Ayur-Veda Medical Center, nestled between a dry coastal canyon and the sparkling Pacific Ocean, offers a Rejuvenation Program founded on the principle of restoring balance. The purpose of the program is to eliminate accumulated impurities from the body before imbalance can manifest as disease. By gently and effectively cleansing the body, digestion, appetite, stamina, and circulation improve, and vitality and mental clarity are restored.

Before beginning the program, patients are asked to begin the rejuvenation process through a cleansing diet in order to prepare the diet. Because everyone is different, the program will vary from person to person, but some elements are common to all. The first day begins with a consultation with an expert in the Maharishi Vedic approach to health to determine which herbal preparations, diet, and daily routine will most benefit the patient. Afterward, a health educator explains the recommendations in detail. For the next three to seven days, the patient undergoes a series of herbalized oil applications, internal purification procedures, steam treatments, and inhalation therapies in a quiet environment intended to induce deep rest. Presentations on health, lifestyle, and spirituality are also a part of the program, complementing the process of "enlivening the inner intelligence" through physical purification.

Hours and Days of Operation: Tue–Fri, 10–4:30; Sat, 10–3:30; 3- to 7-day panchakarma treatment offered year-round.
Accommodations: Single rooms with private bath.
Rates: Vary according to services. Panchakarma treatment $370 per day.
Credit Cards: MC, V.
Meal Plans: All meals provided during residential program and designed to complement the healing process.
Services: Traditional Ayurvedic healing treatments, including pulse readings, oil massage, herbal steams; yoga instruction, educational programs.
Facilities: A large complex with lecture hall, treatment rooms, overnight accommodations, gardens, paved walking paths.
Staff: About 25 total staff, including Ayurvedic physicians, massage therapists, yoga instructors.
Special Notes: Recommended that program be scheduled at least 3 weeks in advance. Women should not undergo the program during the first 3 days of their menstrual cycle.
Nearby Attractions: Topanga Canyon State Park, Will Rogers State Park, miles of beaches, coastal canyons.
Getting There: 25 minutes by car from Los Angeles International Airport, 10 minutes by car from Santa Monica.

Mendocino Summer Camp

2122 Prince Street
Berkeley, CA 94705
(510) 841-8096
E-mail: macrocamp@geocities.com

A clear creek with salmon fry runs through the Mendocino Summer Camp, located in the center of a 2,000-acre redwood forest. For nine years, the camp has offered a program designed to teach people the difference between what appears to be a good lifestyle and what truly is a good lifestyle. Over the course of a week, guests receive nourishment for the mind, body, and spirit and come away with restored vitality. Says founder Yolanda Huang, "We teach people to be aware, to be centered and to enjoy our physical being as the vehicle for our spiritual selves."

A typical day is relaxed and unhurried. The morning starts with gentle exercise or breathing and a warm macrobiotic breakfast. Afterward, adults can attend health lectures or take a walk. Kids can paint tepees; weave baskets; make masks; saw, hammer, and sand wooden boats; or simply play in the creek. Lunch follows a singing circle, and in the afternoon there are more lectures, exercise classes, or simply reading in a hammock under a giant redwood. The day winds down with a large and healthy dinner followed by stories around a campfire.

Body-based health counseling is available by counselors trained either at the Kushi Institute or in the field of holistic bodywork, such as shiatsu or jin shin jyutsu. It starts with an examination of the person's present physical state and whether there are any symptoms of pain or other health concerns. The counselor takes into account the person's family, work, and social environment as well as their emotional and mental states and any seasonal influences. Counselors then recommend any changes in the person's diet, exercise, habits, or environment.

Camp activities also include the unique sea vegetable harvest off the coast of Mendocino. Sea vegetables are plants that grow in the ocean and are an excellent source of plant-based minerals. Because the surrounding farmlands—and, consequently, the food they produce—are mineral depleted, sea vegetables are an excellent way to restore trace minerals to the body. The waters near camp are very clean and produce a high-quality sea vegetable. The group wades out into the pristine waters to collect the evening's dinner.

Hours and Days of Operation: Yearly 9-day summer camp starting the week of Independence Day. Daily participation available for the first half of the program.

Accommodations: Rustic redwood cabins with separate bathhouses. Guests may also pitch tents but will not receive a discount for doing so.

Rates: Children under 2 free; children 2–12 $175 per week; teens 13–18 $300 per week; adults 19 and older $450 per week. Daily rates depend on availability.

Credit Cards: None accepted.

Meal Plans: 3 vegan organic meals a day based on macrobiotic principles. Special diets can be accommodated.

Services: Health lectures, workshops, cooking classes, crafts, bodywork, individual counseling, yoga, tai chi, guided meditation, dance, full-time children's Waldorf program.

Facilities: Cabins, fully equipped kitchen, dining hall, hiking trails.

Special Notes: Alcohol and nonprescription drugs not allowed.

Staff: About 10 total staff, including macrobiotic counselors and therapeutic bodyworkers.

Nearby Attractions: San Francisco, Berkeley, Fourth of July parade in nearby Mendocino, redwoods, wine country.

Getting There: Mendocino is the nearest town; transportation available to and from Mendocino bus station.

Mount Madonna Center

445 Summit Road
Watsonville, CA 95076
(408) 847-0406; fax (408) 847-2683
Web site: www.mountmadonna.org

In the rolling meadows and seaside forests of Santa Cruz County lies the Mount Madonna Center, a residential community offering spiritual and health retreats. In 1978, the Hanuman Fellowship originally purchased 355 acres of land with an expansive view of the Monterey Bay to form what would become the Mount Madonna Center, a community of people united by the study and practice of yoga. The center was founded with the goal of providing a place where people can attain a state of peace.

Mount Madonna is a threefold facility, functioning as a conference and retreat center, a private school, and a community. The center holds about 85 activities a year, including workshops, seminars, intensives, rentals by outside groups, retreats, and other educational gatherings. Programs are primarily spiritual; however, each year several workshops are offered that focus on health and healing. Ayurvedic workshops are hosted by Dr. Vasant Lad, director of the Ayurvedic Institute in Albuquerque, New Mexico.

Yoga is a strong undercurrent at Mount Madonna, and most staff have studied and practiced it for some 20 years under the direction of Baba Hari Dass. Guests on an unscheduled personal retreat can receive yoga instruction as well as acupuncture, massage, and other related services.

Personal retreats of any length can be scheduled year-round at Mount Madonna and are an ideal way for people to take advantage of the beautiful natural setting and community resources. The center provides an ideal location for academic research, personal projects, or simply a quiet place to recuperate.

Hours and Days of Operation: Office hours: Mon–Thu, 9–5; Fri, 9:30–5:30; Sat, 10–5.
Accommodations: Up to 500 in various facilities, including a studio, community lodge, guest house, and dormitory-style conference center. Most bathrooms shared. Campsites, tents, and RV hookups available.
Rates: Vary according to lodging; $24–$73, including meals.
Credit Cards: None accepted.
Meal Plans: 3 healthy vegetarian meals a day served cafeteria style.
Services: Retreats focusing on yoga practice and theory, seasonal celebrations, traditional Vedic healing methods, swedan treatments consisting of body oiling, an herbal steam bath, barley flour rubdown, and hot shower.
Recreational Activities: Swimming.
Facilities: 355-acre estate with private school for grades K–12, library, conference and seminar rooms, bookstore, gift store, Ayurvedic herb store, bathhouse, hot tub, basketball courts, tennis courts, volleyball courts, full-size gym, garden, greenhouse, lake, hiking trails.
Staff: About 100 residents.
Special Notes: Smoking allowed only in designated outdoor areas. Facilities accessible for people with disabilities.
Nearby Attractions: Santa Cruz, Monterey, Pacific Coast Highway, festivals, redwoods.
Getting There: 45 minutes by car from Santa Cruz. From San Francisco or San Jose Airports, take airport shuttle, bus, train, or cab.

Optimum Health Institute of San Diego

6970 Central Avenue
Lemon Grove, CA 91945
(619) 464-3346; fax (619) 589-4098
E-mail: optimumhealth@optimumhealth.org   Web site: www.optimumhealth.org

A diet of live raw foods, exercise, whirlpools, and the opportunity to receive colonics, massage, and chiropractic is what one can expect at the Optimum Health Institute. In three-week sessions, guests have the opportunity to live the institute's philosophy that "the human body is self-regenerating and self-cleansing and if given the proper tools with which to work, it can maintain its natural state of health." The program is structured to address the mental, physical, and emotional aspects of each person, with the ultimate goal of having each guest learn about the body and mind and how the two work together.

In the first week, some of the activities are daily exercise and attending classes that teach proper food combinations, how to build self-esteem, how to mentally and emotionally detoxify, and relaxation techniques that help control pain. Daily exercise continues in the second week, but guests also learn how to grow sprouts, plant wheat grass, organically garden, prepare healthy foods, and plan menus. Communication skills and at-home personal follow-up are also addressed. The third week has guests putting their newfound knowledge to work with hands-on food preparation classes as well as classes on the mind-body connection and diet maintenance.

Since its founding in 1976, more than 50,000 have benefited from the institute's program. Testimonials of lowered blood pressure and blood sugar levels returning to normal are just some of the many shared by former guests. Staff are passionate, knowledgeable, and experienced in the holistic health field.

Hours and Days of Operation: Daily, 7–8:30 p.m. Reservations are available: Mon–Fri, 9–5. 1-, 2-, and 3-week programs year-round.
Accommodations: Standard single, standard double, apartments, townhouse.

Rates: $400–$700 a week, depending on lodgings. Rates include room, meals, and classes. Colonics, massage, and chiropractic available at additional cost.
Credit Cards: D, MC, V. The salon does not take credit cards.
Meal Plans: 3 vegan, raw vegetarian meals a day, including sprouts, greens, fruits, vegetables, fruit juices, enzyme-rich Rejuvelac, wheat grass juice.
Services: Nutritional counseling, massage, chiropractic, and colonic hydrotherapy.
Facilities: Beachfront facility with main building, lounge, exercise room and townhouses, greenhouse, hot tub, skin care center, whirlpool, lawns, gardens, beach access.
Staff: About 70 staff members on a rotating basis, including licensed massage therapists, aestheticians, and a chiropractor. Professional counselors available, depending on capacity.
Special Notes: The institute has a free open house every Sunday at 4:30 p.m. with a live foods meal at 6 p.m. $3 donation requested for the meal. Smoking, alcohol, incense, and heavy perfumes not allowed at the Institute.
Nearby Attractions: San Diego Zoo, San Diego Wild Animal Park, Balboa Park, downtown shopping.
Getting There: The institute has an agreement with Orange Cab for a reduced rate from the San Diego Institute and train station. Fare applies only to phoned-in requests.

Preventive Medicine Research Institute

900 Bridgeway, Suite 1
Sausalito, CA 94965-2100
(800) 775-PMRI, ext. 221; fax (415) 332-5730

The Preventive Medicine Research Institute's rather clinical name belies its luxurious location at the Bay Area's only spa and fitness resort: the Claremont Resort and Spa, named one of the country's top ten by *Vogue* magazine. Nonetheless, luxury is not the main intent of Dr. Ornish's four-times-a-year residential Reversing Heart Disease workshop.

The normal length of Dr. Ornish's program is about three years, and it is aimed specifically at people with heart disease. The program begins with 12 weeks of cardiac care and lifestyle education. Cardiologists, nurse case managers, exercise physiologists, nutritionists, stress management specialists, and group support leaders all work closely with the individual to monitor progress and make the necessary treatment modifications to improve cardiac health. The remaining time involves ongoing opportunities for clinically supervised care and joining a community of program graduates and clinical staff to share successes and offer mutual support.

For those who have heard of Dr. Ornish yet cannot invest the time or do not have heart disease, the one-week retreats are a good way to learn the benefits of making comprehensive changes in diet and lifestyle. Designed for people with or without heart disease who are interested in maximizing their overall wellness, the retreats give the direct experience of all elements of the three-year program. The theory behind the condensed retreat is that people will feel significantly better in a very short time, learning firsthand the benefits of diet and lifestyle change. Increased vitality, enhanced awareness, and a greater sense of peace and well-being are all benefits past participants have claimed as a result of the retreat. An advanced program is offered for people who have participated in one or more retreats.

Hours and Days of Operation: 1-week retreats offered 4 times a year.
Accommodations: Single and double rooms with oversize beds and sitting areas.
Rates: Primary participant $2,900, companions $2,200. Special hotel rate of $125 per night, plus tax, offered to retreat participants.
Credit Cards: MC, V.
Meal Plans: 3 gourmet low-fat, low-cholesterol meals a day.
Services: Health, lifestyle, and nutritional counseling; various types of massage, including Swedish, shiatsu, and sports; acupressure, thalassotherapy, aromatherapy, herbal wraps, body scrubs, facials, salon services, tennis and swimming lessons.
Recreational Activities: Water volleyball, golf, horseback riding, hiking.
Facilities: 22-acre resort with 1915 Victorian castle, minisuites, bay-view café, exercise equipment, 2 lap pools, 10 tennis courts, par course, gardens.
Staff: Physicians, nurses, medical personnel, group support leaders, nutrition specialists, exercise physiologists, certified stress management/yoga instructors. All have collaborated with Dr. Ornish.
Special Notes: Deposit of $1,500 required, fully refundable up to 30 days prior to retreat date. Limited number of financial scholarships available to selected individuals. Call for more information.
Nearby Attractions: San Francisco, Berkeley, Oakland's Jack London Square, museums, beaches, water sports, sports activities, concerts, shopping, theater.
Getting There: From San Francisco, take the Bay Bridge to Highway 24. Take the Claremont Avenue exit to Ashley Avenue.

Quantum Shift

315 First Street, #174
Encinitas, CA 92024
(800) 573-0528

In *The Teachings of Don Juan,* famed anthropologist Carlos Castaneda refers to the exhortation of his teacher, Don Juan Matus, to follow the path with heart. Quantum Shift facilitators Robert Frey and Joy Nelson refer to the six-step process of lifestyle change they have developed as just such a path. Nelson is a chiropractor, author, and dancer; Frey, also an author, is a therapist and singer/songwriter. Both have extensive experience in leading personal growth workshops. Through a combination of movement therapy, guided inner journeys, interactive communications, intellectual dialogue, and vocal expression, guests begin to move beyond their perceived limitations, or, in other words, to make a quantum shift.

Within a safe and loving environment, participants learn the Process of Change and receive the necessary tools to continue the process on their own. The process is applied to a number of specific areas, including unfulfilling relationships, listlessness, and self-sabotage. Though the issues are deep and sometimes painful, the environment is nurturing, engaging, and often lighthearted. Guests are also immersed in nature as a part of the healing experience.

A typical day at Quantum Shift starts on a Monday evening, if guests have not arrived a few days beforehand to prepare and unwind. A gourmet vegetarian dinner is served, and guests get to know one another during an evening of music, song, and playful activities. The following morning begins with light exercise and a guided meditation. After a breakfast of tropical fruits, guests begin learning the first of the six steps to uncover, release, and transform hidden psychological and emotional blocks. Each day the group ventures out to explore the sacred spot of Maui, including journeys to jungle pools, waterfalls, and remote beaches. The remainder of the day is a balance of inner work, play, and connecting with other like-minded individuals. For an additional fee, guests can spend the day on a whale-watching excursion led by a holistic medical doctor.

Hours and Days of Operation: 4- to 8-day retreats offered year-round.
Accommodations: Vary according to location. Lodging typically in a picturesque retreat center with double-occupancy rooms. Bathrooms and showers usually shared and gender separated. Dormitory-style rooms and tent sites available.
Rates: 8-day retreat $1,200. Pre-registration discounts available.
Credit Cards: MC, V.
Meal Plans: 3 healthy gourmet meals a day, including fish and chicken. Meals primarily low-fat vegetarian, with very little dairy or sugar. Special dietary needs can be accommodated with advance notice.
Services: Personal growth programs, including yoga, movement, meditation, art therapy, music/singing, massage, breathwork, neurolinguistic programming, intuition, prosperity work, ceremony, journaling, nature excursions.
Facilities: Retreat centers include conference rooms, hot tubs, saunas, swimming pools.
Staff: In addition to Robert Frey, graduates of previous Quantum Shift retreats help facilitate retreats.
Special Notes: All facilities accessible for people with disabilities.
Nearby Attractions: Remote beaches, tropical jungles, waterfalls and pools, spectacular hiking trails and ancient Indian ruins, giant-redwood groves.
Getting There: Maui retreat center 35 minutes by car from the nearest airport. The Sedona and redwoods retreats are 2 hours by car from the nearest airport.

Redwood River Lodge

639 11th Street
Fortuna, CA 95540-2346
(707) 725-9627; fax (707) 725-2471
E-mail: skyhawk@northcoast.com

The Walake River Valley is found at the northernmost tip of California, and in it lies the home of Dr. Rosaline Skyhawk Ojala, principal chief of the Thunderbird clan. Ojala's home, otherwise known as the Redwood River Lodge, occupies 4 acres of ancient redwoods. She regularly opens her home to the public for private retreats, community sweat lodge ceremonies, and seasonal celebrations. Dr. Ojala is an internationally certified massage therapist since 1974 and a California state-licensed teacher since 1982. She is also the director of the nearby Loving Hands Institute. The institute was established in 1979 and became an incorporated nonprofit organization in 1982. Year-round classes demonstrate various techniques for initiating the natural healing process within the human body. The institute also offers an occasional apprenticeship with Ojala that takes place at the lodge.

One of the more unique courses is a two-week presentation of universal concepts and teachings passed down through the ages in native societies. Students explore the nature, purpose and possibilities of human existence using the Ancient Wheel of Life as a metaphorical mirror which reflects not only what a person is, but also what they might became. The class is a camping experience and provides 14 continuing education units.

Guests who come to the lodge for retreats will most likely sense Ojala's determination to impart a way for people to find spiritual expressions in all the daily activities of life. Personal spiritual counseling can be scheduled, as can massage—or guests can choose to simply soak in a hot tub, nap under a giant redwood, or explore the many hiking trails. Guests are also invited to participate in a sweat lodge ceremony, viewed as a return to the womb of Mother Earth. The sacred ceremony is intended to reconnect the individual with his or her spiritual self as well as cleanse and purify the body, mind, and emotions. A Visions of the Goddess gathering is also open to women on personal retreat.

Hours and Days of Operation: Personal retreats ranging from a few days to a week are offered year-round. Office hours: Mon–Sat, 11–6.

Accommodations: Small garden cottage, single occupancy, with dirt floor; Wikkiup Guest Lodge with queen bed, private bath, and wood stove; double occupancy; tent sites.

Rates: Guest cottage $40 per day. $10–$15 per day, per person, plus cost of workshops, massage sessions, or counseling.

Credit Cards: MC, V.

Meal Plans: Some programs include meals; otherwise, guests supply their own food and cooking equipment. Use of kitchen must be scheduled in advance.

Services: Classes and workshops in Swedish-Esalen, acupressure, reflexology, deep tissue and lymphatic massage, hydrotherapy, herbal remedies, trigger-point therapy, Native American spiritual counseling in earth medicine ways; seasonal celebrations.

Recreational Activities: Swimming, hiking.

Facilities: Loving Hands Institute, kitchen, garden cottage, guest lodge, sweat lodge, outdoor shower, indoor and outdoor bathrooms, hot tub, access to swimming holes on river.

Staff: Dr. Rosalind Skyhawk Ojala, DD ICMT; instructors.

Special Notes: Advance registration required for all visits. Various levels of certification offered, including Swedish-Esalen and holistic massage. Inquire for details.

Nearby Attractions: Fortuna Rodeo, Redwood AutoRama, Civil War Reenactment Days, Eureka Jazz Festival.

Getting There: Directions available on registration.

STAR Foundation

P.O. Box 516
Geyserville, CA 95441
(888)857-STAR or (707) 857-3359; fax (707) 857-3764

STAR is not an acronym; rather, it's a description of what founder Barbara Findeisen believes to be the natural state and birthright of every human being. It describes a state of openness, love, vulnerability, safety, and vibrancy of life. The 17-day STAR retreat helps people recover this natural state through integrating "the wisdom of the heart" with intuitive knowledge. The workshops use a variety of healing techniques, including experiential therapies, breathwork, sand-tray therapy, art therapy, emotional release work, cognitive exercises, bodywork, and more. Findeisen, who is also STAR's director, is a licensed marriage and family counselor internationally recognized for her work in pre- and perinatal psychology and in regressive psychotherapy.

The healing that takes place at STAR cannot be described as a single retreat event but as a catalyst for a lifelong process. The program is designed to allow individuals to journey deeply into themselves and tap the innate wisdom of living, being, and loving in a better way. Various therapeutic techniques are drawn on during the retreat, including art therapy, cognitive exercises, bodywork, breathwork and other experiential methods that form an integrated approach to exploration and healing. Rebirthing, optional therapy during the STAR process, is intended to put the individual in touch with deeply buried memories and patterns that affect the way he or she interacts with the present-day environment.

Staff to participant ratio is nearly one-to-one and includes bodyworkers, marriage and family counselors, social workers, and psychologists. All 1998 workshops will be held at Saratoga Springs in Upper Lake, California. Amidst the high-desert slopes of Lake County, California, is the 260-acre retreat center complete with healing mineral springs. The center boasts a rope swing, old manzanita trees, and maidenhair fern, a fire circle and large, comfortable wood cabins. Built in the late 1800s, the Saratoga Springs provides an isolated natural setting conducive to a sense of privacy as guests undergo deeply personal work.

Hours and Days of Operation: 17-day program offered 4 times per year.
Accommodations: Comfortable dormitory-style bunkrooms in lodge and cottages.
Rates: 17-day retreat $5,200.
Credit Cards: MC, V.
Meal Plans: 3 healthy meals a day using fresh local produce whenever possible. Vegetarian options and special dietary needs can be accommodated with advance notice.
Services: Cognitive exercises, guided imagery, feeling work, art therapy, sand-tray therapy, bodywork, breathwork.
Facilities: 260-acre hillside estate with community lodge, meeting rooms, cabins, hot tub, outdoor swimming pool, roundhouse with 6 different soda mineral springs and several cold mineral springs.
Staff: Ratio of staff to guests is nearly 1-to-1, including licensed bodyworkers, psychologists, social workers, marriage and family counselors, administrative staff.
Special Notes: STAR is a valuable complement to people involved in 12-step programs. Sightseeing only before or after the program.
Nearby Attractions: Sonoma wine country, California's scenic northern coast, Clear Lake, Mount Konocti.
Getting There: 3 hours by car from San Francisco, 2¼ hours by car from Sacramento.

Vega Study Center

720 Bird Street
Oroville, CA 95965
(800) 818-8342 or (916) 533-4777; fax (916) 533-4999
E-mail: VegaStudy@cncnet.com

Vega is an educational institute dedicated to teaching macrobiotic self-healing through diet, attitude, and personal empowerment. All programs are geared toward health education and healing oneself. The staff is internationally recognized by the macrobiotic community for its expertise. Vega's teachers have been actively engaged in macrobiotic education for 20 to 40 years. Cornellia and Herman Aihara founded the institute as a result of a promise to George Ohsawa, one of the founding fathers of macrobiotics, to develop Vega as a profound social force. In 1991, the Aiharas joined forces with Cynthia and David Briscoe to promote the Aihara's Vega traditions well into the next century while further cultivating new macrobiotic customs for a healthy society.

A day at Vega beings with early morning qigong exercise followed by tea and discussion at 8. A morning lecture on the macrobiotic lifestyle is followed by lunch at 11. A cooking class at 2 is the only afternoon activity, leaving guests free to take a sauna, walk through the surrounding countryside replete with organic farms and orchards, or receive personal lifestyle counseling. Dinner is at 5, followed by an evening salt bath before bed.

Probably one of the most intriguing courses offered at Vega is Swingolf with Les Bolland, a 20-year qualified member with the British PGA who has followed the macrobiotic lifestyle for 14 years. The course offers a way to enjoy golf based on holistic laws rather than technique-motivated play. Guests learn to see the golf swing as a means of self-expression. Characteristic of the Vega's unique approach, course requirements include an ability to laugh with oneself and appreciate the moment.

Hours and Days of Operation: Office hours: Mon–Fri, 7–6. 5-day retreats, 1- and 2-week courses, and 6-month residency program offered year-round.

Accommodations: Shared and private rooms containing cotton futons or single beds and half or private bath; 1 private cottage with bedroom, kitchen, bathroom, and dining room available. Weekly bed linens provided.
Rates: Workshops $545–$1,300, depending on length of course. Day classes $150.
Credit Cards: AE, MC, V.
Meal Plans: 3 macrobiotic vegetarian meals a day, with optional fish and locally grown produce and grains.
Services: Macrobiotic clay facials and herbal steams, saunas, salt baths, relaxation techniques, drumming and inner journeying, music, sound and light therapy, acupressure facelifts, macrobiotic cooking lessons; Do-In; qigong; meditation; breathing, movement, and stretching exercises; bioenergetics; morning tea with Herman and Cornellia Aihara.
Recreational Activities: Swimming, biking.
Facilities: Macrobiotic store, lounge with television, library, redwood deck, sauna, salt baths, laundry facility.
Staff: Since Vega is an educational facility, no medical professionals are on staff. Instructors include a master macrobiotic counselor and teacher, senior macrobiotic counselor and teacher, master macrobiotic cooking instructor, senior macrobiotic cooking instructor, licensed shiatsu practitioner.
Special Notes: Vega is not a medical facility. Guests must bring their own towels and toiletries.
Nearby Attractions: Birdcage Theatre; State Theater; Feather River; Chinese Temple and Garden; C. F. Lott Home in Sank Park; Butte County Pioneer Museum; Bedrock Park; Oroville antique shops; Ehmann Home; Nevada City; blues and bluegrass festivals; cultural activities in nearby Chico.
Getting There: 1½ hours by car north of Sacramento. Shuttle service available for a fee.

Vichy Springs Resort

2605 Vichy Springs Road
Ukiah, CA 95482-3507
(707) 462-9515; fax (707) 462-9516
E-mail: vichy@pacific.net   Web site: www.vichysprings.com

There is an old photo of the Vichy Springs Resort that shows Mark Twain in summer suit, necktie, and Panama hat "taking the waters." Twain dips the tip of his long cane into the mineral water that pours from the Mendocino foothills and stares intently at the mouth of a cave. It is obvious that both the resort and the waters have been around a long time. The "Champagne Baths," as they are known at Vichy Springs, were first used by indigenous peoples thousands of years ago and are sought for their healing and restorative qualities. The mineral baths contain the only warm and naturally carbonated water in North America, and their composition is exactly like that of the famous Vichy Springs in France. The mineral water bottled directly from the springs has occasionally been served at the White House.

After the 700-acre resort opened in 1854, it began to gain renown among well-known writers, philosophers, and politicians. Robert Louis Stevenson, Jack London, and Ulysses S. Grant made Vichy a regular retreat spot. The current proprietors of Vichy Springs traveled through 135 countries to gain an intimate knowledge of what visitors need and seek. They then sought out the most unique springs in the United States and developed this small and understated resort for the subtle rest and healing people need today. There are no set programs at Vichy. The naturally occurring springs are therapeutic in themselves and provide relief from a variety of maladies, including arthritis, gout, rheumatism, poison oak, burns, and the general stresses of everyday life. Combined with massage therapy, facials, hiking, and swimming, the benefits of this relaxed and healthy getaway accumulate.

Hours and Days of Operation: Open year-round. Check-in 3–9 p.m.

Accommodations: Rooms or cottages with queen and/or twin beds and individual climate control.
Rates: $99 for a single room; $195 for a double cottage. Massage rates $60–$85. Day use of mineral baths, swimming pool, and property $30 for all-day pass, $18 for 2 hours or less.
Credit Cards: AE, CB, D, DC, JCB, MC, V.
Meal Plans: Full buffet-style breakfast included with room, with vegetarian options.
Services: Therapeutic and Swedish massage, reiki, foot reflexology, herbal facials.
Recreational Activities: Volleyball, basketball, hiking.
Facilities: 700-acre ranch estate with 10 private mineral baths, a communal hot pool, an olympic-sized outdoor pool, massage and treatment rooms, 3 cottages, 5 acres of landscaped gardens, swings, badminton, horseshoes, live stream, waterfall, rolling hills, and miles of hiking trails.
Staff: 10 certified massage therapists.
Special Notes: Bathing suits required in all facilities. Pets not allowed.
Nearby Attractions: The Mendocino coast; lakes and wineries of Sonoma, Lake, and Mendocino Counties; redwood forests; Grace Hudson Museum; water sports; fishing.
Getting There: From San Francisco, follow Highway 101 north 2 hours to Ukiah, then go east on Vichy Springs Road and follow the Historic Landmark signs. From Sacramento, take Highway 5 north, Highway 20 west, and Highway 101 south to Ukiah (2½ hours).

We Care Holistic Health Center

18000 Long Canyon Road
Desert Hot Springs, CA 92241
(800) 888-2523 or (760) 251-2261; fax (760) 251-5399

We Care Holistic Health Center is a family-owned holistic health center dedicated to total well-being through natural health practices. Guests are rejuvenated and detoxified through the combined use of herbs, an all-natural liquid diet, colonics, and massage. This approach is built around the recovery of an impaired immune system. But guests don't have to have an illness caused by a weak immune system to benefit from We Care's program. Founders Susana and Susan Lombardi believe that people who feel sluggish, bloated, or listless or who are prone to gas, indigestion, and constipation are already feeling the effects of immune system damage. Consequently, through participating in the We Care program, guests not only restore healthy immune function but also experience redoubled energy and the need to sleep less.

The Lombardis emphasize improving the mind, body, and spirit through cleansing, relaxation, exercise, and nutritional education. Although guests are technically fasting, they are not on a starvation diet. A regular stay consists of a liquid diet, daily colonic hygiene treatments, reflexology, and the use of products that act as solvents to remove toxins from the body. The cold-press raw fruit and vegetable juices, herb teas, and lemon water ensure that the body receives all the nutrition it needs and sometimes more than most people get from their normal diets. Guests also experience lymphatic massage, reflexology, herbal wraps, salt glows, yoga, mineral water baths, swimming, cooking demonstrations, and daily nutrition classes.

Because it takes several days of cleansing before the body begins to release toxins, the program is one week long; daily and monthly rates are available, as well as a home cleansing program.

Hours and Days of Operation: 1-day to several month programs offered year-round.
Accommodations: 7 spacious private rooms with private bath, 5 small rooms with semi-private bath. Guests have the option of no television or telephone.
Rates: 3-day retreat $250–$300; 8-day wellness package $1,500–$1,800. Second week discounted 10%. Discount rates offered for double occupancy, We Care graduates, and travel agents.
Credit Cards: AE, MC, V.
Meal Plans: We Care is a juice-fasting spa. Raw juices offered hourly, as are herbal teas and detox drinks.
Services: Yoga classes, meditation, guided fasting, colonics, iridology, reflexology, massage, salt glow rubs, herbal wraps, skin brushing, aromatherapy, energy clearing, nutrition and cooking classes, Rolfing, Hellerwork.
Recreational Activities: Desert walks.
Facilities: A desert ranch with sun deck, kitchen, hot mineral pools, outdoor swimming pool.
Staff: Licensed nutritionists, massage therapists, colon therapists, Rolfer, acupuncturist, iridologist, biologist.
Special Notes: A satisfaction guarantee gives guests 24 hours to claim a refund, minus a daily rate charge. Smoking not allowed.
Nearby Attractions: Joshua Tree National Monument; theater, concerts; and galleries of Palm Springs; botanical gardens; jeep tours; hikes.
Getting There: From the Palm Springs Airport, We Care recommends a prearranged arrival with Checker Cab.

Weimar Institute

P.O. Box 486, 20601 West Paoli Lane
Weimar, CA 95736
(916) 637-4111; fax (916) 637-4408

Fresh air, the smell of pine, and the sounds of wild songbirds awaken guests of the Weimar Institute's NEWSTART Lifestyle Program. Since 1978, people have participated in the program to restore health and vitality through a combination of diet, exercise, stress management, medical supervision, and a connection with the divine. The program begins on a Sunday and last for 18 days. "Graduates" participate in a ceremony, complete with graduation certificates, group photo, and an inspirational book autographed by NEWSTART physicians and staff.

A typical day begins at 6:30 a.m. with a breakfast of fresh fruit, oatmeal with raisins, and a warm muffin. Afterward, a chaplain presents strategies for a healthy and fulfilled lifestyle during FRESHSTART, then it's time for a Stretchercise class, designed for bodies unaccustomed to exercise. Free time is from 8:30 to 10, which is a great time for guests to walk one of the many trails throughout the 500 wooded acres. Guests then meet with a doctor who conducts a physical examination while discussing individual health goals and concerns. Lunch follows, usually consisting of something like lentil soup, homemade bread from an on-site bakery, vegetarian lasagna, and fresh steamed vegetables. Hydrotherapy and massage treatments are usually scheduled in the afternoon; lectures on topics ranging from maintaining a healthy body to the importance of low-fat foods begin at 4:30. A light dinner of soup, toast, and fruit follows, and in the evening guests gather for a "Let's Get Acquainted" walk through the landscaped grounds.

Hours and Days of Operation: Weekend seminars offered year-round; NEWSTART program, Jun–mid-Dec.
Accommodations: 29 rooms with sitting area, private bath, and single or king-size beds. 23 additional rooms available for overflow at the Weimar Inn.
Rates: 4-day program $1,200 for individual; $1,025 for companion; $720 for partial program companion. 18-day program $4,670 for individual; $8,790 for couples; $2,370 for partial program companion; $3,220 for alumni. Rates do not include medical costs, which vary according to Medicare coverage.
Credit Cards: AE, D, MC, V.
Meal Plans: 3 vegan meals a day, including fresh baked bread.
Services: Medical consultations, hydrotherapy, massage, Stretchercise, counseling, health lectures, cooking classes, 24-hour nursing staff, videos and group discussions on health-related and inspirational topics.
Recreational Activities: Volleyball, golf, river wading.
Facilities: 457-acre campus with community lodge, Weimar college, whirlpools, Russian-style steam baths, exercise equipment, walking trails, gardens.
Staff: All staff, including doctors, massage therapists, and fitness instructors, are Seventh-Day Adventists.
Special Notes: Smoking not allowed. Although the center is operated by Seventh-Day Adventists, the institute is nondenominational.
Nearby Attractions: Sacramento's Old Towne, Empire Mine State Historic Park, Railroad Museum, Yosemite National Park.
Getting There: 1 hour by car from Sacramento. Transportation from Greyhound or Amtrak station available on request for an additional fee.

Well Within

P.O. Box 1563
Nevada City, CA 95959
(530) 478-1242; fax (530) 478-1572
E-mail: wwithin@nccn.net   Web site: www.nccn.net/~wwithin

Since 1982, Sheri Nakken has been touring the Earth's sacred sites and healing centers. A registered nurse who has been teaching homeopathy workshops for five years, Nakken has been taking groups of people to Kauai, Peru, Ireland, Bali, Greece, and other places where she believes they can experience the power and energy of a natural setting or ancient historical remains. Nakken believes people visiting the sites can tap into ancient memories and teachings that will assist them on their journeys. Well Within sponsors and conducts workshops, conferences, weekend retreats in holistic health, and international tours to sacred sites and alternative healing centers. Through the workshops and tours, as well as through alternative healing therapies and metaphysics, Nakken believes healing can occur for the person and the planet.

The November 1998 trip to Kauai is titled "Healing, Wholeness, and Living Your Vision." For seven nights, guests stay in a comfortable hotel near the beach while they hike the Na Pali coast, walk through Waimea Canyon and the mountains of central Kauai, and visit the Kaduval Hindu Temple, which contains a giant "earthkeeper" crystal. Workshops explore the Kahuna healing teachings, how to "live your vision," and various Hawaiian myths.

In the spring, a one-day "Introduction to Homeopathy" course is offered in Nevada City. The workshop explores the principles of homeopathy and how the healing process begins in the body. Nakken compares homeopathic remedies with allopathic medicine and explains how homeopathic medicine is made and used. Guests learn to evaluate symptoms and discuss how treatment evolves. If participants are nurses, the course provides seven continuing education credits.

Nakken is also the publisher of *The Well-Being Directory*, a directory of professionals involved in the healing arts in Nevada City, California. In the process of publishing the directory, she conducts meetings of the Healing Arts Network, a networking group for practitioners in the healing arts. The meetings are open to all therapists, physicians, nurses, counselors, and teachers who work in the complementary healing arts.

Hours and Days of Operation: Daylong workshops, weekend retreats, and longer international tours offered year-round.

Rates: $185–$250 per weekend, depending on location and lodging. Rates include accommodations, meals, workshop. Inquire for details on international tours.

Credit Cards: MC, V.

Services: Holistic health workshops and lectures, journeys to sacred healing sites, massage, acupuncture, energy healing, homeopathy, acupressure, reiki.

Facilities: Vary according to location. Most retreat centers are in rustic locations with hot tubs.

Staff: In addition to Nakken, support staff are available on an as-needed basis.

Nearby Attractions: Vary according to location. Santa Barbara offers museums, shopping, nightlife, and beaches. Mendocino offers redwood forests and historic coastal towns. Nevada City offers tours through gold-mining country. Kauai's attractions include helicopter trips over the Na Pali coast. Ireland's attractions include a tour of Dublin's museums, parks, and the River Liffey; excursions to Newgrange, a passage "tomb," and the Hill of Tara (a sacred center of Ireland). Peru's attractions include a trip to Ollantaytambo, the Inca town with condor niches and ruins, and 4 days at Machu Picchu during a full moon.

Getting There: Sheri Nakken will help facilitate plane reservations, car rentals, or carpooling.

Wilbur Hot Springs

3375 Wilbur Springs Road
Williams, CA 95987-9709
(530) 473-2306

Gold diggers, silver miners, stagecoach drivers, and weary travelers once flooded the small town of Wilbur Springs, California, during the Victorian era to sit in the natural hot mineral waters and rejuvenate themselves—and perhaps slug a shot of whiskey. Today, Wilbur Hot Springs, billed as a "sanctuary for the self," is a place where people who seek a healing quiet can come to take the waters. The Colusi, Pomo, and Wintun tribes considered these panoramic ridge views and high meadows home for centuries before Columbus found his way to America. The springs were revered as sacred healing grounds. Although it is not the type of healing a naturopathic physician might provide, guests can experience the unmistakably therapeutic experience of a mineral soak amidst serene and remote countryside.

Though founded in 1865, the resort was purchased by the late Dr. Richard Louis Miller in 1970, who emphasized an environment of mutual respect, quietude, conservation, and cooperation. The retreat rests on 240 acres on a 15,000-acre nature preserve in northern California's Coastal Mountain Range. The hotel is solar powered and warmed by centrally located gas fireplaces. The Victorian era lodge is a historic hotel, evidenced by the details of carved flowers in paneled wood within the guest rooms. The bathhouse, a quiet area at all times, is sheltered. Water is channeled into three long baths with temperatures ranging from a mild 98 degrees to a near-scalding 112. A large, cool-water mineral pool offers guests a break from the heat, and an outdoor hot mineral sitting pool is for those who like to scald under the sun. A dry sauna is connected to the bathhouse by a sweeping wood deck. Licensed massage therapists are available with advance reservations.

Hours and Days of Operation: Open year-round. Reservations accepted daily 10 a.m.–9 p.m.; check-in 3 p.m.; quiet hours 10 p.m.–10 a.m. Daytime use of hot springs 10–5.

Accommodations: 17 private guest rooms, one spacious suite with a private bath, kitchen, 3 optional adjoining bedrooms, 11-bed bunk room, campsites (available seasonally).

Rates: Vary according to lodging and time of visit. Single-occupancy room $85 Sun–Thu; $126 Fri, Sat, holidays. Rates include access to all facilities, unlimited use of hot springs, and all taxes. Minimum stay of 2 nights required for weekend bookings.

Credit Cards: MC, V.

Meal Plans: Guests supply their own food and cook their meals in a commercially equipped kitchen. Dry spices, cookware, utensils, and dishes provided.

Services: Esalen/Swedish and deep-tissue massage, hot and cold water mineral soaks.

Recreational Activities: Hiking, mountain biking, stargazing.

Facilities: 240-acre private valley adjacent to a 15,000-acre nature preserve; bathhouse; cool water mineral pool; outdoor hot mineral sitting pool; dry sauna; redwood deck; historic hotel; kitchen; billiards; music room with piano, guitars, and bamboo flutes; Ping Pong; 2 dining rooms; library; nature trails.

Staff: Licensed professional bodyworkers and massage therapists available on call.

Special Notes: Wilbur Hot Springs is clothing optional behind the screened area. Towels are required, and guests supply their own, and all, toiletries. Bunk-room guests must bring their own top bedding. Children under 3 not permitted in baths.

Nearby Attractions: River rafting in the Cache Creek Canyon.

Getting There: 2½ hours by car northeast of San Francisco, 1½ hours by car north of the Sacramento Airport.

Earth Rites, Inc.

1265 South Steele Street
Denver, CO 80210
(303) 733-7465; fax (303) 777-7544
E-mail: clbolender@aol.com

Earth Rites guides lead nine-day rites of passage into Utah's high desert wilderness. Since 1983, the trips have helped participants experience a renewed sense of meaning and life direction. Leav Bolander, director and co-founder of Earth Rites, has been guiding Rites of Passage since 1980. She is an artist, psychotherapist, and licensed clinical social worker who uses traditional clinical approaches—as well as ceremony, experiential activities, and creativity—in her healing work with individuals and groups. Bolander is also a former instructor for Colorado Outward Bound's Community Programs and a certified Emergency Medical Technician. She helped found Earth Rites with the goal of helping people gain a deeper understanding of the interconnectedness and sacredness of all life. During the wilderness retreats, participants learn to go beyond the familiar and discover their physical, emotional, and spiritual potential.

The trips involve three elements: release, solo and fasting, and a return. The release, a group process involving music, dance, and ceremony, serves to focus intentions and allows individuals to bond as a supportive community before they split up for the solo experience. During the solo experience, participants fast to cleanse the body and become receptive to insights. Prayer and ritual are used during this time, and many guests remain awake during an all-night vigil. The return is a celebration of the new beginning that guests feel after the solo and fast. A "give-away" follows in which everyone shares their stories of inward journey. The goal of Earth Rites is to help people gain the clarity, strength, and spiritual power they need to win life's challenges and ride its turning points.

Hours and Days of Operation: 9-day trips offered in spring, summer, and fall.
Accommodations: Participants carry camping equipment on their backpacks.
Rates: $475–$750, depending on program.
Credit Cards: None accepted.
Meal Plans: Meals are community based. Guests bring 4 of their own lunches and 1 community meal to which they are assigned. Directions are provided for wilderness preparation, cooking, and packing. Meals are primarily vegetarian.
Services: Fasting, ritual, ceremony, rites of passage, group discussion, dance.
Staff: Trips are led by Leav Bolender, Margot Smit, and Kathy Karn. All are experienced wilderness Rites of Passage guides and certified in wilderness first aid.
Special Notes: Fasting is an essential element of the Rite of Passage. Guests must be physically able to participate and strong enough to carry a backpack or arrange for a helper to carry their gear.
Nearby Attractions: Colorado mountain and canyonlands wilderness.
Getting There: Journeys originate from Denver. Guests carpool in local vehicles to the site of the passage.

Eden Valley Lifestyle Center

6263 North County Road 29
Loveland, CO 80538
(800) 637-WELL or (970) 669-7730; fax (970) 667-1742

Eden Valley Lifestyle Center is situated on 550 acres of fields, woods, lakes, and streams in Colorado's Rocky Mountains. The center offers seven- to 24-day lifestyle programs providing therapy, nutrition, and exercise for people suffering from chronic conditions like allergies, high blood pressure, and arthritis. The program began as an extension to services offered at the nearby Eden Valley senior citizens' home in 1987. The home can still be found on the grounds, as can a Seventh-Day Adventist medical missionary school.

Natural remedies and a holistic approach are essential elements of the lifestyle programs. A comprehensive physical examination, including a blood chemistry analysis, kicks off the program. Guests can also expect to receive nutritional counseling, daily exercise, paraffin baths for arthritis, health lectures, cooking classes, and herbal remedies. Hydrotherapy, therapeutic massage treatments, and optional guided fasting are also a part of the program. Meals consist of fresh vegan cuisine made with fruit and vegetables from the center's organic garden. During free time, guests can walk along quiet mountain trails or take an excursion to nearby antique shops and ghost towns.

It is Eden Valley's goal to send guests home with improved physical, mental, and social well-being as well as a renewed sense of vitality, strength, and stamina. Because disease is viewed as a result of an unhealthy lifestyle, staff first work to help guests understand the cause of their disease in order to correct it. Guests then learn health-promoting principles to continue their lifelong journey to wellness. A healthy lifestyle consisting of no smoking or alcohol, a high-fiber, low-fat vegetarian diet, and normal weight maintenance is emphasized to prevent illness.

The center has had successful results in treating chronic illnesses, including heart disease, digestive problems, chronic fatigue, high blood pressure, and arthritis. The center's New Start Program is designed, in particular, to combat the effects of stress, obesity, and addiction. Decoding the acronym NEWSTART summarizes the program's basic elements: nutrition, exercise, water, sunlight, temperance, air, rest, and trust in God.

Hours and Days of Operation: Open year-round with monthly scheduled programs. Office hours: Mon–Thu, 8–5; Fri, 8–12:30.
Accommodations: 5 rooms in private homes and 5 in a new guest house, 3 of which have private baths.
Rates: 1-week program $600; 2-week program $1,100; 3-week program $1,500.
Credit Cards: MC, V.
Meal Plans: 3 vegan meals daily for Lifestyle participants.
Services: Lifestyle programs, hydrotherapy/massage treatments, colonics, health lectures, medical examinations, cooking classes.
Recreational Activities: Nearby swimming, horseback riding, hiking, downhill and cross-country skiing, fishing, boating, tennis, golf.
Facilities: 550-acre retreat center with exercise equipment, sundeck, sauna, hot tub, walking trails, garden, lakes, solarium, greenhouses.
Staff: Physicians, massage therapists, lifestyle counselors, hydrotherapy specialists, nutritionists. All staff are Seventh-Day Adventists.
Special Notes: Smoking not allowed.
Nearby Attractions: Outdoor recreations, rodeos, county fair, trail rides, ghost towns, balloon rides.
Getting There: From Denver, take Interstate 25 north to Loveland. Exit on Country Road 27 and continue to County Road 29.

Global Fitness Adventures

P.O. Box 1390
Aspen, CO 81612
(970) 927-9593; fax (970) 927-4793
E-mail: gfadvspa@csn.net   Web site: www.globalfitnessadventure.com

Best described as a "traveling spa," Global Fitness Adventures offers healthy hiking vacations. Expect to get away to remote and breathtaking vacations while having the luxury of returning to a unique hacienda, country inn, villa, or jungle lodge for an evening's rest. Tours are offered to Aspen, Colorado; Santa Barbara, California; Sedona, Arizona; the island of Dominica in the Caribbean; Bali; Indonesia; and Lake Como, Italy.

A vegetarian nutritional program teaches guests an easy and natural approach to eating that produces a healthy, strong body. Fresh fruits and vegetables, sprouts, salads, and legumes are standard fare, with the option of organic chicken or freshly caught fish of the day. Indigenous guides lead a daily hike between 5 and 18 miles through spectacular wilderness settings. Morning yoga and deep-breathing exercises help guests prepare for the hike while teaching them ways to relieve stress. Afternoon is the time for an optional muscle-toning class, horseback riding, biking, fishing, whitewater rafting, kayaking, or other activities. Guests can then have a massage therapist pummel the knots out of tired muscles or let the strong jets of a Jacuzzi take a go at them. Dinner is prepared by a private chef and served by candlelight. Guests can then enjoy local cultural activities or attend a motivational and inspirational group discussion or lecture.

For people who want to focus on improving their health, natural healing bodywork, detoxification techniques, nutritional supplements, and a high-energy personalized diet are available. Dr. Rob Krakovitz, a co-leader on many of the adventures, is a recognized authority in this area.

Hours and Days of Operation: Tours averaging 1 week offered year-round.
Accommodations: Deluxe private rooms with private baths. Some rooms include fireplaces, decks, and stylish furnishings.
Rates: Vary according to location. 7-day all-inclusive package $2,275.
Credit Cards: None accepted.
Meal Plans: 3 meals a day consisting of spa cuisine (vegetarian with some chicken and fish). Full vegetarian options available.
Services: Massage, healing bodywork, yoga, tai chi, nutritional and psychological counseling, detoxification techniques, consultations on health problems with holistic therapies, exercise physiology, motivational talks, outdoor recreation.
Facilities: Vary from location to location; Colorado center maintains a rustic main lodge, cabins, whirlpools. Sweat lodge available in Sedona, Arizona, and Colorado upon request.
Staff: Core staff include a medical doctor and private chef; 4 staff members on each trip consisting of licensed and certified exercise physiologist, nutritional counselors, psychologists, massage therapists and bodyworkers, and movement instructors. All are certified in first aid and CPR. Local guides are used in areas such as Dominica, Italy, and Bali.
Special Notes: For more information, a Global Fitness Adventures video is available on request.
Nearby Attractions: Depends on location. Snorkeling, scuba diving, and windsurfing on the Caribbean island of Dominica; shopping, dining, biking, and botanical gardens of downtown Santa Barbara; tropical gardens and temples of Bali, Indonesia; neoclassical villas, art galleries, and museums of Lake Como, Italy.
Getting There: Depends on location. Inquire for details.

HealthQuarters Lodge

4141 Sinton Road
Colorado Springs, CO 80907
(719) 593-8694; fax (719) 531-7884

The HealthQuarters' 11-day lifestyle program is one aspect of the larger HealthQuarters Ministries. The purpose behind the program is to promote physical and spiritual wellness through nutrition, natural health care practices, and instruction on how to renew one's connection with Jesus through prayer and devotional life. All HealthQuarters programs are based on Christian philosophies.

Guest begin with a seven-day intensive detoxification fast-and-cleansing process. Nine organically grown juice drinks are consumed daily, as are 20 different supplements that aid in the detoxification process while providing necessary nutritional support. Guests receive water or coffee enemas three times a day and one liver/gallbladder flush. Daily dry brushings and three scheduled therapeutic massage sessions help remove dead skin, revive the cells, and improve circulation. A total of eight instructional classes provide nutritional information, and three classes teach guests how to meet their spiritual and emotional needs. The program winds down with a vegetarian banquet, and guests are given access to follow-up with HealthQuarters' staff and resources. Don't expect nursing care, drugs, or medications. The lodge is not a hospital or clinic, and it does not claim to treat specific diseases. Rather, guests learn the principles of nutrition and how to detoxify their bodies and rebuild impaired immune systems. They then get a chance to apply the newly learned habits during the 11-day program.

Only 10 to 15 participants are allowed at a time to preserve the unique group dynamics.

Hours and Days of Operation: 22 11-day sessions offered year-round.
Accommodations: 9 bedrooms in a bed-and-breakfast-style lodge, each with private bath.

Rates: HealthQuarters recommends you call for details. Scholarships available.
Credit Cards: MC, V.
Meal Plans: 7 of the 11 days spent juice fasting. Remaining meals are organic and vegetarian. Only dinner is served hot.
Services: Guided fasting, detoxification programs, enema cleanses, spiritual counseling, massage, herbal supplements, dry brushing, light exercise, nutritional seminars and cooking classes, networking assistance.
Facilities: Lodge with large dining area and treatment rooms.
Staff: 6 staff members with nutritional training and education.
Special Notes: Smoking not allowed. Some facilities accessible for people with disabilities.
Nearby Attractions: Garden of the Gods, Seven Falls, Cave of the Winds, Cheyenne Mountain Zoo, Will Rodgers Shrine, Pro Rodeo Hall of Fame, Mining Museum, cliff dwellings.
Getting There: Transportation provided to and from Colorado Springs Airport.

The Lodge and Spa at Cordillera

P.O. Box 1110, 2205 Cordillera Way
Edwards, CO 81632
(800) 87-RELAX or (970) 926-2200; fax (970) 926-2714

A person could think of many reasons to visit The Lodge and Spa at Cordillera: spectacular hiking and skiing, the glamour of Vail, or to spoil themselves with gourmet dining, an in-room fireplace, and the luxury of a dry brush massage. But wellness? The new Wellness Weekend now provides yet another excuse to visit the plush surroundings and state-of-the-art spa tucked away in Colorado's Rocky Mountains. The weekend is intended not to be a quick cure but to instill in guests the practice of a healthy lifestyle.

Six rooms are held for the event, which takes place in September. The weekend begins on Thursday, when, after check-in and a chance to unpack, guests attend a reception and an introduction to stress-release techniques. The following morning begins with yogic breathing and stretching, followed by a gourmet vegetarian breakfast. A hike follows, and the spa is close to the White River National Forest, which is bound to be not only healthy exercise but an inspiring natural beauty. Aromatherapy follows, with guests learning about the benefits of flower oils and essences. After lunch, guests have free time for spa services, a golf or tennis clinic, or some shopping in nearby Vail. Dinner is combined with a cooking class led and prepared by a spa chef. Saturday starts with an early breakfast, and the routine is similar to the previous day, except for the addition of an aquatics class and a Pilates session. Guests check out at noon on Sunday.

Hours and Days of Operation: 2-night getaways and special packages offered year-round.
Accommodations: 56 deluxe rooms and suites, some with fireplace, sundeck, and balcony.
Rates: Vary according to season and choice of lodging. Wellness Weekend package $710–$1,180.

Credit Cards: AE, D, MC, V.
Meal Plans: Some packages include meals, 3 restaurants on property. Inquire for details.
Services: Massage, hydrotherapy, aromatherapy, watsu exercise equipment, sauna, steam room, lap pool, salon services, yoga, Pilates.
Recreational Activities: Golf, tennis, hiking, mountain biking, fishing, skiing, snowshoeing, snowmobiling, dogsled rides, ski tours, croquet, volleyball, badminton, gourmet picnic lunches.
Facilities: 5,000-acre resort with 3-story lodge, lobby with large limestone fireplace, restaurant, co-ed exercise room, aerobics studio, indoor lap pool, outdoor heated pool, men's and women's saunas, private hiking, biking and cross-country skiing trails, 3 world-class golf courses.
Staff: About 345 total staff with 18 massage therapists, 3 aestheticians, 2 hair technicians, 2 nail technicians, 8 aerobics instructors, 4 yoga and pilates instructors, 5 exercise and wellness specialists. All licensed and certified in their respective fields.
Special Notes: Facilities accessible for people with disabilities.
Nearby Attractions: White River National Forest, Beaver Creek, El Mirador Peak, shopping and dining in downtown Vail.
Getting There: 2½ hours by car from Denver. Complimentary Eagle Airport pick-up with reservation.

Peaceways

P.O. Box 388
Nederland, CO 80466
(303) 258-0421; fax (303) 258-9351

Committed to teaching ways for individuals to empower themselves and each other, Peaceways incorporates the healing properties of Earth-based medicine and spirituality. Workshops and journeys are held both indoors and outdoors throughout the wilderness of the Boulder and Nederland areas. Lynne Ihlstrom, the founder of Peaceways, facilitates all programs. Ihlstrom is a holistic psychotherapist with a degree in counseling psychology, a trained herbalist, and a yoga and meditation teacher. Since 1990, she has led solo quest journeys, drawing on the teachings of her ancestral Celtic, Lapp, and Norse roots while incorporating some Buddhist traditions.

Four approaches to wellness are weaved throughout the various programs offered in remote wilderness settings: the wellness of mind through holistic practices; the wellness of body through nutrition, herbs, yoga, and natural hot springs; the wellness of spirit through solo quests, sacred journeys, meditation, and ceremony; and the wellness of Earth through organic gardening, ethnoherbology, vegetarianism, and environmental consciousness.

Programs range from simple daylong field trips and seminars to spending six to eight days in sacred healing sites. Activity topics include a seminar on Earth- and body-friendly vegetarianism, the two-day Learning the Way of the Wise Woman retreat, and the weeklong Those Who Went Before Us sacred journey. Solo quests are also offered and are intended to allow guests to reflect on their relationship with themselves and the natural world. Solo quests involve guided spiritual, physical, and emotional cleansing and include two to three days of fasting and time alone on a chosen spot. A pre-quest diet is required of participants, who must register at least four weeks in advance to allow for this preparation.

Hours and Days of Operation: Weekend and 1-day workshops and personal retreats offered year-round.
Accommodations: Mountain retreat lodging or campsites.
Rates: Vary according to program; typically $200–$575.
Credit Cards: None accepted.
Meal Plans: 3 vegetarian meals a day, with some fruit and vegetables from the center's organic garden.
Services: Solo quests, massage, tai chi, lectures on healthy eating, group and inner-process work, fasting, spiritual counseling, guided visualization, survival skills, meditation, hiking.
Facilities: 35-acre rustic mountain retreat center with organic garden and hot springs.
Staff: Guest speakers and staff are professionals in the fields of holistic psychotherapy, nutrition, hatha yoga, massage, tai chi, energy systems, Neuromuscular Integrative Action, child care.
Special Notes: Guests with medical conditions can participate in the solo quests that do not require fasting.
Nearby Attractions: Vary according to program. Inquire for details.
Getting There: Varies according to program. Inquire for details.

The Peaks at Telluride

624 Mountain Village Boulevard, Box 2702
Telluride, CO 81435
(800) SPA-KIVA or (970) 728-6800; fax (970) 728-6567

This spa features a wide expanse of slender aspen, regal velvet-green foothills, and carved and solemn rock outcrops topped with pure white. It's no wonder this world-class destination resort and spa is known as The Peaks. For those interested in wellness, the newly launched Next Level Spa offers several "quests" that can be tailored to the individual needs of each guest. Rejuvenation of the mind, body, and spirit is the philosophy behind the spa, with the goal that each guest can transcend the traditional spa experience and achieve the "next level" of his or her well-being. Sixteen rooms connect directly to the spa by way of a separate enclave.

The quest begins with a phone call to 888-SPA-HLTH. Guests are assigned a personal spa concierge who assists them in creating a customized program. Five quests are offered, each exploring various avenues of improved health: rejuvenation, vigor, tranquillity, adventure, and change. A typical day of rejuvenation starts with a 7 a.m. wake-to-oneness ceremony, inspired by the Southern Utes. A breakfast of energy-boosting, low-fat spa cuisine follows. Afterward, guests participate in a mind-body-spirit workshop. Lunch is at noon, then guests receive a private consultation with a health counselor. Free time is followed by a 4 p.m. body treatment. The Alpine Strawberry Rejuvenator sounds heavenly. Guests can expect local produce and regional specialties for dinner at 7.

If it's your first time visiting a spa, be sure to request the brochure "How to Spa like a Pro."

Hours and Days of Operation: 4- and 7-night Next Level Spa packages offered year-round.
Accommodations: 177 rooms in 10-story mountain resort, including 25 luxury suites with terrace and living- and dining-room areas.
Rates: Vary according to season, package, and choice of room; 4-night Next Level Spa package $1,295–$2,115, single occupancy.
Credit Cards: AE, D, MC, V.
Meal Plans: Spa packages include 3 gourmet spa meals a day plus healthy snacks. Meals are very low in fat and use no butter, oil, or cream.
Services: Workshops on astrology, breath work, chakra clearing, homeopathy, therapeutic touch, and Tibetan healing sounds; various types of massage, including shiatsu, shirodhara, and targeted massage with parafango; aromatherapy, hydrotherapy, reiki, reflexology, stress management techniques using biofeedback; body wraps and scrubs; facials; salon services; cooking demonstrations; health lectures; journaling workshops.
Recreational Activities: Racquetball, squash, mountain biking, hiking, wall climbing, skiing, fly-fishing, gondola rides.
Facilities: Luxury mountain resort with 42,000-square-foot spa, 2 restaurants, kiva with purification bath, exercise equipment, weight room, cardiovascular deck, squash and racquetball courts, indoor lap pool connected by a water slide to a lower indoor/outdoor pool, sauna, steam rooms, whirlpools, indoor climbing wall, 5 tennis courts, golf course, television lounge.
Staff: About 400 full-time employees, 70 of whom work in the spa. Spa staff include a fitness director, exercise physiologist, nutritionist, therapists. All therapists have at least 500 hours of training and are trained in specific areas of specialty, such as infant massage and mind-body therapies.
Special Notes: Day care available. Smoking not allowed in spa. All areas wheelchair accessible.
Nearby Attractions: Anasazi cliff dwellings, Ouray and Pagosa hot springs, Million Dollar Highway, Black Canyon National Monument.
Getting There: 7 hours by car from Denver. Complimentary shuttle from Telluride Airport.

Rocky Mountain Ayurveda Health Retreat

P.O. Box 5192
Pagosa Springs, CO 81147
(800) 247-9654 or (970) 264-9224
E-mail: valentines@ayurveda-retreat.com   Web site: www.ayurveda-retreat.com/rockymountain

Visitors to this retreat center can smell the ponderosa pine while gazing at the expansive San Juan Mountains. At this secluded holistic health retreat center located on 20-acres in southwestern Colorado, Cary and Wendy Valentine host the Rocky Mountain Ayurveda Health Retreat. Both have backgrounds in natural healing and Vedic studies and are graduates of Dr. Jay Scherer's Academy of Natural Healing and Dr. David Frawley's American Institute of Vedic Studies. Both also have studied with Dr. Vasant Lad and Dr. Sunil Joshi. By hosting the retreats, the Valentines fulfill their goal to help people "become their own best doctor" through the balancing principles of Ayurveda.

The couple specializes in providing panchakarma experiences. All packages begin with an initial consultation and pulse reading to determine the individual's constitution and current state of health. Based on the results of the consultation, an individualized program is designed, complete with recommendations for diet, herbal preparations, and lifestyle regimes to take home. The Valentine's pride themselves in offering each guest individual attention. Consequently, only two guests are allowed per retreat.

Each luxurious day begins with *snehana*, a full-body warm oil massage carried out by two qualified technicians in a calm environment. Next is *nasya*, an herbalized oil massage to the head and neck, said to be effective in clearing the sinuses and inducing mental clarity. *Swedana*, an herbalized steam bath, comes next. The steam's heat improves circulation and increases the blood flow as well as further loosening impurities. The entire session concludes with a self-administered herbal and oil enema, intended to purify, nourish, and strengthen the large intestine. Throughout the week, guests ingest medicated oil as a part of the *virechana*, or purgation process. As part of *virechana*, a mild laxative is taken at the end of the week to release any remaining impurities.

When they are not being steamed and rubbed, guests can take part in two sessions each of yoga and meditation. The programs also include three hours of verbal or nonverbal assistance, such as counseling, hypnotherapy, inner-child work, and gentle energy balancing. Optional intuitive readings help guests gain access to the inner workings of the subconscious.

Hours and Days of Operation: 1-, 4-, 7-, and 14-day retreats offered year-round.
Accommodations: 8 bedrooms on 3 levels in 4,000-square-foot house. Each bedroom adjacent to full bath.
Rates: 7-day all-inclusive panchakarma program is $2,980.
Credit Cards: D, MC, V.
Meals: 3 organic, vegetarian meals included in cost of program.
Services: Massage, herbalized steam baths, colon therapy, yoga, meditation, lifestyle management program, counseling, hypnotherapy, inner-child work, energy balancing, intuitive readings.
Facilities: 4,000-square-foot main house with large living room, 25-foot stone fireplace, floor-to-ceiling windows, and decking on 3 sides of the house; solarium, library/sitting area; 16-sided House of One, used for prayer, meditation, and quiet time; 22-foot Growing Dome, where organic fruits and vegetables are grown for consumption at the center.
Staff: Carey and Wendy Valentine facilitate retreats.
Special Notes: Because only 2 guests are allowed per retreat, it is recommended that vacation plans be made well in advance.
Nearby Attractions: Hot spring baths; Anasazi ruins; thousands of acres of national forest land; nearby hiking, biking, camping.
Getting There: 3 hours by car north of Santa Fe.

Norwich Inn and Spa

607 West Thames Street, Route 32
Norwich, CT 06360
(800) 275-4772 or (860) 886-2401; fax (860) 886-9483

The Georgian-style Norwich Inn and Spa is located on 40 acres of New England woodlands. Graceful white columns and red brick accentuate the charm of this regal country estate. Intimate breakfast tables open up to old asters and groomed lawns bordered with brilliant flowers. The inn is a perfect getaway for busy city people who need a quiet place to de-stress. Though no specific program is geared toward wellness, all spa staff have backgrounds and training in holistic health, and the philosophy of achieving and maintaining health carries through, if subtly.

Spa treatments, while intended to pamper, are also methods of improving the well-being of body, mind, and spirit through the initial benefits of stress reduction and the more subtle effects of ancient health practices. For example, the ancient Japanese practice of reiki is offered and consists of a practitioner placing the hands over various "energy centers" of the body. It is believed that this noninvasive and gentle healing method realigns energy. An Ayurvedic mud wrap involves the application of rejuvenating muds from India that are said to enhance circulation and pull toxins out of the body. Various hydrotherapy treatments target specific concerns, for example, the Dead Sea salt bath relieves topical skin conditions, the seaweed bath is said to stimulate the circulation, the volcanic mud bath uses mineral-rich mud with anti-inflammatory and muscle-relaxing properties. All baths help eliminate toxins. Body treatments include an acupressure foot massage that not only relaxes but also helps balance the body's vital organs. A session in polarity therapy revives the nervous system and relaxes the mind and body. A registered dietitian is also available to review individual eating habits and make recommendations. Emphasis is placed on balance and moderation rather than deprivation to allow guests to make permanent, as opposed to temporary or drastic, lifestyle changes.

Hours and Days of Operation: Open year-round. High season May–Oct, low season Nov–Apr.

Accommodations: Inn rooms, country rooms, and private villas, all with private bath. Some come with fireplace, deck, and private access to clubhouse.

Rates: Vary according to season, room, and spa package. The Personal Escape Plan $355–$455 per night, single occupancy.

Credit Cards: AE, D, MC, V.

Meal Plans: All meals included with some packages. Inquire for details. Vegetarians and special diets can be accommodated.

Services: Various types of massage, hydrotherapy, thalassotherapy, polarity therapy, acupressure, body wraps, loofah scrubs, salon services, cooking demonstrations, weight training, and fitness lectures.

Recreational Facilities: Tennis, biking, golf.

Facilities: 1920s Georgian-style inn with lakeside villas, taproom with stone fireplace, exercise equipment, indoor and outdoor swimming pools, men's and women's sauna, steam room and whirlpool, golf course.

Staff: About 250 total staff with spa staff of about 75 employees, including 26 massage therapists, 9 aestheticians, 8 hand-and-foot technicians, 15 fitness staff, a tennis pro, 2 nutritional counselors. All licensed, experienced, and certified in their respective fields.

Special Notes: Minimum age for the spa is 18. Smoking not allowed in spa or dining room.

Nearby Attractions: Eugene O'Neill Theater Center, Gillette Castle, Old Lyme Art Center and historic homes, Cathedral of St. Patrick in Old Norwich.

Getting There: About 3 hours by car from New York City.

Dreamtime Cruises

2911 Red Bug Lake Road, Suite 800
Casselberry, FL 32707
(800) 787-8785 or (407) 695-1467; fax (407) 695-8265
E-mail: Dreamtime@aol.com

Dreamtime Cruises offers holistic health and personal growth seminars and workshops aboard a luxury ocean liner. Holistic health cruises include free massage, aromatherapy, reiki, and lectures by well-known authors, energy healers, mind-body psychologists, and urban shamans. Choose a scheduled program, such as the Inner Voyage, presented in collaboration with *New Age Journal,* or create your own healthy vacation. A typical day of the program starts with morning yoga at 7:45, followed by a low-fat, primarily vegetarian breakfast. Programs begin at 9 and conclude at 5. Guests are free to engage in an extensive choice of presentations and workshops or go ashore to shop in local markets or explore a natural crystal cave. Dinner is followed by special nighttime activities, such as the New Moon Ceremony, after which guests can dance all night in the ship's disco.

Cruise packages vary from year to year, and several land packages are now offered in addition to cruises. An example of a typical land package was last year's Energy Healing Journey, presented by Qigong in China. Guests flew to China to study the ancient healing technique with master teachers and healers. The immersion in traditional Chinese energy medicine included qigong, meditation, and acupressure for routine health care and first aid. While staying at the rustic and charming Wuyunshan Health Resort in Hangzhou, China, guests also enjoyed daily tui na (or deep energy massage), acupuncture, and herbal remedies selected for each individual to rebalance internal energy flow. Other land retreats are scheduled at the newly opened retreat center in a Trinidad pine forest and at the new holistically oriented MetaResort in Anguilla.

Hours and Days of Operation: 1- and 2-week cruise and land voyages offered year-round.

Accommodations: Inside standard to deluxe ocean-view staterooms. Inquire for details on land-based voyages.
Rates: Vary according to program. Cruises $749–$1,799, plus a port charge of $169.50. Prices based on double occupancy.
Credit Cards: AE, D, DC, MC, V.
Meal Plans: All meals included. Vegetarian options available.
Services: Workshops and seminars led by well-known healing professionals in massage therapy and intuitive counseling; offshore activities include excursions, golf, tennis.
Facilities: Ocean liner with hot tubs, exercise equipment, restaurants, discos, sitting rooms, view decks. Inquire for details on land-based programs.
Staff: Standard cruise staff, plus 25 recognized health experts as workshop facilitators, such as Ilana Rubenfeld and Raymond Moody. Licensed and certified practitioners of various healing modalities, including qigong and therapeutic bodywork, also available. Dr. Karen Kramer leads the Qigong in China Educational Series.
Special Notes: Smoking allowed only in designated areas. Facilities accessible for people with disabilities.
Nearby Attractions: Vary according to location. Inquire for details.
Getting There: If clients arrange airfare through Dreamtime, free transfers provided from the nearest major airport. Otherwise, taxis and airport shuttles available for a fee.

Fit for Life Health Resort and Spa

1460 South Ocean Boulevard
Pompano Beach, FL 33062
(800) 583-3500 or (954) 941-6688 or (954) 943-1219
E-mail: fitlife@icanect.net   Web site: www.icanect.net/fitlife

Harvey Diamond, co-author of the best-seller *Fit for Life* and the man whose ideas helped found the Fit for Life Health Resort and Spa, gives his professional endorsement to the programs and vegetarian cuisine at this Pompano Beach resort. Not to be confused with a treatment or therapy center, Fit for Life is a health resort with spa amenities. The goal behind its various programs is to teach self-responsibility, self-care, and how to make better choices for a healthier mind, body, and spirit. "We want to emphasize overall good health with the idea to prepare our guests for an improved lifestyle," says director Mort Pine.

The 70-room resort is just 200 feet from the shore of Florida's Gold Coast. Personalized programs are offered for emotional health and stress management, weight reduction, nutritional education, exercise, and fitness—all at affordable prices. The resort is designed to promote a group environment, with the lecture hall, dining room, exercise room, lounge, and kitchen all adjacent to one another and in the same building. A typical eight-day package includes morning walks on the beach, three natural vegetarian meals per day with the option of guided organic juice fasts, nutritional consultations with the health director, an optional weight-loss program, exercise classes, meditation, yoga, daily lectures on health and nutrition, cooking demonstrations, and psychology seminars. The minimum stay is five days, but eight days are recommended to fully benefit from the diet and lifestyle change. A free information video is available to anyone considering the program.

Hours and Days of Operation: 5- to 8-day programs offered year-round.
Accommodations: 70 rooms with single and double occupancy and private bath. Some rooms have private patios and ocean views.

Rates: Vary according to length of stay, season, room, and spa package. An 8-day program with meals and accommodations starts at $999.
Credit Cards: AE, MC, V.
Meal Plans: 3 vegetarian meals a day, with optional juice and water diets.
Services: Nutritional consultations, health and nutrition lectures, psychology seminars, meditation, yoga, massage, body wraps, aromatherapy, hydrotherapy, salon services.
Recreational Activities: Bicycling, snorkeling.
Facilities: Oceanside resort with spa treatment rooms, outdoor pool, poolside dining room, fully equipped gym, sauna, hot tub.
Staff: Licensed and certified massage therapist and fitness instructors. Others are trained in health, fitness, nutrition, yoga, and tai chi.
Special Notes: Minimum age for spa is 18. Smoking not allowed on premises. All facilities wheelchair accessible.
Nearby Attractions: Disney World, beaches, museums, shopping.
Getting There: 20 minutes by car from Fort Lauderdale International Airport.

Hippocrates Health Institute
1443 Palmdale Court
West Palm Beach, FL 33411
(407) 471-8876; fax (407) 471-9464

Founded by Ann Wigmore and Viktoras Kulvinaskas over 40 years ago, the Hippocrates Health Institute is based on the ancient Hippocratic wisdom to "Let food be your medicine." Today, directors Brian and Anna Maria Clement encourage guests to achieve personal goals using healing techniques they can use at home. Brian Clement is also the author of *Living Foods for Optimum Health*.

This holistic health and learning center, located on a 30-acre, tropical, wooded estate, uses an enzyme-rich nutritional regimen and natural oxygenating therapies to detoxify, cleanse, and revitalize the mind, body, and spirit. The three-week Life-Change Program, in particular, integrates this approach. During the program, guests receive private consultations with the resort health team, a live-cell analysis, daily lectures, stress-free exercise, group-sharing therapy, buffet meals of live organic food, weekly massage, and electromagnetic treatments—yet they still have time for excursions to the beach, museums, and shopping areas. Guests also have access to the dry sauna, ozonated outdoor pool, and the Native American–inspired Vapor Cave, which emits a therapeutic warm vapor 24 hours a day.

Food is of primary importance at Hippocrates and is defined as anything that enables one to live and grow. Consequently, daily meals consist of inspired combinations of fresh fruits and vegetables. A sample menu includes an almond basil loaf with red pepper coulis, stuffed avocado platters, cauliflower and mushrooms à la greque, and a broccoli salad with garlic and oregano. Guests also have 24-hour access to a self-help wheat grass juice bar and are served a daily staple Green Power drink consisting of organic vegetables and sprouts.

Hours and Days of Operation: 1-, 2-, and 3-week programs offered year-round.

Accommodations: 23 rooms, on and off the premises, most equipped with queen beds and Jacuzzis.

Rates: $1,650–$3,850 per person, per week. Includes lodging, meals, services, and use of all facilities.

Credit Cards: AE, D, MC, V.

Meal Plans: 2 live organic vegetarian meals a day. Wheat grass, vegetable and fruit juices offered between meals.

Services: Colonic irrigation, Thai massage, hydrotherapy, acupuncture, reflexology, chiropractic, centropic integration, psychotherapy, yoga, shiatsu, watsu, deep-tissue massage, lymphatic drainage, polarity energy balancing, aesthetics.

Facilities: 30-acre estate with Spanish-style haciendas, garden apartments, 4 ozonated outdoor pools, sauna, vapor cave, electromagnetic treatment system, jogging trail, exercise equipment.

Staff: 30 total staff, including 1 consulting medical doctor and 1 on-site medical doctor, a health administrator, 7 massage therapists (some of whom specialize in colonic hydrotherapy and reflexology), 3 psychotherapists; acupuncturist and chiropractor available on call. All licensed and certified.

Special Notes: Cigarettes, alcohol, and meat not allowed on premises.

Nearby Attractions: Palm Beach, Kravis Cultural Center, beaches, shopping, John MacArthur Park nature reserve and beach, museums, Morikame Gardens.

Getting There: 1 hour by car from Miami. Free shuttle available to and from Palm Beach International Airport.

PGA National Resort and Spa

400 Avenue of the Champions
Palm Beach Gardens, FL 33418-3698
(800) 633-9150 (resort) or (800) 843-7725 (spa); fax (561) 622-0261
E-mail: jodic@pga-resorts.com   Web site: www.pga-resorts.com

When most people think of PGA National Resort and Spa, the word "golf" comes to mind. Nonetheless, this AAA Four-Diamond and Mobil Four-Star resort provides guests with a luxurious European spa and programs targeted to benefit mind, body, and spirit. Even the centuries-old spa cure of "taking the waters" has literally been imported to a collection of five mineral pools, known as Waters of the World. Salts from the Dead Sea were flown in for an aquacise pool, and the mineral content of the thermal waters of the French Pyrenees spa town of Salies de Bearn were re-created for a flotation pool. PGA also boasts of an organic herb garden filled with a variety of healing plants, such as ajuga, sweet woodruff, and clary sage.

Nancy Soccorso, spa director at PGA, is dedicated to tailoring each program to the unique needs of guests. A complimentary 25-minute Personal Lifestyle Profile is available to help guests not only select a program but also learn how the services they select can be adapted to their daily lives. Therapists take into account the guest's physical composition, health history, and reasons and goals for visiting the spa.

A unique facet of PGA's spa programs is a 60-minute class that teaches parents massage techniques for their infants. The techniques serve to strengthen the immune system, stimulate weight gain, and aid the baby's overall well-being. The class also teaches parents how to spend quality time with their child and how to support a baby's overall health.

The Bramham Institute at the PGA spa provides training and education for experienced massage and skin care specialists in the fields of health care, spas, dermatology, and plastic surgery. Founder Anne Bramham, a prolific writer and lecturer, is committed to teaching a total-body approach to all aspects of health.

Hours and Days of Operation: Open year-round; half-day and full-day packages available.
Accommodations: Single and double standard rooms, suites, and cottage suites available with Mediterranean-style fabrics and furniture.
Rates: Vary according to room and services. Day Of Beauty spa package $249. Standard rooms $119–$335 per night.
Credit Cards: AE, D, MC, V.
Meal Plans: Spa lunch included with full-day package. Resort offers 7 dining facilities, including tropical poolside indoor/outdoor café serving spa cuisine.
Services: 140 spa services offered, including Swedish, neuromuscular, and lymphatic massage; hydrotherapy tubs; Vichy shower; salt glow rubs; marine algae wraps; aromatherapy; nutritional consultations; facials; salon services.
Facilities: 2,340-acre resort with guest rooms, suites, and cottages; state-of-the-art exercise equipment; spa building with 25 co-ed treatment rooms; hydrotherapy tubs and Vichy shower; 7 restaurants; health and racquet club; 5-lane lap pool; 5 golf courses; 19 outdoor tennis courts; 5 croquet lawns; 3 indoor racquetball courts; sailboats and aquacycles available on 26-acre lake.
Staff: 42 massage therapists, 10 aestheticians, personal grooming assistants.
Special Notes: Child care available; golf and tennis lessons included and private instruction available at certain times during the summer. Specially equipped rooms designed for people with disabilities.
Nearby Attractions: Morikami Museum and gardens, Golf Hall of Fame, Palm Beach Symphony Orchestra.
Getting There: 20 minutes from West Palm Beach. Limousine and van service available for a fee.

Regency House Natural Health Spa

2000 South Ocean Drive
Hallandale, FL 33009
(800) 454-0003 or (954) 454-2220; fax (954) 454-4637
Web site: www.regencyhealthspa.com

Bright blue beach chairs complement the cream-colored stucco and red Spanish tile of the Regency House Natural Health Spa. The spa is only a short walk from the beach, and guests breathing deeply can smell the crisp ocean air. Throughout its 13 years, the spa has had an exceptionally successful history of helping people lose weight and body fat. It also strives to be a comprehensive body-mind health spa. Lifestyle awareness, detoxification, and rejuvenation programs are offered in addition to weight-loss and physical fitness programs.

An average eight-day program begins with each guest personally consulting with director Dr. Frank Sabatino on arrival. A nutrition and exercise program is established here. Guests then settle into a regimen of three gourmet vegetarian meals a day, early morning walks on a white-sand beach, daily health and nutrition lectures, vegetarian cooking demonstrations, psychology seminars, exercise classes, yoga, and meditation. Two free massages come with the seven-night package and include a deep sport, aromatherapy, Swedish, neuromuscular therapy shiatsu, reflexology, or dry skin brush massage. For an additional fee, guests can schedule reiki, hypnotherapy, chiropractic care, bone density testing, lymphatic drainage, psychic astrology, and more. Guided organic juice and water fasting is also available and is supervised by Dr. Sabatino.

An informal atmosphere pervades the spa, and guests are advised not to pack a large wardrobe or bring expensive jewelry. Casual clothes are par for the course, and guests are also advised to supply their own suntan lotion, hair dryer, alarm clocks, personal toiletries, and bathrobe.

Hours and Days of Operation: Programs averaging 1 week offered year-round.

Accommodations: Standard rooms have 2 double beds, cable television, private bath. Studio rooms have ocean views.
Rates: Vary according to room, season, and package. Winter rates for 7-night package $995–$1,095 per person, double occupancy. Summer rates $795–$995.
Credit Cards: AE, D, MC, V.
Meal Plans: 3 gourmet vegetarian meals. Optional juice and water fasting.
Services: Massage, reflexology, facials, body wraps, sea-salt scrubs, hypnotherapy, reiki, yoga, meditation, stress-reduction techniques, wellness counseling, psychic astrology, progressive relaxation/hypnosis, chiropractic, in-depth nutritional profile, health lectures.
Facilities: Oceanside resort with Spanish-style guest and dining rooms, gym, heated outdoor pool, Jacuzzi, sauna, sundeck.
Staff: 48 spa staff, including Dr. Frank Sabatino, D.C.; a fitness director; 10 massage therapists; 2 aestheticians; a reflexologist, 3 yoga instructors, 3 aerobics instructors. All licensed and certified.
Special Notes: The Regency does not provide shuttle service to and from the airport. Pets are not allowed on premises. Minimum age for spa is 16. Smoking not allowed in rooms or grounds. Anyone found smoking will be asked to leave without a refund.
Nearby Attractions: Broward Performing Arts Culture Center, Pro Players baseball stadium, Gulfstream Park, Miami Convention Center, Golden Isle Tennis Center, shopping, cinema, boating, jet skis, golf.
Getting There: 15 minutes by car from Ft. Lauderdale Airport. Grayline Limo Service, Super Shuttle, and taxis available.

Atlanta Center for Chronic Disorders

2020 Howell Mill Road, Box C 359
Atlanta, GA 30318-1732
(404) 351-3650 (phone/fax)
Web site: www.vedic-health.com

The Physicians' Association for Eradicating Chronic Disease was founded in May 1997 with the participation of medical doctors throughout the United States. The association was created to promote a more comprehensive system of health care to prevent illness through treating the root cause of disease and promoting a healthy lifestyle. The Atlanta Center for Chronic Disorders, one of four similar centers currently open in the United States, is part of the association's Campaign to Create a Disease-Free Society. Future plans include the opening of 435 similar centers, with in-residence facilities near 40 of the largest metropolitan areas.

The centers offer integrative health programs that incorporate natural approaches for the prevention and treatment of chronic disorders. Drawing on Vedic and Ayurvedic principles, specialized programs are developed for individuals with virtually any type of chronic condition, from listlessness to Parkinson's disease. Because the centers also function as complementary care, patients are never asked to discontinue seeing a family physician or specialist.

Consultations and rejuvenation treatments are also provided for those who are fortunate not to be suffering from chronic ailments but would like to feel more physically and mentally alive. During consultations, doctors assess the individual's current state of physiological balance and design an at-home program that includes recommendations for diet, exercise, herbal supplements, stress management techniques, and daily and seasonal health routines. The five- to seven-day Rejuvenation Program is tailored to each person's unique needs and involves traditional methods of eliminating impurities from the body due to bad diet, stress, and other factors.

For more serious health concerns, the Chronic Disorder Program, which begins with a thorough medical examination, is recom-

mended. After a highly personalized health regimen is established, patients receive daily treatments and undergo an extensive health education. Habits for maintaining and promoting total well-being are developed alongside a system of continuing self-care.

Hours and Days of Operation: Office hours: 9:30–4. Open 7 days a week, 9:30 a.m.–10 p.m. for treatments. Residential programs vary in length.

Accommodations: Guests reside in nearby luxury hotels and a limited number of private and spacious residential rooms within the center.

Rates: Vary according to services provided, starting at $375 per day.

Credit Cards: MC, V.

Meal Plans: All meals provided in accordance with the dietary needs of each client.

Services: Thorough physical examination, techniques for managing health, pulse diagnosis, purification therapies and herbalized oil applications, special herbal food supplements, diet and exercise programs, instruction in health-promoting behavior, methods for enhancing collective health worldwide.

Facilities: Treatment and residential rooms, small kitchen, dining rooms.

Staff: On-site physician, nurse, health educator, and 2 qualified technicians available for every client. A team of physicians trained in the Chronic Disorders Program available through video conferencing.

Special Notes: Smoking not allowed. Facilities accessible for people with disabilities.

Nearby Attractions: Theater, music, museums, shopping, and dining in Atlanta.

Getting There: About 5 minutes by car northwest of downtown Atlanta on Interstate 75.

Center for New Beginnings

129 Center Point Drive
Dahlonega, GA 30533
(800) 492-1046 or (706) 864-5861; fax (706) 864-7254

Located on 45 acres in the North Georgia woodlands, the Center for New Beginnings has a magnificent view of the Blue Ridge Mountains. The land has been owned for four generations by the Whitner family, and the center was established in 1985. Today, Joseph and Katherine Whitner own these 45 acres of hiking trails, gardens, hot tubs, and a fire circle. It was Joseph's great-grandfather who built a 50-room hotel over a hundred years ago on the property, intended as a place for healing and renewal, surrounding the site of an ancient healing spring. The hotel no longer stands, having been replaced by six sleeping cabins, three meeting rooms, a chapel, kitchens, dining room, and two outdoor hot tubs. The Whitner's vision is to provide a homelike, nurturing environment where groups and individuals can explore personal and spiritual growth. It is their wish that each guest feels a sense of healing while exploring the connection of body, mind, and spirit while at the center.

Many workshops are booked throughout the year, and subjects have included stress reduction, eupsychia healing intensives, couples therapeutic workshops, and an introduction to tai chi. Individuals are also welcome to stay at the center, when space is available, and may design a personal healing retreat. Joseph Whitner, an ordained Presbyterian minister, has practiced psychotherapy full-time for 30 years and is available for private counseling and to lead seminars and study groups. Appointments with other types of counselors and massage therapists are available. Meals are included with the price of lodging and are always healthy and nutritious.

Hours and Days of Operation: Weekend and weeklong workshops and personal retreats offered year-round.

Accommodations: Cedar View Lodge is an 8-bedroom, 8-bath, 2-story lodge with large sitting area and queen beds on second floor. Trahlyta Lodge is a 3-level unit with 2 bedrooms on each floor; each level has a shared bath. Harmony House is a 2-level unit with 2 bedrooms on each floor. Main floor has shared bath. Lower level has 2 baths with a private entrance to each room, opening onto a large deck. Serendipity is a 2-bedroom, 2-bath, spacious duplex. The "Be" Hive is a 2-room cottage with sitting room, desk, and private deck. Dove's Nest is a 2-bedroom cottage with 1 bath. Main House, the Whitneys' private home, has 4 guest rooms with private baths.

Rates: $65 per person, per day, double occupancy; private room $70. Rates include lodging, meals, use of group meeting rooms.

Credit Cards: MC, V.

Meal Plans: 3 meals a day with vegetarian option.

Services: Workshops and retreats hosted by guest facilitators, including cancer healing retreats, yoga and meditation workshops, eupsychia healing intensives, and artistic self-expression retreats; massage, counseling for couples and individuals, group and inner-process work, stress reduction techniques, tai chi, shamanism.

Facilities: 45-acre retreat center with several cabins, main house, community lodge, meeting space, outdoor hot tubs, fire circle, flower and vegetable gardens, hiking trails.

Staff: In addition to guest presenters, professionally trained kitchen staff and licensed massage therapists.

Special Notes: The center offers full-service weddings, including accommodations for guests.

Nearby Attractions: Appalachian Trail, Alpine Village of Helen, Mountain Magic Auto Tour, historic Dahlonega.

Getting There: 65 miles northeast of Atlanta.

The Spa at Chateau Elan

Haven Harbour Drive
Braselton, GA 30517
(770) 271-6064; fax (770) 271-6069
Web site: www.chateauelan.com

Taking in a healthy retreat at Chateau Elan is like ordering the three-layered Tiramisu and learning that it is not only fat-free but also good for you. The health benefits come in a pleasant disguise known as the Luxury Vacation. The resort itself looks like it was imported directly from the French countryside, along with sprawling grape fields for the on-site winery. The building is, in fact, a reproduction of a sixteenth-century French manor house, and within its confines lies a 20-room, world-class spa whose professional staff is supplemented by local medical consultants and nutrition specialists.

Chateau Elan will never be singularly thought of as a health retreat because it offers too many spectacular activities, from wine tasting to golf tournaments. However, for those interested in promoting their well-being through a holistic approach, the Luxury Vacation is the best bet. The program lasts six days, with guests arriving on Sunday. Guests can expect three gourmet spa meals a day, a fitness assessment, a thalassotherapy underwater massage, two Swedish massages, a salt glow with Vichy shower, an antistress wrap, an aromatherapy multijet bath, foot reflexology, salon services, access to the steam room, sauna, whirlpool and indoor resistance pool, afternoon tea, and more. A smaller version of the Luxury Vacation is the Mini Vacation, which has many similar elements. The benefits of the package are primarily to reduce stress through a healthy diet and personalized care, yet many of the treatments promote physical well-being, such as underwater massage, which has been known to relieve arthritis.

Hours and Days of Operation: 2- to 8-day packages offered year-round.
Accommodations: 14 deluxe rooms with queen-size beds; 2 loft suites available. A 274-room French-style inn is also on the property, and 18 villas border the golf course.
Rates: Vary according to room, season, and package. 3-day Spa Getaway $889–$1,489, including 2 breakfasts, 2 lunches, 2 dinners, lodging, spa services.
Credit Cards: AE, D, DC, MC, V.
Meal Plans: Meals included with some packages. Vegetarian options available.
Services: Various types of massage, reflexology, aromatherapy, thalassotherapy, body wraps and scrubs, facials, salon services, yoga, relaxation techniques, exercise equipment, nutritional assessments, fitness evaluations, heated outdoor pool.
Recreational Activities: Bicycling, horseback riding, concerts.
Facilities: 3,400-acre private resort community with a reproduction sixteenth-century French manor chateau, conference center, library, 6 restaurants, shops, spa with 26 treatment rooms, exercise equipment, Vichy shower, sauna, steam bath, co-ed whirlpool, hydro bath, outdoor heated pool, health club, 7 tennis courts, 4 golf courses, bicycles, vineyards, winery, equestrian center, woodland trails, private lake.
Staff: All staff professionally trained and licensed.
Special Notes: Minimum guest age is 18.
Nearby Attractions: Downtown Atlanta's dining, shops, museums, theater.
Getting There: 45 minutes by car from Atlanta. Round-trip limousine service available through prior arrangement.

Wildwood Lifestyle Center and Hospital

P.O. Box 129
Wildwood, GA 30757-0129
(800) 634-9355 or (706) 820-1493; fax (706) 820-1474

Since 1941, people have come to Wildwood's 600 acres of forested Georgia mountainsides to take part in a residential health program. Over the course of 10 or 17 days, guests learn simple methods of attaining the highest possible condition of wellness. Prevention is stressed at Wildwood, and diet is an important element of that. Many serious and chronic conditions are treated at the center, from hypoglycemia to ulcerative colitis. Yet you don't have to be chronically ill to participate in a program. Wildwood is for anyone who wants to improve their health, whether that means learning a healthier way to eat or handle stress or applying lifestyle-changing techniques for preventing heart disease.

The center is run by a staff of Seventh-Day Adventists, but all programs are nondenominational, except for stress-handling methods, which are approached from a Christian perspective. Each program includes the basic elements of a complete medical history, a physical examination, blood chemistry, periodic physician consultations, whirlpool, sauna, massage, hydrotherapy treatments, herbal therapy, guided walks, lectures on health and nutrition, vegetarian cooking classes, meals, and lodging. A typical day starts with a 7 a.m. breakfast followed by a short walk through the 25 miles of trails. A health lecture begins at 9, followed by warm-up exercises. A hydrotherapy session is squeezed in before lunch and another short walk scheduled afterward. The afternoon consists of a health lecture and cooking class. Dinner is at 6, after which is a lecture on spiritual or health-related topics.

A Get Acquainted offer allows for someone to experience Wildwood at a greatly reduced rate. For only $50 a night, guests can attend health lectures, take guided walks, relax with a massage, and enjoy a delicious vegan buffet.

Hours and Days of Operation: 10- and 17-day programs offered year-round, as well as a 3-day Get Acquainted offer.

Accommodations: 26 rooms, double and single occupancy with private and shared baths.

Rates: 10-day program $1,640 with a required $150 deposit; 17-day program $2,575 with a required $250 deposit. Prices subject to change without notice.

Credit Cards: AE, MC, V.

Meal Plans: 3 vegan meals a day.

Services: Seminars on nutrition, stress management, and addiction recovery; massage; hydrotherapy; health lectures; nutrition classes; cooking demonstrations; physical examinations; medical treatments, including surgical procedures and physical therapy; spiritual counseling.

Recreational Activities: Hiking, boating.

Facilities: 600-acre retreat center with medical and dental clinic, lodge with fireplace, chaplain's department, sauna, whirlpool, hydrotherapy showers, exercise equipment, walking trails, lake.

Staff: 50 total staff, including 4 medical doctors, 2 massage therapists, 2 physical therapists, a nutritional counselor, a chaplain, 6 lifestyle counselors.

Special Notes: Smoking not allowed indoors. Phones available only on request and require a $25 deposit.

Nearby Attractions: North Georgia forests, Chattanooga train museums, Point Park Civil War sites.

Getting There: 2 hours by car from Atlanta. Free transportation from Chattanooga.

Angel's Nest of Mother Maui

1135 Makawao Avenue, Suite 220
Makawao, Maui, HI 96768
(888) 222-6295 or (808) 572-6773; fax (808) 573-2213
E-mail: info@anglesnest.com   Web site: www.angelsnest.com

Angel's Nest of Mother Maui is located on ancient sacred grounds overlooking both sides of the island and—to the olfactory benefit of guests—sits right between a pine and eucalyptus forest. The name is a result of a belief that people can sense a universal and angelic presence at this cliffside getaway. Both bed-and-breakfast and retreat center, Angel's Nest offers a high-energy natural location where guests can come to restore the soul and body. Retreat activities include massage and healing sessions, yoga, tai chi, dolphin swims, hikes to hidden waterfalls, and connecting with authentic Hawaiian teachers and kahunas.

The popular Soul Journeys to Paradise program is a seven-night package including round-trip airport transfers, three healthy gourmet meals a day, daily yoga or tai chi, a massage, a copy of *Hiking Maui* by Robert Smith, a custom-designed and -guided Eco-Adventure, and evening group discussions and lectures. Eco-Adventures are a form of nature therapy. These environmentally friendly and ecologically minded tours take guests into Maui's remote and sacred places. A typical tour can involve a hike to one of Hawaii's most ancestral *heiaus,* or sacred spots, in the Iao Valley to get a pounding hydromassage from a waterfall, or it can mean sea kayaking over coral reefs to the home of green sea turtles and perhaps catching a glimpse of spinner dolphins or migrating whales.

A diverse blend visits Angel's Nest, from entertainment executives to nuns, and all in turn learn stress-release and breathing techniques while connecting with the *aina,* or spirit of the land. One way of "connecting" involves a trip to the aquarium, a swimming cove filled with tropical marine life. And all guests can expect a breakfast of fresh organic juice, fruit spread, nut butters, sprouted bagels, whole-grain cereals, and seasonal fruits.

Hours and Days of Operation: Individual retreats and 8-day Soul Journeys to Paradise program offered year-round.
Accommodations: Up to 20 in spacious single and double rooms with "sky beds," affording panoramic views. Private cottages also available.
Rates: Lodging $85–$150 per person, per night.
Credit Cards: AE, D, JCB, MC, V.
Meal Plans: 3 healthy gourmet meals a day with vegetarian option.
Services: Massage, qigong, yoga, tai chi, breathwork, movement therapy, Sufi dancing, group discussions, health lectures, ecotours.
Recreational Activities: Nature hikes, diving, dolphin swims, sea kayaking, surfboarding, bodysurfing, windsurfing.
Facilities: Main house with panoramic view of ocean and eucalyptus and pine forests, cottages, dining room, healing temple, lap pool, hot tub, sauna, steam room, gardens, nearby waterfalls.
Staff: 3 core staff with therapeutic bodyworkers available on call.
Special Notes: Smoking and alcohol not allowed. Angel's Nest is an adult-only retreat.
Nearby Attractions: Shopping, dining, and nightlife in Maui, rain forest, the Bamboo Forest, Iao Valley, Hana, Haleakala National Park, the Aquarium, sacred sites.
Getting There: Round-trip airport transportation provided from Kahului.

Anuhea Health Retreat

3164 Mapu Place
Kihei, Maui, HI 96753
(800) 206-4441 or (808) 874-1490; fax (808) 874-8587
E-mail: anuhea@maui.net   Web site: www.maui.net/~anuhea

Dr. Elaine Willis, Dr. Russel Kolbo, and Cherie Kolbo have blended their vision and talents to create Anuhea, a unique health and healing center in a large home surrounded by palms, plumeria, and fragrant plants and within walking distance of Maui's crystalline waters. Since 1989, this tropical bed-and-breakfast has offered a peaceful healing environment for individuals and groups. Willis is a prominent nutritional consultant and psychologist who has written books on women's nutrition and stress relief. Dr. Russell Kolbo has been a practicing naturopathic physician and chiropractor for 28 years and specializes in allergies, metabolic imbalances, candida, parasites, and detoxification programs. Cherie Kolbo is a certified colonic hydrotherapist and colonic hydrotherapist instructor. She incorporates color, sound, and flower essence therapy in her healing sessions. Cherie and Russell have taught classes on tissue cleansing and proper food combining. Together, the talents of this team offer guests of Anuhea a comprehensive life-enhancing program.

Guests awaken each morning to the sounds of tropical birds and take a healthy gourmet breakfast of fresh live foods, included in the price of the room, on a lanai overlooking lush green gardens and the ocean sparkling beyond. They can then participate in a guided meditation, have a personal health and life plan consultation with Dr. Willis, receive a therapeutic massage, or simply read a book in a hammock. Cleansing programs are available and are tailored to meet each individual's specific needs. Colonic hydrotherapy, transformative bodywork, and juice fasting are methods used to detoxify the body.

Hours and Days of Operation: Personal retreats averaging 3–7 days offered year-round.

Accommodations: 6 bedrooms (each with 2 twin beds), 4 with private baths and 2 set in the tropical gardens with shared bath.

Rates: $60–$110 per night; group rates available. Detoxification programs, guided meditation, personal consultations, bodywork available at an extra charge. Group rates also available.

Credit Cards: MC, V.

Meal Plans: A healthy gourmet breakfast comes with room. For groups, 3 meals a day.

Services: Massage and therapeutic bodywork; nutritional, spiritual, psychological counseling; detoxification programs; meditation; colonics.

Recreational Activities: Guided tours, swimming, snorkeling.

Facilities: The bed-and-breakfast-style retreat center surrounded by tropical gardens has 6 private rooms, large living room, hammock, colonic hydrotherapy room, lanai.

Staff: A naturopathic physician, clinical nutritionist and family therapist, certified colonic hydrotherapist.

Special Notes: Wedding services can be conducted on the premises.

Nearby Attractions: Wailea beaches, world-class restaurants, shops, and galleries.

Getting There: 25 minutes by car from Kahului Airport. Anuhea provides written directions. Car recommended.

Dragonfly Ranch

P.O. Box 675
Honaunau-Kona, HI 96726
(800) 487-2159 or (808) 328-2159; fax (808) 328-9570
E-mail: dfly@aloha.net   Web site: www.dragonflyranch.com

The Dragonfly Ranch is a bed-and-breakfast and ecotourism center located 2 miles above Honaunau Bay, site of a *heiau,* or historic temple. The area is also an ancient "place of sanctuary" blessed with mana, or spiritual power. It's hard to tell whether it is this spiritual power or the lush garden atmosphere that makes Dragonfly the unique and restorative retreat that it is. In addition to personalized individual retreats, proprietor Barbara Kenonilani Moore offers the one-week Hawaiian Rejuvenation Retreat. Retreats are scheduled around the full moon and are designed to relax guests while educating them about the traditional Hawaiian way. Teachers and guides include Aunty Margaret, kahuna of the healing arts, and Kaipo DeGuair, Hawaiian musician, singer, and healer.

The rejuvenation package includes Ohana (Hawaiian family-style) accommodations; three meals a day consisting of fresh homegrown fruits, vegetables, and fish; a hot soak with aromatic oils, massage, aromatherapy, colored light therapy, and the ancient Hawaiian rejuvenation treatment of LomiLomi; an introduction to the health benefits of Noni; visits, lectures, and sharing with native Hawaiian guides and teachers; a luau with live music and hula lessons; and use of snorkel and beach gear along with instructions and round-trip airport shuttle service. During free time, guests can trek to nearby tropical pools long sought for their healing properties. Because sun, wind, and volcanic conditions vary, as do the wishes of the group, the itinerary can be altered when situations or events arise that may be more interesting or important than planned activities.

For those who may want more privacy during the retreat, three suites are available with distinct characters. Take, for example, the Honeymoon Suite. In a junglelike setting with ocean views lies an outdoor king-size bed with a mirrored canopy. The bed and kitchen are screened in under a pavilion roof, with an adjoining indoor redwood living room. Tropical vegetation surrounds an old-fashioned outdoor bathtub and shower, while a private redwood deck overlooks rock walls, gardens, and meadows.

Hours and Days of Operation: Open year-round. Weekend and weeklong programs offered year-round.

Accommodations: 2 main rooms and 3 suites, the Writer's Studio, the Lomilomi Suite, the Honeymoon Suite.

Rates: 7-day Hawaiian Rejuvenation Retreat $1,195. Individual room rates $85–$176 per night. Discounts available for extended stays.

Credit Cards: MC, V.

Meal Plans: 3 healthy, nutritionally balanced meals included with Hawaiian Rejuvenation Retreat. Continental breakfast included with room rate.

Services: Massage, aromatherapy, colored light therapy, lectures by local healers and teachers.

Recreational Activities: Scuba diving, kayaking, dolphin swims.

Facilities: Ranch with tropical garden, main house, 3 studios.

Staff: Barbara Kenonilani Moore and native Hawaiian healers, guides, teachers.

Special Notes: Weddings or renewal vows can be accommodated at Dragonfly.

Nearby Attractions: Pu'uhonuaa O Honaunau National Park—Ancient "Place of Refuge," kayaking, world-class diving and snorkeling on the Kona coast, dolphin swims.

Getting There: 40 minutes south of Keahole KONA Airport. Private transportation can be pre-arranged at discount rates.

Express Your Truth, Creativity, Passion and Power

Mailing address:
359 Arapahoe
Boulder, CO 80302
(800) 932-2483 or (303) 442-2486 (phone/fax)

Joy Lynn Freeman, Ph.D., a physician and body-mind therapist, has been a leader in the healing arts for 20 years. An author and nationwide lecturer, Freeman also produced five body-mind yoga videos and was the creator of Quantum Shift, a series of transformational retreats and workshops. Paul Cicco has incorporated rhythm and psychospiritual teachings into the group seminars he has led for many large corporations, government agencies, and educational institutions. Together, Freeman and Cicco lead the Express Your Truth retreats, designed for rejuvenation, healing, and empowerment of the body.

The retreats are intended to help guests discover a deeper connection to their souls while providing the optimal environment for healing the body, mind, and spirit. Freeman believes that through transforming judgmental or fear-based thoughts, opening the heart, connecting with the power of nature, engaging in daily health practices, and expressing individual truth and creativity, the body is restored to a natural state of health. Both Freeman and Cicco contend that guests not only have a healing and transformative experience but also learn and take home with them the many tools and practices that allow the healing process to continue.

Methods used during the retreat are creative expression through art, music, and writing; daily body movement; various forms of meditation; a natural healthy diet; vocal expressions; and dance and rhythmic drumming. Through experiencing what it means to "live from the soul" during the five-day retreat, guests create a foundation for positive change and a state of well-being. During free time, guests can soak in an outdoor hot tub, hike across the surrounding tropical hillside, or receive therapeutic body treatments.

Hours and Days of Operation: Weeklong retreats offered several times throughout the year. Inquire for details.
Accommodations: Private and semiprivate rooms and dormitories, newly decorated in Balinese style.
Rates: $1,200–$1,500 per person, $2,700 for couples. Therapeutic body services available on an à la carte basis.
Credit Cards: MC, V.
Meal Plans: 3 gourmet vegetarian meals a day, including local organic fruits and vegetables.
Services: Personal growth workshops incorporating music, various forms of meditation, dance, storytelling, drumming, psychospiritual teachings, daily body movement and health practices, vocal expression, massage and therapeutic bodywork, naturopathic healing and psychic arts session, yoga instruction, chiropractic.
Recreational Activities: Sailing, snorkeling, scuba, windsurfing.
Facilities: 55-acre tropical retreat center with massage therapy center, private and dormitory-style rooms, spacious community lodge with fireplace, 2 hot tubs, sauna, outdoor pool, Native American sweat lodge, watsu pool, washer and dryer, 75-foot water slide, tropical gardens, ocean-view meadows and walking paths.
Staff: Joy Lynn Freeman, D.C., Ph.D., and Paul Cicco are experienced group facilitators. All bodyworkers licensed and certified.
Special Notes: Guests are asked not to bring bar soap and to bring a flashlight, beach towels, biodegradable bath articles, suntan lotion, and appropriate seasonal clothing.
Nearby Attractions: Beaches, nature excursions, and historic attractions.
Getting There: About 30 minutes by car from the nearest airport. Inquire for directions.

Grand Wailea Resort Hotel and Spa

3850 Wailea Alanui Drive
Wailea, Maui, HI 96753
(800) SPA-1933 or (808) 875-1234, ext. 4949; fax (808) 874-2424

Failing to mention the Grand Wailea when talking about healthy vacations in Hawaii is like failing to mention the Chrysler Building when talking about New York City's finest architecture. The Grand Wailea Resort's Spa Grande, alone covering 50,000 square feet, is Hawaii's most extensive health and fitness facility. Opulence is the key word at Grand Wailea, with some suites going for as much as $10,000 a night—but this doesn't mean that health and well-being are overlooked.

All visits to the spa begin with the Terme Wailea Hydrotherapy Circuit, which consists of a brief shower, a soak in a Roman tub for relaxation, a cold plunge, a steam and sauna, and then a sit under the cascading waterfall shower. A specialty bath of either Moor mud, seaweed, aromatherapy, tropical enzymes, or mineral salts follows, all of which have curative properties. Guests also have the option of taking a traditional Japanese-style bath.

Several packages are available, ranging from half- to full-day. Each package includes a sampling of spa services, from a LomiLomi massage to a seaweed body mask. Natural Hawaiian plants are used in treatments and are selected for their particular healing properties, such as kelp, ginger, and papaya. The spa also offers a collection of Ayurvedic revitalization therapies. The goal is to help guests achieve an inherent balance and improve overall wellness—in addition to the luxury pampering. The abhyanga, pizichili, and shirodhara treatments, once reserved for the kings and queens of India, are intended to energize and detoxify. Private consultations are available in stress management, nutrition, movement therapy, psychic therapy, and more.

Hours and Days of Operation: 9–8 daily.
Accommodations: Deluxe rooms in 8-story tower with ocean views and private decks.

Rates: Vary according to room, services, and season. The Terme Wailea Hydrotherapy Circuit is $50 for hotel guests, $100 for nonhotel guests. Rooms $380–$10,000.
Credit Cards: AE, D, MC, V.
Meal Plans: Meals not included in packages, but gourmet spa cuisine available à la carte.
Services: Various types of massage, including LomiLomi, shiatsu, Swedish; aromatherapy; reflexology; hydrotherapy; herbal baths; Ayurvedic body treatments; body wraps and scrubs; facials; salon services; private consultations on health, nutrition, stress management.
Recreational Activities: Catamaran cruises, snorkeling, windsurfing, scuba diving, kids' programs.
Facilities: 40-acre luxury resort with 8-story hotel, 50,000-square-foot spa with Roman-style whirlpools, 42 treatment rooms, 3 restaurants, exercise equipment, weight-training room, racquetball court, 14 tennis courts, 2 swimming pools, 2 golf courses, billiards, gardens.
Staff: Over 1,000 total staff, with spa staff of about 59 massage therapists, 5 Ayurvedic body-workers, 15 aestheticians, 20 Terme attendants, 12 program specialists. All licensed and certified in their respective fields.
Special Notes: Facilities accessible for people with disabilities.
Nearby Attractions: Seven Sacred Pools, Skyline Drive, Haleakala National Park, horseback riding.
Getting There: From Maui's Kahului Airport, either take a transfer or take Highway 380 to Highway 350 via Kihei Highway 31.

Hale Akua Shangri-La Bed and Breakfast Health Retreat

Star Route 1, Box 161
Haiku, Maui, HI 96708
(888) 368-5305 or (808) 572-9300; fax (808) 572-6666
E-mail: shangrla@maui.net   Web site: www.maui.net/~shangrla/ha.html

Sitting in the cliffside hot tub at the clothing-optional Hale Akua Shangri-La Resort, guests can relax while gazing into the Hale Akua Crater. The health and yoga center is dedicated to the rejuvenation of body, mind, and spirit and is designed as a place to experience nature while receiving therapeutic bodywork, learning relaxation techniques, and consulting with local healers. Maui's waterfalls, bamboo forests, lava beds, and snorkeling bays are all within hiking distance, and seasoned guides will accompany those who request them. A set program does not exist at the Shangri-La. The most routine feature is a continental breakfast included in the room rate and a fully equipped vegetarian kitchen to prepare all other meals.

The best way to describe the healing activities at Shangri-La is to describe some of its healers, all available on an individual basis at an additional charge. Jeff Dobbins has over 13 years' experience as a licensed massage therapist and specializes in structural integration, LomiLomi, and neuromuscular therapy. His goal is to help clients get relief from pain and tension. Passion Flower is a certified Thai massage instructor and therapist who studied at the Old Medicine Hospital in Chiang Mai, Thailand. She works on specific problems, such as back pain, headaches, and shoulder and wrist pain. Sandra Be Taylor, a psychic healer, is also the staff psychic for the Grand Wailea Resort and Spa. She takes a holistic approach and tries to get people to "tune in" to the connection between mind, body, and spirit. She uses a combination of humor, psychology, nurturing compassion, physics, and psychic revelation. Both Manon and Shinzo are trained in the healing arts and together help people create balance and harmony within the body, mind, and spirit using Tantric healing methods.

Hours and Days of Operation: Weekend and weeklong personal retreats offered year-round. Office hours: Mon–Fri, 9–noon; Sat, 11–1.
Accommodations: 3 buildings holding 12 rooms in all, with ocean views and vegetarian kitchen in each building.
Rates: $50–$140 per day; $300–$840 per week.
Credit Cards: AE, D, MC, V.
Meal Plans: Continental breakfast included with room rate.
Services: Various types of massage including LomiLomi, Thai, neuromuscular, Swedish, structural integration, reflexology, acupressure; energy healing; organic healing herbs; aura soma; hatha yoga; Ayurvedic healing treatments; polarity therapy; psychic therapy; Tantric counseling and meditation sessions.
Recreational Activities: Swimming, whale watching, kayaking, biking, nature walks.
Facilities: 2-acre cliffside retreat center with spacious main house, cabana building, flower cottage for body treatments, hammocks, 2 hot tubs, outdoor ozonated pool, tropical flower gardens, natural pools and waterfalls.
Staff: All therapeutic bodywork, counseling, and massage therapy staff on call and licensed and/or certified in their respective fields.
Special Notes: The resort is clothing optional.
Nearby Attractions: Baldwin Beach, Hale Akala Crater, Seven Sacred Pools, shopping and dining in Makawao and Paia, Hana, bamboo forest, beaches, waterfalls, lagoons.
Getting There: 40 minutes by car from Kahului Airport.

Hawaiian Wellness Holiday

P.O. Box 279
Koloa, Kauai, HI 96756
(800) 338-6977 or (808) 332-9244

Dr. Grady Deal is a holistic, nutritional chiropractor who holds a doctorate in psychological counseling and a master's in sociology. He is also a licensed massage therapist, lecturer, gourmet cook, and author of *Dr. Deal's Delicious Detox Diet and Wellness Lifestyle*. His wife, Roberleigh Deal, is a licensed massage therapist and professional astrologer and numerologist and has delivered health lectures throughout the country. Both work together to form the Hawaiian Wellness Holiday, a health vacation program, and Hawaiian Metaphysical Vacation, a personal transformation program. Guests can participate in either vacations or in both simultaneously. The groups are kept small to allow for personal attention. The vacations are a great idea for people who want to give themselves a leg up on their personal journey to health.

The vacations are available in increments from as small as three days to as long as four weeks. The Hawaiian Wellness Holiday includes an initial nutrition, weight-loss, and health consultation that results in recommendations for correcting nutritional deficiencies and excesses and methods to improve lifestyle habits and health problems. A diagnosis is made to determine which diet and lifestyle habits have poisoned the body. Healthy foods, cleansing herbs, self-administered colonics, fasting, raw juicing, and lots of water usually follow the diagnosis. Guests are also tested for a number of conditions, such as free radical pathology, which may result in joint stiffness, chronic pain, and arthritis. Massage, reflexology, chiropractic adjustments, and hot packs are also a part of the therapeutic bodywork included in the program. Other healing activities include hikes to sacred sites and energy vortexes, yoga, aquacise, aura balancing by Roberleigh Deal, lessons in Hawaiian history, and health and personal transformation lectures.

Hours and Days of Operation: 3-day and 1-, 2-, and 3-week programs offered year-round.

Accommodations: Single and double rooms with private bath in a condominium on Poipu Beach.

Rates: Vary according to room. 3 days $895–$1,030 single occupancy; $1,395–$1,575 double occupancy. 1-, 2-, 3-, and 4-week options. 3- and 4-week rates eligible for 10% discount.

Credit Cards: MC, V.

Meal Plans: 3 meals a day with option of vegetarian, macrobiotic, raw foods, juice fasting, Fit for Life, or Dr. Deal's Delicious Detox Diet. Fish and eggs available.

Services: Massage, chiropractic, reflexology, exercise equipment, detoxification programs, colonics, nutritional counseling, lectures and slide show on health-related subjects, cooking classes.

Recreational Activities: Golf, tennis, horseback riding, hiking, water sports.

Facilities: Guests have access to the health spa at the Hyatt Hotel, which has a steam room, sauna, hot tub, exercise equipment, outdoor pool, beach access.

Staff: Dr. Grady and Roberleigh Deal.

Special Notes: Smoking not allowed in program areas. Facilities accessible for people with disabilities.

Nearby Attractions: Waimea Canyon, Kokee State Park, Waimea Canyon, botanical garden, fern grotto, golf courses, bicycle rental, horseback riding, water sports, helicopter tours, day cruises.

Getting There: From Koloa, take Poipu Road to Poipu Beach. Complimentary round-trip airport service.

Hono Hu'Aka Tropical Plantation

P.O. Box 600
Haiku, Maui, HI 96708
(808) 573-1391; fax (808) 573-0191
Web site: www.maui.net/~bnb/BB.html

Hono Hu'Aka Tropical Plantation, which translates as "Valley of Rainbows, Sky, and Healing Waters," is not only a retreat and healing center but also a certified organic farm. Orchards and bamboo grow on the 38 acres of permaculture in addition to the natural tropical vegetation. Situated on the lush North Shore in the middle of a jungle, the oasis of a quiet and clean environment pervades Hono Hu'Aka. The healing center serves to support and facilitate total health in mind, body, and spirit, while the plantation is vital in creating a sustainable living environment.

Director Leonard Keith's vision for Hono Hu'Aka is to build a community of people who celebrate awareness of the Earth, mind, and spirit. The center is still in its early stages, and improvements are made every day. Call it an in-process educational and healing facility. When completed, Hono Hu'Aka will be a school and elder center as well as a balanced community with artists and healers in residence. A complete cycle of harmony is the motivating philosophy at the retreat center and is represented through a totally sustainable plantation and through working closely with indigenous peoples.

Retreats are highly individualized, and Keith works with guests ahead of time to arrange the type of experience they seek. Healing activities include therapeutic massage, watsu, Pilates, Rolfing, homeopathy, astrology readings, yogic exercise, meditation, and reconnecting to the Earth through hands-on experiences in organic gardening and permaculture. The plantation is also an ecocenter where reforestation is a consistent effort and sanctuary provided for endangered Hawaiian species of flowers and fruit.

Hours and Days of Operation: Personal retreats averaging 1 week are offered year-round. Office hours: 9–6.

Accommodations: Private and shared rooms with kitchenettes, filtered water, microwaves, and barbecues.
Rates: Vary according to room and services. Lodging with breakfast $85–$175 per person, per night.
Credit Cards: MC, V.
Meal Plans: Continental breakfast included with room rate. Inquire about catered meals.
Services: Women's retreats, various types of massage including Feldenkrais, LomiLomi, Thai, and deep tissue; watsu, Pilates, Rolfing, homeopathy, aromatherapy, meditation, astrology readings, yogic exercise, organic gardening, art and dance classes, rituals.
Recreational Activities: Horseback riding, hiking, bicycling.
Facilities: A tropical plantation and organic farm with pool, hot tubs, waterfall, kiva, community gathering tent, orchards.
Staff: About 5 residential staff with backgrounds in various healing modalities, dance, ecotourism, gardening. Massage therapists and health practitioners contracted on an as-needed basis. All therapists licensed and certified.
Special Notes: Facilities accessible for people with disabilities. The plantation can accommodate weddings.
Nearby Attractions: Hana, Haleahala volcano, world-renowned surfing beach, whale watching, dolphin swims, waterfalls, lagoons.
Getting There: 40 minutes from Kahalui Airport. Call for directions.

Kai Mana

P.O. Box 612
Kilauea, Kauai, HI 96754
(800) 837-1782 or (808) 828-1280; fax (808) 828-6670

On a 5-acre estate overlooking the ocean lies Kai Mana, the home of well-known consciousness teacher Shakti Gawain. The main house and private guest cottages provide a secluded and restful stay. The house is at the edge of a gardenlike open field and is literally perched on a precipice from which the Pacific's breaking waves can be seen. Sitting in an outdoor hot tub, guests can get a front-row view of the Bali Hai cliffs. All rooms have a private entrance that opens onto a lanai, and a kitchenette is available for guests to prepare meals. During free time, they can stretch out in a hammock for a nap.

Gawain is also a prolific author whose books include *Creative Visualization* and *The Path of Transformation*. Throughout the year, she hosts weeklong intensives that focus on healing and balancing all levels of being—spiritual, mental, emotional, and physical. The technique of Voice Dialogue, developed by Drs. Hal and Sidra Stone, is used to help guests discover, explore, and integrate their personal life energies. The program also includes massage, meditation, guided visualization, and nature attunement rituals and excursions. The week is intended to be a catalyst toward meaningful and lasting change. The program is also a good way for health professionals to learn the Voice Dialogue technique.

A typical day during the intensive can include a group session facilitated by Gawain, individual Voice Dialogue sessions with a staff member, therapeutic massage, meditation and movement classes, or a walk down a cliffside trail to breathe the aroma of exotic tropical flowers and explore some of Kauai's most secluded beaches. Group sessions take place at a nearby location. Guests wishing to stay a few extra days at Kai Mana can make arrangements to do so.

Hours and Days of Operation: Open year-round, with blackout periods that vary from year to year. Inquire for details.
Accommodations: Single and double rooms with private bath and entrance in Shakti Gawain's home. Separate cottages also available. Overflow guests are referred to nearby bed-and-breakfasts.
Rates: $75–$150 per person, per night, plus 10% tax.
Credit Cards: MC, DC, JCB, V.
Meal Plans: Continental breakfast included with room.
Services: Personal growth workshops including group sessions facilitated by Shakti Gawain, Voice Dialogue sessions, therapeutic bodywork, meditation and movement classes, nature attunement exercises.
Recreational Activities: Hiking, tennis, horseback riding, swimming, snorkeling.
Facilities: 5-acre estate with main house and private guest cottages with hot tub, cliffside trails to secluded beaches.
Staff: In addition to Shakti Gawain, all therapists and bodyworkers are licensed and certified.
Special Notes: Smoking allowed only outside.
Nearby Attractions: Bird sanctuary, historical park with interpretive museum and lighthouse, whale watching, dolphin swims, windsurfing. Princeville is 5 minutes by car, and Hanalei Bay is 10 minutes by car.
Getting There: Call for directions from the Linhue airport.

Kalani Oceanside Retreat

RR 2, Box 4500
Pahoa, HI 96778
(800) 800-6886 or (808) 965-7828; fax (808) 965-9613
E-mail: kh@ILHawaii.net or kalani@kalani.com   Web site: www.kalani.com

Located on 113 acres of rural and sunny southeastern Hawaii is Kalani Honua Eco-Resort. The resort offers a variety of vacations, workshops, and retreats and is the only coastal lodging facility within Hawaii's largest conservation area. Orchid farms and botanical gardens border Kalani, while the sea cliffs in the surrounding coastal area allow for close-up views of sea turtles, dolphins, and migrating whales. The resort, whose name translates as "harmony of heaven and earth," has been offering unique and comfortable getaways since 1975. Kalani is also a member of the Hawaii Ecotourism Association and seeks to protect the natural environment through cultural education and responsible travel. Their not-for-profit status means Kalani not only provides visitors with rich, healing experiences but also helps support the well-being of local communities.

Guests come to Kalani either for any one of the myriad scheduled activities or simply to settle into a cottage and take advantage of its many services and facilities. For those traveling to Kalani for an unscheduled event, options include various types of bodywork, watsu, tai chi, yoga, lei making, a natural steam bath, dolphin swims, and treks to rare thermal springs and spectacular waterfalls. Scheduled programs vary from year to year. Some samples of last year's included an Ayurvedic fasting retreat led by Nora and Gabrielle Cousins; a mind-body dynamics workshop that taught Eastern methods of breathwork, meditation, yoga, and martial arts; and a neurolinguistic program led by Maureen Morgan that explored the relationship between consciousness and the healing arts. A residency program was established for artists and volunteers.

Hours and Days of Operation: Workshops and personal retreats offered year-round from 2 days to 2 weeks.

Accommodations: 8 private cottages and 4-story cedar lodges with a capacity of 75–85. Orchard campsites available.
Rates: Vary according to program and usually include room and board. Lodge $75–$730 per night, double occupancy. Campsites $20.
Credit Cards: AE, MC, V.
Meal Plans: 3 meals a day. Meals are $25 a day and can be purchased individually. Produce comes from the Kalani Honua herb garden and local farms. The lodge has kitchen facilities for use by guests.
Services: Various types of massage, LomiLomi, watsu, yoga, counseling on nutrition, diet and weight loss, health workshops.
Recreational Activities: Tennis, horseback riding, hiking, volleyball, golf.
Facilities: 113-acre oceanside estate with outdoor pool, whirlpool, steam baths, thermal springs, orchard.
Staff: About 30 staff members, including 10 licensed massage therapists, 3 watsu practitioners, LomiLomi specialist.
Special Notes: Smoking allowed only in designated areas. Facilities accessible for people with disabilities. Bug spray, sunscreen, and flashlights are available at gift shop.
Nearby Attractions: Volcanoes National Park, King Kamehameha historic site, Mauna Kea observatory telescope, Hawaii Tropical Botanical Garden, MacKenzie State Park, thermal spring parks.
Getting There: 45 minutes from Hilo Airport. Taxi service is available, or guests can arrange for a rental car at the airport.

Keali'i Nui Retreat

Well Being International, Inc.—Keali'i Nui Retreat
P.O. Box 1277, Haiku, HI 96708
(800) FOR-YOGA or (808) 572-2300 (phone/fax)
E-mail: yoga@aloha.net

Well Being International is located in a nature sanctuary known as Keali'i Nui, or "the highest royalty." It's an appropriate name for this 11-acre retreat center stretched across a remote private valley with a meandering stream and a waterfall pool cascading toward the Pacific. The name Keali'i Nui also indicates that the location occupies a sacred and historical site marked by ancient Taro fields. To maintain a balance with nature, this oceanside retreat uses a windmill to generate electricity and solar panels to heat water. Year-round workshops focus on a healthy lifestyle.

The brother-and-sister team of Meenakshi and Frederick Honig offer more than 50 years of combined teaching experience. For 23 years, Frederick Honig studied with the same teacher as Dr. Dean Ornish—the renowned yoga master Reverend Sri Swami Satchidananda. Frederick is a certified instructor of integral yoga and known for his warm and lighthearted approach. As director of Keali'i Nui, Frederick's program is similar to that of Dr. Ornish, yet it is more relaxed and targets a broad range of health concerns. "We've made significant advances with chronic fatigue," says Frederick. "This is a place where people can genuinely heal."

During the retreat, guests learn the benefits of a vegan diet and receive health, lifestyle, and nutritional counseling. The Honigs work closely with each person to design a program best suited to promoting total well-being. Each day, guests learn skills for creative stress management, participate in yoga and meditation, or take a guided nature hike to the Bamboo Forest, Twin Falls, the Queens Pool Waterfall, or Kuliki Bay.

Keali'i Nui also accommodates persons on private retreats, and guests are free to pick and choose from the menu of personal services. Two state-licensed ministers are also on staff to perform wedding services.

Hours and Days of Operation: Programs average 1 week and are offered year-round. Extensive sabbaticals available.

Accommodations: Private cottages with full bath, deck, kitchenettes; rustic tent cabins.

Rates: Vary according to lodging and package. 7-night vacation package with a private cottage and daily services $895.

Credit Cards: MC, V.

Meal Plans: Guests either purchase meals à la carte from a gourmet, multicultural vegan menu or provide their own meals. Cottages equipped with kitchenettes.

Services: Group and private instruction in yoga, meditation, stress management, goals clarification, healthy back care and vegan nutrition; guided nature adventures, licensed spiritual weddings, teachers' certification programs.

Recreational Activities: Swimming.

Facilities: 11-acre oceanfront retreat center, private cottages, windmill, orchard, organic garden, outdoor bathtub and outdoor shower, waterfall for swimming, hiking trails.

Staff: About 8 full-time staff, including Meenakshi and Frederick Honig, plus volunteers.

Special Notes: Cigarettes, alcohol, and nonprescription drugs not allowed.

Nearby Attractions: Haleakala Crater, Uaoa Bay, Hana, bamboo forests, waterfalls, beaches, windsurfing.

Getting There: 25 minutes by car from the Kahului Airport. Airport shuttles and rental cars available.

Mana Le'a Gardens

1055 Kaupakalua Drive
Haiku, Maui, HI 96708
(800) 233-6467 or (808) 572-8795; fax (808) 572-3499
E-mail: mlg@maui.net Web site: www.maui.net/~mlg

Mana Le'a is a sort of private clubhouse for spiritual, health, and personal growth retreats. Each year, this lush tropical garden retreat hosts dozens of seminars and workshops covering topics as diverse as sound and movement integration to drumming as a means to psychological and physical healing. Though Mana Le'a does not open its doors to private retreatants, opportunities are more than plenty to experience the calm and nurturing atmosphere the garden center provides. In fact, it is director Michael Corwin's goal to provide a serene, sacred, and safe environment to nourish the mind, body, and spirit.

The setting is a high-ceilinged wooden lodge with a fireplace and floor-to-ceiling windows that look out on the green Hawaiian hillside. Workshop schedules vary but usually take place in the spacious meditation hall, which is also ideal for tai chi, zazen, and dance. During free time, therapeutic bodyworkers offer treatments on an outdoor slate deck, and guests relax in an outdoor hot tub or take an invigorating hike through the rain forest. Nutritional counseling, naturopathic healing, psychic arts sessions, yoga instruction, and chiropractic are also available at an additional cost.

Retreats in 1998 include, among others, two workshops held in the fall, sponsored by the Worldwide Aquatic Bodywork Association. For five days, Harold Dull, the director of the School of Shiatsu and Massage at Harbin Hot Springs, will teach his therapeutic in-water body treatment known as watsu. Alan Cohen, contributing editor for the Chicken Soup for the Soul series and author of 12 books including *The Dragon Doesn't Live Here Anymore,* will lead a master training workshop in December.

To register for a workshop, obtain a listing of events through Mana Le'a, then contact the sponsoring group.

Hours and Days of Operation: Workshops and retreats sponsored by various groups offered year-round.
Accommodations: Cottages, private and semi-private standard rooms, dormitory rooms.
Rates: $80 per person, per day.
Credit Cards: MC, V.
Meal Plans: Gourmet vegetarian food included with room rate. Chefs handpick local produce, most of which is organically grown. Dietary needs can be accommodated.
Services: Massage therapy, nutritional counseling, naturopathic healing, psychic arts sessions, 1-on-1 yoga instruction, and chiropractic.
Facilities: 55-acre estate with 1,000-square-foot group room, 2 massage rooms, meditation hall, community lodge with fireplace, full kitchen facilities with covered lanai, solar heated bathhouse, 2 hot tubs, tiled swimming pool with 75-foot water slide, Native American sweat lodge, watsu tub, washer and dryer, walking paths through ocean-view meadows, tropical gardens.
Staff: In addition to guest workshop facilitators, such as Harold Dull, nutritional counselors, bodyworkers, and movement instructors available on call.
Special Notes: Mana Le'a does not allow individual guests to visit for private, unscheduled retreats. Guests are asked not to bring bar soap. Guests are asked to bring a flashlight, beach towels, biodegradable bath articles, suntan lotion, appropriate seasonal clothing.
Nearby Attractions: Volcanoes National Park and over 100 activities available on Maui, including whale watching, dolphin swims, and rain-forest hikes.
Getting There: 30 minutes by car from the Maui Airport. Inquire for details.

Far and Away Adventures

Middle Fork River Company, P.O. Box 54
Sun Valley, ID 83353
(208) 726-8888; fax (208) 726-2288
E-mail: adventures@far-away.com

For 18 years, Far and Away Adventures has spirited thrill seekers around the globe. Vacations traditionally are designed to combine an adventurous experience with a high level of comfort, service, and safety. Just recently a river jaunt has been added to the menu of journeys that also promotes well-being. Call it a wilderness spa, if you will. The Luxury Adventure Fitness Tour has guests rafting down Idaho whitewater with the intention of linking mind, body, and spirit with the outdoors. Guests return physically fit, spiritually recharged, and totally relaxed.

While floating past forests and rock formations, guests are as physically challenged or as laid-back as they choose. The tour begins with an initial assessment to determine toning and strength-training goals. Yoga and kinesthetic awareness activities are combined with aerobic interval workouts to prepare guests for the river ride. Guests benefit from professional masseuses who assess individuals' needs to provide the bodywork they require after a rigorous day of activities. Nutritionists and fitness and relaxation trainers conduct workshops and design personal fitness agendas. Deep-water workouts, nature hikes, and discussions on long-term fitness and nutrition goals are available throughout the journey.

Guests also learn the basics of ecotravel during the adventure. Techniques on how to keep the wilderness pristine are taught during a pretrip orientation that emphasizes conservation and preservation practices, including the principles of low-impact camping and tips on locating the "high water line" in order to properly dispose of water, what kind of biodegradable soap to use, and even where to brush your teeth. Since its inception, Far and Away has been active in protecting natural resources, participating in letter-writing campaigns, attending public hearings, and writing letters and articles to magazines and newspapers to promote a clean environment.

Hours and Days of Operation: Mon–Fri, 9–5. Trips averaging 1 week offered year-round.
Accommodations: Campsites during trip. Far and Away helps arrange pre- and posttrip lodging.
Rates: $2,100 for 6-day Luxury Fitness Adventure program.
Credit Cards: MC, V.
Meal Plans: 3 nutritionally balanced meals a day, with a gourmet presentation.
Services: Therapeutic bodywork, photography workshops, fitness and relaxation training, nutritional counseling, kinesthetic awareness activities, deep-water exercise.
Recreational Activities: Fly-fishing, whitewater rafting, wilderness hikes.
Facilities: North Face tents and sleeping bags, foam sleeping pads, cotton sheet liners, pillows, life jackets, wetsuits, wetsuit booties, rain gear and bedding that can be zipped together for couples, Mad River canoes, self-bailing rafts, inflatable kayaks, and whitewater dories.
Staff: Guides are certified in advanced first aid, and most are either emergency medical technicians, registered nurses, or first-response ambulance drivers. Guides who started with Far and Away 10 years ago are still with them. The Luxury Fitness Adventure also includes licensed bodyworkers and counselors.
Special Notes: Groups have a minimum number of 12 people and a maximum of 24.
Nearby Attractions: Sun Valley's outdoor recreation, Frank Church Wilderness Area, Moon National Park, Stanley Basin/Sawtooth Mountain Range, Bruneau Sand Dunes, City of Rocks, Sun Valley Ski Resort.
Getting There: Take airport shuttle, taxi, or rental car from Friedman Memorial Airport, Boise Airport, or Salt Lake International Airport.

Chicago Center for Chronic Disorders

636 South Michigan Avenue
Chicago, IL 60605
(312) 431-1452; fax (312) 431-1561
Web site: www.vedic-health.com

The Physicians' Association for Eradicating Chronic Disease was founded in May 1997 with the participation of medical doctors throughout the United States. The association was created to promote a more comprehensive system of health care to prevent illness through treating the root cause of disease and promoting a healthy lifestyle. The Chicago Center for Chronic Disorders, one of four similar centers currently open in the United States, is part of the association's Campaign to Create a Disease-Free Society. Future plans include the opening of 435 similar centers, with in-residence facilities near 40 of the largest metropolitan areas.

The centers offer integrative health programs that incorporate natural approaches for the prevention and treatment of chronic disorders. Drawing on Vedic and Ayurvedic principles, specialized programs are developed for individuals with virtually any type of chronic condition, from listlessness to Parkinson's disease. Because the centers also function as complementary care, patients are never asked to discontinue seeing a family physician or specialist.

Consultations and rejuvenation treatments are also provided for those who are fortunate not to be suffering from chronic ailments but would like to feel more physically and mentally alive. During consultations, doctors assess the individual's current state of physiological balance and design an at-home program that includes recommendations for diet, exercise, herbal supplements, stress management techniques, and daily and seasonal health routines. The five- to seven-day Rejuvenation Program is tailored to each person's unique needs and involves traditional methods of eliminating impurities from the body due to bad diet, stress, and other factors.

For more serious health concerns, the Chronic Disorders Program, which begins with a thorough medical examination, is recommended. After a highly personalized health regimen is established, patients receive daily treatments and undergo an extensive health education. Habits for maintaining and promoting total well-being are developed alongside a system of continuing self-care.

Hours and Days of Operation: Office hours: 9:30–4. Open 7 days a week, 9:30 a.m.–10 p.m. for treatments. Residential programs vary in length.
Accommodations: Comfortable hotel accommodations with private bath.
Rates: Vary according to services provided. Initial consultations $275. Rejuvenation Program $365–$515 per day.
Credit Cards: MC, V.
Meal Plans: All meals provided in accord with the dietary recommendations for each client.
Services: Thorough physical examination, techniques for managing health from its foundation, pulse diagnosis, purification therapies and herbalized oil applications, special herbal food supplements, diet and exercise programs, instruction in health-promoting behavior, methods for enhancing collective health throughout the world.
Facilities: Treatment rooms, small kitchen, dining rooms.
Staff: On-site physician, nurse, health educator, and 2 qualified technicians available for every client. A team of physicians trained in the Chronic Disorders Program is available by video conferencing.
Special Notes: Smoking not allowed. Facilities accessible for people with disabilities.
Nearby Attractions: Theater, music, museums, shopping, and restaurants in Chicago.
Getting There: Transportation available from O'Hare International Airport.

Heartland Spa, Kam Lake Estate

1237 East 1600 North Road
Gilman, IL 60938
(815) 683-2182; fax (815) 683-2144

On the 31-acre Kam Lake Estate in the heart of rural Iroquois County lies one of the Midwest's most recognized spas, the Heartland Spa. Heartland was recently included in *Condé Nast Traveler* magazine's "25 of the Best" spas throughout the world. Helping guests achieve lasting wellness is emphasized at this secluded health retreat, just 80 miles south of Chicago. Programs are designed to provide guests the knowledge and skills to utilize the current wealth of information regarding health, nutrition, and stress management. Guests leave Heartland revitalized and inspired to make positive lifestyle changes.

Heartland's programs can be divided into four basic categories: general lifestyle, nutrition, stress management, and beauty. General lifestyle programs start with a detailed questionnaire, after which guests receive individual counseling on the most effective ways to make the desired healthy changes. During the stress management program, guests receive therapeutic massage; learn yoga, tai chi, relaxation, and meditation techniques; and participate in gentle movement exercises. The nutritional program emphasizes a sound diet as the first step toward living a full life with the health and stamina required to achieve personal goals. Guests learn about nutrition, food preparation, and behavior modification techniques for weight loss. Beauty programs spoil guests with a laundry list of personal services, including loofah scrubs, manicures, pedicures, massage, and aromatherapy relaxation treatments.

Because of the voluminous offering of daily classes and activities, guests are encouraged to participate only in those activities that address their personal goals. The weekend and five- and seven-day program rates include taxes and lodging, meals, classes, use of spa and sport and exercise facilities, lectures, massages, facials, complementary exercise, and clothing.

Hours and Days of Operation: Weekend and 1-week packages offered year-round.
Accommodations: 14 rooms, single or double occupancy, with antique furnishings, twin beds, private bath.
Rates: Vary according to lodging, program, and season. Winter rates for a 5-night all-inclusive program $945–$1,131.
Credit Cards: AE, D, DC, MC, V.
Meal Plans: 3 gourmet low-fat meals a day and snacks.
Services: Massage, reflexology, facials, body wraps, sea-salt scrubs, salon services, tai chi, Brazilian martial arts, yoga, nutrition evaluation and counseling, resistance conditioning, boxercise, manicures, pedicures, group discussion on health-related topics, lectures on stress management, life enhancement, fitness assessment.
Recreational Activities: Country line dancing, aerobics, racewalking, horseback riding, fishing.
Facilities: 30-acre estate with challenge course, exercise equipment, indoor pool, 3-acre lake, steam room, whirlpool, tennis, hiking, par course, quarter-mile track, high-ropes course, water bikes, cross-country skiing, paddleboats.
Staff: About 50 staff, including massage therapists, nutritional counselors, fitness, meditation and yoga instructors, aestheticians, and nutritional counselors. All staff professionally licensed and certified. Olympian Augie Hirt teaches racewalking.
Special Notes: Smoking not allowed indoors.
Nearby Attractions: Tall Grass Farms, Frank Lloyd Wright's architecture in Oak Park, home and tomb of Abraham Lincoln in nearby Springfield.
Getting There: 1½ hours by car south of Chicago.

Lomax Wellness Center and Retreat

Lomax Station, Inc.
3153 South 900 West
San Pierre, IN 46374
(219) 896-2600

In 1853, the Junction Railway Company installed tracks, switches, lights, and crossings throughout the town of Lomax, Indiana. As central railroad access to outlying towns, Lomax witnessed a burst of economic growth. During the 1930s, however, electricity replaced steam power, and the town's progress slowed to a halt. Today, this historic railroad and pipeline town has transformed into Lomax Station, a holistic residential community offering health and rejuvenation programs for the mind and body. Some interesting new takes on old functions include the historic Telegraph Office, now a center for transcendental meditation and creative visualization.

Lomax is also on the migratory path for sandhill cranes, which fly past in the fall and return in April. Along with the three wildlife preserves that border the center, Lomax works to protect and restore the surrounding natural environment, which is home to a wide variety of medicinal plants and herbs. Each year, 300 to 350 trees are planted at and around the center.

Wellness retreats and programs at Lomax emphasize disease prevention and anti-aging, though stress management, weight reduction, and chronic ailments are also addressed. Programs are individualized. Most begin with a comprehensive medical examination. Then a nutritionist makes dietary recommendations and, in some cases, prescribes nutritional supplements. Biofeedback, yoga, meditation, massage, and exercise may all be a part of the daily routine. A psychotherapist specializing in the use of flower essences is also available. Lomax however, does not promise to cure all. "We try to educate people along their path," says Chief Business Consultant Michael Anthony. "They may be here for just one week, but the program is the rest of their lives."

Hours and Days of Operation: Programs averaging a week in length offered year-round.

Accommodations: Single- or double-occupancy cottages with fireplace, wood floors, screened porch, sleeping loft, small galley kitchen, and whirlpools; log cabins and dormitories.
Rates: Vary according to lodging and services. Accommodations $35–$125 per night. Holistic treatments $50 for initial colonic therapy session, $240 for initial medical examination.
Credit Cards: MC, V.
Meal Plans: 3 vegetarian meals a day.
Services: Nutritional medicine, traditional Chinese medicine, herbology, colonic therapy, massage, reflexology, Feldenkrais, aromatherapy, chiropractic, acupuncture, acupressure, homeopathy, biofeedback, expressive therapy, transcendental meditation.
Recreational Activities: Hiking, cross-country skiing, canoeing, fishing, boating.
Facilities: 29½ acres bordering the southern shore of the Kankakee River, 27 homes with whirlpools and fireplaces serving as B&Bs, educational facility, wellness center, restaurant, Anglican church, woodworking company, trails.
Staff: Dr. Steven Novil, an internationally recognized authority on metabolic and eating disorders who now specializes in anti-aging treatments; medical doctors specializing in mind-body medicine, acupuncture, and traditional Chinese medicine; psychotherapist; certified biofeedback specialist; transcendental meditation specialist.
Special Notes: Many wellness programs reimbursable by insurance. Facilities accessible for people with disabilities.
Nearby Attractions: Kankakee Fish and Wildlife Wetland Preserve, Jasper-Pulaski State Fish and Wildlife Nursery Area, Tippecanoe River State Park, historic Knox.
Getting There: 1½ hours by car from Chicago or South Bend, Indiana. Lomax has an FAA-approved airstrip.

The Raj

1734 Jasmine Avenue
Fairfield, IA 52556-9005
(515) 472-9580; fax (515) 472-2496

The Raj is a Maharishi Ayur-Veda Health Center that invites guests to experience perfect health. The center uses the 6,000-year-old Ayurvedic system of natural care, with the goal of preventing disease and promoting perfect health. All programs are designed to restore balance throughout the mind and body. Although it offers a variety of programs, each one is based on one comprehensive system of health care. Consequently, whether it's aroma- and sound therapy or learning a way to work out to relieve stress, each step supports every other to accelerate the process of increasing vitality and well-being.

The Maharishi Rejuvenation Program is offered for a minimum of three days, though one week is recommended for first-time guests. As Ayurveda has been known to be particularly helpful with chronic disease, the program begins with an in-depth health evaluation and includes the ancient pulse diagnostic technique to determine an individual's mind-body balance and to detect any pre-illness imbalances. After specific recommendations are made regarding diet, herbs, daily routine, exercise, and behavior, guests experience powerful detoxification treatments. Two and a half hours each day are spent receiving shirodhara oil massages, herbalized steam baths, aromatherapy, and gentle oil enemas, after which the effects of stress, fatigue, and environmental toxins are eliminated. The program also includes a gourmet vegetarian diet, health education courses, yoga, and lectures from visiting experts. Because the program is meant to be a foundation for long and lasting well-being, guests are given a home program to continue working toward a health-promoting lifestyle.

The Raj has also established an information office with a toll-free number for people wanting to know of an Ayurvedic physician in their area—(800) 248-9050.

Hours and Days of Operation: 3- to 14-day programs offered year-round.
Accommodations: Capacity for about 50 guests in 46 deluxe rooms and various 2-story villas. All villas have 3 guest suites.
Rates: Vary according to room and services. Maharishi Rejuvenation Program $1,611 for 3 days; $2,685 for 5 days; $3,760 for 7 days.
Credit Cards: AE, MC, V.
Meal Plans: 3 organic vegetarian meals a day.
Services: Ayurvedic purification therapies, consultations with medical doctors and Ayurvedic experts, yoga classes, transcendental meditation classes, Royal Skin Rejuvenation programs, nutrition and diet counseling, lectures on health-related topics.
Recreational Activities: Tennis, golf, horseback riding.
Facilities: 100-acre wooded estate with 3-story, French-country-style main building including a health center, private guest living room, 18 bedrooms, herb and gift shop, medical offices, exercise room, conference and meeting rooms, and Raj Restaurant; 5 private villas, 18-room hotel, reflecting pond, Osage orange grove.
Staff: 50 staff members, with a 2-to-1 staff-to-guest ratio; 2 medical doctors, full-time nurse, Ayurvedic technicians, visiting expert from India.
Special Notes: Smoking not allowed. Facilities accessible for people with disabilities.
Nearby Attractions: Dutch historic settlement of Pella, southeast Iowa woodlands and meadows, Amish communities.
Getting There: 1 hour and 15 minutes by car from Cedar Rapids. Transfers can be arranged for a fee from the Cedar Rapids, Burlington, and Des Moines, Iowa, airports.

Foxhollow Life Enrichment and Healing Center

8909 Highway 329
Crestwood, KY 40014
(502) 241-8621; fax (502) 241-3935

Like a scene from *The Great Gatsby,* guests approach Foxhollow from a long drive lined with dogwoods and evergreens to arrive at the 100-year-old Manor House on an old-fashioned Kentucky estate. Though it sounds elegant, the reason people visit this life enrichment and healing center is to initiate or continue the path toward mental, physical, and spiritual well-being. Programs and activities at Foxhollow are designed to help people learn and implement what they need to maximize their inner and outer health. The center is truly holistic in the sense that guests can consult a medical doctor, a nutritionist, a doctor of oriental medicine, or a colonic hydrotherapist and spend the rest of the afternoon in a pottery class or studying yoga. The spa itself is in a renovated farmhouse and is equipped with a luxurious Vichy shower. Between treatments and classes, guests can walk through a meditation and herb garden or explore the many trails on the 700-acre estate.

The center is the realization of founder Mary Norton Shands' determination to provide a place where people can come for health and well-being. "Ever since I was very young, I always wanted people to be well," she says. Shands is a living example of what Foxhollow can do for guests. She has maintained a healthy lifestyle based on exercise, nutrition, yoga, meditation, and vegetarianism for a number of years, and her vibrant health is more than evident.

In the spring of 1998, Foxhollow unveiled its new partnership with the Switzerland-based Paracelsus Klinik Lustmuhle. The clinic, founded in 1958 by a team of doctors, dentists, and therapists, is dedicated to the science and philosophy of holistic medicine. The recently opened Paracelsus Clinic at Foxhollow will provide guests with a combination of holistic biological medicine and conventional modern methods of holistic dentistry.

Hours and Days of Operation: Office hours: Mon–Sat, 9–6. One-day, weekend, and week-long programs offered year-round.

Accommodations: 14 rooms in 4 guest houses with a capacity for 22 guests.

Rates: $55–$80 per person, per night.

Credit Cards: MC, V.

Meal Plans: Gourmet vegetarian meals, with seafood options à la carte.

Services: Various types of massage including acupressure and Feldenkrais, iridology, acupuncture, oriental medicine, herbalism, naturopathy, comprehensive medical examinations, facials, body wraps and scrubs, hydrotherapy, aromatherapy, manicures, pedicures, astrology readings, yoga, healing circle, health and nutritional counseling, relaxation techniques, weekly classes on subjects like pottery and gourmet vegetarianism, informal personal growth workshops on subjects like journaling and expanding mental power.

Facilities: 700-acre country estate with 100-year-old Manor House, health spa, fitness center, medical clinic, steam, sauna, herb and meditation garden, tennis court, outdoor swimming pool, walking trails.

Staff: 20 medical and naturopathic doctors, registered nurses, homeopaths, nutritionists, acupuncturists, herbalists, massage therapists, colonic hydrotherapists. All professionally licensed and certified.

Special Notes: Smoking not allowed indoors. Facilities accessible for people with disabilities.

Nearby Attractions: Churchill Downs, Louisville Slugger Museum, horseback riding.

Getting There: 30 minutes by car from Louisville airport or 1½ hours from the Cincinnati airport. Round-trip shuttle available for a fee.

Healing of Persons Exceptional (H.O.P.E.) and Interface Integrative Health Services

52 High Street, P.O. Box 276, South Paris, ME 04281
(207) 743-9373; fax (207) 743-0540
E-mail: hopeheal@megalink.net

In 1910, the construction was completed on the Victorian-style Ripley House. This style included a large downstairs parlor for greeting guests and an upstairs parlor for the homeowners to enjoy themselves in a comfortable, open space. Perley and Mary Ripley bought the house in the 1930s. Perley was a philanthropist and entrepreneur, known for his local Ford car dealership. When he died childless in 1945, Mary decided to donate their home to the community for the purpose of health care. Following the dictates of Ripley's will, Healing of Persons Exceptional, or H.O.P.E., was awarded the full use of the buildings and grounds in 1989. What started out as a center offering cognitive-attitudinal work to create successful lives has developed into the holistic, integrative center of today. The center has helped people with cancer, heart disease, AIDS, chronic fatigue syndrome, depression, anxiety, and arthritis make significant changes.

H.O.P.E. was created during the surgical career of Dr. Ken Hamilton to support his patients who were battling cancer. The program grew from his success in guiding his patients toward healthy lives in spite of challenging diagnoses. During support groups, people learn to shift their focus from a fear-filled perspective to one of joy and appreciation. H.O.P.E is also the foundation for other health services, including those available at the Ripley Center. Within its umbrella is the Interface Integrative Health Services Healing (IIHS) Intensive, a three- to five-day residential program designed to evoke the healer within each individual.

A typical day during the IIHS intensive might include a consultation with Dr. Hamilton to establish a program best suited to the individual's specific health needs. A mask- and breastplate-making session might follow. This sacred process of celebration and healing has patients casting their faces and torsos with plaster-impregnated gauze. Through worship, prayer, song, and movement, the casting is developed into a finished sculpture based on its meaning and story. A therapeutic massage might follow, as might a reiki or acupuncture treatment or stress management workshop.

Hours and Days of Operation: 3-day intensive offered Tue–Thu; 5-day intensives offered Mon–Fri.

Accommodations: Guests referred to nearby bed-and-breakfasts or hotels.

Rates: 3-day intensive starts at $870.

Credit Cards: None accepted.

Meal Plans: IIHS facilities include a kitchen where guests can cook their own meals. Many restaurants in the surrounding area.

Services: Reiki, jin shin jyutsu, attitudinal healing, soul mapping and soul crystals, cognitive restructuring, relaxation, hypnosis, biofeedback, guided imagery, conscious behavior modification, therapeutic massage, acupuncture, psychological and nutritional counseling, art therapy, tai chi, chi kung, mask and breastplate making to get a deeper look at the self, shamanic practices, stress management, and rehabilitation counseling.

Facilities: The 10-room H.O.P.E. Ripley Center.

Staff: About 11 total staff, including a medical doctor, reiki masters, certified massage therapists, registered nurse, licensed acupuncturist, visual artist, nutritional counselor, movement instructor.

Special Notes: Smoking not allowed.

Nearby Attractions: Brunswick, Orr's and Bailey's Islands, picturesque Bowdoin College, Joshua Chamberlain Museum, L.L. Bean in Freeport, western mountain ski areas.

Getting There: 1 hour by car north of the Portland International Jetport.

Northern Pines Health Resort

559 Route 85
Raymond, ME 04071-6248
(207) 655-7624; fax (207) 655-3321
E-mail: norpines@maine.com

Located on 70 acres of pine forests in the Sebago Lake Region of southern Maine is the Northern Pines Health Resort. Situated on a mile of Lake Crescent waterfront, the resort offers a secluded natural environment to improve overall well-being. Owner Marlee Turner co-founded Northern Pines in 1980 based on the methods she used to overcome thyroid cancer. A simple program of meditation, daily walks, quiet time, and vegetarian meals made with natural, whole foods are the ingredients of the Pines' mind, body, and spirit revitalization program. Even the water is wholesome, burbling up from two deep artesian wells. If guests are up for it, they can hike to the top of Rattlesnake Mountain—where not one snake has been spotted since 1870—and get a lookout over the New England hillside covered with pines, some 300 years old.

The center operates under the small group concept to ensure each guest receives the personal attention required to meet his or her goals. No more than 20 people at a time participate in summer programs, and the number drops to 15 during winter, as it is a time reserved for personal retreats.

In the warm summer months, classes are offered every day on a variety of natural health subjects. Classes are intended to encourage guests to pursue their personal health goals and to teach them ways to develop more energy and greater awareness. Throughout summer and fall, guest speakers present programs on related subjects. Topics vary, but a recent year's schedule included Women's Health and Menopause, Homeopathy for You, and Relief from Arthritis Now.

Fasting programs are offered and recommended for periods of three to seven days. Guests are required to follow the Northern Pines' fasting program, which consists of two days of raw fresh fruits and vegetables before beginning a fast and three days of transition afterward.

Hours and Days of Operation: Programs averaging 1 week offered Jun 27–Sep 1, full-time. Private retreats available in winter.
Accommodations: Range of original 1920s cedar cabins and modern rooms.
Rates: $130–$195 per person, per day.
Credit Cards: D, MC, V.
Meal Plans: 3 vegetarian meals a day. Fasting options available.
Services: Various types of massage, reflexology, rebirthing, Moor mud body wrap, acupressure, aroma salt glow, transformational breathwork, tai chi, folk dancing, hiking.
Facilities: 68-acre rustic retreat center on a ⅔-mile stretch of lakefront with cabins, lodge, treatment room, exercise and yoga room, yurt, sauna with wood-burning stove, hot tub, flotation tank.
Staff: About 18 staff, including massage therapists, vegetarian chefs, aestheticians, yoga and tai chi instructors, medical social worker. All therapists licensed and certified.
Special Notes: Only 2 rooms accessible for people with disabilities. Northern Pines is not a medical facility.
Nearby Attractions: Rattlesnake Mountain, Shaker Village, Gray Animal Farm, shopping at L.L. Bean in Freeport.
Getting There: From Portland, take Interstate 95 to Exit 8. Follow to Route 302 and go northwest to Route 85.

Poland Spring Health Institute

32 Summit Spring Road
Poland, ME 04274-6704
(207) 998-2894; fax (207) 998-2164
E-mail: 71041.2216@compuserve.com   Web site: www.sms-witness.org

A stay at Poland Spring means living in the guest room of a large New England farmhouse for one to three weeks, surrounded by 135 acres of woodlands and garden. Programs emphasize the center's philosophy that health is not an accident but an achievement gained through following the laws of nature. The program involves a simple lifestyle, using the elements of natural food, exercise, rest, body therapies, a supportive family-like atmosphere, clean air, and pure water. The famous Poland Spring drinking water complements a vegetarian diet, and guests drink eight to ten glasses a day directly from the spring-fed well. Spring water is also piped into the steam room, hydrotherapy baths, whirlpools, and shower.

Never more than ten guests at a time participate in the programs offered at this Christian "health reconditioning facility." Prevention is emphasized during the one-, two-, or three-week stay, and a wide variety of natural remedies and alternative approaches are used to treat chronic degenerative diseases such as hypertension, diabetes, and arthritis. Stress management and smoking cessation programs are also offered. Dr. Richard Hansen, medical director and president of Poland Spring, advocates and teaches plant-based cooking schools. Author of *Get Well at Home*, Dr. Hansen is also an associate editor for the *Journal of Health and Healing*, a Christian wellness magazine advocating natural approaches to wellness.

The 14-day "Steps to Wellness" program includes a complete medical and diagnostic evaluation, nutrition and health-related instruction, hydrotherapy, and exercise. Therapists administer hot packs, steam baths, massage, and hydrotherapy to help each guest relax, eliminate toxins, and improve muscle tone. Guests maintain a vegan diet, served buffet style.

Hours and Days of Operation: 1-, 2-, and 3-week programs offered year-round.
Accommodations: 5 large rooms, 1 with private bath. Single or double occupancy.
Rates: Vary according to length of stay and lodging. 7-day Health and Healing Program $745–$950. Medical visits and diagnostic testing are extra.
Credit Cards: None accepted.
Meal Plans: 3 vegetarian meals a day consisting of salads and steamed, homegrown vegetables, fresh-baked bread, and seasonal fruit. Half of Poland Spring's food is grown on the property.
Services: Hot packs, hydrotherapy, massage, steam baths, therapeutic bodywork, lectures on health-related subjects, exercise equipment.
Recreational Activities: Canoeing, biking, horseback riding, ice-skating, swimming, sleigh rides.
Facilities: 135 acres with 3 large farmhouses, whirlpool, walking trails, rural lake, hay fields, bee farm, and 2 sheep whose wool provides mittens and socks.
Staff: Doctors, nurses, and licensed therapists, including Dr. Richard Hansen and program director Melody Wallace, R.N. All staff are Seventh-Day Adventists.
Special Notes: Alcohol not allowed. Smoking allowed only outdoors. Guests should remember to bring sturdy walking shoes, sweater or jacket, rain gear, and personal medical records as requested.
Nearby Attractions: Shopping and sightseeing trips to Portland and surrounding towns and Historic Shaker Village tours at nearby Sabbathday Lake.
Getting There: Rates include shuttle from Portland International Jetport and Lewiston Greyhound station.

Canyon Ranch in the Berkshires

165 Kemble Street
Lenox, MA 01240
(800) 726-9900 or (413) 637-4100; fax (413) 637-0057
Web site: www.canyonranch.com

Sloping lawns and a symmetric reflecting pool lead toward the centerpiece of Canyon Ranch in the Berkshires—the historic brick and marble Bellefontaine Mansion, built in 1897 as a copy of Louis XIV's Petit Trianon. This sister resort of the world-renowned Canyon Ranch in Tucson, Arizona, is situated on 120 acres of New England woodlands. The 100,000-square-foot spa opened in 1989 and was named Best Spa by the readers of *Condé Nast Traveler* magazine in 1991, 1994, and 1995.

The spa offers award-winning luxury vacations that promote healthy living through fitness, nutrition, and lifestyle education. An emphasis is placed on lifestyle, prevention, and awareness. The center offers an array of indoor and outdoor fitness activities, hiking and biking programs, spa and beauty services, nutritious gourmet dining, private consultations, and workshops. The goal is to teach people to take responsibility for their own well-being.

Program coordinators assist guests in arranging a schedule of individualized programs. All packages include accommodations, three nutritious and balanced gourmet meals a day, use of spa and resort facilities, fitness classes and sports activities, airport transfers, gratuities, and a selection of services. Preventive health care assessments can also be arranged, and the on-site Health and Healing Center offers the professional services of medical staff, exercise physiologists, behavioral health professionals, and movement therapists. Healthful cooking classes and nutrition consultations are also available.

Hours and Days of Operation: Various programs offered year-round.
Accommodations: 120 guest rooms and suites in a New England–style inn.
Rates: Vary according to season and package. A 3-night package starts at $1,955 single occupancy, $1,670 per person, double occupancy, in the fall. Rates do not include 18% service charge and sales tax. Discounts for longer stays.
Credit Cards: AE, D, MC, V.
Meal Plans: 3 healthy gourmet meals a day, plus snacks. Vegetarian options.
Services: Lifestyle programs; acupuncture; massage; therapeutic bodywork including craniosacral therapy, reiki, energy balancing; thalassotherapy; aromatherapy; medical and behavioral health services; salon services; nutritional and psychological counseling; lectures.
Recreational Activities: Hiking, biking, tennis, skiing, swimming, canoeing.
Facilities: 120-acre woodland retreat with the historic Bellefontaine Mansion; reflecting pool; formal gardens; demonstration kitchen; exercise and weight-training rooms; indoor tennis courts; racquetball and squash courts; indoor swimming pool; indoor jogging track; herbal and massage rooms; beauty salon; men's and women's sauna; steam and inhalation rooms.
Staff: 550 employees with an almost 3-to-1 staff-to-guest ratio. Health and wellness experts include doctors, nurses, nutritionists, exercise physiologists, psychologists, health educators, behavioral counselors, movement therapists, acupuncturists, Chinese herbalists, art and music therapists.
Special Notes: Minimum age of spa guests is 14. Alcoholic beverages not permitted in public areas, and smoking not permitted indoors or in public areas. All facilities provide access for people with disabilities.
Nearby Attractions: Tanglewood Music Festival, Jacob's Pillow Dance Festival, Williamstown Summer Theatre, Appalachian Trail, museums.
Getting There: About 3 hours by car from Boston and New York City. Van transportation for guests provided from Albany Airport and Bradley International Airport in Hartford, Connecticut, and at the Albany train stations.

Kushi Institute of the Berkshires

P.O. Box 7
Becket, MA 01223
(800) 975-8744 or (413) 623-5741; fax (413) 623-8827
E-mail: kushi@macrobiotics.org   Web site: www.macrobiotics.org

Michio Kushi, founder of the Kushi Institute and the One Peaceful World Society, is an internationally recognized teacher and spokesperson for the macrobiotic philosophy. Kushi is also the author of several books, including *The Macrobiotic Way*, and has won the Award of Excellence from the United Nations Society of Writers. For the uninitiated, the macrobiotic philosophy includes eliminating animal products and sugars from the diet, staying mentally and physically fit, spending time outdoors, and keeping your home in good order. Macrobiotic cooking and lifestyle also offers remedies for a variety of chronic conditions, including fatigue, digestive disorders, and aches and pains. Yet the institute's programs are designed to benefit everyone, including those who only wish to explore methods of achieving total wellness.

The institute is housed in a former Franciscan abbey on 600 acres of meadows, woodlands, and streams in the heart of the Berkshire Mountains. Dozens of programs are offered year-round focusing on natural approaches to health, healing, and personal development. The Women's Health workshop explores methods for improving, regaining, and optimizing health through a natural diet and healthy lifestyle. Women discuss health issues that are particular to their needs and bodies, such as menstrual difficulties; breast, ovarian, and cervical cancers; hormone imbalances; osteoporosis; and healthy skin, hair, and nails. The three-day workshop also includes a Home Remedy workshop that demonstrates ways to make baths, teas, drinks, and compresses. A cooking class teaches women ways to enhance their feminine health through diet. Women also learn self-massage, meditation, ways to perform Do-In and shiatsu facials, and how to make a hot ginger compress.

Whatever the workshop subject, a typical day begins with a gentle stretching exercise followed by breakfast at 9. A three-hour cooking class begins at 10, and guests taste the fruit of their labors with a lunch at 1. A class at 3:30 is followed by free time until dinner at 6, after which is an evening lecture. Guests on retreat are offered over 125 classes on topics like Healing the Environment, Cancer Prevention and Recovery, Strengthening Natural Immunity, Remedies from the Kitchen, and more. Each of the more than 75 teachers and counselors has 20 to 30 years of training with Michio Kushi and has been approved by Kushi.

Hours and Days of Operation: Open year-round. Office hours: 9–6 daily.

Accommodations: 10 country manor–style guest rooms in main lodge, single and double occupancy. Dormitory facility can accommodate 15 guests.

Rates: Vary according to length of stay and program; weekend program $350; per month $2,900. All prices include program, meals, and accommodations.

Credit Cards: AE, D, JCB, MC, V.

Meal Plans: 3 macrobiotic meals a day, Mon–Sat. Brunch and dinner on Sun.

Services: Seminars and workshops on macrobiotic cooking, women's health and natural weight-loss programs, health evaluation and consultations, shiatsu massage.

Facilities: 600-acre Berkshire Mountain educational center with bedrooms, lecture and workshop spaces, organic garden, nearby lake.

Staff: 10 experienced macrobiotic teachers and counselors.

Special Notes: Smoking allowed only in designated area.

Nearby Attractions: Tanglewood Music Festival, Jacob's Pillow Dance Festival.

Getting There: Pre-arranged shuttle service from Bradley International Airport and Albany Airport.

Maharishi Ayur-Veda Health Center

679 George Hill Road
Lancaster, MA 01523
(978) 365-4549; fax (978) 368-7557

Thirty miles northwest of Boston lies the Maharishi Ayur-Veda Health Center, a restorative health farm offering the 3,000-year-old Indian system of rejuvenation for mind, body, and spirit. Despite the luxurious 1920s furnishings and celebrity clientele—Calvin Klein and Cindy Crawford are known to have stayed for a week or more—the center offers powerful cleansing treatments and methods for creating a health maintenance program at home.

Because the programs emphasize prevention, an initial evaluation is conducted by a physician trained in Maharishi Ayur-Veda. The consultation includes a pulse diagnosis, a detailed medical history, and an evaluation of the dosha, or psychophysiological type, and any underlying patterns of imbalances that coincide with that particular dosha. Doshas are divided into three categories: vata, pitta, and kapha, also defined as the three elements of nature. The theory is that each person has elements of all three, with one or two usually dominating.

Laboratory tests are also done at the time of the initial evaluation, if necessary. Afterward, recommendations are made to tailor a program specifically around an individual's health needs. The program consists of any one of 20 approaches to Maharishi Ayur-Veda. Individuals are placed on a diet suited to their dosha, with recommendations for herbal food supplements. Health and behavioral routines are prescribed daily and can vary from daily hatha yoga to a course in transcendental meditation. Two hours a day are spent receiving panchakarma rejuvenation treatments, which include massage, steam baths, mild enemas, and pouring warm oil across the forehead.

The center also offers educational programs that teach introductory methods for detecting imbalances and the practical knowledge necessary to promote good health. Topics include the Good Health Through Prevention Course; the Diet, Digestion, and Nutrition Course; and the Self-Pulse Reading Course for Prevention. Sixteen-hour courses are available during seven-day stays for an additional fee.

Hours and Days of Operation: Programs averaging 1 week offered year-round.

Accommodations: 14 rooms and some suites in country house estate with four-poster beds and marble fireplaces.

Rates: 1-week stay $3,190–$4,190. To minimize monetary exchange concerns, international guests are requested to wire full payment in U.S. funds at least 1 month in advance.

Credit Cards: MC, V.

Meal Plans: Three vegetarian meals a day, with optional fish and chicken.

Services: Ayurvedic evaluation, massage, herbal steam bath, heat treatments, colonic cleansing, aromatherapy, transcendental meditation, courses on preventive health care, self-pulse reading and nutrition, lectures and videotapes on health-related subjects.

Facilities: 260 acres of woodland forest with red brick mansion, sunken gardens, walking trails.

Staff: Doctors, trained clinical technicians, massage therapists who are specially trained in Maharishi Ayur-Veda, chefs.

Special Notes: Smoking not allowed; guests who do will receive dry-cleaning and fumigation bills.

Nearby Attractions: Thayer Estate, Wachusetts Mountain Range.

Getting There: About 1 hour by car from Boston. The center recommends calling Continental Limo (800/666-4252) or Premier (800/240 5466) to make pickup arrangements at least 2 weeks in advance.

New Life Health Center, Inc.

12 Harris Avenue
Jamaica Plain, MA 02130
(617) 524-9551; fax (617) 524-0345
E-mail: NHLCenter@aol.com   Web site: www.anewlife.com

Bo-In Lee, founder of the New Life Health Center, is the author of *Wake Up! You Can Heal Yourself.* Educated in oriental medicine in Korea, Japan, and India, Lee is a licensed acupuncturist, yoga master, master of meditation, and grand master in taekwondo.

The three-story center opened in 1980 and contains a natural foods kitchen; dining area; guest rooms; yoga and meditation hall; lecture, physical therapy, and treatment rooms; and organic vegetable garden. A Resident Healing Program is offered in addition to outpatient care for people with degenerative and chronic illnesses. Treatments consist of traditional oriental medicine, including acupuncture, herbal therapy, and natural healing. Fasting is also prescribed when deemed necessary. Eastern medicine is complemented by Western technology at the center. X rays, EKGs, MRIs, CAT scans, and laboratory tests are obtained on an as-needed basis to accurately diagnose a patient's condition. Dr. Lee's programs have been reportedly successful with chronic pain, immune disorders, ulcers, addictions, diabetes, and cancer.

The Residential Healing Program lasts for an average of three weeks and is designed to facilitate self-healing and balance the body, mind, and spirit. The program begins with an in-depth evaluation by Dr. Lee. Morning treatments are administered as needed six days a week and can include acupuncture, cupping, infrared heat treatments, electrical stimulation, and moxabustion. Mahayana yoga and meditation classes are offered five days a week, as are lectures and training in holistic self-healing. Unless the body is undergoing a supervised cleansing fast, a diet of natural foods complements the healing process. A peaceful, supportive environment is provided to help guests make healthy and lasting changes in their lives. Optional services include acupressure massage, corrective exercises to reduce muscle strain and balance posture, and herbal teas and nutritional supplements.

Hours and Days of Operation: 1-, 2-, and 3-week programs offered year-round. Outpatient treatment available.

Accommodations: Capacity for 11 in comfortable private and semiprivate rooms.

Rates: 1-week program $995; 2-week $1,990; 3-week $2,985.

Credit Cards: None accepted.

Meal Plans: 3 vegetarian meals a day, with occasional fish and chicken. Fasting programs available.

Services: In-depth health evaluation, acupuncture, acupressure, cupping, electrical stimulation, herbal teas, cleansing fasts, health lectures and training in holistic self-healing, yoga classes, meditation, corrective exercise.

Facilities: 3-story building in Boston's Jamaica Plain section with yoga and meditation hall, guest rooms, natural food kitchen and dining area, physical therapy and treatment rooms, lecture room, garden.

Staff: Dr. Bo-In Lee, founder and director; Namye Lee, co-director; Dr. Asha Saxena, general practitioner and acupuncturist; and several health care assistants.

Special Notes: Special companion rates available for residents in need of support. Smoking not allowed.

Nearby Attractions: Jamaica Pond, Arnold Arboretum, shopping, museums and theater of Boston.

Getting There: Located in the Jamaica Plain section of greater Boston and accessible by car and public transportation. Call for directions.

Option Institute

2080 South Undermountain Road
Sheffield, MA 01257-9643
(413) 229-2100; fax (413) 229-8931
E-mail: happiness@option.org   Web site: www.option.org

When Barry Neil Kaufman's one-year-old son Raun was diagnosed as incurably autistic, functionally retarded, and possessing an IQ below 30, he and his wife, Samahria, refused to accept the sad and empathetic response of medical professionals. For 12 hours a day, seven days a week, the Kaufmans skipped regular meals and got down on the floor to play with, encourage, and respond with love and attention to their son. Over time, Raun completely recovered from his autism and by age 3½ had mastered first- and second-grade reading texts. By age 16, Raun's IQ tests were at near-genius levels. From this experience, the Option Institute and Fellowship was born, a personal growth retreat center in Sheffield, Massachusetts.

Since its founding in 1983, the institute has offered year-round programs that help people improve various aspects of their lives, including relationships, career, parenting skills, and ways to achieve peace of mind. The Body Vital is the institute's only program that focuses exclusively on health and healing. Over the course of five days, participants learn about the relationship between personal beliefs and physical health. Although The Body Vital is recommended for anyone facing an immediate health concern, it also benefits those who may already be healthy but who would like to feel more vitality and joy.

Acceptance and self-empowerment are underlying themes of The Body Vital. Participants learn to befriend their bodies and to discover negative belief systems that can destroy good health. Program facilitators help participants explore the relationship between healing and spirituality and teach techniques for building and maintaining lasting well-being. During optional sessions, guest speakers discuss natural methods for successfully challenging chronic ailments such as fibromyalgia, anxiety, hypertension, and high blood pressure.

How effective are the programs? Says one participant of the Healing the Mind and Body program, "When I dressed the morning I left the Option Institute, it was the first time [in 6 months] it didn't hurt to raise my arm."

Hours and Days of Operation: 3- to 8-day programs offered year-round.
Accommodations: Up to 55 in guest houses, including double rooms, triple rooms, and a few private rooms available on special request.
Rates: Vary according to program. The Body Vital program $1,225. Rates include meals, lodging, workshops.
Credit Cards: MC, V,
Meal Plans: 3 vegetarian meals a day.
Services: Programs for improving relationships, health, career, parenting skills, and peace of mind; personal consultations and dialogues with professional mentors; group discussion; massage; nature walks.
Facilities: 95-acre mountainside campus with comfortable rustic buildings nestled throughout the woods, swimming pond, volleyball court, recreation room, sweeping lawns, and waterfalls.
Staff: 60 full-time staff. Happiness Coaches have professional experience and training in group facilitation, pastoral and substance abuse counseling, elementary and secondary education, and special education. A licensed massage therapist is available on call.
Special Notes: Free information packets available on request. Volunteer and training programs available. Inquire for details.
Nearby Attractions: Boston Symphony at Tanglewood, Jacob's Pillow, Shakespeare and Company Theater, museums, bird sanctuary, botanical gardens, the Appalachian Trail, downhill and cross-country skiing.
Getting There: About 3 hours by car from Boston and New York City airports.

Rowe Conference Center

Kings Highway Road, Box 273
Rowe, MA 01367
(413) 339-4216; fax (413) 339-5728
E-mail: Retreat@RoweCenter.org   Web site: www.RoweCenter.org

What began as a simple Unitarian summer camp in 1924 has grown to become Rowe Conference Center, the three-story white clapboard farmhouse that draws internationally recognized healers and speakers throughout the year to host workshops and retreats. Still much like the original camp, there are no daily regimens guests must adhere to. Visitors are free to attend workshops or simply walk through some of the 1,400 acres of Berkshire forests, streams, and rolling hills adjacent to Rowe.

Workshops primarily focus on personal growth, drawing such names as Starhawk, ecofeminist and author of several books, including *The Spiral Dance*, and Grandfather Wallace Black Elk, grandson of the legendary Nicholas Black Elk and author of *Black Elk: The Sacred Ways of the Lakota*.

Several workshops throughout the year focus on healing, including Shamanism, Healing and the End of Time, led by Dr. Alberto Villoldo, who traveled to the Amazon in 1973 and spent 14 years as the apprentice of Don Jicaram, a Q'ero (Inka) shaman. Villoldo reveals ancient shamanic healing techniques and modern psychological insights as he teaches guests how to heal the past in order to "summon destiny from the future." Ilana Rubenfeld hosts the Healing the Emotional/Spiritual Body workshop, in which she demonstrates the Rubenfeld Synergy Method, which synthesizes gentle touch, movement, verbal intervention, body posture, imagination, music, and humor. Deena Metzger, who has led workshops nationally and internationally for 30 years, hosts The Creative, Ethical, and Spiritual Aspects of Healing in the 21st Century. The workshop is aimed primarily at health professionals, but anyone committed to healing the community and the land is invited. Metzger is the author of *Tree*, a pioneering book on breast cancer that has been republished with four new essays.

Hours and Days of Operation: Weekend workshops and personal retreats offered fall, winter, and spring. Summer camp for young people, teenagers, and families.

Accommodations: Capacity for 120 in dormitory-style housing and winterized 1-room cabins with wood-burning stoves. A limited number of single- and double-occupancy private rooms in Orchard Guest House, Rec Hall, Farmhouse, and Fromson House. Option of women-only, men-only, or co-ed housing.

Rates: Vary according to income $145–$205. Meals and lodging $80–$165 per person, per night. Members receive a $15 discount. Bartering is possible with advance notice.

Credit Cards: D, MC, V.

Meal Plans: 3 healthy vegetarian meals a day. Special dietary needs can be accommodated.

Services: Health and personal growth workshops including drumming, shamanism, healing touch, growing old courageously, discussion groups, massage.

Recreational Activities: Swimming, hiking, cross-country skiing.

Facilities: White clapboard farmhouse with recreation hall, cabins, nearby lake, sauna, sweat lodge, adjacent to 1,400 acres of Berkshire forest.

Staff: In addition to guest facilitators such as John Bradshaw, Marianne Williamson, Jean Houston, and Babatunde Olatunji, support staff include spiritual and personal growth counselors.

Special Notes: Smoking not allowed indoors. Bring your own toiletries, towels, bedding. Guest houses wheelchair accessible.

Nearby Attractions: Clark Art Museum in Williamstown, historical Deerfield, glass blowing studio, Bridge of Flowers, glacial potholes and candle factory in Shelburne Falls.

Getting There: The center will send you a map with special directions from New York, Vermont, and Connecticut.

Creative Health Institute

918 Union City Road
Union City, MI 49094
(517) 278-6260

In rural Michigan, the Coldwater River runs past the Creative Health Institute, a 300-acre health and lifestyle institute and home to abundant natural wildlife. The center is dedicated to the "living foods" principles of the Ann Wigmore Center in Boston, which operated for more than 30 years. Creative Health offers an unpretentious and simple approach to wellness education and practice, with the ultimate goal of teaching people to heal themselves in mind, body, and spirit.

The institute was founded in 1982 by Don Haughey. After Haughey was treated with over 116 different medications for a chronic illness, he was told there was nothing more to be done. Haughey tried the "living foods" lifestyle and has been healthy for more than 21 years. The lifestyle encompasses not only a diet of organic living foods but also methods for colonic cleansing and developing a positive outlook. It is presented as an alternative to the high cost of medicine and processed unhealthy foods. A typical diet consists of organic produce and greens, fermented foods, "Energy Soup," Rejuvelac, enzyme-rich foods, and sprouts. The program has had proven success with people suffering from heart disease, diabetes, arthritis, cancer, asthma, and other chronic diseases.

A one-week intensive starts on Sunday and ends Saturday. An emphasis is placed on hands-on, experiential learning. The program includes a diet of wheat grass and living foods, learning about living-foods theory, sprouting, indoor gardening and composting, raising and using wheat grass, colonic health and elimination, lymphatic circulation, exercise and breathing, living-foods preparation, alternative healing methods, food combining, video- and audiotapes on health, and ways to continue the program at home.

Hours and Days of Operation: Open year-round. Average program 2 weeks; shorter and longer stays available.

Accommodations: 20 standard dormitories, with semiprivate and private rooms available.

Rates: Vary according to room and length of stay. 1-week intensive in dormitory-style rooms $560, additional weeks $360. Rates include lodging, meals, videos, class instruction, educational material. Discounts apply to longer stays.

Credit Cards: None accepted.

Meal Plans: 3 live, organic vegan meals a day.

Services: Hands-on experience in vegetable and herb sprouting, growing greens indoors and living-food preparation, massage, hydrotherapy, daily exercise classes, stress reduction techniques, nutritional and lifestyle counseling, colonics, educational videos, courses on various aspects of health and cleansing, wheat grass juice therapy consisting of wheat grass implants, skin poultices, mouth, eye, nose, and ear washes.

Facilities: 9-acre estate bordering 2 rivers with informal community lodge including lodging for guests, classrooms, walking trails.

Staff: No medical doctors, but massage and colonic therapists are licensed. The center cannot accept guests who are unable to care for themselves.

Special Notes: Smoking and alcohol not allowed.

Nearby Attractions: Coldwater Lake, golf, horseback riding.

Getting There: 3 hours by car from Chicago.

Song of the Morning

9607 Sturgeon Valley Road
Vanderbilt, MI 49795-9742
(517) 983-4107; fax (517) 983-2102
E-mail: gli@goldenlotus.org

In 1951, former airline pilot Bob Raymer was ordained by Paramahansa Yogananda to teach the science of self-realization. Today, Raymer is the spiritual director for Song of the Morning, an 800-acre retreat located 40 miles south of the the Mackinac Straits in Michigan's lake and forest country. Though scheduled weekend workshops occur throughout the year, anyone is invited to come to Song of the Morning to enjoy kayaking on the Pigeon River, swimming, hiking, cross-country skiing, and some daily yoga and meditation.

Primarily a retreat center dedicated to the practice and teaching of yoga, Song of the Morning offers a few weekend workshops that address physical health through cleansing fasts, therapeutic bodywork, and vibrational healing. The Clear Light Healing Retreat is designed to recharge body, mind, and spirit through methods that help participants let go of subconscious blockages. The retreat, which lasts from a weekend to five days, includes purifying the body through a diet of fresh vegetables, breathwork sessions, vibrational healing, mantra yoga, chanting, and satsangs, or spiritual services. Chad Ulmer teaches the Functional Normalization Cranio-Sacral Workshop, which teaches guests how to use the holistic massage and healing energy technique known as Functional Normalization. The technique serves as a catalyst to the body's natural healing abilities while balancing mind, body, and spirit. Ulmer has been a certified Functional Normalization instructor and practitioner since 1983 and teaches workshops throughout Ohio and Michigan. Ulmer also hosts the Rejuvenation Retreat for Holistic Healthcare Providers, designed to teach guests how to relax and reconnect with their own innate healing abilities while exchanging knowledge and bodywork with fellow healers.

Hours and Days of Operation: Daylong and weekend events held throughout the year.
Accommodations: Capacity for 75 in private, semiprivate, and dormitory rooms. Tent and RV space available.
Rates: Range from $120 per day for private apartment with kitchen to $20 per day for camping (members receive 10% discount).
Credit Cards: AE, MC, V.
Meal Plans: A vegetarian brunch and dinner available daily except Tue; dinner only on Sun.
Services: Daily meditation service, Clear Light Healing Retreats, breathwork, hatha yoga, meditation, chi kung, tai chi, cooking classes.
Recreational Activities: Swimming, hiking.
Facilities: An 800-acre forested retreat center with dormitory, campsites, main house, vegetable garden, conference and meeting rooms, bookstore.
Staff: 8 resident staff, including spiritual director, yoga and meditation instructors, chef.
Special Notes: Pets, smoking, and alcohol not allowed. Children 12 and under stay for free. The center's driveway and back gate are locked between 10 p.m. and 8:30 a.m., so guests must schedule arrivals accordingly.
Nearby Attractions: Elk-viewing in Pigeon River Country Forest, Mackinac Island, mile-long Mackinac Bridge, scenic Petoskey/Harbor Springs area, cross-country skiing, hiking, windsurfing.
Getting There: About 4 hours by car north of the greater metropolitan Detroit area and 1 hour south of the Straits of Mackinac. Shuttle service available from local airports and from Detroit Metro Airport.

Birdwing Spa

21398 575th Avenue
Litchfield, MN 55355
(320) 693-6064; fax (320) 693-7026
E-mail: birdwing@hutehtel.net   Web site: www.birdwing-spa.com

The area surrounding Birdwing Spa is so pristine that it was once the sight of a Disney nature movie. Located on a former bird sanctuary, this upper Midwest spa is the perfect getaway for those who want to ignore phones, traffic, or 9-to-5 drudgery for a few days. And they do it with style—*McCall's* magazine recently featured Birdwing as one of the "Ten Best Spas." Says owner Richard Carlson, "We provide an island where people can get away from stress and bad habits, and we get them started on a better course of life."

Only 18 guests are allowed at a time on this 300-acre estate. Though Birdwing will never claim to be a health center, the Extended Life Enhancement package provides enough healthy air, food, exercise, education, and spa services to give guests the jump start they need toward a healthier lifestyle. The package includes a detailed lifestyle assessment and a consultation with a dietitian. Nutritious gourmet food is combined with the pampering pleasures of full-body massage, herbal wraps, and body polishes. Guests also get the chance to explore the rich natural scenery through bicycling, skiing, hiking, or canoeing. If it's too cold to get outdoors, they can work out in the fitness building or relax in the spa's sauna and whirlpool. Evening activities include guest speakers on stress control, nutrition and cardiac health, and cooking classes, and feature films. The spa also offers special weeks for art and nature studies.

Birdwing's philosophy is to offer "a balance of pampering, relaxation time, fitness activities, and a nutritionally balanced cuisine." And in its thirteenth year of operation, Birdwing's philosophy is serving them well. Owner Carlson relates a story of how in 1993 a sheik from Saudi Arabia visited the spa. No one knew he was a sheik until he had left and staff members were nervous about whether his expectations had been met. After a few weeks, a formal invitation arrived for Carlson to attend the wedding of the sheik's son.

Hours and Days of Operation: Weekend and 5- and 7-day packages offered year-round.
Accommodations: Standard single, standard double, barn Jacuzzi suite, master suite.
Rates: Vary according to length of stay and lodging. 5-day packages $1,050–$1,350. Rates include meals, accommodations, all services. Discounts available for extended stays.
Credit Cards: MC, V.
Meal Plans: 3 healthy, low-calorie meals a day.
Services: Facials, massage, paraffin treatments, manicures, pedicures, herbal wrap, body polish, nutritional counseling.
Facilities: 300-acre wooded estate with renovated barn, outdoor swimming pool, aerobics room, saunas, co-ed whirlpool, massage room, bicycling, canoeing, cross-country skiing, bird-watching.
Staff: 15 total spa staff including 4 massage therapists, an aesthetician, 2 cosmetologists.
Special Notes: Smoking not allowed indoors in public areas. Guests must be at least 16.
Nearby Attractions: Sioux uprising historic sites, Civil War museum, Mall of America, tennis, golf.
Getting There: 1½ hours by car from Minneapolis. Birdwing makes arrangements for local transportation on request.

IIHS Summer Symposium

P.O. Box 1309
Minnetonka, MN 55345
(612) 934-6516 (phone/fax)
E-mail: MANelson@CompuServe.com

Since the founding of the International Institute of Integral Human Sciences (IIHS) in Montreal, Quebec, in 1974, more than 10,000 members have joined worldwide. The Midwest Chapter is dedicated to exploring the mind, body, and spirit within a holistic and respectful atmosphere. The institute's goal is to help individuals live their lives more fully. The Summer Odyssey, as well as year-round workshops, lectures, and other events, provide participants the opportunity to delve into spiritual, philosophical, psychic, scientific, and cultural subjects.

Between 350 and 450 people meet each summer at the University of Wisconsin campus, located on the south fork of the Kinnickinnic River within blocks of quaint River Falls. Each year focuses on a new theme. The average day is spent attending at least two keynote events, two workshops, and optional meditation and yoga. Free time can be spent either donating or receiving therapeutic bodywork or psychic readings at the Healing Center.

Daily keynote events might be a seminar led by a renowned healer, a musical performance, or an interactive panel of speakers. Last year's keynote guests included Dr. Amar Kapoor, a renowned cardiologist and author. Dr. Kapoor, an Associate Clinical Professor of Medicine at the UCLA School of Medicine, has written several textbooks on cardiology. He recently developed a breakthrough in the field of mind-body medicine as it is used to combat coronary heart disease.

The IIHS is also dedicated to honoring diversity and works toward building harmony and a sense of community throughout the world. As evidence, the organization is an affiliated nongovernment agency.

Accommodations: Standard college dormitory rooms with mini-refrigerators and shared bath. **Rates:** All-inclusive rate for 5-day annual Summer Odyssey $425. Daily registration accepted on a space-available basis. Bodywork sessions and psychic readings available for an additional fee. **Credit Cards:** V.

Meal Plans: 3 meals a day with choice of meat-based, vegetarian, or vegan diet. Meals not included with daily registration but can be purchased from the college cafeteria. Campus within walking distance of coffeehouses, health food stores, and restaurants.

Services: Annual summer workshops and keynote events, optional daily meditation, yoga, therapeutic bodywork, psychic readings, nature walks.

Facilities: The Summer Odyssey is held at the University of Wisconsin, River Falls, campus. The buildings that IIHS utilizes is located in the middle of campus. Individual programs throughout the year held in rented churches, community centers, and other facilities in the Twin Cities metro area.

Staff: About 30 volunteers and an international faculty of 30–40 guest speakers including healers, shamans, authors, artists, theologians, teachers, psychologists, anthropologists, and medical, health, and scientific professionals.

Special Notes: Early registration encouraged for best workshop choices. Catalogs available in March. All facilities for the Summer Odyssey accessible for people with disabilities.

Nearby Attractions: Summer training camp for the National Football League's Kansas City Chiefs, dog racing in nearby Hudson, antiquing in nearby Stillwater, St. Croix River, Valleyfair amusement park, Omnitheater and Science Museum, Ft. Snelling, Murphey's Landing, Mall of America, Camp Snoopy, Canterbury Downs.

Getting There: 45 minutes by car east of the Minneapolis/St. Paul International Airport. Odyssey volunteers help match up drivers and riders in carpools.

Ruth Stricker's The Marsh, A Center for Balance and Fitness

15000 Minnetonka
Minnetonka, MN 55345
(612) 935-2202; fax (612) 935-9685

Situated literally in a marsh surrounded by natural wetlands, The Marsh, A Center for Balance and Fitness, was built on the philosophy that health goes beyond a physically fit body. The mind, spirit, and emotions are seen as integral aspects of total health, and the center offers an eclectic menu of activities, programs, and services designed to promote it. Inspired by the meditation and movement therapies she used to overcome a debilitating case of lupus, founder Ruth Stricker opened the center in 1985.

The center takes a traditional Western approach to health combined with complementary Eastern practices. The center houses a climbing wall, flotation tank, and a meditation tower with a view of natural Minnesota wetlands. Guests can work out on an underwater treadmill or practice their backstroke in the 75-foot lap pool. The training center is stocked with state-of-the art aerobic and resistance equipment.

Memberships, rather than programs, are the modus operandi at The Marsh. Member privileges include a fitness assessment, health history review, total blood cholesterol level test, body composition analysis, an electrocardiogram, and a personalized exercise program. Members also receive discounts on health and nutrition consultations, spa therapies, sleep fitness screening, cooking and nutrition classes, and workshops and special events. Overnight guests have full use of all facilities and classes.

The Marsh 24-Hour Get-Away is designed as a personal mini-retreat for mind and body and begins with an aroma steam shower followed by a full body wrap or Moor mud therapy. A 12-jet Swiss shower is next, followed by a one-hour deep-tissue massage and a one-hour custom facial. Plenty of time is allowed for classes and meditation. Dinner is taken on the Moon Terrace. The following morning begins with a spa breakfast before a pedicure, manicure, and scalp massage; a shampoo and style finish off the program. Before leaving, visit the Mental Gym, a unique space below the Meditation Tower stocked with rain sticks and other tools that visually stimulate the mind.

Hours and Days of Operation: Open year-round, Mon–Fri, 5:30 a.m.–10:30 p.m.; Sat and Sun, 7 a.m.–9 p.m.

Accommodations: 6 overnight guest rooms available, double and single occupancy.

Rates: Single $100 per night; double $115.

Credit Cards: AE, MC, V.

Meal Plans: Continental breakfast included with room. On-site restaurant provides a variety of fresh, healthful menu items served in both informal and fine-dining settings.

Services: Tai chi, qigong, yoga, meditation, acupuncture, acupressure, therapeutic massage, shiatsu, watsu, craniosacral therapy, trigger-point therapy, Feldenkrais, Alexander technique, Core Method (based on Pilates), body wraps, herbal wraps, salon services.

Recreational Activities: Hiking, biking, cross-country skiing, snowshoeing.

Facilities: 27,000-square-foot structure built on marsh with wraparound deck, 75-foot lap pool, exercise equipment, warm-water therapy pool, flotation tank, indoor and outdoor tracks, 4-level silo with Meditation Tower and Mental Gym, underwater treadmill, hydrotherapy tub, physiogymnastic balls, training center, gift shop.

Staff: Clinical exercise physiologists, board-certified cardiologists, registered dietitians, licensed psychologists, doctor of Chinese medicine, registered physical therapists.

Special Notes: All facilities, pools, and some guest rooms handicapped accessible.

Nearby Attractions: Minneapolis Art Institute, Mall of America.

Getting There: 30 minutes by car from Minneapolis.

Wholistic Life Center

Route 1, Box 1783
Washburn, MO 65772
(417) 435-2212; fax (417) 435-2211

Located on 900 acres of Ozark countryside, the Wholistic Life Center offers year-round residential detoxification and rejuvenation workshops. The center, which was originally designed as a martial arts training camp, now offers programs individually tailored to meet the specific health needs of each guest.

Health and lifestyle programs are based on the belief that "dis-ease" is a state of imbalance within the body and that true healing comes from within. The underlying philosophy of the center's programs is that in order to be truly happy, healthy, and fulfilled in life, one must work toward a state of physical, emotional, mental, and spiritual balance, thus the name Wholistic Life Center. Fruit and vegetable juicing is also a vital element of the center's programs. Raw and cooked whole food is used in every meal with an emphasis on the importance of eating "live" foods to promote health and healing.

A typical day at the center starts with morning light movement and stretching classes, which might be followed by a workshop on the mind-body connection. A colonic therapy treatment might then be followed by a class in food combining, nutrition, juicing, or stress management. After a lunch of natural whole foods, light exercise prepares guests for an afternoon hydrotherapy, massage, or reflexology treatment. The evening might include a group discussion on the universal concepts of life or a private session with a counselor aimed at dealing with any personal problems of an emotional or spiritual nature. The center's staff work to create a supportive and nurturing atmosphere to facilitate a profound level of healing.

Hours and Days of Operation: Programs averaging 2 weeks offered year-round.

Accommodations: 10 shared cabins and a limited number of private rooms.
Rates: 1-week program $850, on average; 2-week program $1,600; 1-month program $3,000. Because the center is a nonprofit organization, all rates are "suggested donations."
Credit Cards: MC, V.
Meal Plans: Vegan meals included with residential programs.
Services: Health lectures, group discussion, art and meditation classes, hydrotherapy, yoga, massage, colonic irrigation, reflexology, iridology, chiropractic, naturopathy, pastoral counseling.
Recreational Activities: Swimming, Ping-Pong, singing and dancing.
Facilities: A 900-acre wooded estate with 10 cabins in a hostel-style 2-story lodge, main activity building, exercise gym, hot tub, cafeteria and kitchen, organic greenhouse, basketball and tennis courts, walking trails and pond.
Staff: 11 full-time staff, including retired psychiatrist, doctors of chiropractic and naturopathy, yoga instructor, massage therapists.
Special Notes: Smoking not allowed.
Nearby Attractions: Branson, Missouri, home of many well-known country music stars, is within 2 hours. Beaver and Table Rock Lakes for swimming, boating, picnicking, fishing, camping.
Getting There: About 2 hours by car from Branson, Missouri. Regional airports in Tulsa, Oklahoma, and Springfield, Missouri.

Feathered Pipe Foundation

P.O. Box 1682
Helena, MT 59624
(406) 442-8196; fax (406) 442-8110
E-mail: fpranch@initco.net

For 22 years, the Feathered Pipe Ranch, located in the heart of the Montana Rockies, has symbolized the spirit of the feathered pipe—that of connecting with the circle of life—through its workshops and programs. The goal behind the Feathered Pipe Foundation, the nonprofit educational umbrella under which the ranch operates, is to provide learning experiences that provide the knowledge and commitment necessary for healthy living.

Programs are offered not only at the Montana home base but throughout the world. During ranch seminars, a broad spectrum of natural health, spirituality, and lifestyle topics are covered, such as power yoga, holistic health, shamanism, drum building, and natural healing. Guests also have time to take in a sauna and massage or to hike through the miles of forested mountains, pristine lakes, and abundant plant and wildlife. A short hike to the "sacred rocks" above the 110-acre ranch affords panoramic views. A typical day includes drumming, song, dance, shamanic dream work, prayer, and purification ceremonies with the Huichol shaman Brant Secunda. As part of his workshop, Secunda leads guests down a 40-foot chamber in a mountain cave, used as a sacred ceremonial site by prehistoric indigenous people.

Travel seminars are intended to foster personal growth while enabling guests to study ancient traditions and experience the healing energies of a place. Past workshops have included the four-day Power of Healing: Science, Nature and Spirit intensive with Dr. Andrew Weil and Dr. Christiane Northrup. Participants learned about the costs and benefits of traditional and natural medicine, how to prevent disease and promote health, herbs everyone should know, how to create health during menopause, how thoughts and feelings influence health and disease, and more.

Hours and Days of Operation: 3-day to 1-week programs offered year-round.

Accommodations: Dormitory-style rooms that hold up to 4 persons; camping in tepees, tents, or yurts; limited number of double rooms with private or semiprivate baths available at an additional $250 and $150, respectively, per person.

Rates: Vary according to program chosen. Cost for each program includes all instruction, lodging, meals, and general use of bathhouse and ranch facilities. Discounts available. Scholarships available for those who need financial assistance (please inquire).

Credit Cards: MC, V; checks or money orders preferred.

Meal Plans: 3 organic, vegetarian meals a day, with the option of chicken or fish.

Services: Health, spirituality, and lifestyle programs; therapeutic bodywork; meditation.

Recreational Activities: Swimming, volleyball, hiking.

Facilities: 110-acre ranch with main lodge, meeting rooms, tepees, yurts, tents, laundry facilities, hot tub, sauna, hiking trails, swimming pond.

Staff: About 20 permanent staff with guest lecturers like Dr. Andrew Weil and Dr. Christiane Northrup, Judith Lasater, Rodney Yee.

Special Notes: Smoking not allowed. Facilities accessible for people with disabilities.

Nearby Attractions: Helena, Montana; Yellowstone National Park; Glacier National Park.

Getting There: 15 minutes by car from Helena, Montana. A detailed information packet including map will be sent on registration. Round-trip van transportation available.

Free Enterprise Radon Health Mine

P.O. Box 67
Boulder, MT 59632
(800) 474-8657 or (406) 225-3383; fax (406) 225-4259
E-mail: hlthmine@mt.net   Web site: www.mt.net/~hlthmine

In 1951, a woman from Los Angeles noticed that her bursitis had disappeared after visiting her husband several times while he worked in a Montana ore excavation mine. Word spread, and the pilgrimage began. While miners attempted to put in a day's work, over 1,000 people suffering from chronic pain demanded access to the curing radiation. At first, they were allowed in for observation purposes only. After reports of pain relief ran consistently high, the operators of the mine decided to transform the mining operation into a health facility. It seems incongruous to expose oneself to radon for health purposes, yet radon and radium spas are found all over the world. In Hungary, radioactive caves are used to treat lung disorders. The Gasteiner spa in Austria states the value of radon in treating rheumatic disease, hormone imbalances, and problems with circulation.

The Montana mine markets itself as a holistic alternative to pain relief from immune system disorders such as arthritis, fibromyalgia, gout, asthma, and migraine headaches. Since its official transformation in 1952, tens of thousands of visitors have traveled to the mine to expose themselves to a little natural ionizing radiation therapy. Visitors travel underground to a depth of 85 feet and sit in a dry and well-lit 400-foot-long sitting room. The room is kept at a cool year-round temperature of 56 to 60 degrees. Comfortable chairs, couches, tables, heat lamps, and blankets are available during visits, and low-heeled rubber-soled shoes are highly recommended. For those who are uncomfortable with sitting underground at such a deep level, a surface-level sitting room was built.

Hours and Days of Operation: Mar–Oct. Winter hours 8–4 daily; summer hours 7–6 daily.

Accommodations: List of motels, bed-and-breakfasts, and RV campgrounds provided on request. Reservations must be made in advance.

Rates: 32 1-hour visits $140 per person; 16 1-hour visits $75 per person; individual 1-hour visits $5. Rates, though good through 1998, are subject to change.

Credit Cards: D, MC, V.

Meal Plans: No meals provided.

Services: Ionizing radiation therapy (Radium emanation).

Facilities: Above-ground building with lobby, reception area, surface-level therapy room; an Otis elevator that takes guests 85 feet underground to a 400-foot-long therapy room with comfortable chairs, tables, heat lamps. Two kennels for pet therapy.

Staff: No medical doctors on staff. One full-time employee attends the reception and lobby area; other staff maintain the premises, both above and below ground.

Special Notes: Free tours available. No scents, perfumes, or tobacco of any kind allowed. Children under 18 must have written approval by a physician. Anyone with a contagious cold or flu not permitted underground. Pregnant women advised to consult a physician before entering the mine. All facilities wheelchair accessible; wheelchair available for use on premises.

Nearby Attractions: Boulder Hot Springs, Glacier National Park, Yellowstone National Park.

Getting There: Boulder is on the Interstate 15 corridor halfway between Helena and Butte. Call for directions.

HealthQuest Clinics and Resorts

24 High Street
Hampton, NH 03842
(603) 929-4161
Web site: http://www.dr-hoyt.com

A modest New England address might cause someone looking for an exotic locale to skip over HealthQuest. However, this company provides healing spa packages in locations as diverse as Grande Cayman, Cayman Islands; Portofino, Italy; Nice, France; St. Moritz, Switzerland; Reykjavik, Iceland; and Palm Springs, California. The worldwide clinics and resorts focus on promoting and maintaining optimal health as well as restoring wellness regardless of the individual's present condition. In a naturally stunning environment removed from daily stress, guests are encouraged to take control of their health and lifestyle.

Because some sites are booked fully from year to year, advance reservations are required. Therapies run the full range of noninvasive modalities and integrate both ancient and modern techniques, including Chinese medicine, Ayurveda, European spa therapies, nutritional medicine, and naturopathy.

Therapies are tailored to an individual's needs, yet fundamental programs are similar from one location to another. For example, the rejuvenation/detoxification process starts with a prescribed diet broken into three phases. Fresh organic fruit and vegetables, followed by the addition of concentrated food supplements, comprise the first week's menu. Detoxifying teas and botanical medicines are also prescribed and taken in five-day cycles. Daily hydrotherapies, mineral baths, therapeutic massage, exercise, relaxation techniques, colonics, and personal counseling are usually included in the cleansing and healing of the whole person. Diets are slowly modified to reintroduce organic whole food, and quality rest and sleep are always recommended.

Hours and Days of Operation: Programs offered year-round. Stays average 3 weeks; 2-week minimum required for residential sites.

Outpatient programs 2 days–3 weeks.
Accommodations: Lodging ranges from site to site depending on exchange rates and local economies.
Rates: Comprehensive health plans average $345 per day and include meals, lodging, diagnostic work-up, and services. HealthQuest strives to accommodate people with limited financial means. Inquire for details.
Credit Cards: MC, V. Some locations may require advance payment when using credit cards.
Meal Plans: All meals included; diet prescribed according to the individual needs of each person.
Services: Chinese medicine; qigong; therapeutic massage; balneotherapies, including wraps and packs; hydrotherapies, including Floyer, Priessnitz, Kneipp, Baruch, Kellogg; botanical cures; Ayurveda; naturopathic internal medicine and cardiology; classical homeopathy; cosmetic and nutritional medicine; life path counseling.
Facilities: HealthQuest is currently investing $1.2 billion in 12 new clinic/resort facilities. Current affiliate clinic/resort locations in Grande Cayman; Lake Como, Portofino, and Sorrento Italy; St. Mortiz and Lausanne, Switzerland; Marco Island, Florida; Palma, Spain; Palm Springs, California; Reykjavik, Iceland; Nice and St. Tropes, France.
Staff: Vary according to size of facility. On average, 3-to-7 staff-to-patient ratio.
Special Notes: HealthQuest requires guests to provide a complete medical history, including typed transcriptions of all chart notes from all doctors, complete lab reports, lists of medications, and dietary supplements with dosages and potencies.
Nearby Attractions: Inquire for details, as locations vary. All locations in picturesque, health-promoting environments.
Getting There: Depends on location. Inquire for details.

Ann Wigmore Foundation

P.O. Box 399
San Fidel, NM 87049
(505) 552-0595 (phone, fax)

Dr. Ann Wigmore was the founding mother of the Living Foods Lifestyle. After 35 years of research, Wigmore drew a correlation between disease and the toxicity and nutritional deficiencies resulting from cooked and processed foods, drugs, and a negative mental attitude. Her theories proved successful, as evidenced by testimonials from people suffering from various chronic and degenerative diseases such as arthritis, hypoglycemia, chronic fatigue, and cancerous tumors.

The Lifestyle consists of a live-food organic diet that includes the famous Energy Soup, made with sprouts, watermelon rind, carrots, buckwheat greens, apples, avocado, and more. Wheat grass is an essential element of the living-foods program, believed to have profound detoxifying effects. The diet also excludes all breads, meats, dairy products, and cooked or processed foods. In addition to the diet, students go through an internal cleansing process while taking classes in growing greens and wheat grass, composting and soil management, indoor gardening, sprouting, food combining, meditation, self-improvement, positive thinking, breathing, stress reduction, visualization, and more. The environment is supportive and family-like, with all staff having gone through the program themselves. The standard two-week course ends with a celebration and diploma. Because the center is adjacent to two indigenous tribes, many cultural activities are incorporated into the program as well, such as adobe brick making.

Dr. Wigmore was director of the Ann Wigmore Foundation in Boston for more than 30 years. In 1994, she died from smoke inhalation when the foundation caught fire. Since that time, the Boston school has closed, and the property has been sold to acquire a new site in New Mexico. As of fall 1997, plans for the new school were blocked by the local zoning board, but the foundation expects to begin giving classes by fall 1998.

Hours and Days of Operation: 2-week classes offered year-round.
Accommodations: 15 rooms, single and double, with private and shared baths in simple 2-story dormitory-style building.
Rates: 2-week program $800–$1,500.
Credit Cards: MC, V.
Meal Plans: 3 live, organic vegan meals a day.
Services: Living foods program, colonics, yoga, self-sufficiency skills, relaxation, transformational and cultural activities.
Recreational Activities: Hiking.
Facilities: 2-story lodge with classrooms, kitchen, dining room and community space, hot tub, sauna, outdoor organic garden, indoor greenhouse.
Staff: 7 instructors, including a colonic hydrotherapist. Licensed massage therapists and therapeutic bodyworkers available on call.
Special Notes: Smoking and alcohol not allowed.
Nearby Attractions: Sky City; University of New Mexico's observation towers; dining, galleries, museums, and shopping in Santa Fe.
Getting There: 1 hour by car west of Albuquerque.

Ayurvedic Institute

P.O. Box 23445
Albuquerque, NM 87192-1445
(505) 291-9698; fax (505) 294-7572
Web site: Ayurveda.com

The snow-covered Sandia Mountains rise to the east of the Ayurvedic Institute. Founded in 1984 as an educational nonprofit corporation, the institute has expanded each year, adding new courses, treatments, and facilities. A two-year course in Ayurveda is offered, as is a rejuvenating panchakarma cleansing program at the institute's healing center. Dr. Vasant Lad, an Ayurvedic physician, teaches many courses at the institute, and panchakarma clients are welcome to attend his evening health lectures while they participate in the program.

The healing center at the Institute offers the five-day panchakarma programs, which are designed to bring the body, mind, and spirit back into balance. The program begins with an orientation, consultation, and pulse diagnosis with Dr. Lad or his assistant, after which an individualized series of treatments is recommended, as is a special diet, herbal teas, yoga, and health classes. Panchakarma therapies include an oil massage performed by two therapists in synchrony, herbal steam baths, herbal skin care, and a treatment that involves pouring warm oil onto the forehead. Oils and specific services are chosen according to the individual's unique constitution. Although extremely relaxing, the treatments act as vehicles to more or less force toxins to travel through the tissues and into the organs, where they can be eliminated. Guests also meet with department staff throughout the week to discuss the Ayurvedic diet and lifestyle and monitor progress. Because of the program's immense popularity, scheduling for panchakarma is normally made six to nine months in advance, although a waiting list is available for cancellations.

Hours and Days of Operation: Office hours: Mon–Fri, 9–6. Phone calls taken until 5 p.m. Residential panchakarma treatments offered year-round.

Accommodations: A nearby house accommodates 3–4 panchakarma clients. Because the house is booked well in advance, a list of motels and bed-and-breakfasts is available. Some bed-and-breakfasts will arrange to drive you back and forth to the institute for an additional fee.

Rates: Daily panchakarma services, without lodging, $240 per day, $1,200 per week. Lodging rates vary. Inquire for details.

Credit Cards: MC, V.

Meal Plans: All meals included with panchakarma treatment; diet designed to support the prescribed regimen of therapy.

Services: Orientation, consultation, and pulse diagnosis with an Ayurvedic specialist; herbal steam treatments; herbal skin treatments; Ayurvedic treatments such as abhyanga, netra basti, shirodhara, and nasya; color therapy; marma point therapy; therapeutic and Ayurvedic massage; private yoga lessons; evening health lectures.

Facilities: The institute comprises a large single structure divided into classrooms, offices, store, health center, meditation room and panchakarma department, hiking trails.

Staff: In addition to Dr. Vasant Lad, the Panchakarma Department has 14 staff members, including 6 licensed massage therapists, 3 shirodhara technicians, and 2 Ayurvedic specialists.

Special Notes: Smoking not allowed. Facilities accessible for people with disabilities.

Nearby Attractions: Restaurants and sightseeing in Albuquerque, Santa Fe, and Taos; downhill skiing; hiking; boating.

Getting There: About 25 minutes by car from the Albuquerque International Sunport. Shuttle service available through Airport Express.

Light Institute of Galisteo

HC 75
Galisteo, NM 87540
(800) 983-1975 or (505) 466-1975; fax (505) 466-7217

The Light Institute of Galisteo is a spiritual counseling organization established by Chris Griscom, known worldwide from actress Shirley MacLaine's writings as well as Griscom's own books. Exercises in consciousness, emotional body exploration, soul centering, and multi-incarnational regression are some of the methods used to enable guests to explore the spiritual purpose of a particular problem, ailment, or disease. This approach can provide an effective method of self-healing. A variety of workshops are held throughout the year, lasting from five to eight days. Workshops provide an opportunity for guests to work directly with Griscom as well as other therapists. Light Institute sessions are also offered and consist of daily three-hour sessions for four days.

Griscom has also developed the Light Institute Cranial, which subtly works to expand consciousness and dissolve accumulated emotional and karmic blockages within the cranium, spinal, and sacral areas of the body. The goal is to bring the entire body into a more healthy spiritual alignment. Cranial therapists are authorized by Griscom to conduct the spiritually focused and transformational technique.

Once a year, the institute offers an intensive called Soul Lessons Through the Body, intended for individuals with AIDS, cancer, and other life-threatening diseases. Guests discover the soul lessons of their particular disease and learn that disease is not a punishment but a path to self-awareness and enlightenment.

Free public meditation is held every Wednesday from 4:00 to 4:30 p.m., after which is an informal one-hour class led by the Nizhoni College of Divinity Students. The meditations are intended to revive the spirit while the class aims to get people in touch with their spiritual nature.

Hours and Days of Operation: Open year-round. 4-day sessions and 5-day intensives available.
Accommodations: Lodging provided in Galisteo guest house at additional cost from sessions. Lodging for intensives provided at the Nizhoni School for Global Consciousness and is included in cost.
Rates: Vary according to program. 5-day workshops $1,900–$2,300.
Credit Cards: MC, V.
Meal Plans: 3 vegetarian meals consisting of organic fruits and vegetables whenever possible.
Services: Exercises in consciousness, craniosacral therapy, emotional body exploration techniques, multi-incarnational sessions, soul centering.
Facilities: 50-acre campus with meditation hall, the Nizhoni boarding and day care school, guest house, organic garden, hiking trails.
Staff: 15 ministers, trained at the Sanctuary of Light Divinity School.
Special Notes: Smoking not allowed. Facilities accessible for people with disabilities.
Nearby Attractions: Indian villages and pueblos; shopping, sightseeing, and dining in Santa Fe; skiing and art community in Taos.
Getting There: 24 miles south of Santa Fe. Call for directions.

New Mexico Center for Chronic Disorders

2721 Arizona Street NE
Albuquerque, NM 87110
(888) 895-2614 or (505) 830-0435; fax (505) 830-0538
Web site: www.vedic-health.com

The Physicians' Association for Eradicating Chronic Disease was founded in May 1997 with the participation of medical doctors throughout the United States. The association was created to promote a more comprehensive system of health care to prevent illness through treating the root cause of disease and promoting a healthy lifestyle. The New Mexico Center for Chronic Disorders, one of four similar centers currently open in the United States, is part of the association's Campaign to Create a Disease-Free Society. Future plans include the opening of 435 similar centers, with in-residence facilities near 40 of the largest metropolitan areas.

The centers offer integrative health programs that incorporate natural approaches for the prevention and treatment of chronic disorders. Drawing on Vedic and Ayurvedic principles, specialized programs are developed for individuals with virtually any type of chronic condition, from listlessness to Parkinson's disease. Because the centers also function as complementary care, patients are never asked to discontinue seeing a family physician or specialist.

Consultations and rejuvenation treatments are also provided for those not suffering from chronic ailments but who would like to feel more physically and mentally alive. During consultations, doctors assess the individual's current state of physiological balance and design an at-home program that includes recommendations for diet, exercise, herbal supplements, stress management techniques, and daily and seasonal health routines. The five- to seven-day Rejuvenation Program involves traditional methods of eliminating impurities from the body due to bad diet, stress, and other factors.

For more serious health concerns, the Chronic Disorder Program is recommended. After a highly personalized health regimen is established, patients receive daily treatments and undergo an extensive health education. Habits for maintaining and promoting total well-being are developed alongside a system of continuing self-care.

Hours and Days of Operation: Office hours: 9:30–4. Open 7 days a week, 9:30 a.m.–10 p.m. for treatments. Residential programs vary in length.

Accommodations: Guests reside in nearby luxury hotels until the completion of the new facility, which is designed according to the health-promoting principles of Sthapatya-Veda architecture.

Rates: Vary according to services provided. Full-time, 3-week program $25,000.

Credit Cards: MC, V.

Meal Plans: All meals may be provided according to the dietary needs of each client.

Services: Thorough physical examination, techniques for managing health from its foundation, pulse diagnosis, purification therapies and herbalized oil applications, special herbal food supplements, diet and exercise programs, instruction in health-promoting behavior, methods for enhancing collective health throughout the world.

Facilities: Treatment rooms, classrooms, kitchen, dining rooms.

Staff: On-site physician, nurse, health educator, 2 qualified technicians available for every client. A team of physicians trained in the Chronic Disorders Program available by video conferencing.

Special Notes: Treatment is full-time, so sightseeing may be done before or after the residential program.

Nearby Attractions: Sandia Mountains, Indian Pueblo Cultural Center, Old Town Albuquerque, Santa Fe, Taos, petroglyphs, zoological park.

Getting There: About 20 minutes by car from the Albuquerque Airport. Transportation provided to and from the airport.

Takoja Retreat Center

656 North Star Route
Questa, NM 87556
(505) 586-1086 or (303) 934-3607 (winter)

Takoja is Lakota for "grandchildren" or "seventh generation." Dr. Judith Sauceda (pronounced sow-SEH-dah) uses the word to symbolize the dedication to Mother Earth and all life that she helps foster through programs at the Takoja Retreat Center. Sauceda is both founder and executive director of the center, which offers three- to seven-day programs throughout the summer on 40 spectacular acres in the mountains of northern New Mexico. Programs at the center, which are based on Native American and Taoist spirituality, teach ceremony and ritual, environmental awareness, and a proactive approach to conflict resolution.

At press time, eight summer programs were offered, though schedules are subject to change. Some of the programs are primarily spiritual, while others address therapeutic healing. One of the programs is an ongoing apprenticeship. The three-day Circle of Life retreat helps people going through personal transitions to align themselves with the Earth's natural changes. Guests learn to maintain balance and harmony with society and with themselves. This program helps people who suffer from anxiety to establish an equilibrium, heal themselves, and support loved ones through difficult transitions. Through ritual, painting, dance, and other forms of creative expression, Sauceda aims for each guest to leave the retreat with a sense of "the big picture."

Internal martial arts are explored during the Gateway to the Warrior Within retreat, taught by Sifu Mario Sauceda, Dr. Sauceda's son. Participants learn tai chi chuan, kung fu, and pakua chang, a sister to tai chi. No previous experience is necessary to partake in these intensive session. Practitioners of the healing arts will be interested in the Shamanic Practices for Healers retreat. Facilitated by both Mario and Judith Sauceda, the workshop teaches spiritually oriented therapeutics with hands-on techniques. The Saucedas demonstrate ways to create power objects for healing and self-transformation. Yoga exercises are implemented throughout the workshop, and guests can also participate in tai chi.

Hours and Days of Operation: 3- to 7-day programs offered June through Sept.

Accommodations: Can accommodate up to 20 people in domes, loft, tipis, small cabin, and campgrounds. Domes contain futons and bathrooms, and the small cabin has a solar shower and an outhouse.

Rates: $55 per day for lodging and breakfast. $250 per day for workshop with private instructor. Lunch and dinner included in package for nominal additional fee with advance notice.

Credit Cards: None accepted.

Meals: Homecooked meals; vegetarian options.

Services: Ceremony and ritual, shamanic healing practices, stress reduction skills, martial arts, yoga, tai chi.

Facilities: 40-acre retreat center with kitchen, lodging domes, tipis, loft, cabin, and campfire.

Staff: Dr. Judith Sauceda and guest retreat facilitators.

Special Notes: Smoking allowed only outside. Alcohol not permitted.

Nearby Attractions: Abundant fishing and hiking, Taos Red River Amalia, Kit Carson National Forest, Cabresto Park, Sulphur Springs, Rio Grande Gorge Park, Latier Lakes, Villa Vidal.

Getting There: About 30 minutes by car north of Taos, New Mexico.

Ten Thousand Waves

P.O. Box 10200
Santa Fe, NM 87504
(505) 982-9304; fax (505) 989-5077

For centuries the Japanese have known about the health benefits of "taking the waters," and at Ten Thousand Waves in Santa Fe, this ancient tradition of healing and relaxation takes place against a backdrop of New Mexico's serene and beautiful Sangre de Cristo Mountains.

People visit this Japanese health spa mainly to relax and enjoy themselves, but therapeutic massage is also provided, offering relief from physical pain as well as stress reduction and deep relaxation. As for healing modalities, Ten Thousand Waves also offers Watsu, the in-water form of massage developed by Harold Dull, director of Harbin Hot Springs in Middletown, California. The treatment involves cradling, pulling, and stretching, and the application of pressure to "energy centers," described in the Taoist creation myth. Watsu has proved to be a valuable treatment in aquatic rehabilitation, especially for cerebral palsy and sleep disorders and for people recovering from stroke, injury, or emotional disabilities.

Spa treatments are also available at Ten Thousand Waves. The 5,000-year-old Ayurvedic tradition is drawn on with the East Indian cleansing treatment. First, hot oil scented with sandalwood, orange, and lavender is massaged into the skin. Then, calamus root powder is massaged in as a stimulant, mild exfoliant, and rejuvenater. Afterward, guests are wrapped in hot linen soaked in herbs, allowing the calamus and essential oils to penetrate the skin and pull the toxins out.

Hours and Days of Operation: Sun, Mon, Wed, Thu, 10 a.m.–9:30 p.m.; Tue, 4:30 p.m.–9:30 p.m.; Fri, Sat, 10 a.m.–11 p.m. Day visits and weekend retreats offered year-round.
Accommodations: 8 lodging units available, each housing 1–5 people.
Rates: Vary according to services. Lodging $125–$200 per night.

Credit Cards: D, MC, V.
Meal Plans: No meals provided, though there is a healthful snack bar.
Services: Private and communal hot tubs, massage, Watsu, facials, herbal wrap, salt-glow scrub, East Indian cleansing treatments.
Facilities: 7-acre spa with Japanese- and Southwest-style treatment rooms and lodge; outdoor hot tubs spaced all over the mountain, including Japanese-style wood tubs.
Staff: All therapists certified by an AMTA Inquire–affiliated school with 2–30 years professional experience.
Special Notes: Discounts available for New Mexico residents. Reservations should be made in advance for all baths and treatments except communal tubs. Gift certificates available.
Nearby Attractions: Bandelier National Monument; Abiquiu; Taos; Santa Fe museums, galleries, restaurants, and other attractions.
Getting There: 3½ miles from downtown Santa Fe on Hyde Park Road. Taxis and rental cars available downtown.

Vista Clara Ranch

HC 75, Box 111
Galisteo, NM 87540
(505) 466-4772; fax (505) 466-1942
E-mail: vclara@newmexico.com   Web site: www.vistaclara.com

Vista Clara Ranch is named appropriately. The ranch affords 80-mile views across the Dali-esque New Mexico landscape. The site of the ranch itself is considered sacred by the Tewa Indians. Closed as the ultra-chic spa that drew an elite celebrity clientele in 1990, the ranch reopened in 1993 as a fully self-sustained non-profit wellness center and spa. All profits benefit the Juvenile Diabetes Foundation. Expansion for 1998 includes programs in nutritional education, an organic greenhouse, an observatory for guests to learn about astronomy, a multitude of conservation equipment, and more.

The ranch aims to nurture the growth of wellness in mind, body, and spirit. Designed primarily for baby-boomers, programs focus on maintaining good health and anti-aging therapies. The diverse spa menu reflects the belief that each guest needs to learn about and experiment with health treatments to discover what works best for them in achieving optimal wellness. This includes all facets of living, including a nutritious diet, proper exercise, body therapies, spiritual discovery, and the development of the mind. Through these facets, it is hoped that guests will gain an understanding of how mind, body, and spirit are connected in a holistic sense and how personal wellness is connected with the wellness of the Earth. Native American spiritual ceremonies are recent additions to the programs, including a traditional sweat. Native American facilitators conduct the ceremonies, following traditions handed down over many generations.

The eight-day package includes accommodations; three gourmet spa meals a day plus two snacks; six massage therapies; three body therapies; two beauty treatments; fitness classes and nature hikes; use of all facilities including steam, sauna, and Swiss shower; astrological chart and reading; round-trip transportation from Santa Fe.

Hours and Days of Operation: Open year-round. 1-, 4-, 6-, and 8-day spa packages available.
Accommodations: View rooms with balconies, hardwood floors, 2 double beds, full bath; lower-level with king and double rooms with hardwood floors, full bath, private garden.
Rates: 4-day package $700–$950; 8-day package $1,750–$2,300.
Credit Cards: MC, V.
Meal Plans: All meals are included with package. On-premise restaurant serves Southwestern cuisine.
Services: Therapeutic bodywork, shiatsu and Swedish massage, salt scrubs and herbal wraps, cranial sacral therapy, personal trainers, Native American ceremonies, astrology, salon services, yoga, tai chi, activity and fitness classes.
Recreational Activities: Horseback riding, nature and petroglyph hikes.
Facilities: 80 acres with a pueblo-style adobe main lodge, dining rooms, ozonated pool, glass-enclosed outdoor hot tub, fully equipped gym, kiva room, sweat lodge, orchard, pond, organic vegetable and herb garden.
Staff: About 30 staff, including 8 massage therapists, 3 aestheticians, 2 dance instructors, personal trainers, 2 craniosacral therapists. All licensed and certified in their respective fields.
Special Notes: Smoking allowed only in designated outdoor areas. Facilities accessible for people with disabilities.
Nearby Attractions: Santa Fe shopping, dining, and museums; downhill skiing; historic Indian ruins; petroglyphs.
Getting There: About 1 hour and 15 minutes from Albuquerque Airport. Transportation available from Albuquerque and Santa Fe airports.

Abode of the Message

5 Abode Road
New Lebanon, NY 12125
(518) 794-8095; fax (518) 794-8060
E-mail: aefis@sufiorder.org   Web site: http://www.sufiorder.org/aegis/

The Abode of the Message, a facet of the larger Sufi Community, is located on 430 acres of forest in upstate New York's Berkshire Hills. The retreat center is the site of a historic Shaker village. The Abode's Healing Arts Center, which functions to integrate the benefits of the retreat process—foods with hands-on healing practices—was built by the Shakers and is one of several in the complex that housed the South family of the Mount Lebanon Shaker Community.

Scheduled retreats are offered year-round, addressing a variety of subjects, for example, "Awakening the Life Force: Lotus Tai Chi" and "Mystical Astrology." Last year's "Being a Healer for the Self" was led by Zehra-Latif Williams, a senior conductor, teacher, and guide of the International Sufi Order with over 20 years of experience as a healer. Williams has developed a unique healing modality based on her training in shabd and kriya yoga; osteopathy, chiropractic, and craniosacral work; kinesiology; Gestalt; herbology; and more. The retreat taught people to look into the physiology of their bodies, from cell to tissue, and become familiar with their unique internal structure. Case studies from Williams' work were presented with hands-on training and short healing sessions.

A personal retreat at the Abode usually lasts three to six days, though longer retreats are available. To reside in an environment conducive to reflection, guests stay in hillside huts adjacent to the Meditation Hall. Retreats can include any combination of meditation practices, breathwork, light and sound therapy, guided imagery, or a therapeutic bodywork session with a healing arts practitioner. Fresh vegetarian meals and lodging are included in the rate, and guests are also encouraged to walk through the Berkshire forests, herb garden, or organic farm.

Hours and Days of Operation: Weekend to 10-day programs offered year-round.
Accommodations: Private retreat huts, shared cabin rooms, tent sites. The camp can accommodate up to 300, including tent sites. On-site housing is limited to 50.
Rates: Vary according to program. Tuition assistance available. Call for information.
Credit Cards: MC, V.
Meal Plans: Three wholesome vegetarian meals daily, with nondairy alternative. Special diet needs accommodated.
Services: Daily meditation, spiritual healing, therapeutic massage, reflexology, life path counseling, energy balancing, singing, dance, child care.
Recreational Activities: Swimming, hiking.
Facilities: 430-acre mountain retreat camp with Healing Arts Center, bookstore, private retreat huts, shared cabin rooms, showers, washrooms, outhouses, tent space, kitchen, dining pavilion, sweat lodge, large organic garden, walking trails, pond.
Staff: A core staff of 6, with guest facilitators like Dr. Atum Thomas O'Kane, Vice President of the International Sufi Order.
Special Notes: Many work-exchange programs available. Facilities available for rent by private groups.
Nearby Attractions: Berkshire Mountains, Shaker community, Living History Museum.
Getting There: 1 hour by car east of Albany and 3 hours north of New York City. Albany is the closest airport. Shuttles can be arranged from Albany and Pittsfield with advanced notice.

Body/Mind Restoration Retreat, Ithaca Zen Center

56 Lieb Road
Spencer, NY 14883
(607) 272-0694 (phone/fax)
E-mail: bodymindr@aol.com   Web site: http://users.aol.com/bodymindr/

On 60 acres of gently rolling hills, woods, and meadows lies the Ithaca Zen Center. The center hosts the Body/Mind Restoration Retreat, a two-week program designed to guide the body and mind toward optimal health. The one-week Meditation/Living Foods Retreat is also held at the center and is intended for graduates of the Body/Mind program. Both retreats are dedicated to the memory of Dr. Ann Wigmore, whose life and work served as inspiration. The retreats are designed to effectively cleanse the body of toxins while helping it easily assimilate nutrition. For this reason, it is recommended that guests prepare for the program by eating only raw fruits and vegetables for two days before the retreat.

Because the Body/Mind Restoration Retreat is a prerequisite to the Meditation/Living Retreat, it is assumed guests who forgo the initial Body/Mind program are already familiar with Dr. Wigmore's philosophy. A typical day during both programs begins with a 6 a.m. wake-up followed by nonsectarian meditation at 6:30. Beginners need not feel intimidated, as instructors will provide guidance. A breakfast of raw foods and wheat grass juice is followed by a brisk walk and, for returning participants, an advanced kinesiology class. At 9:30, guests receive instruction in preparing raw foods during a recipe class, followed by instruction in preventive medicine at 10:30. Lunch is at 11:30, followed by low impact aerobics and toning exercises. Afternoon is time for a swim, and perhaps a sauna and shower. A brief snack and a kinesiology course are offered before dinner at 5:45, and in the evening, guests gather for meditation and group discussion.

Hours and Days of Operation: 2-week retreats offered each year, Jun–Aug.
Accommodations: Cabins with bath sleep 4, private rooms with no bath, semiprivate rooms with bath, dormitory with shared bath, double or single cabin tents, campsites.
Rates: Rates vary according to new or returning participant and choice of lodging. Accommodations for Meditation/Living Foods Retreat are 50% of full retreat. Scholarships are available. No charge for camping.
Credit Cards: None accepted.
Meal Plans: 3 vegetarian meals a day. Retreats are designed to detoxify the body, and watermelon is emphasized as a cleansing food. It is recommended to eat only raw fruits and vegetables 2 days before arrival.
Services: Meditation, nutritional counseling, cognitive kinesiology, aerobics.
Recreational Activities: Swimming, hiking.
Facilities: 60-acre estate with only 5 acres cleared for the retreat facility, which includes dining hall, large dance studio, sauna, showers, campgrounds, swimming pond.
Staff: 3–5 staff members, including founder Marcia Radin, Dr. Richard Cohen, and David Radin, who leads meditation and evening group discussion.
Special Notes: A doctor's consultation recommended before enrollment. Smoking not allowed.
Nearby Attractions: Antiquing in nearby Ithaca, forests, streams, waterfalls.
Getting There: 45 minutes by car from Ithaca, New York. Shuttle service available from the airport for a fee; pickup arranged for guests who arrive by bus.

Cardiovascular Wellness Center

1600 Stewart Avenue
Westbury, NY 11590
(516) 222-2288; fax (516) 745-0976

"Arteriosclerosis is a preventable disease," says Dr. Frederic Vagnini, founder and director of the Cardiovascular Wellness Center, "and it is preventable by early detection and nutrition." Vagnini should know. After 25 years as a leading cardiovascular surgeon, he founded the center with the primary goal of promoting good health through early detection and nutrition. The center is based on his belief that a patient's health is in his or her own hands. "Once I saw the possibility to attack disease before it becomes serious and attacks the patient, I knew I'd found a method of halting the advance of cardiovascular diseases like arteriosclerosis, and actually reversing them."

Patients become familiar with their cardiovascular health through noninvasive, painless, ultrasound imaging at the center. Injections, X rays, and dyes are not used. Next, they receive a personalized regimen of diet, exercise, lifestyle adjustments, stress reduction and vitamin recommendations—the core elements of Dr. Vagnini's program. A Nutri-Scan blood chemistry evaluation assesses a patient's functional blood vitamin and mineral levels, including antioxidants.

The center has been so successful utilizing nutrition and natural therapies in the prevention and treatment of cardiovascular diseases that additional programs have been created to reduce dependence on medical drugs and surgery, including one for osteoporosis prevention and treatment.

Vagnini places strong emphasis on his assertion that medical drugs and surgery are not always necessary for the prevention, treatment, and care of heart disease. Through proper health management learned at the center, patients have a viable alternative to angiograms, angioplasty, or bypass surgery. Nonetheless, Vagnini will still recommend the appropriate surgical procedure if he believes there is no other alternative.

Hours and Days of Operation: Mon–Fri, 8–4:30; alternate Saturdays.

Accommodations: The Marriot and Garden City hotels conveniently located within 1 mile of the office.

Rates: Determined on an individual basis: $350–$1500.

Credit Cards: D, MC, V.

Meal Plans: No meals provided, but many restaurants in the surrounding area.

Services: Clinical nutrition and preventative medicine, physical examination, high-resolution blood-vessel imaging, Nutri-Scan blood chemistry evaluation, blood chemistry analysis, extensive lipid studies, functional cardiac exercise tolerance test, ambulatory and transtelephonic cardiac monitoring when deemed necessary.

Staff: All staff have extensive medical education and training, including specialized training in nutritional and cardiovascular medicine, and are handpicked by Dr. Vagnini.

Special Notes: Dr. Vagnini's "Heart Show" can be heard every Sunday from 4–5 p.m. on radio station WOR 710 AM. The Wellness Center now accepts most insurance, including HMOs, Union, GHI, and Medicare. Smoking not allowed. Facilities accessible for people with disabilities.

Nearby Attractions: Museums, restaurants, shopping, and nightlife in New York City.

Getting There: The office is right off the Meadowbrook Parkway and easily accessible by the Long Island Railroad.

Elat Chayyim, A Center for Healing and Renewal

99 Mill Hook Road
Accord, NY 12404
(800) 398-2630 or (914) 626-0157; fax (914) 626-2037
E-mail: elatchayyi@aol.com   Web site: http://members.aol.com/elatchayyi

The Catskill Mountains are home to Elat Chayyim, the six-year-old retreat center offering classes and programs centered around Jewish spiritual renewal. Courses focus on spiritual, environmental, and emotional healing, with one or two weeks of the year devoted specifically to physical health. All programs are designed to encourage learning about the Four Worlds as defined in the philosophy of Jewish mysticism. These four principles are *assiyah*, how the divine manifests in with the physical world; *yetsirah*, how God is present in the emotional world; *beriyah*, the intellectual world and how God is experienced through conceptions; and *atzilut*, the underlying oneness of God throughout all.

Retreats at Elat Chayyim are a community experience. Guests are invited to join a *mishpacha*, or family group, during their stay. The small groups meet for informal discussions and to reflect on the retreat experience. Optional groups for gay and lesbian guests, as well as those undergoing the 12-step program, are offered. At the end of the week, guests light candles together in preparation for the weekly Shabbat, or sabbath, celebration.

Based on the idea that the body and spirit must work together, Elat Chayyim also offers health and healing services to complement the retreat process. Practitioners have been chosen for their ability to harmonize the body and mind while guiding clients to health and well-being. Guests can receive a deep-muscle therapeutic massage and relax in an indoor whirlpool afterward. The diet is not only kosher but organic and vegetarian as well, and brachot, or blessings, are said over meals to encourage conscious eating.

Hours and Days of Operation: The center is open 7 days a week, Jul–Aug. Weekend retreats offered year-round.

Accommodations: Standard rooms with double occupancy and private bath. Some single and family rooms available.
Rates: Average $100 per day, all-inclusive.
Credit Cards: MC, V.
Meal Plans: 3 kosher vegetarian meals a day.
Services: Courses on spirituality, healing, and creative expression; rabbis to officiate events or conduct services; classes in Jewish spirituality; Swedish massage; deep-muscle work; acupressure; foot reflexology; yoga; meditation; children's programs.
Recreational Activities: Hiking.
Facilities: 35-acre Catskills retreat center with kosher kitchen, workshop, and meeting space, organic vegetable garden, swimming pool, indoor hot tub, tennis, Ping Pong table, volleyball court, year-round hot tub.
Staff: Core staff of 6, including some with training in rabbinical and social work, and a licensed massage therapist.
Special Notes: Smoking not allowed indoors. Facilities accessible for people with disabilities.
Nearby Attractions: Minnewaska State Park; Mohonk Preserve; Woodstock, New York; Catskill Mountains.
Getting There: 2½ hours by car from New York City. Flights available from New York City and Stewart International Airport in Newburgh.

Healing Tao USA

P.O. Box 20028
New York, NY 10014
(888) HEAL-TAO or (212) 925-7139; fax (201) 656-2346
Web site: www.healing-tao.com

As its name implies, Healing Tao is dedicated to presenting the best instruction of Taoist practices and other healing arts. Workshops and retreats are offered worldwide and differ from year to year. One recent year's subjects included the two-day Tao of Doing Nothing Together and the three-month Total Body-Mind-Spirit Rejuvenation Retreat at Tao Garden Thailand. Regionally, retreats take place in settings like the Big Indian Retreat Center, located in the Catskills just 100 miles north of New York City. The 300-acre site is recognized by Native Americans as spiritually powerful. It contains, among other things, a 40-foot meditation stupa.

The Iron Shirt Chi Kung retreat—typical of most programs at Big Indian—is designed as a starting point for learning chi kung. Separated into three levels, the first relaxes the body, emphasizes skeletal alignment, and teaches breathing techniques that enhance immune system responses. The second level develops open joints and tendon elasticity while teaching guests how to absorb and discharge energy safely. The third level targets bones and connective tissues surrounding the vital organs with the goal of strengthening them against injuries. The goal is to attain a "Steel Body," prized in ancient Chinese medicine and the martial arts.

Participants of the Tao Garden program experienced and learned techniques for cleansing and toning the body, cell by cell, with the intent of attaining mental clarity and developing inner wisdom. Guests could choose from a three-week intensive to a six-month stay. Chronic illnesses as well as short-term acute imbalances were addressed through the practices of chi kung, cleansing, and meditation and through gourmet vegetarian food and herbal steam baths. Guests experienced a complete body cleansing consisting of natural colonics and parasite cleaning. Chi nei tsang and Thai therapeutic massage were available by special arrangement.

Hours and Days of Operation: Retreats and workshops offered year-round in the United States and Thailand, 2 days–3 months.
Accommodations: Vary according to location. Range from campsites and double-occupancy rooms to shared and private condos and townhouses. In Tao Garden Thailand location, a townhouse is available for 3 guests sharing 1 large room with private bath and balcony and a communal living room.
Rates: Vary according to lodging and program. Basic tuition for a 6-day retreat in the United States $695, which includes double-occupancy room and meals.
Credit Cards: MC, V.
Meal Plans: 3 gourmet vegetarian meals a day.
Services: Tai chi, chi kung, meditation, breathwork, hands-on healing, energy work, relaxation techniques, self-massage techniques, natural colonics, detoxification programs, skin brushing, gentle exercise, courses, workshops, retreats.
Facilities: Vary according to location.
Staff: Master Mantak Chia and Maneewan Chia, 24 senior instructors, 4 consultants.
Special Notes: Certification programs are available.
Nearby Attractions: Vary according to location. Big Indian center is near Woodstock, New York, in the heart of the Catskill Mountains.
Getting There: Varies according to location. Big Indian Retreat Center is 100 miles north of New York City.

New Age Health Spa

P. O. Box 658
Route 55
Neversink, NY 12765
(800) 682-4348 or (914) 985-7600; fax (914) 985-2467

Rural luxury mixed with a holistic approach to wellness—this is the New Age Health Spa in Neversink, New York. The spa claims 155 acres of Catskill Mountain foothills, with a converted farm as the inviting focal point. The motivating philosophy behind all spa programs is to create an environment where people can learn to make lasting and positive lifestyle changes.

Programs, tailored around each guest's individual needs, can keep guests busy for as many as 12 hours a day—or allow them to lie back in a hammock for quiet reflection. The spa promotes the concept of balance in nutrition, fitness, and personal growth, and for this reason many activities are available in all three areas. This might mean hiking to the stone ridge of a Catskills overlook, learning how to prepare the delicious and low-fat treat of bananas in a crepe with orange-ginger sauce, or participating in guided visualization. Guests also have the option of climbing the 50-foot Alpine Tower (weather permitting) or scaling the challenge-ropes course, intended to get guests in shape and boost self-esteem.

The new Pathways to Wellness Project promotes overall wellness—mental, physical, spiritual, and social—through self-healing strategies. The new Lifestyle Management Program focuses on increasing wellness, self-awareness, and a healthy lifestyle. The two- to five-day program consists of facilitators helping guests to develop their own holistic approach to daily living.

Another addition to New Age's serving plate is the recently opened Wholistic Health Care Center. The center offers traditional mind-body, complimentary, and alternative treatments. Dr. Paul Salzberg, staff medical director, assesses the needs of each guest and develops a personalized wellness plan suited to his or her needs.

Hours and Days of Operation: Programs averaging 1 week offered year-round.

Accommodations: Single, double, triple cottages with private bath.

Rates: Vary according to lodging and services. Spa services $30–$175

Credit Cards: AE, D, MC, V.

Meal Plans: 3 meals a day, including vegetarian and nonvegetarian entrées. A salad bar is filled with organic vegetables, soups.

Services: Health planning consultations, Ayurvedic botanical therapy and body treatments, therapeutic massage, aromatherapy, reflexology, hydro-colonic therapy, hypnotherapy, loofah scrubs, mud, algae and herbal wraps, facials, fitness consultations, aerobics, tai chi, yoga, meditation, nutritional counseling, guided fasting, astrological charting.

Recreational Activities: Snowshoeing, cross-country skiing.

Facilities: 160-acre country estate with 2-story main house, cottages, gym, exercise equipment, indoor and outdoor pools, men's and women's steam rooms and saunas, treatment rooms, Alpine climbing tower and challenge-ropes course, yoga, weight and exercise rooms, tennis courts, hiking trails, corporate meeting rooms.

Staff: About 80 staff, including massage therapists, nutritional counselors, yoga, meditation and fitness instructors. Medical doctors available for the Pathways to Wellness Program.

Special Notes: Smoking, alcohol, and nonprescription drugs not allowed.

Nearby Attractions: Woodstock, New York; New York City; Catskills Forest Preserve.

Getting There: Shoreline bus service provides transportation between the Port Authority Bus Terminal in New York City and Liberty, New York. Cabs available at Liberty. Spa provides a minivan service from Madison Avenue and 72nd Street to Neversink on Fridays, Sundays, and holidays.

New York Open Center, Inc.

83 Spring Street
New York, NY 10012
(212) 219-2527; fax (212) 226-4056
E-mail: box@opencenter.org   Web site: http://www.opencenter.org

Just about the only thing you can't do at the New York Open Center is stay overnight. The program guide is thick enough to be confused with *The New Yorker* magazine, and it is virtually impossible to take in all the workshops, classes, and lectures offered within it. All programs at this nonprofit center address, in a more or less introductory style, holistic practices. Conferences and journeys are scheduled yearly; in 1997 guests traveled to Prague for four days of workshops on alchemy and the hermetic tradition. In 1998 two European conferences will be held on the "deepest mystical subjects." One group will travel to the west coast of Ireland to discuss Celtic vision and spirituality. Another group will travel to Wales to discuss the earliest references to Arthurian stories and legends.

It is best to contact the center, or the center's Web site, for the most recent catalogue before scheduling a trip. Some samples of last year's events included a mini-workshop on rejuvenation rituals led by Horst Rechelbacher, founder of Aveda. Participants learned about the practical daily uses of essential oils for physical and psychological rejuvenation. The four-day Transformational Breathwork Workshop explored the relationship between repressed emotions, healing, and breath. Guests were advised to bring pillows and blankets and to wear loose clothing for the experiential focused breathing techniques. Dr. Roger Jahnke, author of *The Healer Within*, led the Way of Self-Healing and Transcendence Workshop. Participants learned various self-healing chi kung practices, considered to be the mother of Taoism, Chinese medicine, and tai chi chuan.

The center is supported by its membership program, but nonmembers are welcome to participate in all programs—they just have to pay more. Volunteers are an integral aspect of the center and are needed in virtually every area, including catalog writing. Special volunteers-only events and eligibility for free programs are exchanged for a few hours of work each week.

Hours and Days of Operation: Classes and lectures held year-round.
Accommodations: On-site accommodations not available. Arrangements will be made for those traveling in from out of town.
Rates: Prices for classes and lectures vary according to the intensity and length of program and speaker. Group rates available. Scholarships awarded on the basis of need—call ext. 100 for details.
Credit Cards: AE, MC, V.
Meal Plans: Meals not included, although restaurants abound in the heart of Soho.
Services: Personal growth, spiritual and creative expression classes and workshops, a variety of massage and bodywork.
Facilities: Classic Soho cast-iron building has classrooms, a gallery, performance space, and a bookstore.
Staff: Lectures, classes, and workshops offered by renowned leaders in their fields. Practitioners and therapist certified and licensed.
Special Notes: Smoking not allowed. Facilities accessible for people with disabilities.
Nearby Attractions: Angelika Film Center, Soho Guggenheim Museum, Puck Building.
Getting There: Located in the heart of Soho on Spring Street in New York City. Center easily accessible by subway, bus, taxi.

Omega Institute for Holistic Studies

260 Lake Drive
Rhinebeck, NY 12572
(800) 944-1001 or (914) 266-4444; fax (914)266-4828
Web site: www.omega-inst.org

Ram Dass, Maya Angelou, Andrew Weil, Deepak Chopra, and Bobby McFerrin—just some of the guest speakers at the Omega Institute for Holistic Studies in Rhinebeck, New York. But Omega is more than just big names. The center, founded in 1977, was formed by three friends who met at a nearby Sufi Center in Lebanon, New York. What was once a handful of people attending weekend seminars in the remote rolling hills of upstate New York has become one of North America's best attended holistic centers. More than 10,000 people participated in Omega's myriad workshops and retreats in 1994. The 80 acres of apple trees, organic garden, and rolling lake mists are now capable of providing space for 600 people at a time who come to the institute for anything from curing burn-out to in-depth instruction in the traditional Chinese healing arts. With the kaleidoscope of programs offered at Omega, it may be necessary for newcomers to experience an introductory weekend, offered five times throughout the center's May-through-October season.

The five-day Wellness Week, the institute's most popular retreat, uses a mind-body approach. Diet, nutrition, fitness, exercise, lifestyle, and attitude are all addressed during daily core program workshops between 9 a.m. and noon. Muscle strengthening, creative movement, stretching, and low-impact aerobics are also a part of the week. After the three-hour daily workshop, free time is allowed for massage, fitness activities, music making, or simply walking through the trees.

It is not unusual for some Omega guests to wake up at 4:30 for tai chi at the lakeside, but for late sleepers, the blast of a blown conch shell bellows throughout the center at 7, announcing breakfast. From there, a day of learning begins, usually ending between 5 and 6 with dinner. Afterward, expect anything from a concert with a well-known musician to a community gathering, a dance, or a film.

Hours and Days of Operation: Weekend and weeklong workshops offered spring through fall. Registration available Mon–Sat, 9–6.

Accommodations: Double cabin rooms with roommate and either private bath, adjoining room, or shared bath. Dormitory space with bath shared by 8. Campsites available. No vehicle camping. Bring your own towels and linens for dorm space.

Rates: As low as $300 for a 2-day seminar with campsite to $1,545 for a monthlong retreat in a shared double cabin with private bath. A 10% discount applies to early registration, full-time students, senior citizens.

Credit Cards: MC, V.

Meal Plans: 3 meals a day, mostly vegetarian with produce from the organic garden.

Services: A wide variety of body therapies, including aromatherapy, shiatsu, reflexology and therapeutic massage, sauna, fitness, nutrition and stress reduction counseling.

Facilities: 80-acre upstate New York campus, including dormitories, cottages, campsites, Omega's Wellness Center, theater, gift shop, bookstore, café, garden, woods, and lake.

Staff: 250 seasonal staff, including massage therapists, movement and fitness instructors, various guest speakers.

Special Notes: Smoking not allowed in or close to any building, including housing. Omega provides child care for pre-registered children ages 4–12. Scholarship, work-study, and community exchange programs available.

Nearby Attractions: Catskill Mountains, Hudson River Valley, 90 miles north of New York City, local vineyards and farms.

Getting There: 2 hours by car from New York City. Check with registration office for available ride shares.

Omega in the Caribbean

260 Lake Drive
Rhinebeck, NY 12572-3212
(800) 944-1001 or (914) 266-4444; fax (914) 266-4828
Web site: www.omega-inst.org

The founders of the Omega Institute have the right idea: When one of the nation's leading holistic centers is buried under several feet of winter snow, move it to the Maho Bay Resort in the U.S. Virgin Islands. While still participating in one of Omega's myriad personal growth and holistic health seminars, guests can lie on a massage table set up on crystal-white sands and listen to the gentle lapping of aquamarine waves while they receive a deep-tissue massage. The Maho Bay Resort is within the boundaries of the Virgin Islands National Park. Mahogany and bay trees surround the tropical tent village, and guests are free to snorkel through coral reefs or hike to the ruins of an eighteenth-century sugar mill.

Caribbean programs take place over five weeks starting the first week of January and ending usually in the first week of February. Each week is selected to appeal to a diverse spectrum of interests, though some programs are offered throughout all five weeks, such as Dr. Stephan Rechtschaffen's "Timeshifting: Creating Time to Enjoy Your Life," which explores holistic approaches to nutrition, longevity, stress reduction, and well-being.

As in New York, a typical day starts with sunrise meditation, tai chi, or yoga. After breakfast in an open-air pavilion, one of the two daily workshops begins. Guests can spend the entire week sampling the Omega faculty's programs or instead focus on one or two teachers. Omega's natural foods chefs also migrate to the Caribbean to prepare daily buffets of vegetables and tropical fruits.

Hours and Days of Operation: 1- to 5-week programs offered Jan–Feb.
Accommodations: Single and double canvas cottages with comfortable furnishings.
Rates: Average weeklong course $1,025–$1,190, which includes lodging and food. $100 weekly discount offered to guests who wish to stay longer.
Credit Cards: MC, V.
Meal Plans: 3 vegetarian meals a day using natural foods and fresh tropical fruit. Fish and dairy optional. Meals served community style, overlooking the ocean.
Services: Personal growth and spiritual workshops such as Mindfulness-Based Stress Reduction and Moving Toward Wholeness; massage; meditation; energy training; nutritional counseling; yoga.
Recreational Activities: Snorkeling, swimming, hiking.
Facilities: Canvas cottages, a network of boardwalks connecting the resort to beaches, miles of marked hiking trails.
Staff: Facilitators, therapists, chefs selected from Omega faculty.
Special Notes: Omega's travel agent has a limited number of seats blocked at a special rate on American Airlines and USAir. Call (800) 516-4265. Guests are asked to bring a flashlight, all-terrain shoes, bug spray. Smoking not allowed indoors.
Nearby Attractions: Virgin Islands National Park, Annaberg Plantation, Bordeaux Mountain rain forest, catamaran trips, dining and nightlife on St. Thomas, coral reefs of Trunk Bay.
Getting There: Fly to St. Thomas and take the ferry to St. John.

Phoenicia Pathwork Center

P.O. Box 66
Phoenicia, NY 12464
(914) 688-2211; fax (914) 688-2007

Since 1972, the Phoenicia Pathwork Center has offered seminars and intensives based on 258 lectures channeled through the late Eva Pierrakos. The Pathwork is a spiritual path of self-transformation, offering a map to the human personality and the soul's evolutionary journey. The Path is a grounded approach using practical tools to guide retreatants toward self-responsibility, self-knowledge, and self-acceptance. Individual sessions with retreat facilitators, group lectures and discussion, prayer, and meditative exercises are all elements of the program. The retreat center is located on 300 acres of forest in the Catskill Mountains. During free time, guests might spot a wild turkey while wandering in and exploring the surrounding woods, or they might release toxins in a Native American sweat lodge.

Pathwork programs are integrated with Core Energetics, a method of bodywork developed by Dr. John Pierrakos, Eva's husband. The belief is that energy and consciousness work together in the transformative process of healing. The method, which is founded on the teachings of Sigmund Freud, Carl Jung, and Wilhelm Reich, is based on the idea that all experiences are physically stored in the body and manifest through emotional and muscular blocks. The work serves to energize the body through breath and movement, with the goal of breaking down and transforming defense mechanisms. The result is increased energy and vitality as well as a greater sense of fulfillment and joy. The effect of combining the two approaches is that guests are able to express dormant feelings, connect more fully during meditation and prayer, and expand their minds through the study of spiritual concepts.

Hours and Days of Operation: 2- to 6-night programs offered year-round. Long-term residential and work-exchange programs available.

Accommodations: Up to 200 in standard double and single rooms. Some rooms sleep up to 4. Limited number of private rooms and cottages available.

Rates: $70–$95 per night, including meals and snacks.

Credit Cards: MC, V.

Meal Plans: 3 buffet-style meals a day, with chicken, fish, and vegetarian entrées; fresh fruit; whole grains; freshly baked bread.

Services: Bodywork, meditation, prayer, lectures, group discussion, workshops, seminars.

Facilities: 300-acre estate with meeting facilities, Native American sweat lodge, low-ropes course, 7-sided sanctuary, tennis courts, swimming pool, hiking trails.

Staff: 35 total staff members including Pathwork counselors, Core Energetic therapists, residents studying Pathwork.

Special Notes: Smoking allowed only in designated outdoor areas. Facilities accessible for people with disabilities. Individuals must participate in a program to stay at the center.

Nearby Attractions: Catskill Game Farm, Woodstock, Hunter Mountain, horseback riding.

Getting There: 2½ hours by car from New York City. Bus pickup available in Phoenicia.

Pumpkin Hollow Farm

1184 Route 11
Craryville, NY 12521
(518) 325-3583 or (518) 325-5633
E-mail: pumpkin@taconic.net

The worldwide Theosophical Society, established in 1875, is devoted to promoting harmony among all people. The society encourages the search for an understanding of nature's laws and the inherent—yet latent—powers within humanity. Founded in 1938, Pumpkin Hollow Farm is the society's nonprofit retreat center of the Northeast. The 130-acre farm lies between the Berkshire and Taconic Mountains, with open fields, flower beds, forests, and an organic vegetable garden comprising the landscape. A bucolic charm permeates Pumpkin Hollow, where the Taconic Stream meanders through the property and over a rocky waterfall, making its way down a tree-lined gorge.

For more than 25 years, the center has offered workshops addressing spiritual and personal growth, such as Conscious Dreaming and Healing Cumulative Grief. Several workshops throughout the year teach both beginners and advanced therapeutic touch, the modern method of healing that draws on ancient practices. Workshops are open to health professionals and a general, interested public. A typical workshop includes lecture, small-group discussions, audiovisual aids, and hands-on experience. Dora Kunz, author of *The Personal Aura, Chakras and the Human Energy Fields,* leads several workshops on healing and therapeutic touch. Together, Kunz and Dolores Krieger, Professor Emerita of the State University of New York, developed therapeutic touch specifically for health professionals. Both women host a yearly Invitational Healers Workshop for those in health-related professions to further understand the principles of healing.

Workshop prices are reasonable, as is lodging and food. In addition to scheduled programs, the farm is open year-round for personal retreats. Pumpkin Hollow fosters a community atmosphere. Sunrise ceremonies, group meditation, storytelling, singing, swimming, and campfires are all a part of daily life. Guests are also invited to share in the daily chores of kitchen work and gardening and see that their rooms are picked up. A healer's sanctuary is open to those on personal retreat for quiet reflection and meditation.

Hours and Days of Operation: 2- to 5-day seminars offered year-round. Midweek personal retreats by reservation.
Accommodations: Dormitory-style rooms, cabins, campsites, limited number of single rooms.
Rates: Room and board $50–$100; program fees vary, though generally $25–$75. Contributions beyond the cost of program fees are tax deductible.
Credit Cards: None accepted.
Meal Plans: 3 vegetarian meals a day, fresh fruits and vegetables from the organic garden.
Services: Personal growth and health workshops, campfires, study, singing, dancing, nature walks, meditation, ceremony, meditation, tai chi, therapeutic touch.
Facilities: 130-acre estate with main farmhouse, 2 dozen bungalows, healer's sanctuary, organic garden, fields, forest, farmland.
Staff: Small, permanent staff; residential volunteers and guests; workshop facilitators, such as Dora Kunz and Dolores Krieger.
Special Notes: Continuing education credits available for some workshops.
Nearby Attractions: Taconic Mountains, Copake golf courses, Mount Washington State Park.
Getting There: 3 hours by car north of New York City, off the Taconic Parkway.

Triquetra Journeys
26 Third Street, #1R
Brooklyn, NY 11231
(718) 858-7271; fax (718) 858-7302
E-mail: 76352.3250@compuserve.com   Web site: www.triquetra.netgate.net/~lorna

It's easy enough to find a cab in New York City, but a shaman? Lorna Roberts apprenticed with the shaman/neuropsychologist Dr. Alberto Villoldo in 1983 and the Peruvian shaman/sculptor Agustin Rivas in 1984. In 1988 and again in 1990, Roberts was initiated into the Peruvian shamanic lineage. Her most recent accomplishment is an initiation by shaman/anthropologist Juan Nunez del Prado into the fourth level of the Alto Masayoq lineage of the Andes Mountains in Peru. For six years, Roberts has led people to power spots throughout the United States, Peru, and Bolivia to participate in shamanic workshops. She makes it clear that her programs are cross-cultural journeys and not spiritual tourism. When at home in New York, she conducts cleansing fire ceremonies each month and has a private healing practice.

Triquetra Journeys aims to provide an authentic experience of indigenous ceremony and ritual. Roberts teaches from traditions born of a direct experience with nature rather than from dry doctrine. The traditional shaman is a priest-doctor who uses magic to heal, and healing is a strong undercurrent of all journeys. The Peruvian Amazon journey takes participants to the Amazon rain forest to work with master shaman Agustin Rivas at his healing site. Days are spent bathing in the creek, eating locally grown food; taking clay, magnesium, and herbal baths; and participating in a fire ceremony. Personal cleansing and transformation through traditional Amazon medicines and healing techniques are emphasized throughout the 12-day trip.

In the United States, journeys are offered to remote natural sites, such as the Kansas Flint Hills trip, which takes place on a rocky hilltop above the bluestem and prairie switchgrass of the Great Plains.

Hours and Days of Operation: 1- to 2-week journeys and vision quests offered year-round.
Accommodations: Vary according to location and can range from tents and huts to hotels. When traveling through France, lodging arranged in classic European hotels. Participants of the Amazon journey stay in a jungle shaman's healing compound.
Rates: $750–$3,200.
Credit Cards: None accepted.
Meal Plans: Vary according to program. Vision Quests entail fasting. European trips include lavish gourmet meals.
Services: Shamanic and spiritual workshops and journeys, quests, fasting, healing sessions, therapeutic bodywork, fire ceremonies.
Facilities: Vary according to location. Inquire for details.
Staff: Typically, a shamanic assistant and a translator accompany Lorna Roberts on each journey. Participants of the Amazon journey receive massage from a therapist at a jungle shaman's healing compound.
Special Notes: People with disabilities should inquire about choosing a destination with wheelchair accessibility.
Nearby Attractions: Vary according to location. Inquire for details.
Getting There: Participants meet in Miami and fly to the specified destination.

Vatra Mountain Valley Lodge and Spa

Route 214, Box F
Hunter, NY 12442
(800) 232-2772 or (518) 263-4919; fax (518) 263-4994

Health and weight-loss programs are offered at the 12-year-old Vatra Mountain Valley Lodge and Spa. The lodge is located at the base of Hunter Mountain, just two and a half hours north of New York City. Programs emphasize wellness as a lifelong commitment and activities integrate the elements of mind, body, and spirit.

On arrival, guests meet with the spa director to schedule a program of diet, fitness, and spa treatments. The wellness director then meets with guests to discuss their overall health and well-being and any nutritional or herbal needs. Spa programs include three vegetarian meals a day, with the option of juice fasting; a choice of reflexology, shiatsu, aromatherapy, or hydrotherapy massage; a personalized fitness program; use of all spa facilities; access to walking trails, tennis courts; a year-round heated indoor pool and outdoor pool in season; and a wide range of winter sports. Evening group discussions address topics like herbal wellness, dealing with stress, and how to cook "lite."

An intimate lodge atmosphere pervades at Vatra. Guests dine by candlelight together in the dining room. Juice or Vegetable Happy Hour affords guests a predinner chance to socialize. During the summer, evening group discussions can take place on a deck overlooking the majestic North Range of the Catksill Mountains. In winter, evening programs take place around the lodge fireplace, surrounded by fresh-picked mountain wildflowers and festive decorations.

Personal retreats can last from a weekend to a week or longer. Theme programs include a women's health care week, singles weekend, and retreats for business- and professional women.

Hours and Days of Operation: Weekend, weeklong, and extended retreats available. Lodge operates as a ski resort with a limited spa program in winter.

Accommodations: Private rooms with bath, television, phones. Some rooms have balconies and skylights.

Rates: Vary; 2- to 3-day program $495–$695.

Credit Cards: MC, V.

Meal Plans: 3 vegetarian meals a day.

Services: Individualized diet, fitness and treatment plans, therapeutic massage, facials, salon services, aromatherapy, body wraps and polishes, yoga, meditation, aerobics, hiking, and dance. Winter ski clinic available for various levels of skiers and cross-country lessons.

Facilities: Chalet-style main house, fitness room, sauna, indoor and outdoor pools, tennis, basketball and volleyball courts, walking trails.

Staff: 25 total staff, including 5 massage therapists, 2 aestheticians, nutritionist, 5 workshop facilitators, including herbalist, astrologer, tarot card reader.

Special Notes: Smoking and nonsmoking rooms available. Ramps and ground-floor rooms accessible for people with disabilities.

Nearby Attractions: Woodstock, antique stores, horseback riding, golf.

Getting There: 2½ hours by car north of New York City.

Wainwright House

260 Stuyvesant Avenue
Rye, NY 10580
(914) 967-6080; fax (914) 967-6114
E-mail: registrar@wainwright.org

Built in the manner of a seventeenth-century French chateau, Wainwright sits regally on 5 acres of rolling lawn overlooking Long Island Sound. The center is the oldest nonprofit holistic educational center in America. An impressive list of teachers have facilitated some of the many classes and workshops over the years, including Aldous Huxley, Joseph Campbell, and Rosalyn Bruyere. Wainwright also holds status as a nongovernmental organization of the United Nations and has hosted UN conferences on conflict resolution. The center's meditation room contains an altar made from a 300-year-old giant agma tree found in Africa, a gift from former UN Secretary General Dag Hammarskjold.

Classes and workshops scheduled throughout the year are designed to explore the integration of body, mind, and spirit. Subjects cover diverse ground, from the basics of astrology to shamanic journeys, yoga, spiritual transformation, and global issues. Several workshops offered each quarter specifically address holistic health, like the Letting Like Cure Like workshop held recently. Here, participants learned about the healing potential of homeopathy. The Edgar Cayce Remedies workshop focused on Cayce's readings about diet, meditation, prayer, herbs, and other natural remedies. The three-part Aromatherapy Workshop covered the extraction and chemical constituents of essential oils as well as their pharmacology, psychology, and safe use. Guests ended the workshop by blending their own unique essences. For program participants, meals and lodging are available with advance reservation.

A recent innovation in Wainwright's health and healing programs is the exploration of ways to integrate traditional and alternative methods of health care, with the goal of providing the public enough information to make informed choices. Wainwright is currently in the process of forging a relationship with hospitals and insurance companies that also seek to incorporate these concepts.

Once a year, usually in the fall, a Holistic Health Day is offered. For $10, people can meet with holistic health experts and receive demonstrations of everything from acupressure to yoga. Free lectures and workshops explore the latest discoveries in the mind-body relationship as it pertains to physical health.

Hours and Days of Operation: Office hours: Mon–Fri, 9–5; 2- and 3-day retreats and 1-day programs available. Facility available for group rental.

Accommodations: Dormitory style and single and double rooms.

Rates: Room and board $55–$75 per night. Workshops $15–$200.

Credit Cards: MC, V.

Meal Plans: Buffet-style meals available with advance reservation.

Services: Workshops on personal and spiritual growth, alternative medicine, yoga, reflexology, reiki, and other healing energies.

Facilities: 5-acre estate with large stone mansion on sloping lawns with a meditation room, meeting rooms, library, dining rooms, solarium.

Staff: A broad base of scholars and professionals in various fields, including psychotherapists, writers, herbalists, yoga practitioners.

Special Notes: Smoking not allowed.

Nearby Attractions: Shops, restaurants, museums, and theater in New York City; Playland Beach; amusement park.

Getting There: 40 minutes by car north of New York City. Rye, New York, is a regular stop on Metro North from Grand Central Station.

Pavillon International Retreat and Renewal Center

500 Pavillon Place, P.O. Box 189
Mill Spring, NC 28756
(800) 392-4808 or (704) 625-8210

Pavillon International integrates a healing natural environment with 12-step recovery programs. The center is located on 160 acres of mountain forests, overlooking a waterfall and tranquil mountain lake. Over 20 years of experience have resulted in programs based on the belief that to look into the decision-making process and to examine emotions is a spiritual practice. Ultimately, the goal is to enhance not only mental, physical, and emotional health but spiritual well-being as well.

Liliane and Gilles Desjardis, recognized for their innovative recovery work, facilitate all programs. Both are graduates of the programs, as is Father Leo Booth, Pavillon's spiritual director. Dr. Douglas Ziedonis, a Yale faculty member and director of its Dual Diagnosis Program, is a consultant for Pavillon's treatment effectiveness.

Guests can choose from one-day and weekend seminars, four- and nine-day residential programs, or a 28-day intensive. "Pre-care" is available through phone consultations, educational materials, and written assignments. A G.R.A.D. program is included in the package price, which includes several phone counseling sessions spread out over a period of three months. Unlike other recovery programs that have a revolving-door policy, groups begin and end the 28-day program together. This allows supportive bonds to grow between participants. Meditation, self-exploration, breathwork, and therapeutic bodywork are just some of the methods used to treat addiction, and individual counselors are available 24-hours a day.

Pavillon's Treatment and Renewal Center is staffed with a psychiatrist, physician, and a team of clinic technicians and counselors. In addition to alcohol and chemical dependency, care and counseling are provided for a variety of conditions such as anxiety, stress, eating disorders, and depression.

Hours and Days of Operation: 4- and 9-day and 4-week residential programs; also 1-day and weekend seminars.
Accommodations: Lodging for up to 30 in double-occupancy rooms with private bath.
Rates: 4-week program $8,900; 9-day program $2,900; 4-day program $700.
Credit Cards: MC, V.
Meal Plans: 3 nutritionally balanced meals a day. All diets can be accommodated with advance notice.
Services: Alternative treatment recovery programs for addictions and related affective and family dysfunctions. Program includes group therapy, psychoeducation, individual and family therapy, psychiatric evaluations, medical and nursing care, case management, vocational guidance and counseling, grief work and healing sessions, massage, meditation, breathwork, self-exploration techniques, accountability and empowerment support groups, nature walks.
Facilities: 168-acre estate with main house, exercise room, 10-acre lake, forest trails.
Staff: Psychiatrist, nurse, certified alcohol and drug counselors.
Special Notes: Before their arrival, clients are screened for eligibility. Criteria include symptoms of drug and alcohol dependence, co-dependency, compulsive behavior and dysfunctional family dynamics, complete detoxification, emotional and physical stamina, willingness to work on personal issues, minimum age 18. Smoking allowed but not encouraged. Facilities accessible for people with disabilities.
Nearby Attractions: Chimney Rock, forests and lakes in the Blue Ridge Mountains.
Getting There: 30 miles by car southeast of Asheville.

Spirit Journeys

P.O. Box 3046
Asheville, NC 28802
(800) 490-3684 or (704) 258-8880; fax (704) 281-0334
E-mail: spiritjourneys@worldnet.att.net   Web site: www.spiritjourneys.com

David Frechter founded Spirit Journeys with the intent of providing a communal and non-judgmental environment for gay and bisexual men to spend time together while exploring their brotherhood and self-awareness. Spirit Journeys has also recently begun to offer a limited numbers of trips for lesbians and "nongay" men and women. Three types of events occur through Spirit Journeys: workshops, retreats, and journeys. Workshops take place over a weekend and have specific themes, usually revolving around personal exploration. Retreats usually last five days and serve to rejuvenate participants as they relax in a lighthearted and supportive environment. Journeys can take place as far away as the Peruvian Andes and as close as Big Bend National Park, Texas. They serve to collaborate a profound inner experience with a powerful and mysterious natural setting. Dolphin swims, therapeutic natural pools, ancient oracle sites, and Hopi mesas are just some of the journey options.

Group size can range from a dozen to more than twice that, and a diverse range of backgrounds and ages is represented. Although journeys can involve adventurous physical activities, including snorkeling, hiking, and canoeing, most guests who are in generally good physical shape will be able to participate. For those worried about traveling with a group, daily schedules are balanced to allow for personal time.

Though focused primarily on emotional well-being and spirituality, the adventures also consider healing, including time spent with Incan mystics, shamans, and healers, as in the Pilgrimage to the Mystic Andes Tour; soaking in the hot mineral springs of the Bodhi Mandal Zen Center on the R and R Summer Retreat; exploring the 2,857-foot-deep Waimae Canyon, recognized by many as a place of energy and healing, during the Hawaiian Adventure in Kauai; or simply taking the time to contemplate the red rock mesas of Sedona—a magnetic natural landscape that draws thousands every year—while participating in the Arizona Autumn Quest.

Hours and Days of Operation: Journeys averaging 3–7 days offered year-round.
Accommodations: Vary from journey to journey. Lodging can be either in a bed-and-breakfast, retreat center, lodge, or hotel. Rooms usually double occupancy with private baths; some 3 to a room with shared bath.
Rates: Weekend workshop $350; 2 weeks in Greece $2,995.
Credit Cards: None accepted.
Meal Plans: 3 nutritionally balanced meals a day, with vegetarian options.
Services: Bodywork, breathwork, ceremony, group and inner-process work, yoga, guided hikes, dolphin swims, therapeutic soaks, deep-tissue and Swedish massage (some journeys), energy work, polarity therapy.
Facilities: Depends on location. Inquire for details.
Staff: Journeys usually include David Frechter and at least 2 or 3 guides with backgrounds in group facilitation and social work. Support staff varies according to location and can include a licensed massage therapist, yoga instructor, meditation instructor.
Special Notes: If necessary, air transportation can be arranged by Spirit Journeys.
Nearby Attractions: Depends on location. Inquire for details.
Getting There: Depends on location. Inquire for details.

Beechwold Natural Clinic

4191 North High Street
Columbus, OH 43214
(614) 262-1308

"I was a sick boy," says Dr. Ernest Shearer, founder of America's oldest natural clinic. At a young age he fell victim to the infamous Spanish flu epidemic. His condition worsened until a naturopath helped him to recover. In the 1920s, naturopathic doctors broke ground for today's "alternative" practitioners. The recovery made a strong impression on the young Ernest Shearer. "With $85 and a wife and one child coming," says Shearer, he went on to pursue a medical practice in nearby Kirksville. Shearer blazed a trail for others to follow and has been the inspiration and mentor of many of today's well-known leaders in the alternative health field. He has been before the Supreme Court of Ohio twice to defend his health practices. "I'm a fighter," he says of his fierce determination. "I've always been guided."

For more than half a century, Dr. Shearer, chief of staff at the Beechwold Natural Clinic, has provided a holistic approach to the well-being of mind, body, and spirit. Referred to as "Ohio's Shangri-La," the clinic provides an alternative for people who want to take responsibility for their health. Services emphasize a lifestyle of disease prevention and health maintenance. An initial visit to the clinic may include a consultation with members of the health team to determine the patient's specific needs. Methods of diagnosis include foot reflexology, structural analysis of the spine through osteopathic manipulation, chiropractic or Rolfing, acupuncture point analysis, iris analysis, and more. "We don't guess, and we don't experiment," says Shearer. "We are very spiritual and we have a lot of experience rebuilding people." Overnight and extended-stay programs are recommended on the basis of the results of the initial analysis.

The clinic is widely known for its work with chronic fatigue and other serious health concerns, including cancer. But patients don't have to be sick to visit Beechwold. The clinic emphasizes prevention, and people who want to learn how to maintain good health and increase their vitality would benefit from a visit to the good doctor.

Hours and Days of Operation: Office hours: Mon–Fri, 8–6. Every month the center holds informal workshops for health professionals.
Accommodations: Patients referred to nearby comfortable housing.
Rates: Average $100 per day.
Credit Cards: MC, V.
Meal Plans: A kitchen and health food store are located at the clinic for guests to provide and prepare their own meals.
Services: Homeopathic medicine, chelation therapy, nutritional supplementation and counseling, osteopathic manipulation, acupressure, acupuncture, iridology, colonic therapy, massage, Rolfing, reflexology, biofeedback, relaxation therapy, pastoral counseling, polarity therapy, oxygen bath treatments, transformational and educational kinesiology.
Facilities: Health clinic, kitchen, health food store, German Mora instruments.
Staff: In addition to Dr. Shearer, 2 medical doctors, 3 osteopathic doctors, 3 chiropractic doctors, 2 nurses, 2 acupuncturists, 2 nutritionists, 3 counselors, 6 massage therapists.
Special Notes: Facilities are accessible for people with disabilities. Smoking not allowed.
Nearby Attractions: Park of Roses, zoo, theater, concerts, and museums in Columbus.
Getting There: Centrally located in the Columbus business district.

Kerr House

17777 Beaver Street, P.O. Box 363
Grand Rapids, OH 43522
(419) 832-1733; fax (419) 832-4303

Laurie Hostetler, director of the Kerr House, knows how to do things right. A stay at this Victorian mansion cum holistic rejuvenation center begins with breakfast in bed. Programs are primarily targeted for women, but occasional one-week and weekend programs for couples, co-eds, and men only are offered throughout the year. Only eight guests are taking the program at any one time to allow for a staff-to-guest ratio of about three to one. All programs are meant to leave guests with a renewed sense of life and self.

After the luxury of being awakened with a wicker tray filled with wholesome natural foods, guests attend an exercise class at 8. Exercises take place in the mansion's picturesque loft and are meant to do more than get a body in shape. Better described as mind-body exercises, guests learn relaxation techniques, body appreciation, breathing exercises, and intensive stretches. Afterward, it's an herbal tea break and then off for a morning treatment, which could mean anything from reflexology to an herbal body wrap. Lunch is at noon, followed by quiet time and the option of a counseling session on how to reduce stress. Outdoor activities are encouraged in the afternoon, and guests can choose to walk along the nearby towpath. At 6, guests relax and prepare for dinner, which is served by candlelight in the formal dining room at 7. A whirlpool and sauna might follow, and perhaps listening to the melodies of a harpist plucking strings, before lights go out at 11.

Hours and Days of Operation: Daily, weekend, and weekly sessions. Facility can be reserved for private groups.
Accommodations: A maximum of 8 guests in Victorian-style rooms with high ceilings, lace curtains, antique furniture.

Rates: 1 week $2,150.
Credit Cards: AE, MC, V.
Meal Plans: 3 meals a day with natural ingredients and no additives, dyes, white flour, processed sugar. Breakfast served in bed.
Services: Foot reflexology, body wraps, mud baths, massage, facials, exercise classes.
Recreational Activities: Hiking.
Facilities: Whirlpool, sauna, Nordic track, treadmill, swing.
Staff: Professional cosmetologist, masseurs, applied kinesiologists, yoga instructors. Staff-to-guest ratio 3 to 1.
Special Notes: Programs are primarily for women, though co-ed, couples, and men-only specialized programs available.
Nearby Attractions: Shopping in Grand Rapids, exercise paths along Miami and Erie canals.
Getting There: Grand Rapids is 20 minutes south of Toledo Express Airport and 1 hour from the Detroit Metro Airport. Limousine service can be arranged at no extra cost from the Toledo Airport.

Breitenbush Hot Springs and Retreat

P.O. Box 578
Detroit, OR 97342
(503) 854-3321; fax (503) 854-3819

This Oregon Cascades retreat is as famous for its location as it is for its atmosphere. Guests can soak in a natural hot mineral spring lined with large smooth stones overlooking a valley with a glacial river cutting through it and the forested mountain slopes. Or they can float in one of the four Medicine Wheel tubs in the "sacred circle" and receive a Watsu treatment under a sky full of brilliant stars. This is Breitenbush Hot Springs and wildlife sanctuary, set in one of the last temperate rain forests in the world.

A 70-year-old lodge is the center of activity on this 86-acre holistic health retreat, providing space for guests to read one of the many library books on an oversized couch in the study or to feast on a fresh vegetarian lunch in the dining room. Shared community spaces include the Sanctuary, or sacred temple, where Daily Well Being programs such as meditation and yoga are held. The Forest Shelter is commonly used for workshops and yoga, and floor-to-ceiling glass provides an incredible view of the forest. The Villa is a community kitchen for staff and guests. The Vista Healing Arts Center is where guests come for a variety of therapeutic bodywork and energy healing treatments such as LomiLomi, craniosacral therapy, somato-emotional release, or reiki.

People come to Breitenbush for one- and two-hour workshops, for unscheduled Personal Visits, or for one of the many workshops held throughout the year. The annual Women's Renewal Weekend, limited to 20 women, is intended to relax and renew guests with healing arts and laughter. Women learn techniques to promote relaxation, stress reduction, and spiritual awareness, such as partner massage, group discussion, polarity energy balancing, conscious eating, and expressive movement. Because the center is situated just below the Pacific Crest Trail, backpackers have been known to drop down for a hot mineral bath and a soothing massage.

Hours and Days of Operation: Workshops and retreats generally run 2–5 days.
Accommodations: Cabins with heat and electricity available for 2–4 people; single-occupancy cabins available on limited basis; 20 tents with mattresses and campsites.
Rates: $55–$90 per night for adults. Children's rates range from no fee to $30.
Credit Cards: MC, V.
Meal Plans: 3 organic vegetarian meals a day.
Services: Meditation, relaxation techniques, dance, yoga, music therapy, recovery programs, healing rituals, herb walks, drum circles, journaling.
Recreational Activities: Hiking.
Facilities: Natural hot springs, steam and sauna, sweat lodge, community temple, healing arts center, greenhouse, organic garden, kitchen and dining villa.
Staff: 5 regular staff members specializing in healing arts. Workshop leaders are professionals in their fields.
Special Notes: Bring warm bedding, towels, pillow, flashlight, swimsuit, rain gear and boots, caffeinated beverages if desired, plastic water bottle, slip-on shoes and robe, battery-operated alarm clock, snacks sealed in critter-proof containers. Smoking allowed only in designated areas.
Nearby Attractions: Mount Jefferson Wilderness, Gorge Trail, Lake Detroit recreation area, Pacific Crest Trail, cross-country skiing.
Getting There: 2 hours southeast of Portland.

Namaste Retreat Center

29500 Southwest Grahams Ferry Road
Wilsonville, OR 97070-9516
(800) 893-1000 or (503) 682-5683; fax (503) 682-4275

Situated on 95 peaceful acres of woodlands next to Oregon's beaches, mountains, and desert is the Namaste Retreat Center, one of the Northwest's leading spiritual centers. Cabins, gardens, and a serene pond provide an atmosphere perfect for spiritual renewal through quiet rest. A large cozy living room with oversized fireplace is ideal for small-group discussion or curling up with a book. Though Namaste is not a health center in the sense that it offers the services of naturopathic doctors, counselors, or massage therapists, groups who rent out Namaste's facilities often include health professionals.

Namaste can also be described as a living enrichment center. Each year it hosts a series of programs on personal growth and inner exploration. Visiting speakers like Barbara Marx Hubbard and Joan Borysenko present talks on different aspects of alternative health. Programs encourage the exploration of personal relationships to gain deeper levels of physical, emotional, and spiritual intimacy. Guests also discover ways to energize the body, focus the mind, and unleash creativity.

One can go to Namaste Retreat Center alone and enjoy the natural solitude, or visitors can request a catalog of upcoming events to participate in one or more of their retreats. Because Namaste is central to many of Oregon's natural attractions, scheduling a few extra days before or after the retreat may be a good way to spend a family vacation.

Hours and Days of Operation: Weekend and weeklong workshops offered year-round, as are occasional 10-day experiential conferences.
Accommodations: Private 4-room cabins accommodating up to 158.
Rates: Single room with meals $58.50; double room with meals $49.
Credit Cards: MC, V.

Meal Plans: Freshly prepared home-style meals served buffet style are available à la carte. Special dietary needs can be accommodated with prior notice.
Services: Weekend and weeklong workshops, indoor pool, hot tubs.
Recreational Activities: Volleyball, basketball, badminton, hiking, nature walks.
Facilities: Community living room with oversized fireplace, lap-size indoor swimming pool, 16 meeting and banquet rooms, full-service audiovisual department, washers and dryers, game field, horseshoe pits.
Staff: Vary according to the group renting Namaste facilities.
Special Notes: Round-trip shuttle service available for a fee. Guests are asked to bring a flashlight, umbrella, all-terrain shoes, swimsuit, soap, shampoo.
Nearby Attractions: Mount Hood ski areas, Oregon Museum of Science and Industry, Multnomah Falls, Portland Art Museum, Japanese Gardens, Carson Hot Springs, Pittock Mansion, Washington Park, ocean beaches.
Getting There: 30 miles from Portland International Airport.

Deerfield Manor Spa

650 Resica Falls Road
East Stroudsburg, PA 18301
(800) 852-4494 or (717) 223-0160; fax (717) 223-8270
E-mail: DEERSPA@PTD.NET

Deerfield Manor is a tranquil destination spa tucked away in Pennsylvania's Poconos mountain range. Twelve acres of forest surround an elegant, rambling country house, and every day guests explore the various walking trails throughout them. Selected as one of America's best new spas by *Shape* magazine, Deerfield offers a variety of programs designed to relieve everyday stress, tone the body, and ultimately lead to a lasting healthy lifestyle. Attitude is viewed as the essential starting ingredient of health, and guests are encouraged to set and visualize their goals.

As a destination spa, Deerfield can boast that all programs are geared toward the guests' health and well-being—with no diversions—and to maintain an intimate atmosphere, no more than 33 people at a time participate in programs. All programs are personalized for individual self-improvement. Fitness programs, in particular, take a holistic approach, integrating the elements of exercise, healthy nutrition, and stress management techniques. A typical day might start at 8 with a breakfast of whole-grain cereal and fresh seasonal fruit, followed by tai chi. Ambitious guests might squeeze in a neuromuscular massage and a reiki hands-on healing session before lunch, which might consist of locally grown and deliciously prepared vegetables and perhaps some chicken or fish. Afterward, guests can either board a shuttle to embark for a Poconos Mountain trailhead or attend a fitness class of African dance or aquatic exercise in the heated outdoor pool. After dinner, guests might gather in the lounge for a mind-body-spirit lecture or take part in an informal group discussion. Personal counseling and group discussions are available.

Hours and Days of Operation: Weekend and weekly programs offered year-round.

Accommodations: Double and single rooms with private baths. Rooms have wicker furniture, antique furnishings, air conditioning, cable television, pleasant views.

Rates: Weekends $210–$390; weeklong $699–$1,125.

Credit Cards: MC, V.

Meal Plans: 3 low-cal meals a day with locally grown produce, fresh fruit, optional fish and chicken.

Services: Reiki, reflexology, shiatsu, Swedish and neuromuscular massage, body treatments, salon services, personal counseling, group discussions, customized fitness programs, aerobics, dance, aquatic exercise, body sculpting, circuit training, hiking, step aerobics, tai chi, yoga, mind-body-spirit lectures.

Facilities: Main country house with 3 informal lounges, dining rooms, sauna, spa, fully equipped gym, hot tub.

Staff: 28 total staff, including 2 chefs, 4 massage therapists, 4 exercise instructors, 1 aesthetician, 2 yoga and tai chi instructors. All licensed, trained, certified.

Special Notes: Smoking not allowed indoors. Ramps and lodging available for people with disabilities.

Nearby Attractions: Poconos Mountains, shopping in nearby Stroudsburg, summer theater.

Getting There: 1½ hours by car from New York City, on US 80W. Call for directions.

Himalayan Institute

RR 1, Box 400
Honesdale, PA 18431
(800) 822-4547 or (717) 253-5551; fax (717) 253-9078
E-mail: himalaya@epix.net   Web site: www.himalayainstitute.org

Forested hills, a spring-fed pond, and abundant wildlife surround the Himalayan Institute, the international headquarters for the Himalayan Institute of Yoga Science and Philosophy of the USA. The late Swami Rama founded the institute in 1971 after training in the cave monasteries of the Himalayas. The institute is designed to help people grow physically, mentally, and spiritually through programs that combine ancient Eastern teachings and modern scientific approaches. Workshop subjects range from holistic health to hatha yoga, meditation, psychology, and more.

Programming changes from year to year, but guests can usually count on subjects such as meditation, hatha yoga, psychology, and holistic health. Seminar packages include accommodations and three nutritionally balanced vegetarian meals a day. One recent year's topics included Food for Body, Mind and Soul: An Ayurvedic Perspective; Herbs, Cleansing and Fasting; and Freedom from Stress.

The institute's Center for Health and Healing provides the individualized Ayurvedic Rejuvenation Program. The program is available through a custom-designed weekend or through a ten-day residential program. It is designed to reduce the effects of stress and fatigue and restore good health after an extended chronic illness, surgery, or accident. For those who already maintain general good health, the intended effect is a state of dynamic wellness. Included in the program are holistic medical consultation, yoga therapy, ohashiatsu, biofeedback sessions, restorative Ayurvedic herbs, and cleansing therapies.

Hours and Days of Operation: Weekend and 3- to 5-day seminars offered year-round, as well as personal retreats. 10-day and 4-week residential programs and internships available.
Accommodations: Main 3-story brick building accommodates up to 100 in 1- and 2-bedroom units with sinks. Toilets and showers shared; bed linens and towels provided. A small number of single-occupancy rooms available; limited accommodations for families with children.
Rates: Vary according to lodging and Himalayan Institute membership. 2-night program in double room $200 for members, $260 for nonmembers; includes lodging, meals, seminars. A 2-week advance registration is required.
Credit Cards: MC, V.
Meal Plans: 3 nutritionally balanced vegetarian meals a day, with vegetables from the organic garden. Vegan options available.
Services: Meditation; holistic medical consultations; detoxification programs and cleansing therapies; workshops on yoga, holistic health, and self-development; fasting; homeopathy; Ayurvedic body treatments; restorative Ayurvedic herbs; hatha yoga; biofeedback; cooking classes; relaxation techniques.
Recreational Activities: Ice-skating.
Facilities: 400-acre campus with 3-story main building, vegetable and flower gardens, orchard, exercise equipment, bookstore, gift shop, tennis and basketball courts, hiking trails, spring-fed pond, nearby waterfall.
Staff: 2 medical doctors, Ayurvedic physician, acupuncturist, 2 biofeedback specialists, 3 yoga instructors, massage therapist.
Special Notes: Smoking not allowed indoors. Guests are recommended to bring soap, a bathrobe and slippers, alarm clock, flashlight, and sports equipment for tennis, basketball, and ski resorts. Other suggested items include a yoga mat, umbrella, and warm clothing.
Nearby Attractions: Lake Wallenpaupack, ski resorts.
Getting There: 6 miles north of Honesdale in northeastern Pennsylvania and about 3 hours by car from New York City.

Kirkridge Retreat and Study Center

2495 Fox Gap Road
Bangor, PA 18013-6028
(610) 588-1793; fax (610) 588-8510
Web site: www.kirkridge.com

Though rooted in the Christian faith, a diverse cross-section of cultures and faiths benefit from Kirkridge Retreat and Study Center's enriching, spiritually-based programs. The center is an hour-and-a-half drive from Philadelphia. On its 270 acres, guests enjoy the extraordinary views from Kittatinny ridge, also known as "Endless Hills." Programs are primarily structured around spiritual renewal, and individual retreats at this quiet and secluded center are a perfect opportunity to reduce stress. Guests of Kirkridge have a chance to absorb the healing power of the surrounding natural beauty, including forests, lakes, gentle pasturelands, and a 180-year-old farmhouse at the retreat's center. The motivating philosophy behind programs is to offer a place for profound self-discovery while providing a nurturing and refreshing environment.

Workshops address topics as varied as the exploration of ecological traditions in Judaism and Christianity; the examination of Martin Luther King Jr.'s philosophy of nonviolence; and ways of creating a community of trust for gay, lesbian, bisexual, and transgendered adults. The mind-body connection is emphasized in a recovery weekend for male survivors of abuse. Participants of the program attend by way of recommendation from a therapist, with the goal being to allow men to physically release stored anger.

For those interested in holistic health, opportunities arise, such as the Retreat to Wilderness. Throughout this two-day workshop, facilitators weave movement, yoga, meditation practices, ceremony, breathwork, sound, and poetry readings. The workshop is led by Jane Ely, a holistic health practitioner and shamanic counselor; Anita Bondi, a teacher of sacred dance and a therapeutic bodyworker; and Kate Roche, an instructor of hatha yoga.

Hours and Days of Operation: Office hours: Mon–Fri, 9–4. Weekend and weekday workshops offered year-round.

Accommodations: Double rooms and twin beds in 4 facilities for private retreats, some with fireplaces, kitchens, mountain views. Groups of up to 96 are accommodated in similar, larger facilities.

Rates: Workshops $60–$395. Lodging $42–$70 per night.

Credit Cards: MC, V.

Meal Plans: 3 nutritious, well-balanced meals a day served buffet style with no red meat.

Services: Workshops on personal growth, healing, the arts, social transformation; informal group discussions.

Recreational Activities: Hiking, swimming, bird-watching.

Facilities: Nineteenth-century farmhouse, library, kitchens, bookstore, private and group retreat space in Nelson Lodge, the Apartment, the Undercroft, the Hermitage, the Folly, the Turning Point, the Van der Bent House, walking and hiking trails.

Staff: Kirkridge is maintained by 19 staff members. Workshops led by authors, professors, psychotherapists, religious leaders.

Special Notes: Guests must bring their own flashlight and whatever provisions they may need. Pets and radios not allowed. Child care not available. Facilities can be reserved for private groups.

Nearby Attractions: The Appalachian Trail, Delaware Water Gap National Recreation Area, outlet stores in nearby Tannersville, skiing at Camelback resort.

Getting There: About 1½ hours by car from New York City and Philadelphia.

Ann Wigmore Institute

P.O. Box 429
Rincon, PR 00677
(787) 868-6307; fax (787) 868-2430
E-mail: wigmore@caribe.net   Web site: www.holistic.com/listing/00677awl.html

The late Dr. Ann Wigmore was the founding mother of the Living Foods Lifestyle. As a girl, Wigmore helped her grandmother, a natural healer, attend to the many casualties in her small village during World War I through the use of grasses and herbs. As an adult, Wigmore was diagnosed with cancer and not only applied the techniques she learned from her grandmother but revived and expanded them as well. Without resorting to drugs or surgery, Wigmore sent her cancer into complete remission. After 35 years of research, she drew a correlation between disease and the toxicity and nutritional deficiencies resulting from cooked and processed foods, drugs, and a negative mental attitude. Her theories proved successful, as evidenced by the many testimonials from people suffering from various chronic and degenerative diseases such as arthritis, hypoglycemia, chronic fatigue, and cancerous tumors.

The Puerto Rico institute sits within 50 yards of the tropical west coast. Two white stucco buildings are surrounded by papaya, banana, and coconut trees. Visitors arrive in a village of sleepy cottages and fishermen's homes, and from the second-story verandah of the institute they can hear and see the ocean. Staff emphasize that the center is neither a spa nor a clinic but an educational institution.

The Lifestyle consists of a live organic diet including the famous Energy Soup, made with sprouts, watermelon rind, carrots, buckwheat greens, apples, avocado, and more. Wheat grass is an essential element of the living-foods program, believed to have profound detoxifying effects. In addition to the diet, students go through an internal cleansing process while taking classes in how to grow greens and wheat grass, composting and soil management, indoor gardening, sprouting, food combining, meditation, self-improvement, positive thinking, breathing, stress reduction, visualization, and more. The standard two-week course ends with a graduation ceremony banquet.

Hours and Days of Operation: Office hours: 9–5:30, 7 days a week. 1-week and 19- and 26-day programs available year-round.

Accommodations: Lodging for up to 25 in men's and women's dormitory-style rooms; private and semiprivate rooms with full, half, and shared baths.

Rates: $830–$1,750 per week. Discounted rates apply to the 19- and 26-day programs.

Credit Cards: MC, V.

Meal Plans: 3 vegan, raw, vegetarian meals a day (sprouts, greens, fruits, vegetables, fruit juices, enzyme-rich Rejuvelac, and wheat grass juice).

Services: Nutritional counseling, colonic hydrotherapy, massage, chiropractic.

Recreational Activities: Hiking, swimming.

Facilities: Dining area, upstairs lounge, limited exercise equipment, picnic tables, hammocks, coconut slicing area.

Staff: About 6 teachers, some of whom worked directly with Ann Wigmore; 2 licensed massage therapists; colonic hydrotherapist; support staff.

Special Notes: The institute has a certification program for Living Foods Lifestyle graduates. Cigarettes, alcohol, illicit drugs, and heavy perfumes not allowed. Limited access for people with disabilities.

Nearby Attractions: Atlantic and Caribbean beaches, caves, Phosphorescent Bay, Old San Juan, El Yunque rain forest, whale watching, scuba diving, snorkeling.

Getting There: 2½ hours by car from San Juan Airport. Connecting flights available to Mayaguez Airport and direct flights available to Aguadilla. The center provides transportation to and from Mayaguez and Aguadilla.

La Casa de Vida Natural

P.O. Box 1916
Rio Grande, PR 00745
(888) 3-LA CASA or (787) 887-4259
E-mail: lacasa@lacasaspa.com

Lying in a hammock under a fragrant ylang ylang tree, foraging for edible plants in a tropical forest, or getting buried in therapeutic mud gathered from the peaks of El Yunque mountain are what a typical day holds for visitors to La Casa de Vida Natural. This Puerto Rican paradise is the brainchild of New York–based psychoanalyst Jane Goldberg, who specializes in mind-body health. The natural world permeates the philosophy of La Casa, nearly hidden in the foothills of the Caribbean National Forest. The spa is designed to be a rejuvenation and resource center that guests not only escape to for relaxation but from which they obtain the information and skills necessary to make natural health practices an element of their everyday lives. A naturopathic doctor and certified acupuncturist are among the holistic health practitioners at La Casa.

Each day begins with an early morning walk along a mountain trail. Afterward, guests participate in yogic breathing, practice an ancient Tibetan eye-cleansing ritual, or learn any number of ancient cleansing techniques passed down through the ages. Breakfast follows this daily ritual, and then it's time for a half-hour guided meditation. Excursions usually begin at 9:30, and guests return to the spa for a healthy lunch at 1:30. Afternoons are devoted to therapies and classes. Options include instruction in Ayurvedic self-massage, colonic therapy, or the famous Body Polish described by the *New York Times* as "close to magical realism" and "leaving you feeling otherworldly." Guests stretch, relax, and align muscles in a before-dinner yoga class, and evening activities include candle-gazing meditation, board games, or slipping away to the night life of Old San Juan.

Hours and Days of Operation: Open year-round; 5-day workshops available.

Accommodations: 6 guest rooms accommodate up to 10 guests in a renovated farmhouse and cottage. Single, double, or queen-size beds with private or semiprivate bathrooms.

Rates: 5-day workshops $535–$595; lodging $45–$125 per night.

Credit Cards: MC, V.

Meal Plans: 3 vegetarian meals a day made with fresh unprocessed food, some of which is grown on Casa's own farm. Each day features a different culture, including Puerto Rican, Nepalese, Caribbean, and Indian as well as macrobiotic and raw foods.

Services: Meditation, yoga, natural healing rituals, water aerobics, sand and seaweed rubs, massage and mud therapies, body wraps, facials, colonic therapy, whole-body skin exfoliations and massage.

Recreational Activities: Swimming.

Facilities: 9-acre estate including farm located in the foothills of the rain forest, steam cabinets, outdoor hot tub, trampoline, gardens, river, 2 treatment rooms, cottage, greenhouse, walking trails, meditation shrine.

Staff: 6 staff, including massage therapist, colonic hydrotherapists, New York–trained chefs doing internships.

Special Notes: Smoking not allowed.

Nearby Attractions: El Yunque rain forest, Luquillo Beach, historic Old San Juan, ferry service to Vieques and St. Thomas, nearby hot sulphur springs.

Getting There: Shuttle service available from San Juan Airport.

Carolina Wellness Retreat

P.O. Box 4797
Hilton Head Island, SC 29938
(888) 842-7797; fax (803) 341-3117
E-mail: HJR45650@aol.com

The Carolina Wellness Retreat offers guests three locale choices for its programs on stress, lifestyle, and weight management. The Pine Crest Inn, tucked away in the Blue Ridge Mountains, is situated on 9 acres in historic Tryon, North Carolina. The site includes a 200-year-old cabin, part of the original structure. The Fripp Island retreat site is located next to a wildlife sanctuary. Giant sea turtles nest on the beach of this center, which is so picturesque that several movies have been shot there. The Sea Pines Plantation, adjacent to the 90-foot Harbour Town Lighthouse, lies on 5 miles of sandy beach next to a 605-acre forest preserve. All centers offer the signature programs of Dr. Howard Rankin for weight, stress, and lifestyle management. Rankin, a psychologist and prolific writer, heads a team of psychologists, physicians, dietitians, exercise physiologists, and health educators, all of whom provide services for guests at the Carolina Wellness Retreat.

Programs run an average length of one to two weeks, though longer stays, as well as abbreviated Wellness Weekends, are offered. An emphasis is placed on active participation and life-skills acquisition learned during interactive seminars and group and individual sessions. A typical day starts with an optional water exercise or a walk followed by a balanced, healthy breakfast. At 8:45 guests attend the Skills Practice: Motivational Links group discussion, followed by the session How to Change Your Life and Keep Your Friends. By midmorning, guests choose between walking or step training and can squeeze in an optional group session before lunch. Body conditioning is scheduled for 1:45, leaving guests an afternoon of free time until the Guided Practice: Self Control session at 5:30. After dinner, guests attend the Mindfulness Training seminar before retiring.

Hours and Days of Operation: Office hours: Mon–Fri, 8:30–5. Programs averaging 2 weeks offered year-round.

Accommodations: Single and double rooms with private bath in townhouses and villas near the beach.

Rates: $1,000 a week, including meals, lodging, services.

Credit Cards: MC, V.

Meal Plans: 3 healthy, low-fat meals a day.

Services: Programs for stress, weight, and lifestyle management; step training; body conditioning; Mindfulness Training; interactive seminars; personal counseling; massage; aromatherapy.

Recreational Activities: Horseback riding, water sports.

Facilities: 3 island retreat centers with a spa, fitness center, lighted tennis courts, golf courses, walking and bike trails, beach.

Staff: Each center is staffed with psychologists, nutritionists, physicians, qualified fitness and spa personnel.

Special Notes: Smoking not allowed. Facilities accessible for people with disabilities.

Nearby Attractions: Beach resort community of Hilton Head; dining, museums, and theater of Savannah, Charleston, and Beaufort.

Getting There: Inquire for details. All 3 locations are close to Hilton Head Airport and within an hour's drive of Savannah, Georgia.

Black Hills Health and Education Center

P.O. Box 19
Hermosa, SD 57744
(800) 658-5433 or (605) 255-4101; fax (605) 255-4687
E-mail: bhhec@juno.com

The Black Hills Center, which claims 450 acres of creeks, canyons, and farmland, is located in what is described as the Banana Belt because of its year-round temperate climate. The center draws guests from around the country for its residential wellness programs. The 13- and 20-day programs, designed to help mind, body, and soul, are based on the belief that God has given everyone eight natural remedies: nutrition, exercise, water, sunshine, temperance, air, rest, and trust in divine power.

The center has been particularly successful in controlling heart disease, diabetes, arthritis, hypertension, strokes, depression, addictions, osteoporosis, and obesity. The medically supervised programs begin with a complete physical examination, blood tests, and counseling. Hydrotherapy treatments are included in the program fee, and guests also have access to a Russian steam cabinet, whirlpool, and showers with alternating hot and cold sprays. Outings to a local supermarket and restaurant teach staff how to choose and order healthy foods.

The day starts at 6:15 with an inspirational thought followed by a medical lecture at 6:30. By 7:15 guests are garbed in exercise gear for aerobics, and by 8:15 they sit down for breakfast. At 9:15 a physiology lecture begins, and resistance training is scheduled for 10. A cooking lab is scheduled for noon, and stress class follows at 1:30. An early dinner is served at 2:15, and guests walk through the valley trails. Hydrotherapy or massage treatments are scheduled for 4, and at 7 guests gather to share the day's experiences and watch a health-related video.

Hours and Days of Operation: Office hours: Mon–Fri, 9–5; 13- and 20-day wellness programs offered year-round.
Accommodations: 12 single and double rooms with private bath in 2-story lodge with modern furnishings. Motor home camping facilities available as well.
Rates: 20-day program $2,315–$2,600; 18-day program $1,620–$1,800; 5-day tune-up $500.
Credit Cards: D, MC, V.
Meal Plans: 2 buffet-style vegan meals a day, with an optional third.
Services: Massage, hydrotherapy, medical consultations, health lectures, hot and cold fomentations, exercise rehabilitation, group discussions, excursions to a natural indoor pool fed by a hot mineral spring.
Facilities: Guest rooms, cooking lab, lecture room, cafeteria, exercise equipment, Russian steam cabinet, whirlpool, hot and cold shower with 6 sprays.
Staff: 2 medical doctors, 3 registered nurses, licensed massage therapist, certified personal trainer, fitness therapist.
Special Notes: Smoking not allowed indoors. Specially equipped rooms designed for people with disabilities.
Nearby Attractions: Mount Rushmore, Crazy Horse Memorial, Badlands National Park, Reptile Gardens, Evans Plunge hot springs, Wind Cave National Park, Custer State Park, many Old West towns such as Deadwood, where Wild Bill Hickok was shot.
Getting There: Round-trip shuttle available from Rapid City.

Alamo Plaza Spa at the Menger Hotel

204 Alamo Plaza
San Antonio, TX 78205
(210) 223-5772; fax (210) 228-0022
E-mail: alamospa@swbell.net

One cannot visit the Alamo Plaza Spa without experiencing a kur treatment—a program encompassing relaxing spa treatments and a series of rejuvenating all-natural body therapies. Kneipp herbal baths, an essential element of the kur treatment, were developed by Bavarian priest Father Sebastian Kneipp almost a century ago. Kneipp combined his knowledge of herbs and water therapy to develop the practice of warm bathing with aromatic natural herbs. It was Kneipp's belief that through a combination of healthy eating, exercise, sunlight, and adequate rest, the effects of a detrimental lifestyle can be reversed. Dr. Jonathan Paul de Vierville, director of the Alamo Plaza Spa, studied at the Kneipp center in Bad Worishofen and consequently adapted this popular European tradition for this luxury spa.

De Vierville, author of *American Healing Waters*, believes that spas should serve the whole person. "Traditional and classic spa treatments in places like Bath, Karlsbad, Baden-Baden, and Vichy are profoundly relaxing while regenerating and enriching one's physical, mental, emotional and social energies," he says. "I see the programs at Alamo Plaza Spa as a significant resource for anyone desiring time and space for renewal, restoration, and total regeneration."

The San Antonio Kur Spa Program is the ideal way to experience de Vierville's philosophy. It combines spa services with healthful treatments and cultural activities. Guests also have access to a heated outdoor pool filled with spring water, a tropical shaded patio, solarium, heated whirlpool, and exercise and fitness rooms. The day concludes with a visit to San Antonio's historical sites, art museums, cultural activities, and seasonal festivals.

Hours and Days of Operation: 1- to 7-day custom program offered year-round.

Accommodations: Standard and deluxe rooms with twin or king-size beds in the 320-room Menger Hotel, including the historic nineteenth-century wing.

Rates: Vary according to program. San Antonio Kur Spa Day, including 2 hours of relaxation treatments, lunch, aromatherapy facial, herbal bath, segmental massage, and use of all spa facilities, $215.

Credit Cards: AE, D, MC, V.

Meal Plans: Breakfast, lunch, and dinner included in spa program. Meals a combination of vegetables, fresh fruit, high-protein and whole-grain foods.

Services: Massage, kur program using Kneipp herbal essences, body scrubs, herbal wraps with Egyptian linens, hand and foot reflexology treatments, facials, stress reduction treatments, movement therapy, lifestyle and nutritional counseling, mind-body programs, dream and journal-writing workshops.

Recreational Activities: Golf, self-guided walking and jogging.

Facilities: Finnish sauna, steam room, aquifer-filled swimming pool, heated whirlpool, tropical palm-shaded patio and solarium, exercise and fitness room, ballroom and conference facilities, gardens.

Staff: 20, including 10 massage therapists, aesthetician, personal trainer. All licensed and certified in their respective fields.

Special Notes: Smoking not allowed in spa. Spa and hotel facilities accessible for people with disabilities.

Nearby Attractions: San Antonio's Riverwalk, Institute of Texan Cultures, HemisFair Water Park, Tower of the Americas, Alamodome, Mexican Cultural Institute, Guadalupe Cultural Arts Center, river barge cruises, performing arts centers, museums, and galleries.

Getting There: 20 minutes by car from San Antonio Airport.

Cooper Wellness Program

12230 Preston Road
Dallas, TX 75230
(800) 444-5192 or (972) 386-4777; fax (972) 386-0039

Dr. Kenneth Cooper, whose 13 books have sold more than 30 million copies in 41 languages, is founder and director of the Cooper Aerobics Center. A 63-room colonial-style hotel houses guests at this 30-acre health retreat in Dallas, Texas. Programs are tailored to the unique needs and goals of each guest.

The Cooper Wellness Program is a facet of the center, developed for anyone committed to rejuvenation, fitness, and good health. The program specializes in stress management, nutrition, preventive medicine, and overall well-being. Each day, guests learn strategies intended to guide them toward lasting good health, based on Dr. Cooper's philosophy that, "It is easier to maintain good health through proper exercise, diet, and emotional balance than it is to regain it once it is lost." Options include the four-day Wellness Retreat or one to two weeks of the Wellness Program.

The weeklong program starts with a physical fitness assessment followed by a workshop. Workshop topics vary daily and range from successful lifestyle changes to maximizing natural immunity. Two personal fitness training sessions are included in the program, as are presentations by Dr. Cooper or Dr. Tedd Mitchell, the center's medical director. Also included are three nutritious gourmet meals, plus snacks and dining opportunities at nearby heart-healthy restaurants. Guests attend lectures in goal setting and motivation, take cooking classes, learn relaxation techniques, and receive a wellness workbook and a Cooper T-shirt.

Special one-day-only programs are offered with short courses on specific health behaviors that provide an encapsulated version of the longer wellness weeks.

Hours and Days of Operation: Office hours: Mon–Fri, 8–5; 4-day to 2-week programs offered year-round.

Accommodations: Standard single and double rooms with king or twin beds in full-service guest lodge; 1- and 2-bedroom suites available with private bath and king-size beds.

Rates: Vary according to room and program. 1-day workshop $350; 4-day program $2,095; 2-week program $3,595. Lodging not included in package price. Rooms $110–$260.

Credit Cards: AE, D, MC, V.

Meal Plans: 3 calorie-controlled gourmet meals a day, plus snacks.

Services: Wellness workshops and health lectures on subjects like health, wellness, and total well-being; relaxation techniques; motivation and goal setting and healthy dining; cooking classes; comprehensive medical examination; hearing and vision tests; relaxation and stress management techniques; nutrition assessment; strength training; swimming; water exercise; strength training; yoga; tai chi; boxing; massage.

Facilities: 30-acre estate including fitness center with weight-training equipment, sauna, steam room, 2 heated outdoor pools, whirlpool, lap pools, 4 lighted tennis courts, racquetball court, padded indoor and outdoor jogging tracks, walking trails, duck pond.

Staff: Registered dietitians, medical doctors, exercise physiologists, health psychologists. Workshops led by medical professionals from the Cooper Clinic and the Cooper Institute for Aerobic's Research as well as other health care professionals.

Special Notes: Smoking not allowed indoors. Ramps and elevators provide access to all areas for people with disabilities.

Nearby Attractions: White Rock Lake, Dallas Museum of Art, Kennedy Memorial, Fort Worth Science Center, Dallas Arboretum and Botanical Garden.

Getting There: 20 minutes by car from Dallas.

Dallas Center for Chronic Disorders

5600 North Central at Mockingbird Lane, 4th Floor
Dallas, TX 75206
(214) 824-0027; fax (214) 826-7825
Web site: www.vedic-health.com

The Physicians' Association for Eradicating Chronic Disease was founded in May 1997 with the participation of medical doctors throughout the United States. The association was created to promote a more comprehensive system of health care to prevent illness through treating the root cause of disease and promoting a healthy lifestyle. The Dallas Center for Chronic Disorders, one of four similar centers currently open in the United States, is part of the association's Campaign to Create a Disease-Free Society. Future plans include the opening of 435 similar centers, with in-residence facilities near 40 of the largest metropolitan areas.

The centers offer integrative health programs that incorporate natural approaches for the prevention and treatment of chronic disorders. Drawing on Vedic and Ayurvedic principles, specialized programs are developed for individuals with virtually any type or chronic condition, from listlessness to Parkinson's disease. Because the centers also function as complementary care, patients are never asked to discontinue seeing a family physician or specialist.

Consultations and rejuvenation treatments are also provided for those who are fortunate not to be suffering from chronic ailments but would like to feel more physically and mentally alive. During consultations, doctors assess the individual's current state of physiological balance and design an at-home program that includes recommendations for diet, exercise, herbal supplements, stress management techniques, and daily and seasonal health routines. The five- to seven-day Rejuvenation Program is tailored to each person's unique needs and involves traditional methods of eliminating impurities from the body due to bad diet, stress, and other factors.

For more serious health concerns, the Chronic Disorder Program, which begins with a thorough medical examination, is recommended. After a highly personalized health regimen is established, patients receive daily treatments and undergo an extensive health education. Habits for maintaining and promoting total well-being are developed alongside a system of continuing self-care.

Hours and Days of Operation: Office hours: Mon–Fri, 10–5. Individualized programs varying in length offered year-round.
Accommodations: Comfortable hotel accommodations are provided with all residential programs.
Rates: Initial consultations $275; Rejuvenation Program $365–$515 per day; Chronic Disorders Program $1,200 per day.
Credit Cards: MC, V (all programs except Chronic Disorders).
Meal Plans: Nutritionally balanced meals included in residence program designed to support the prescribed regimen of therapy.
Services: Thorough physical examination, techniques for managing health from its foundation, pulse diagnosis, purification therapies and herbalized oil applications, special herbal food supplements, diet and exercise programs, instruction in health-promoting behavior, methods for enhancing collective health throughout the world.
Facilities: Treatment rooms, small kitchen, dining rooms, and residential guest rooms.
Staff: Medical doctors, doctors of osteopathy, nurses, technicians. All are trained in natural medicine.
Special Notes: Smoking not allowed in the center.
Nearby Attractions: Southern Methodist University, museums, restaurants, world-class shopping in downtown Dallas.
Getting There: 30 minutes by car from the Dallas/Fort Worth Airport.

Eupsychia, Inc.

P.O. Box 3090
Austin, TX 78764-3090
(800) 546-2795 or (512) 327-2795; fax (512) 327-6043
E-mail: Eupsychia1@aol.com   Web site: www.jacquelynsmall.com

In 1975, Jacquelyn Small founded the Eupsychia Institute with the intention of providing training and healing programs throughout the country to people seeking knowledge and the experience of personal transformation. Eupsychia is Greek for "good psyche" or "well-being." The word summarizes the philosophy of healing behind Eupsychia's schedule of events. Small, a former faculty member of the Institute of Transpersonal Psychology in Palo Alto, California, is the author of six books on healing, including *Becoming Naturally Therapeutic.*

The Healing Into Wholeness Program is a ten-day psychospiritual retreat. Stress, depression, repressed trauma, and other issues are addressed during the programs. Retreat locations vary, but a residential healing community is always chosen as the site for an evolution toward well-being. The Blue Ridge Mountains provide a backdrop for 1998's programs, which take place in Dahlonega, Georgia. Techniques combine mainstream psychology, emerging spiritual trends, and a 12-step recovery program. Throughout the retreat, guests experience integrative breathwork, guided imagery, mask making, expressive artwork, psychospiritual small-group work, journaling, silent time, and philosophical chalk talks on how to use transformative thought to everyday advantage. Optional activities include bodywork, nutritional counseling, sacred ceremony, daily yoga classes, 12-step meetings, or simply walking through the grounds of a restorative natural setting.

Other programs include workshops and seminars, such as the two-day Birthing a New Consciousness! workshop on breathwork. All workshops are open to both health professionals and an interested, general public. Because schedules can change from month to month, it's best to contact Eupsychia before purchasing a plane ticket.

Hours and Days of Operation: 2-day workshops and 6- to 10-day intensives usually offered in spring, summer, and fall.

Accommodations: Single and double spacious lodge rooms with heat, air conditioning, private bath.

Rates: Vary according to program. 10-day Healing Into Wholeness Program $2,995, and includes lodging and meals.

Credit Cards: MC, V.

Meal Plans: 3 nutritious meals a day, served buffet style. Meals primarily vegetarian though meat served on occasion.

Services: Therapeutic bodywork, psychospiritual small-group work, integrative breathwork, group discussions, art therapy, guided imagery, mask making, movement and music therapy, journaling, yoga, meditation, nutritional counseling, 12-step meetings, nature walks.

Facilities: 45-acre retreat center with 10 lodges, including large meeting rooms and an octagonal chapel, 2 hot tubs, fire circle, laundry facilities.

Staff: In addition to Jacquelyn Small, the center has a licensed massage therapist and a craniosacral therapist, 1 registered nurse, 2 additional therapists.

Special Notes: Some facilities accessible for people with disabilities.

Nearby Attractions: Sacred Native American sites; North Georgia Mountains; dining, theater, shopping, museums in Atlanta.

Getting There: About 80 miles by car north of Atlanta. Shuttle service available to and from Atlanta's Hartsfield Airport.

Lake Austin Spa Resort

1705 South Quinlan Park Road
Austin, TX 78732
(800) 847-5637 or (512) 372-7300; fax (512) 372-7370
E-mail: reserve@lakeaustin.com   Web site: www.lakeaustin.com

About 20 miles from Austin lies the Lake Austin Spa Resort. This resort would be more aptly named the Colorado River Spa Resort, as it is this actual body of water that collects in the gentle bends of Texas hill country to form a popular site for water-skiing, sculling, and canoeing. It is no coincidence that the spa offers the Healing Waters body treatments, open to both in-residence spa-goers and day visitors. The treatments are intended to reduce stress, increase inner strength, and revitalize the mind, body, and spirit. All treatments are based on ancient healing techniques, such as Ayurveda and thalassotherapy.

Packages at Lake Austin are also designed to rejuvenate the whole person and include lodging, meals, and snacks; unlimited fitness and discovery programs; round-trip transportation to the airport; spa treatments; and personal consultations and/or training sessions. Guests have the option to do as much or as little as they like, such as climbing aboard a 15-person Northern Explorer canoe to glide over the waters of Lake Austin, which turn a stunning green and gold in the afternoon. The Water Relaxation treatment is a unique option consisting of a therapist gently guiding the body through warm water.

In addition to the spa's regular programming, the Gathering of Wise Women program is offered in the fall. The program pools the resources of a panel of experts to examine women's health issues. Surgeons, dermatologists, oncologists, nurses, psychologists, dietitians, and noted speakers gather for one week in October to share knowledge and explore new ground.

The spa has recently compiled a collection of its best recipes into the cookbook *Lean Star Cuisine,* available at Lake Austin.

Hours and Days of Operation: 3-, 4-, and 7-night packages, day packages offered year-round.

Accommodations: 40 rooms facing the lake in bed-and-breakfast-style connecting cottages with comfortable furnishings, down comforters, private bath.

Rates: Nightly room rates from $345. A $500 nonrefundable prepayment required at time of booking and applied toward the last 2 nights. Minimum stay may apply for peak periods.

Credit Cards: AE, D, DC, MC, V.

Meal Plans: 3 low-fat gourmet spa meals a day.

Services: Personal growth and stress-reduction programs, holistic health workshops, nutritional counseling, massage, hydrotherapy, aromatherapy, reflexology, body polishes and wraps, tai chi, meditation, yoga, cooking classes, toning and stretching, circuit training.

Recreational Activities: Hiking, tennis, gardening, water biking, canoeing, lake cruises, nature walks, mountain biking, kayaking, sculling.

Facilities: Indoor and outdoor pools, lakeside exercise equipment, 24-hour gym, activity center, guest dining room, tennis courts, sauna, steam room, hydrobikes, small boats, walking trails, organic gardens.

Staff: 30 massage therapists, 5 aestheticians, 2 nail technicians, acupuncturist, Rolfing specialist.

Special Notes: Smoking allowed only in outdoor nonpublic areas. Minimum age of spa guest is 14.

Nearby Attractions: Steiner Cattle Ranch, Lady Bird Johnson Wildflower Research Center, L. B. Johnson Library and Museum, winery tours.

Getting There: Courtesy transportation provided to and from airport.

Optimum Health Institute of Austin

Route 1, Box 339J
Cedar Creek, TX 78612
(800) 993-4325 or (512) 303-4817; fax (512) 343-0106
E-mail: optimum@optimum.org   Web site: www.optimumhealth.org

Like its California counterpart, the Optimum Health Institute of Austin offers a diet of live raw foods, exercise, whirlpools, and the opportunity to receive colonics, massage, and chiropractic. The institute, which officially opened in March 1996, is a mission of the Free Sacred Trinity Church and provides guests with the opportunity to live the institute's philosophy that "the human body is self-regenerating and self cleansing and if given the proper tools with which to work, it can maintain its natural state of health."

The three-week program is structured to address the mental, physical, and emotional aspects of each person, with the ultimate goal of having each guest learn about the body and mind and how the two work together. In the first week, some of the activities are daily exercise and attending classes that teach proper food combinations, how to build self-esteem, how to mentally and emotionally detoxify, and relaxation techniques to help control pain. Daily exercise continues in the second week, but guests now learn how to grow sprouts, plant wheat grass, organically garden, prepare healthy foods, and plan menus. Communication skills and at-home personal follow-up are also addressed. The third week has guests putting their newfound knowledge to work with hands-on food preparation classes. Guests also take classes on the mind-body connection and diet maintenance.

Since its founding in 1976, more than 50,000 have benefited from the institute's program. Testimonials of lowered blood pressure and blood sugar levels returning to normal are just some of the many former guests have shared. Staff are passionate, knowledgeable, and experienced in the holistic health field.

Hours and Days of Operation: Open year-round. Average stay 3 weeks; 1- and 2-week programs available. Registration office hours: Mon–Fri, 9–5.

Accommodations: Single and double rooms with private bath in new 20,000-square-foot 2-story Southwestern-style lodge built around a grand atrium.

Rates: $500–$700 per week.

Credit Cards: MC, V (the salon does not take credit cards).

Meal Plans: 3 vegan, raw, vegetarian meals a day (sprouts, greens, fruits, vegetables, fruit juices, enzyme-rich Rejuvelac, wheat grass juice).

Services: Colonic hydrotherapy, massage, chiropractic, detoxification.

Facilities: 14 wooded acres with main lodge containing community living room, outdoor pool, hot tub, exercise room, salon, walking trails through cedar and oak trees.

Staff: About 15, all experienced graduates of the Optimum Health Program; professional counselors available at no additional cost.

Special Notes: Buildings as environmentally clean as possible. Smoking not allowed.

Nearby Attractions: L. B. Johnson Library, golf, shopping in downtown Austin, 3 18-hole golf courses.

Getting There: 20 minutes by car from Austin's new airport. The institute has an agreement with Star Shuttle for a reduced rate.

The Last Resort Retreat Center

P.O. Box 707
Cedar City, UT 84721
(435) 682-2289

The Last Resort is, well, at the end of the road. A dirt road winds 30 miles up a mountain from Cedar City to the home of Abhilasha and Pujari, dubbed The Last Resort. The retreat center is the culmination of Abhilasha and Pujari's efforts to create a place where people can come to heal, to reflect on different aspects of their lives, and to revitalize themselves. In an intimate log home, guests participate in daily yoga and meditation, group and individual discussion, or guided hikes to nearby hot springs. Abhilasha, a nutrition teacher and gourmet cook, studied nutrition with the renowned health and nutrition expert Dr. Bernard Jensen. Pujari, also a student of Dr. Jensen, is a rebirther, counselor, and therapist. He has conducted therapy groups in India and throughout the United States since 1974.

Five different types of workshops and retreats are scheduled throughout the year: the Vipassana Meditation Retreat, the Yoga Retreat, a relationship workshop, the yearly Spring Cleaning Retreat, and a natural foods cooking workshop, which is designed to help guests develop good eating habits and eliminate cravings while learning to prepare natural, whole foods. Participants learn how to create tasty well-balanced meals using a variety of whole grains, fresh vegetables, beans, and other natural ingredients. Two-and-a-half–hour classes are held twice a day and cover topics like nutritious food combining, how to cook with tofu and tempeh, and how to cook a healthy meal in less time with proper planning. A morning meditation and yoga class is also part of the daily regimen. The Spring Cleaning Retreat is held in June and includes three to four days of juice fasting, colonics, light yoga, and silent meditation every morning and evening. One morning is spent trekking down to the Pah Tempe Hot Springs for a luxurious mineral water soak. Guests also watch videos by well-known experts on health and nutrition.

Pujari also offers phone counseling, with appointment times scheduled between retreats.

Hours and Days of Operation: 4- to 30-day workshops and retreats offered year-round.
Accommodations: Up to 10 in log home with private and dormitory-style rooms.
Rates: Vary according to program. Vipassana Meditation Retreat $425 for 5 days; $650 for 10 days; $1,650 for 30 days; Yoga Retreat $750 for 7 days.
Credit Cards: None accepted.
Meal Plans: 2 balanced vegetarian meals a day, plus snacks.
Services: Vipassana meditation, yoga, natural foods cooking classes, relationship workshops, nutrition and health education, phone counseling, hiking, mineral baths.
Facilities: A large log home on a ridge overlooking Sunset Cliff, dry sauna, hiking trails.
Staff: Abhilasha, nutrition teacher, gourmet vegetarian cook, and student of Dr. Bernard Jensen, a recognized authority in the fields of nutrition and natural foods cooking; Pujari, meditation and yoga teacher, certified rebirther, counselor, therapist, and founder and former director of the Yoga Institute in San Diego.
Special Notes: Smoking not allowed.
Nearby Attractions: Pah Tempe Hot Springs; central to the major national parks of Utah, such as Bryce Canyon, Dixie, Zion.
Getting There: 30 miles by car from Cedar City on Highway 14.

The Equinox

Historic Route 7A
Manchester Village, VT 05254
(800) 362-4747 or (802) 362-4700; fax (802) 362-1595

To ensure that a critical element of Vermont's heritage remains development free, the owners of the historic Equinox hotel established a preservation trust to protect 900 acres of Equinox Mountain, the 3,800-foot peak rising behind historic Manchester Village. The trust serves the purpose of bringing the local community, as well as resort guests, closer to the natural environment. The 2,300-acre New England resort began as the stoic, two-story wooden Marsh Tavern in 1769. Today, it is devoted to the type of luxury reminiscent of an old Bogart movie, with an amenity spa offering the European ideal of culture, nature, and rejuvenation. Guests have many reasons to visit Equinox, including the award-winning Gleneagles Golf Course designed by the legendary Walter Travis, the first falconry school in America, and the first year-round land rover driving school.

The spa offers treatments primarily designed to relax and revitalize. The Spa Rejuvenation Package is a good prescription for anyone who is stressed, overworked, or fatigued. The package includes accommodations, with the option of upgrading to the nineteenth-century Orviss Inn; three nutritious gourmet meals a day; daily steam and sauna; daily nature walks; informal group discussions on exercise, nutrition, and stress management; and a sampling of spa treatments. Treatments range from an exfoliation with a massage, an herbal wrap with a massage, aromatherapy, reiki, reflexology, and an algae body mask. Fly-fishing, snowshoeing and skiing—both downhill and cross-country—are also outdoor options during the program. Skiers will be happy to know the spa has one of the first physiotherapy centers in New England.

Hours and Days of Operation: 2- to 5-day packages offered year-round.

Accommodations: 183 guest rooms and suites with antique furnishings and Audubon prints. Some rooms have fireplaces, kitchens, porches, mountain views. The historic Charles Orvis Inn offers 9 deluxe 1- and 2-bedroom suites with marble baths, cherry-paneled kitchens, living and dining areas.
Rates: Vary according to room, season, and package. The 4-day Spa Rejuvenation Package $939–$1,217 in May.
Credit Cards: AE, D, MC, V.
Meal Plans: 3 low-fat, nutritionally balanced meals a day with spa package. Vegetarian and special diets can be accommodated with advance notice.
Services: Body composition analysis, physical therapy assessment, informal discussion on stress management and nutrition, massage, reflexology, reiki, herbal wraps, exfoliation treatments, aromatherapy.
Recreational Activities: Falconry training, canoeing, mountain biking, hiking, nature walks, horseback riding and carriage rides, nearby fly-fishing.
Facilities: Physiotherapy center, Turkish steam bath, Swedish sauna, whirlpools, exercise equipment, indoor and outdoor heated pools, boardroom, billiard room, 4-diamond Colonnade restaurant, Gleneagles Golf Course, cross-country ski center, 3 tennis courts.
Staff: Up to 350 staff in prime season with spa staff of 8–10 employees, including bodyworkers and hair and skin technicians.
Special Notes: Smoking allowed only in designated areas.
Nearby Attractions: Historic homes, antique shops, art galleries, theater in Manchester Village; Stratton Mountain ski resort; Norman Rockwell Museum; Marlboro Music Festival; Brattleboro Museum; Bennington crafts center.
Getting There: 4 hours by car from New York City.

Four Seasons Healing

961 New Boston Road
Norwich, VT 05055
(802) 649-5104
E-mail: Four.Seasons.Counseling@Valley.Net

Soul Awakenings, the signature program at Four Seasons Healing, is beneficial for people suffering from chronic pain and stored emotional trauma—in addition to instilling a renewed sense of well-being and energy in burned-out 9-to-5ers. Dr. Israel Helfand, a New York state wilderness guide, and wife, Cathie Helfand, facilitate the program and together have more than 35 years of experience as marriage counselors and family educators. The Helfands have recently been extended a grant from the Department of Psychiatry at the Cambridge Hospital of Harvard Medical School to develop this program as a syllabus for graduate study in ecopsychology. The course will take students out to a secluded homestead for a residential camping experience, much like the one offered to the general public.

Workshops begin at the Cabot, Vermont, homestead, built in 1850. Guests rediscover their relationship with nature and invent personal ceremonies. The group then branches out, so to speak, to the woods to set up camp, cook, wash, gather firewood and water, gaze at stars, and continue the transition from workaday life to a mindful existence in communion with nature. All this is meant to prepare guests for one to four days of fasting and solo quests, after which the community rejoins for shared stories and acclimatizing for the return home.

Essentially, the retreat offers a time of solitude and "moving slowly," as well as team-building experiences and a sense of community. The philosophy behind the nature-oriented activities is that spending time in nature can help people find deeper meaning, enable them to face important transitions, and facilitate spiritual growth.

Hours and Days of Operation: 8-day Awakenings program and weekend retreats offered year-round.

Accommodations: First few nights of the Awakenings program are spent in a sleeping bag in the Vermont homestead; the remaining time is spent camping.

Rates: 8-day Awakening program, including breakfast and dinner, $825. Private programs run about $100 per day. Barter and trade can be arranged.

Credit Cards: None accepted.

Meal Plans: 2 healthy meals a day. Special dietary needs can be accommodated with advance notice.

Services: Ceremony, group discussion, fasting, solo quests, past-life regression, guided imagery, ritual, psychodrama, art therapy, journaling, camping, backpacking.

Facilities: 40-acre estate with rustic homestead, campfire circle, gardens, creekside swimming hole, hiking trails.

Staff: Dr. Israel Helfand, Cathie Helfand, Eve Greenberg.

Special Notes: Smoking not allowed. Guests must provide their own camping and backpacking gear.

Nearby Attractions: Groton State Forest adjacent to Cabot homestead. Norwich office close to Dartmouth.

Getting There: 1 hour by car east of Burlington; 3 hours by car northwest of Boston.

Jimmy LeSage's New Life Fitness Vacations at the Inn of the Six Mountains

P.O. Box 395
Killington, VT 05751
(802) 422-4302

Though it sounds like a workout, the benefits of a New Life Fitness Vacation go deeper than skin, muscle, and bones. Guests return from a rigorous five days of hiking, exercise, meditation, and massage feeling revitalized and optimistic. For 20 years, Jimmy LeSage, the former chef-turned-fitness guru, has offered his down-to-earth wellness vacations to an intimate group of no more than 25. Guests breathe the fresh Vermont air and venture out over mountain streams, working farms, and sections of the Appalachian and Long Trails. Hiking options accommodate all fitness levels, so beginners need not worry about being force-marched up the second-highest peak in Vermont. The advanced level has participants trekking across Pico Peak to take a spirited ride down an Alpine slide.

A typical day begins with a morning stretch and half-hour walk at 7:30. Breakfast is served at 8, followed by a stretch before the five- to seven-mile hike over various types of terrain. Each day, hikers progressively take on more challenging trails. At noon, a 20-minute post-hike stretch counteracts muscle contractions due to exertion and allows muscles to lengthen, relax, and regain oxygen. A lunch of chicken curry salad or perhaps a sandwich with spicy tofu filling is served, and guests have a few minutes to rest before the 2 p.m. water workout. Both swimmers and nonswimmers will benefit from the toning and conditioning the aquacise provides. At 3:15, an aerobic movement class is scheduled, followed by body conditioning at 4 intended to target specific muscle groups. Yoga, breathing, guided imagery, visualization, and postural alignment methods are taught during the 5 p.m. relaxation class. The methods are meant to allow the body and mind to rest while creating greater self-awareness. Dinner is scheduled for 6:30, followed by an evening health lecture.

Guests can wind up the evening with a full-body massage before crashing into a soft pillow in preparation for the next day's hike.

Hours and Days of Operation: Programs averaging 5 days offered May–Oct.
Accommodations: 100 single and double rooms with private bath.
Rates: Vary according to lodging and package. 6-day Classic New Life Program $899–$999.
Credit Cards: MC. V.
Meal Plans: 3 low-fat meals a day consisting of food high in complex carbohydrates. Special dietary needs can be accommodated with advance notice.
Services: Stress-reduction and fitness programs, therapeutic and relaxing massage, Sivananda-style yoga, tai chi, aerobics, aquacise, body-toning, facials.
Recreational Activities: Hiking, swimming, biking, golf, horseback riding.
Facilities: The Inn at Six Mountains resort complex complete with exercise equipment, indoor lap pool, steam room, sauna, heated outdoor pool, tennis and racquetball courts, mountain bikes, hiking trails.
Staff: In addition to resort employees, including licensed bodyworkers and aestheticians, Jimmy LeSage and New Life and a small support staff facilitate all programs.
Special Notes: Smoking allowed only in designated areas.
Nearby Attractions: Appalachian Trail, Marlboro Music Festival, Manchester Village, the performing arts center at Woodstock, Dartmouth College Hopkins Center, antiquing, summer stock theater, concerts.
Getting There: 5 hours by car from New York City. Limousine service and car rental available from the airport in Lebanon, New Hampshire.

Association for Research and Enlightenment (A.R.E)

215 67th Street
Virginia Beach, VA 23451
(757) 437-7202—health services or (757) 428-3588—conferences; fax (757) 422-4631
E-mail: are@are-cayce.com   Web site: www.are-cayce.com

A stately two-story white-clapboard mansion houses the Virginia Beach headquarters of the Association for Research and Enlightenment (A.R.E.). The building, within walking distance of the Atlantic Ocean, houses an association dedicated to preserving, researching, and making available the teachings of Edgar Cayce, the "sleeping psychic" profiled earlier in this book (page 4). On the main floor of the association's large modern library is the conference center, site of the many workshops and lectures on holistic health, meditation, extrasensory perception, reincarnation, and dreams. The second floor contains all the Cayce "readings" as well as one of the most extensive metaphysical libraries in the world.

Conferences, held throughout the year, feature respected authorities in a particular field. Topics relate to personal growth or spiritual evolution. A typical day begins with breakfast followed by small-group discussions. Meditation led by staff in the center's Meditation Garden takes place before lunch. Afternoon and evening presentations are scheduled with free time allowed for dinner and exploring nearby beaches, shops, and cafés.

Staff of the Health Services Department provide and administer the various healing treatments recommended in the Cayce readings. Helping individuals activate their innate healing abilities is a fundamental principle behind the treatments. Spa packages are available between 8:30 and 1:30 and last almost half a day. The day includes a castor oil pack applied to the abdomen during a foot reflexology treatment. A colonic hydrotherapy session and aromatherapy steam bath follow. Guests then receive a Cayce/Reilly massage and facial and are free to finish off the experience relaxing in the Meditation Garden or attending one of the many workshops on healing touch, yoga, or meditation.

Hours and Days of Operation: Center hours are Mon–Sat 9–8; Sun 11–8. Health services available Mon, Tue, Wed, and Fri 8–7, Thu 8–8, and Sat 9:30–5:30. 3- to 5-day conferences held year-round.

Accommodations: A list of hotels along the Virginia Beach oceanfront is available, as is a list of A.R.E. member housing participants.

Rates: Vary depending on conference, services, and season. Conference tuition $255–$315.

Credit Cards: D, MC, V.

Meal Plans: Meals not provided, but lunch may be purchased on site or at several surrounding restaurants.

Services: Personal growth and spiritual conferences, massage, acupressure, colonic hydrotherapy, foot reflexology, manual lymph drainage, castor oil packs, Epsom salt baths, steam and fume baths, craniosacral therapy, reiki, therapeutic touch.

Facilities: Beachfront headquarters complex with original hospital that Edgar Cayce built, now functioning as office space and health services, library and conference center, meditation room and garden, lotus pond, steam bath, bookstore.

Staff: 49 massage therapists, including 15 trained in colonic hydrotherapy, 17 in acupressure, and the rest in specialized healing modalities, such as reflexology, Cayce remedies, and massage. All therapists receive training that exceeds local requirements at the COMTAA-accredited massotherapy school approved by the Virginia Department of Education.

Special Notes: Facilities accessible for people with disabilities.

Nearby Attractions: Virginia Marine Science Museum, Seashore State Park, Cape Henry Lighthouse, oceanfront boardwalk.

Getting There: 30 minutes by car from Norfolk International Airport.

Hartland Wellness Center

P.O. Box 1
Rapidan, VA 22733
(800) 763-9355 or (540) 672-3100; (540) 672-2584
E-mail: nuhealth@aol.com   Web site: www.hartland.edu/nuhealth

The Hartland Wellness Center, founded in 1983, is situated on 760 acres of the picturesque Piedmont Valley, just 40 miles north of Charlottesville. This health retreat and missionary college, located in a regal two-story mansion, can accommodate up to 30 guests at a time. Residential programs approach health from the perspective of prevention and lifestyle management. All staff are Seventh-Day Adventists, but people of different religious backgrounds participate in Hartland's programs throughout the year because religious beliefs are not taught during the retreats.

Hartland's guests include those who may already be healthy and simply want a refreshing tune-up, whereas others may be experiencing chronic ailments such as diabetes, arthritis, cancer, and heart disease. The 10- and 18-day Lifestyle to Health intensive, Hartland's signature program, is designed as a therapeutic reconditioning and health education experience for people wanting to establish lasting good health. It starts with an initial health evaluation, which includes two blood profiles. The remainder of the time, guests can expect health lectures, nutritional counseling, stress management seminars, personal wellness evaluations, updates with the resident physician, massage and hydrotherapy treatments, gentle exercise, and recreational outings. Lodging is comfortable, and meals consist of low-fat natural cuisine. A tour of James Madison's home, Montpelier, is scheduled during the stay, and Monticello, Thomas Jefferson's plantation, is also in the area. During free time, guests can enjoy the indoor swimming pool, sauna, sundeck, garden, and walking trails.

For those who want to learn more about Hartland before committing to a residential retreat, the center opens its doors to the public for a complimentary low-fat vegetarian lunch. Anyone interested can call to make arrangements.

Hours and Days of Operation: 10- and 18-day programs offered year-round.
Accommodations: Up to 15 in 2-story colonial-style building with queen-size beds and private bath.
Rates: 18-day program $2,995, includes lodging, meals, services.
Credit Cards: None accepted.
Meal Plans: 3 low-fat vegetarian meals included in program.
Services: Personal consultations with resident physician, 2 blood profiles, personal wellness evaluations, stress management presentations, massage, hydrotherapy, calisthenics classes, nutrition instruction, health lectures, individual counseling, Christian-based spiritual guidance, recreational outings.
Facilities: 760-acre estate with 2-story residential and treatment building, exercise equipment, sundeck, sauna, steam bath, indoor pool, garden, walking trails.
Staff: 10, including a doctor, nurse, 3 massage therapists.
Special Notes: Smoking not allowed. Facilities accessible for people with disabilities.
Nearby Attractions: Thomas Jefferson's Monticello, James Madison's Montpelier, Skyline Drive in Shenandoah National Park, the Appalachian Trail, Civil War sites.
Getting There: 40 miles by car north of Charlottesville, Virginia.

Homestead Resort and Spa

Hot Springs, VA 24445
(540) 839-7547; fax (540) 839-7670

The story goes that an Indian messenger discovered the rejuvenating qualities of the hot springs surrounding the Homestead Resort and Spa as early as the 1600s when he warmed himself from the winter's chill by sleeping in the hot mineral water. Many also believe that it was Thomas Jefferson who designed the Homestead's original Men's Bathhouse in 1761. It took 75 years for the Ladies Pool to be built, and once it was, anxious mothers began bringing their debutante daughters for a dip in hopes of scouting a potential match amongst the aristocracy who pilgrimaged en masse to the mineral pools, aptly named Warm, Hot, Sweet, and White. In 1832, Dr. Thomas Goode acquired the property and began touting the water's ability to cure gout, rheumatism, liver disease, paralysis, neuralgia, enlarged glands, and spinal irritations. Whether it was Goode's publicity or the simple natural draw of the healing waters, many famous and notable personalities have visited the homestead for a healing soak, including 13 former United States presidents.

Spa services at the Homestead revolve around these historic and therapeutic waters. Guests rent individual bathhouses built in the late 1700s and early 1800s with 98-degree water piped in from the warm spring. A variety of hydrotherapy treatments are offered, including Dr. Goode's spout bath, which begins with a mineral bath to target specific muscle pains and follows with a 100-year-old technique of water-induced massage. A blend of massage, loofah scrubs, herbal wraps, and aromatherapy treatments is also available. More than 100 miles of hiking trails wind through the surrounding 15,000-acre mountain preserve in Virginia's Allegheny Mountains. And, for guests who want a more adventurous form of nature therapy, canoe trips with experienced guides are offered during the warmer months along the Jackson River and over the calm waters of nearby Lake Moomaw.

Hours and Days of Operation: Special packages offered year-round and tailored around the individual interests and availability of guests.

Accommodations: 200 renovated guest rooms in East Wing and Main Building.

Rates: Vary according to room, season, and package. Rooms range $125–$1,000 per night.

Credit Cards: AE, MC, V.

Meal Plans: Some packages include dinner and breakfast, with low-fat spa cuisine and vegetarian options available by request.

Services: Massage, loofah body scrubs, aromatherapy, herbal wraps, facials, manicures, pedicures, salon services, children's programs.

Recreational Activities: Skiing, ice-skating, skeet and trapshooting, trout fishing, mountain biking, canoeing, hiking, nature walks, children's programs, movies, horseback and carriage rides.

Facilities: New fitness center, weight room, aerobics room, therapeutic whirlpool, individual bathhouses, indoor and outdoor swimming pools, 3 golf courses and driving range, 4 tennis courts, equestrian center, lawn bowling, archery, walking trails, game room with 8-lane bowling alley, 10 dining rooms, conference rooms.

Staff: 13 massage therapists, 5 hydrotherapists, 8 aestheticians. All licensed and certified.

Special Notes: On-site full-service travel agency assists guests with travel plans. Smoking not allowed in spa or designated areas.

Nearby Attractions: Jefferson Pools, historic Lexington, Allegheny Mountains, shopping.

Getting There: 20 miles by car from Covington, Virginia; 75 miles by car from Roanoke, Virginia.

Annapurna Inn and Retreat Center

538 Adams Street
Port Townsend, WA 98368
(800) 868-ANNA or (360) 385-2909
E-mail: annapurna@olympus.net

The Sanskrit name Annapurna refers to the goddess of fertility and nutritional healing. What better way to describe this warm and relaxed retreat in one of the Northwest's most picturesque harbor towns? An organic garden filled with plums, echinacea, yarrow, strawberries, and more surrounds the inn while a cottage in back houses a luxurious tiled steam bath and wood sauna. A sign at the front door tells guests which of the six rooms—each named for their individual character—will be theirs.

After checking in, guests are invited to take a steam bath and sauna. Eucalyptus oil in the bath clears congestion while the steam relaxes, physically preparing guests for the three-day retreat package. In the morning, guests find breakfast plates filled, literally, with the fruit of owner Robin Sharan's labor. Along with vegan cuisine comes reflexology, therapeutic massage, nature walks, educational videos, and yoga classes in the retreat package. Combine this with in-room whirlpool baths and you get a small piece of heaven.

Sharan, recently recognized by the *American Directory of Who's Who in Executives and Businesses*, promotes a healthy lifestyle through a plant-based diet and educates her guests on the benefits of various healing modalities, including reflexology and self-massage. "Many times the origin of pain is not where one feels it," she says. "Therefore it is important to go to the source of the irritation to alleviate the condition. For example, painful feet could be a result of an injury to fascial tissue in the calf muscles." Sharon believes that by deeply nourishing the body, assisting in detoxification, and moving the fluids to release soft-tissue restrictions, the body is exponentially assisted in healing itself. Craniosacral therapy, known to alleviate headaches, back pain, head trauma injuries, and emotional stress, is also offered.

The inn is available on an overnight basis in addition to the retreat package. It is best to leave Seattle with a few hours of sunlight left for the two-hour trip in order to witness the drama of the Olympic Peninsula's mountainous ridge and see the densely forested pine groves and pastoral meadows along the way.

Hours and Days of Operation: Apr 1–Oct 31, 7 days a week. Nov 1–Mar 31, weekend retreat packages and mid-week large group packages.
Accommodations: 6 rooms, 3 with private baths and 3 with semiprivate baths.
Rates: $108–$128 for room with private bath; $80–$95 for room with semi-private bath. All overnight rates include access to spa facilities, including sauna and steambath, and full organic vegan breakfast. $252–$552 for 3-day retreat package, including 1-hour reflexology, 2 yoga classes, 1½-hour theraputic massage, 2 nights, 2 breakfasts. À la carte prices for theraputic sessions available.
Credit Cards: MC, V.
Meal Plans: Daily organic vegan breakfast. Other meals—vegan only and livefood style—upon request ($15–$30 per meal). Special meal accommodations for people with food sensitivities and special needs.
Services: Reflexology, therapeutic massage, craniosacral therapy, yoga classes, seminars on nutrition and reflexology.
Facilities: Conferencing for groups up to 18. Sauna and steam bath, sitting room, dining room, kitchen, garden, porch.
Staff: Licensed massage therapists, certified reflexologist, certified yoga instructor.
Special Notes: Smoking not allowed.
Nearby Attractions: The Victorian charm of Port Townsend, hiking through scenic Northwest terrain, kayaking in Puget Sound, whale watching.
Getting There: About 2 hours by car and ferry northwest of Seattle.

Ayurvedic and Naturopathic Medical Clinic

2115 112th Avenue NE
Bellevue, WA 98004
(425) 453-8022; fax (425) 451-2670
E-mail: Ayurveda@Ayush.com   Web site: www.ayush.com

This modern clinic, just 40 minutes east of Seattle, offers the ancient treatment of Ayurveda combined with naturopathic medicine. Ayurvedic philosophy maintains that within each person is an innate knowledge stemming from the Universal Consciousness. The science of Ayurveda also recognizes that each person is different and therefore has unique illness and healing capacities. These differences form into the prakriti, or individual psychosomatic constitution of each person. The prakriti is formed through a combination of the three basic elements of vat, pit, and kaph. Ether and air, fir and water, and water and earth, respectively, comprise the elements. Through an understanding of these elements, various techniques are used to stimulate inner intelligence and bring the body and mind into a state of balance.

Though primarily a family practice, the clinic does offer a two-week panchakarma intensive, a treatment designed to eliminate the body of poisons through a combination of massage, herbal saunas, special foods and dietary patterns, mild fasting, and colonic therapy. When entering the clinic for panchakarma, a physician uses pulse diagnosis to determine the patient's prakriti and recommend the various herbs, vitamins, exercise, and diet to bring the elements into balance and promote good health.

The clinic also offers classes addressing various aspects of health, which are open to panchakarma recipients as well as the general public. The Women's Health and Ayurveda class offers an introduction to Ayurveda, provides health tips specifically for women, and explains how Ayurveda relates to menstrual irregularities, hormonal imbalances, and the prevention of osteoporosis.

Hours and Days of Operation: 2-week panchakarma treatments offered year-round.

Accommodations: Guests are referred to the East King County Convention and Visitor's Bureau at (800) 252-1926, ext. 44.

Rates: Panchakarma services for 2 weeks $1,405.

Credit Cards: V.

Meal Plans: 3 organic meals a day designed to complement the specific Ayurvedic treatment.

Services: Physical examination, mild fasting, herbal massage, herbal steam therapy, Ayurvedic poultices, herbal masks, juice fasting, mild herbal colonics.

Facilities: 40-acre estate with community building containing large hall with pine floors, 3 fireplaces, sauna, whirlpools, treatment rooms, dining room, walking trails, private lake.

Staff: Physician staff include Virender Sodhi, MD, ND; Shailinder Sodhi, BAMS, ND; Anju Sodhi, BAMS, ND. Dr. Sodhi lectures extensively throughout the United States and other countries and is the founder and instructor of the new Sri Chinmoy Institute of Ayurvedic Sciences adjacent to the clinic.

Special Notes: Smoking not allowed. Facilities accessible for people with disabilities.

Nearby Attractions: Museums, shopping, dining and theater in Seattle, whale watching, Snoqualmie Falls, Mounts Rainier and Baker.

Getting There: 40 minutes by car from Seattle.

Camp Indralaya

Route 1, Box 86
Eastsound, WA 98245
(360) 376-4526; fax (360) 376-5977
E-mail: oif@rockisland.com

Camp Indralaya is situated on 78 acres of forests and meadows on Orcas Island in Washington's San Juan Islands. Founded in 1927 by the Theosophical Society, Indralaya is an independent nonprofit organization formed with the goal of exploring the potential for human development in a community that functions in cooperation with nature.

Program topics vary, from developing the creative spirit to exploring the divine in nature. Membership in the Theosophical Society is not required to participate in Indralaya's programs or to schedule a personal retreat. Last year's Breath, Health and Wholeness retreat was led by Erik Peper, professor and associate director of the Institute for Holistic Healing Studies at San Francisco State University. For three days, guests learned a variety of healthy breathing practices and techniques, with the goal of maintaining and enhancing total well-being.

In addition to workshops, guests can expect cabins with wood-burning stoves, three vegetarian meals a day, daily meditation, a bookshop, and a well-stocked library. Everyone is asked to share in daily chores and to bring any musical or artistic talents for evening campfires. Indralaya is also home to rabbits, deer, owls, sea otters, bald eagles, and other wildlife. Walking trails are maintained along three-quarter miles of shoreline, and plenty of free time is allowed to explore the unforgettable natural beauty of this Pacific Northwest island.

Hours and Days of Operation: 2- to 7-day workshops offered spring, summer, and fall. Residential fellowships offered with a minimum 2-week commitment.

Accommodations: Up to 100 in rustic sleeping cabins with wood-burning stoves and shared bathhouse; plumbing cabins with shower, sink, toilet; the Round House, with 7 sleeping rooms and shared bath.

Rates: Lodging $39–$59 per night including meals. Discounted rates apply to children. Program fees are charged in addition to room and board; program fee $40.

Credit Cards: MC, V.

Meal Plans: 3 meals a day served communally in large dining hall. Nondairy and nonwheat options available. Special dietary needs can be accommodated with advance notice. All meals are vegetarian.

Services: Workshops on topics like therapeutic touch, yoga, tai chi, meditation, mask making, breathwork, and sacred community; holiday and solstice celebrations.

Facilities: 78-acre island retreat with cabins, library, bookshop, meadows, trails situated along ¾-mile of shoreline.

Staff: As Indralaya is a community, staff consists of resident managers and volunteers. Workshop facilitators include Ken Jackson Grey Eagle, journalist, professor, and author of a guidebook to sacred healing circles. Dora Kunz and Dolores Krieger lead a workshop on advanced therapeutic touch. Both women helped found the technique. Krieger is a Professor Emeritus of New York University, and Kunz is past president of the Theosophical Society in America and co-founder of Camp Indralaya.

Special Notes: Guests are asked to bring pillows, sleeping bags, sheets, blankets, towels, a flashlight, and any toiletries. Smoking allowed only in the smoking lounge or in guests' cars. Telephone available for outgoing calls only. Alcohol, nonprescription drugs, and any products containing meat, fish, or fowl not allowed.

Nearby Attractions: Hurricane Ridge, San Juan Islands, Hoh National Rain Forest, Pacific Northwest coast and mountain wilderness.

Getting There: About 3 hours by car and ferry northwest of Seattle.

Harmony Hill of Union

East 7362, Highway 106
Union, WA 98592-9781
(360) 898-2363; fax (360) 898-2364
E-mail: harmonyh@halcyon.com

Harmony Hill of Union, a wellness learning center with a stunning view of the Olympic Mountains, is located in a rural setting on the picturesque Hood Canal. First formed in 1986 by Gretchen Schodde, Harmony Hill is one of the few centers of its kind in the Pacific Northwest. Schodde, a nurse practitioner who set up rural health clinics throughout Washington in the 1970s, formed Harmony out of an awareness of the need for a preventive self-care training site in the state. The goal of Harmony is to provide a means for people to make significant and healthy lifestyle changes.

Programs, retreats, and classes are dedicated to health education, positive living strategies, stress management, recovery enhancement, and skills for developing a profound relationship with the Earth. Harmony is designed to serve individuals recovering from substance abuse illness, the physically challenged, the actively aging, people on the verge of burn-out, those with life-threatening illness, and health care professionals. Individuals and groups are referred to Harmony through a public or nonprofit social service organization, a health professional, or a member of the clergy.

Individual and small-group retreats are available, as are facilitated programs and classes. Lodging rates include a shared bedroom and bathroom; gourmet, semivegetarian meals; group access to meeting rooms; library/meditation room; garden; yurt; and walking path. Guests assist a volunteer staff with simple household chores, kitchen duty, and gardening.

The program Healing Into Wholeness: Women and the Power of the Land is designed for women challenged by a major life crisis. The retreat Embracing the Sacredness of Life, specifically for people living with cancer, promotes the nourishment, care, and calming of the body, mind, and soul.

Hours and Days of Operation: In addition to being open for private retreats, 1- to 5-day scheduled programs offered year-round.
Accommodations: Up to 10 may be accommodated in the main house overlooking Hood Canal; a cottage or a yurt will sleep up to 6.
Rates: Harmony relies on donations for about half of its revenue. All contributions, whether of volunteer time or supplies, appreciated. Financial contributions beyond the cost of actual programs and services eligible for tax deduction.
Credit Cards: MC, V (checks preferred).
Meal Plans: 3 healthy vegetarian meals a day, plus snacks.
Services: Annual wellness festival offering lifestyle evaluations; stress management techniques; blood pressure and cholesterol checks; osteoporosis risk assessments; massage; aromatherapy; exercise; chiropractic; foot care and healing touch; structured retreats incorporating wellness activities such as walking, stretching, meditation, nutritional education, cooking classes; qigong; guided meditation; music therapy; guided imagery; dream work; art and sand-tray expressions. Massage scheduled at guest's individual requests and Embracing the Sacredness of Life cancer retreat.
Facilities: Main house, cottage, 3 gardens, greenhouse, 30-foot-diameter yurt, 2 labyrinths with walking paths, walking trails.
Staff: 4 permanent staff, including an ARNP and an MN; contracted staff including medical and naturopathic doctors, psychologists, wellness educators, licensed massage therapists, certified qigong instructor.
Special Notes: Main house wheelchair accessible.
Nearby Attractions: Hurricane Ridge, Olympic National Forest, Union Country Store, Came Boutique, Victoria's Restaurant.
Getting There: About 2 hours by car and ferry west of Seattle.

Pacific Center for Naturopathic Medicine

1919 Broadway, Suite 204
Bellingham, WA 98225
(360) 734-0045; fax (360) 738-4955

Dr. Rachelle Herdman received a doctorate in naturopathy from Bastyr University in Seattle after working as a pathologist at London University in England. She has established a private practice in the small Northwest port town of Bellingham. As a result of Herdman's commitment to caring for the whole person and getting people to understand the roots of their illness, she offers five-day intensives designed to promote the understanding that to comprehend nature is to comprehend one's own body. A lot of time is spent in the natural world during the intensives, as Herdman's treatment center is very close to scenic Chuckanut Drive, which winds past nature reserves filled with dark firs, rocky coastline, and views of the San Juan Islands.

Healing methods vary from person to person. The program is scheduled over a period of five days, and treatments last six hours a day, separated into two- and three-hour blocks. Options include nutritional medicine, which employs a diet of whole foods and supplements; classical homeopathy, designed to match trace plant or mineral elements with the individual's unique constitution; psychoneuroimmunology, or mind-body medicine, intended to cultivate a relationship between the individual's inner life and the nervous and immune systems; botanical medicine, using hand-mixed prescriptions of plants, herbs, and tinctures; and craniosacral therapy, intended to restore the innate rhythms of the organs. Herdman and guests prepare food together, and guests learn how to combine medicinal foods into tasty nutritional meals. Personal counseling, in-depth exploration of dreams, art, and skills for practical reflection on life are also provided. When guests leave, they have an easy-to-follow program they can take home with them and a profound understanding of what their illness means.

Hours and Days of Operation: 3–5-day intensives offered year-round.
Accommodations: Guests referred to local hotels.
Rates: $1,500–$2,500 for meals and services.
Credit Cards: None accepted.
Meal Plans: Vary according to the individual's health requirements. Natural whole foods are used.
Services: Nutritional medicine, cooking classes, Ayurveda, lifestyle and exercise guidance, Chinese medicine, homeopathy, mind-body medicine, Jungian counseling, journaling, guided imagery, botanical medicine, custimized herb blends, craniosacral therapy.
Facilities: Medical clinic and teaching kitchen close to trees, mountains, ocean.
Staff: Dr. Rachelle Herdman, M.D., N.D., and clinical assistant.
Special Notes: All chronic illnesses are treated. Preventive medicine is addressed.
Nearby Attractions: Shopping and dining in Bellingham, whale watching, sightseeing, museums and theater in Seattle.
Getting There: 90 minutes by car north of Seattle.

Sacred Healing, Sacred Retreats

18910 33rd Avenue NE
Seattle, WA 98155-2528
(206) 368-3881
E-mail: SuraChar@aol.com

"Healing is a combination of joy and peace," says Sura Charlier, founder of Sacred Healing, Sacred Retreats. "Joy in our relationship with the outside, and peace in our discovery of the source of our being." Charlier, a student of the Sufi tradition for 14 years and an ordained Interfaith minister, leads both retreats and workshops designed to facilitate well-being, renewal, and transformation. Retreats are tailored to each individual and are intended to support the process of healing and revitalization. Charlier draws on diverse techniques, such as rituals and meditations from various world religions, sound and light therapy, breathwork, magnets, guided self-inquiry, energy centers, regression therapy, creative visualization, music therapy, and prayer.

Silence, solitude, watchfulness, and fasting are elements of the retreats, which take place next to a small creek in a residential forest of North Seattle. Practices vary from day to day and revolve around a pre-retreat consultation with Charlier, who helps guests determine their goals. A typical day begins with a pre-dawn practice using a combination of breathwork, magnets, sound, light, prayer, and journaling. Afterward, guests meet with a retreat guide to discuss the results of the morning's work and follow up with a hot shower and breakfast. Midmorning activities include similar practices as well as reading inspirational material. Noon prayers and a hot lunch precede an afternoon of rest, walking, and more self-exploration practices. Dinner is served at 6:00, followed by sharing the day's experiences with other guests and facilitators. Guests are free to listen to music, sing, create a personal altar, or sit under the stars in a hot tub.

Hours and Days of Operation: 1- to 15-day retreats offered year-round.
Accommodations: Rustic stand-alone structure for cots and sleeping bags.

Rates: 1–3 days $70 per person; 5–7 days $60 per person; 10–15 days $50 per person.
Credit Cards: None accepted.
Meal Plans: 3 healthy vegetarian meals a day, plus snacks and fresh juices.
Services: Guided meditation, prayer, sound, music and light therapy, creative visualization, regression therapy, energy work, journaling, therapeutic bodywork.
Facilities: Hot tub, bath, shower facilities.
Staff: Sura Charlier, an ordained Interfaith minister, counselor, and student of the Sufi tradition.
Special Notes: Smoking not allowed.
Nearby Attractions: Museums, dining, shopping, whale watching in Seattle, Mount Rainier, Snoqualmie Falls.
Getting There: Retreat is in North Seattle, about 45 minutes by car from Sea-Tac International Airport.

Trillium Retreat Center

12810 SW 236th Street
Vashon Island, WA 98070
(206) 463-5509
E-mail: Trillium@wolfenet.com

Janice Lehrer had a vision. On Vashon Island, just 15 minutes by ferry from West Seattle, Lehrer wanted to create a space in a natural environment where people could take time out to recharge, reflect, and receive healing treatments. Trillium Retreat Center, a 15-acre rural getaway surrounded by forests and meadows, is the actualization of her vision. The center provides space for personal retreats designed to relax and rejuvenate. Lehrer is a licensed massage practitioner, registered counselor, certified colonic hydrotherapist, and hatha yoga instructor who specializes in body-mind healing. She and her husband, Jake, a master craftsman and the man responsible for building and designing Trillium, have offered group and personal retreats since 1989.

Retreats are personal, and it is up to guests to orchestrate a daily schedule. Guests either camp or stay in cabins that accommodate up to four. Inside the cabin, a spiral staircase leads up to a loft with a queen-size bed dressed in flannel, cotton, or down. Hand-painted mirrors and furniture, a loveseat that folds out into a bed, a propane stove, a cold-water spigot, and a porch swing are the only amenities, providing a rustic elegance. They walk down a wooded trail to the bathhouse for a soak in a covered outdoor hot tub, a Russian steam bath, and a cold plunge. They can then schedule colonic hydrotherapy or a number of therapeutic treatments including deep-tissue massage, breathwork, and hypnotherapy. Afternoons can consist of guided meditation and yoga; exploring surrounding meadows, gardens, and woods; or venturing into downtown Vashon.

Hours and Days of Operation: Office hours: 9–9, 7 days a week. Weekend and weeklong retreats and workshops offered year-round. Longer stays available.

Accommodations: 30 beds total: 3 rustic cabins with 4 sets of bunk beds, garden cottage for 2, private furnished cabin for up to 4; tent sites.

Rates: Group retreats are $45 per person, per night, not including meals; includes use of yurt as gathering space, cabins, bathhouse, grounds, and kitchen. Daily rate for bathhouse rental, 90 minutes, $15. Massage and colonic hydrotherapy are à la carte.

Credit Cards: MC, V.

Meal Plans: Cabin equipped with small refrigerator, microwave, coffee, tea. Meals can be provided with advance notice.

Services: Massage, colonic hydrotherapy.

Facilities: 15 acres of forest and meadows, hot tub on covered deck, Russian steam bath, cold plunge, 700-square-foot carpeted yurt with timber-frame deck, main kitchen dining room. Rustic cabins to be added in the near future.

Staff: Janice Lehrer, LMP, registered counselor, certified colonic hydrotherapist, and hatha yoga instructor specializing in mindbody healing.

Special Notes: Drugs, alcohol, and pets not allowed. Minimum age is 18.

Nearby Attractions: Lisabuela park, lighthouse on Port Robinson, Blue Heron Cultural Center, dining in Vashon, bicycling, whale watching, kayaking.

Getting There: 15 minutes by ferry from West Seattle.

Coolfont Resort and Wellness Spa

1777 Cold Run Valley Road
Berkeley Springs, WV 25411
(800) 888-8768 or (304) 258-4500; fax (304) 258-5499
Web site: www.coolfont.com

Some attribute the founding of Coolfont Resort and Spa to a snowstorm. In 1961, Sam Ashelman drove to the eastern panhandle of West Virginia for an Easter vacation with his young son. A heavy snowfall forced him to spend the night in nearby Berkeley Springs. It was here that Ashelman saw a "for sale" sign on a 1,200-acre estate. Today, the stately Manor House, lakes, streams, cabins, and hiking trails provide guests with an idyllic escape for rejuvenation, renewal, and relaxation.

Spa programs at Coolfont are designed to achieve and maintain a balance of the different elements of the wellness spectrum. These elements include fitness, nutrition, and stress reduction. A typical package includes lodging and three low-fat, high-fiber spa meals a day; walking and hiking programs; stress management sessions; yoga, tai chi, and relaxation techniques; and access to the spa dining room, indoor solar heated swimming pool, sauna and whirlpool tub, and Cybex exercise equipment. Throughout the year, Coolfont offers Spectrum of Learning courses covering a variety of health-related topics. Courses average three to five days, and room and board are included in tuition. Some of last year's topics included the five-day course Introduction to the World of Herbs and the three-day course Touch for Health Kinesiology: Balance the Energy Flow.

Coolfont also takes an active role in protecting the environment. Since 1965, owners Sam and Martha Ashelman have been committed to providing a demonstration center for environmental preservation. Last year the resort hosted a panel discussion on Earth's deteriorating condition, based on astronaut Mary Cleave's recent observation of how much worse Earth looks from space now than it did four years ago. Cleave and Nature Conservancy author Bruce Rich hosted the discussion.

Hours and Days of Operation: 2-, 5-, and 7-night packages offered year-round.

Accommodations: Single and double rooms with private baths in lodge rooms and chalets with wood-burning stoves and whirlpools. Private vacation homes also available.

Rates: Vary according to room, program, and season. 2-night spa packages start at $250.

Credit Cards: AE, D, MC, V.

Meal Plans: 3 low-fat, high-fiber meals a day with lots of fresh fruit, vegetables, whole grains. Fish, poultry, vegetarian entrées are available.

Services: Workshops on natural foods, stress reduction and problem solving, team-building programs sponsored by Outward Bound, nutritional consultations, massage, craniosacral therapy, herbal wraps, facials, meditation, yoga, tai chi, relaxation techniques, salon services, aquacise, body sculpting, weight training, fitness classes, walking and hiking programs.

Recreational Activities: Horseshoes, horseback riding, snow-tubing in park in winter.

Facilities: 1,350-acre estate with lodges, chalets, log cabins, indoor solar heated pool, sauna, whirlpool tub, exercise equipment, basketball and volleyball courts, beach on private lake.

Staff: 60 total staff, including learning program coordinator, 20 massage therapists, 5 aestheticians, personal trainer, 10 fitness instructors including body sculpting, tai chi, yoga.

Special Notes: Smoking allowed only in designated areas. Facilities accessible for people with disabilities.

Nearby Attractions: Championship golf at Cacapon State Park, White Tail Ski Resort, Berkeley Springs State Park.

Getting There: 2 hours by car from Washington, D.C.

The Greenbrier

300 West Main Street
White Sulphur Springs, WV 24986
(800) 624-6070 or (304) 536-1110; fax (304) 536-7854
Web site: www.greenbrier.com

What look like slender White House columns protrude from the regal facade of the Greenbrier, a Mobil Five-Star, AAA Five-Diamond resort. Greenbrier began as a cottage community more than 200 years ago and now claims 6,500 acres of an Allegheny Mountain valley. The community evolved around the famed mineral baths, first discovered in 1778. When word got out that a woman's rheumatism was "cured" minutes after immersion in the sulphur water, the migration began.

The spa has changed face since 1912, with a $7 million renovation. Today, the 25,000-square-foot wing contains an indoor pool and a Rhododendron Terrace Lounge—along with the historic baths. "We offered hydrotherapy in 1912 and still offer it today," says Greenbrier president Ted Kleisner. Fresh, natural mineral waters fill private walk-in whirlpool baths. Treatments are patterned after European spas, which emphasize water therapy, massage, body wraps, and skin care.

A unique facet of this luxury resort is the Greenbrier Clinic. Based on the reasoning that healthy people make healthy corporations, the clinic was founded in 1948 to offer prevention-oriented health care in a luxury setting to the nation's top executives. The spa works in conjunction with the clinic to offer a five-day Spa and Clinic Program. Guests receive lodging for five nights, daily breakfast and dinner, a complete diagnostic evaluation, a fitness evaluation with a follow-up consultation, two full-body massages, a mineral bath and soak in White Sulphur Springs' waters, a Swiss shower and Scotch spray, a European pressure-point facial, a manicure with paraffin, a haircut and blow dry, an exfoliation treatment, and unlimited use of exercise facilities.

Hours and Days of Operation: Open year-round, with specialty packages offered at the request of guests.

Accommodations: 639 guest rooms, including 121 guest houses and cottages, 53 suites.
Rates: Vary according to room, services, and season. Children stay and eat free when sharing a room with their parents.
Credit Cards: AE, D, MC, V.
Meal Plans: The Modified American Plan includes breakfast in the main dining room and dinner either in the main dining room or at Sam Snead's at the golf club. The main dining room breakfast offers low-calorie and standard eggs-and-bacon choices; Sam Snead's offers gourmet entrées, with meat, poultry, fish, and vegetable options.
Services: Swedish and aromatherapy massage, herbal body wraps, hydrotherapy, facials, salon services, aerobics, body composition assessments, weight training, internal medicine, radiology, cardiology, nursing, mammography, ultrasound, lab work, nutritional and psychological counseling, kids' programs.
Recreational Activities: Fly-fishing, skeet and trapshooting, croquet, carriage rides, horseback riding, hiking, nature walks.
Facilities: Scotch spray; steam, sauna, and therapy rooms; private walk-in mineral baths; indoor and outdoor swimming pool; exercise equipment; health clinic; lounge; 6 dining rooms; game room with billiards and bowling alley; 3 18-hole golf courses; 20 indoor and outdoor tennis courts; shops.
Staff: 8 medical doctors, cardiologist, 2 radiologists, nutritionist.
Special Notes: Smoking not allowed in spa. Facilities accessible for people with disabilities.
Nearby Attractions: Shopping in White Sulfur Springs, Presidents' Cottage Museum.
Getting There: About 4½ hours by car southwest of Washington, D.C. Greenbrier Travel Service assists guest with travel arrangements and makes all necessary reservations.

Aveda Spa Retreat

1015 Cascade Street North
Osceola, WI 54020
(800) 283-3202 or (715) 294-4465; fax (715) 294-4478
Web site: www.aveda.com

The Aveda Spa Retreat is set in the St. Croix River Valley, where health resorts built around local spring water flourished in the 1800s. The retreat is situated on 300 acres of Wisconsin woodlands, complete with waterfalls, rocky bluffs, and expansive fields—once home to several Native American tribes. Intended to provide a setting for relaxation, contemplation, and motivation, this nurturing environment promotes an awareness of the relationship between the earth and the human body. The Barn, which contains luxury suites and rooms for educational seminars and conferences, is a remodeled farm building dating back to 1908. "There's something special about the way the place partners the historical, the natural, and the personal," says Horst Rechelbacher, founder and CEO of Aveda Corporation. "Being here helps attune us to the very real connection between ourselves—our histories and cultures—and the natural environment that sustains us."

Despite its rustic beginnings, the retreat, and particularly the spa, is visually stunning. The spa sitting room looks like the grand hall of a country home for a seventeenth-century French lord. But looks are not everything at Aveda. In addition to its regular spa services, Aveda also hosts workshops for individuals designed to teach techniques for living a healthy, balanced lifestyle. Lifestyle Rejuvenation, a five-day program, teaches guests about the body's potential as well as the necessary skills for managing its unique composition with greater wisdom and joy. During the program, trained instructors teach posture, breathing, adjustments for physical limitations, and beauty techniques—all designed to coincide with an individual's lifestyle. Guests also take part in daily physical activities that are selected to match their needs and interests. Fresh, healthy organic foods are served daily in the Aveda Organica Restaurant.

Hours and Days of Operation: 1-day, weekend, and weeklong packages offered year-round.
Accommodations: Lodging in main house and 15 guest rooms and suites. Rooms come with plush down bedding; some suites have whirlpools.
Rates: Vary according to room and services. 5-day Himalayan Rejuvenation Retreat $2,500 and includes lodging, meals, services.
Credit Cards: AE, D, MC, V.
Meal Plans: 3 organic vegetarian meals a day included in some packages and served in the Aveda Organica Restaurant. Special dietary needs accommodated with advance notice.
Services: Education and consumer lifestyle workshops, rejuvenation retreats, massage, hydrotherapy, facials, flower essence whirlpool with body wrap, scalp treatments, exfoliation, manicures, pedicures, salon services, yoga.
Recreational Activities: Bicycling, cross-country skiing, snowshoeing, nature walks.
Facilities: 80-acre estate with mansion, restaurant, whirlpool, steam room, European shampoo bed, fitness equipment, Native American sweat lodge, tennis courts, hiking trails.
Staff: Spa staff include 20 licensed massage therapists, 6 salon cosmetologists.
Special Notes: Smoking not allowed in the mansion. Minimum age of spa guest is 18. Only limited access provided for people with disabilities. Guests are asked to bring slippers, loose comfortable clothes, all-terrain shoes, and bug spray in warmer months.
Nearby Attractions: Antiquing in Osceola, Como Conservatory, Walker Art Center, rock climbing at Taylor's Falls, golf, canoeing, downhill skiing.
Getting There: 1½ hours by car from Minneapolis/St. Paul International Airport, 1 hour by car from the Twin Cities. Transportation from airport available for a fee.

Christine Center

W8291 Mann Road
Willard, WI 54493
(715) 267-7507; fax (715) 267-7512
E-mail: weareone@christinecenter.org

In 1997, ABC's *Good Morning America* highlighted the Christine Center during a two-day program on retreat centers. Commenting on the pristine natural setting and rustic hermitages of this rural Wisconsin retreat, the Christine Center was described as a vacation where guests take home "more than just a suntan." No surprise, considering that for 17 years the center has welcomed visitors throughout the country who have come for a quiet place to gain insight and perspective in a rejuvenating, spiritually based community. The center was founded in 1980 with the aid of the Wheaton Franciscans in the Spirit of St. Francis, under the direction of Sister Virginia Mary Barta. Intended as a place for solitude and meditation, 20 cabins were built—each in a carefully designated forest setting—of local natural materials. In 1990 the center became an independent not-for-profit corporation embracing Unitive Spirituality, which recognizes the diversity and commonality of all spiritual traditions.

Workshops, scheduled throughout the year, address various aspects of health and personal growth. For example, last year's retreats included the Healing Science of Homeopathy, Feminism and the Path of Meditation, and Mask Making as Creative Initiation. Private retreats offered at the Christine Center provide the solitude necessary to pursue personal goals in an environment of contemplation and renewal. Guests have the option of seeking spiritual guidance or working part of the day in exchange for discounted lodging. The Rejuvenation Retreats can last from a few days to a few weeks. Staff consult with guests to design a schedule of activities intended to nurture the mind, body, and soul. Options include bodywork, traditional Chinese medicine, meditation instruction, natural skin and hair treatments, acupuncture, spiritual guidance, nutritional counseling, qigong, breathwork, and more.

Hours and Days of Operation: Office hours: Mon–Sat, 9–6:00; Sun, 11:00 a.m.–12:30 p.m. Workshops, seminars, and personal retreats offered year-round. Workshops average 2–3 days.
Accommodations: 20 cabins ranging in size from a small rustic hermitage with a woodstove to a large cabin with gas heat, full bath, kitchenette. All cabins have electricity; several are multiple occupancy, accommodating as many as 6 people.
Rates: $30–$90, including meals.
Credit Cards: None accepted.
Meal Plans: 3 nutritionally balanced meals a day, primarily vegetarian and whole foods.
Services: Workshops and seminars, individual and couple counseling, therapeutic massage, breathwork, acupuncture, herbal therapies, dietary counseling, qigong, reflexology and neck release, jin shin do, transpersonal counseling, Rah energy balancing, Enneagram work.
Recreational Activities: Long and short nature walks, biking, cross-country skiing, nearby swimming, climbing, canoeing.
Facilities: Conference room, meditation loft, dining room, chapel, pond, creek, nearby sleds, snowmobiles.
Staff: Doctor of oriental medicine, licensed acupuncturist, massage therapist, homeopathic practitioner, transpersonal psychologist.
Special Notes: Smoking not allowed.
Nearby Attractions: Cross-country skiing, kayaking, remote Wisconsin woodlands.
Getting There: 2½ hours by car from Minneapolis, 5 hours by car from Chicago. Airport pickup available at Central Wisconsin Airport.

Kopp Center for Continuing Education

N6360 ValleyView Road
HoneyCreek, WI 53138
(414) 763-7591; fax (414) 763-4491
E-mail: HoneyCree@aol.com   Web site: www.honeycree.mia.net

Twenty years ago, Dr. Anne Kopp Hyman established the Kopp Center as a retreat center offering training programs for health professionals to earn academic credits. In addition to a long history of training group facilitators, Dr. Kopp has studied with a number of recognized authorities in the fields of family therapy, Gestalt, and psychosynthesis. She has also found time to write three books on the subject of continuing education and working with groups. Dr. Manuel Nakanishi, former president of the Florida chapter of the Association for the Advancement of Social Work, is a cofacilitator and Associate Professor at Barry University in Florida. He has extensive experience working with children.

Only recently has the Kopp Center opened to the public, and today workshops are held in three locations: the rural Wisconsin retreat center, the beachfront Lido Spa in Miami, and at sea aboard the *Island Princess*. The 15-hour seminars aboard the ocean liner and at the Lido Spa are designed for psychologists, psychiatrists, social workers, and mental health counselors who want to learn strategies for experiential group work.

The same seminar is also available at the HoneyCreek, Wisconsin, retreat center, though the site is also open to the public for personal retreats. During personal retreats, guests have access to weekend workshops focusing on a variety of personal growth disciplines, including journal writing, dance therapy, and artistic expression. The center is located on 55 acres just 30 miles from Milwaukee. Daily kripalu yoga sessions and weekend aqua-aerobics in a private lake are offered in addition to free time for swimming, boating, and hiking through numerous trails over meadows and woods.

Hours and Days of Operation: Weekend workshops at HoneyCreek location offered year-round. 15-day group-work seminars usually offered Jul–Jan.

Accommodations: HoneyCreek: dormitory, semiprivate and single chalet rooms with shared bathrooms; Lido Spa: single and double standard rooms in 1- and 2-story garden wings; *Island Princess:* inside and view cabins.

Rates: Vary according to location and program. Lodging at HoneyCreek $35–$65 per night; 2-day workshop $175.

Credit Cards: AE, MC, V.

Meal Plans: Gourmet natural foods included with some programs. Community kitchen available at HoneyCreek center. Inquire for details regarding Lido Spa and *Island Princess* cuisine.

Services: Weekend workshops, massage, kripalu yoga, aqua-aerobics, dance and art therapy, journaling.

Recreational Activities: Swimming, boating, hiking.

Facilities: 55-acre country retreat, community kitchen, private lake. Inquire for details regarding Lido Spa and *Island Princess* facilities.

Staff: Dr. Anne Hyman, Dr. Manual Nakanishi, support staff.

Special Notes: Facilities accessible for people with disabilities.

Nearby Attractions: Woods, meadows, shopping, dining, and theater in Milwaukee.

Getting There: 30 miles by car from Milwaukee, 80 miles by car from Chicago.

Antelope Retreat and Education Center

P.O. Box 156
Savery, WY 82332-0156
(888) 268-2732 or (317) 722-1916
E-mail: ohmakasu@earthlink.net   Web site: www.anteloperetreat.org

For nine years, Antelope Retreat and Education Center has offered spiritually based wilderness retreats and vision quests designed to balance the body and soul. All programs allow guests the opportunity to understand the interconnectedness between their own lives and the natural world. The center is located in the foothills of the Rocky Mountains, just a few miles west of Medicine Bow National Forest. Guests share in communal ranch life, do solo fasts, learn fire building and other primitive skills, work in the garden, or go swimming in a nearby creek. Each day, guests can also venture out with a guide on long walks either to the mountains to the east or the desert to the west. During the walks, guides explain the physical and spiritual landscape. Those who hang back at the ranch can participate in Earth-centered meditation, sweat lodge ceremonies, listening exercises, or bioenergetics. All guests learn ways to develop a lifestyle that can be sustained without further environmental damage to the Earth.

Summer programs, retreats, and vacations are offered throughout the year, with specialized weeks focusing on women's healing, one-week wilderness quests, one-day solo fasts, and a Native American teachings week led by Native American elders. Antelope facilitators Gina, Liz, John, Jean, and Tom give family-like support and have extensive experiential training as well as experience leading groups. Weeklong and weekend wilderness programs are also offered in western Massachusetts and occasionally in Indiana.

No one will be turned away for lack of funds at Antelope; for those who cannot afford program fees, scholarships are available. As a nonprofit organization, all costs exceeding actual program rates are credited to guests as a tax-deductible contribution.

Hours and Days of Operation: Weekend and weeklong programs offered year-round. No scheduled programs during winter.

Accommodations: 5 bedrooms in a 100-year-old ranch house; yurt space for sleeping bags.

Rates: Vary according to season. Day rates $38–$60; programs $500–$1,000.

Credit Cards: None accepted.

Meal Plans: Healthy home-cooked meals included with a vegetarian option.

Services: Earth-centered meditation, listening, sweat lodge ceremonies, bioenergetics, primitive survival skills, community living experience.

Recreational Activities: Hiking, swimming, cross-country skiing.

Facilities: Rustic wooden ranch house, yurt, garden.

Staff: 5 staff members trained in Native American teachings, survival and wilderness skills, bioenergetics, meditation, bodywork, and therapy.

Special Notes: Smoking not allowed indoors.

Nearby Attractions: Steamboat Springs, Colorado; the Snowy Range; Medicine Bow National Forest; the Red Desert; Flaming Gorge; Dinosaur National Monument; Saratoga, Wyoming (hot springs and resort); Little Snake River Museum; hiking; camping and fishing.

Getting There: 6 hours by car from Denver or Salt Lake City; transportation provided to and from Hayden/Steamboat Airport in Colorado. Antelope strongly recommends that you contact them to coordinate travel plans.

Healing Centers & Retreats

in

Canada

Mountain Escape Health and Lifestyle Retreat at Lake Louise Inn

210 Village Road, Box 209
Lake Louise, Alberta, Canada T0L 1E0
(800) 661-9237 or (403) 522-3791; fax (403) 522-2018

Amid the heart of the Canadian Rockies with a view of Victoria Glacier, the Mountain Escape at Lake Louise Inn offers a biannual stress-relieving and health-oriented getaway within a luxury resort. For five weeks in spring and again in fall, the Inn offers the Health and Lifestyle Retreat. Inspired by today's need for restorative vacations, the package teaches the basics of eating sensibly, practical fitness, and positive self-esteem. Visitors can expect daily yoga and meditation, massage techniques, an evening lifestyle program, nature walks, and a take-home educational package.

A typical day starts with a walk through the village of Lake Louise, followed by a breakfast of Irish soda bread and fresh fruit with yogurt. Guests then have the choice of group-led muscle work or aquacise in the heated indoor pool. Aerobics follow the vigorous schedule, and afterward guests climb aboard the bus for Stanley Glacier. Daily mountain walks can lead hikers through dense subalpine forests, mountain panoramas, and along the edge of glacial moraines. For those who choose not to pack a lunch, a second bus departs for Marble Canyon in the afternoon. Yoga class is at 4:30, followed by dinner and an evening presentation on vegetarianism or health and wellness.

Individuals visiting the Lake Louise Inn for a personal retreat can take advantage of spa services and the Nature Walk/Aerobic Hike Program. Spa treatments vary, from the hands-on healing of reiki to shiatsu and reflexology. The Nature Walk Program offers a series of wilderness outings designed to highlight the profound natural beauty of the Canadian Rockies. Treks are geared toward two different fitness levels; destinations vary according to weather and trail conditions.

Hours and Days of Operation: 1-week health and lifestyle program offered Apr 27–May 31, Sep 27–Oct 31.

Accommodations: 232 rooms ranging from Superior Queen rooms to Superior Loft condo-style units.
Rates: Vary according to lodging and package. Condensed week $489–$665 per person, double occupancy.
Credit Cards: AE, D, DC, MC, V.
Meal Plans: 3 calorie-wise meals with snack breads.
Services: Massage, reiki, kinesiology, reflexology, health and lifestyle lectures, salon services.
Recreational Activities: Downhill and cross-country skiing, hiking, mountain biking.
Facilities: Heated indoor pool, steam room, 2 whirlpools, gazebo with outdoor exercise deck and fireplace, exercise equipment.
Staff: About 15 spa staff, including massage therapists, aestheticians, yoga and fitness instructors.
Special Notes: Guests should bring warm clothing, gloves, hiking boots.
Nearby Attractions: Chateau Lake Louise, Banff National Park, Jasper, Lake Agnes Tea House.
Getting There: 2 hours by car west of Calgary Airport.

EcoMed Natural Health Spa

Pacific Shores Nature Resort 515
1600 Strougler Road
Nanoose Bay, British Columbia, Canada V9P 9B7
(250) 468-7133; fax (250) 468-7135

On the tip of Vancouver Island overlooking Nanoose Bay lies the EcoMed Natural Health Spa, North America's first integrated naturopathic spa. Dr. Stefan Kuprowsky founded EcoMed Wellness Centre in 1985, and it quickly became one of Vancouver's busiest and most progressive naturopathic health care centers. In 1993 the operation not only moved but evolved into the five-star luxury spa offering comprehensive wellness and naturopathic services that it is today. Kuprowsky, who is currently studying mind-body medicine with Dr. Deepak Chopra, also integrates the Ayurvedic approach with EcoMed's healing programs.

Retreat packages range from weekend escapes to seven-day retreat packages. Programs combine detoxification and healing-intensive programs with spa and beauty treatments. A range of issues is addressed in programs, such as holistic health, stress management, weight control, and spiritual exploration. The week-long Inner Cleanse Wellness Retreat combines a body tune-up with healing-group sessions and lifestyle education. A typical day begins at 8 with a choice of walking the beach or sitting in a glass-enclosed whirlpool overlooking the Northwest's dramatic rocky Pacific Coast. A healthy vegetarian breakfast of fresh local ingredients is followed by a personal health consultation at 9. An aroma steam and a trigger-point treatment can be scheduled before lunch, after which guests are free to take a hike through the adjacent bird sanctuary and nature preserve or go kayaking on an estuary with an experienced guide. Dinner starts at 6, and evening activities include a Wellness Lecture Series or a drum and music workshop. The evening draws to a close with group-led meditation at 9.

Hours and Days of Operation: 2- to 7-night programs offered year-round.
Accommodations: 6 standard rooms with private bath and garden patio and 6 ocean-view or river suites with fireplace, whirlpool, living room, kitchenette, bedroom.
Rates: Vary according to room and services. 2-night Spa Escape Weekend $370–$500.
Credit Cards: MC, V.
Meal Plans: 3 gourmet vegetarian meals a day, made with fresh local organic ingredients. All special dietary needs can be accommodated with advance notice.
Services: Comprehensive detoxification/inner cleansing and healing programs, comprehensive health assessment, nutritional therapies, herbs and supplements, health lectures, healing-group sessions, acupuncture, massage, meditation, tai chi, myotherapy, aromatherapy, Moor mud and herbal baths, seaweed wraps, aroma-steam treatments, colonic hydrotherapy, manicures, pedicures, facials, nonsurgical facelifts.
Recreational Activities: Hiking, nature walks.
Facilities: Condominium complex on ocean, ozonated swimming pool, sauna and indoor hot tub, oceanfront gazebo with hot tub, canoes, kayaks, mountain bikes, beachfront nature trails, bird sanctuary.
Staff: In addition to Dr. Kuprowsky, spa and clinic staff consist of an aesthetician, registered nurse, licensed massage therapist, colonic hydrotherapist, myotherapist, reflexologist.
Special Notes: Smoking not allowed.
Nearby Attractions: Rathtrevor Park nature reserve, rain forest, horseback riding, kayaking, waterfalls, golf, tennis, shopping.
Getting There: 2 hours by car from Vancouver Tsawwassen or Horseshoe Bay ferry to Nanaimo. Complimentary round-trip transportation from Nanaimo Ferry for weekend and extended stays.

Haven by the Sea

RR 1, Site 9, Davis Road
Gabriola Island, British Columbia, Canada V0R 1X0
(250) 247-9211; fax (250) 247-8454
E-mail: havreg@island.net   Web site: http://www.island.net/~jockben/

Haven by the Sea is a residential educational retreat center on the shores of picturesque Gabriola Island. Only 20 minutes by ferry from Nanaimo on Vancouver Island, Gabriola is among a chain of Gulf Islands on Canada's west coast. On 9 acres of waterfront property, guests have access to outdoor hot tubs overlooking the water, ocean-view dining, a fully equipped gymnasium and sauna, and therapeutic treatments.

PD Seminars provides workshops for personal and professional development at Haven by the Sea. The seminars are recognized as a certified educational institution by British Columbia's Education Commission and are open to both health professionals and people who simply want to improve their lives. Topics vary from personal growth to health awareness.

Some typical workshops include the five-day Body, Breath and Energy Training workshop, hosted by PD Seminar manager Linda Nicholls and counselor David Raithby. The workshop establishes a solid foundation in the concepts and methods of bodywork and energy release work. Guests are encouraged to explore personal issues through a variety of energetic and expressive means. The purpose is for guests to develop and learn to use their intuition and creativity; to encounter buried feelings, memories, and behavior patterns as they are held in the body; and to increase the depth and effectiveness of interpersonal relationships. The three-day Stress and Healing workshop, in addition to addressing the needs of anyone with daily stresses, is designed for those experiencing chronic pain. The format allows guests a chance to identify stressful events and to develop a personal stress management plan. Activities include visualization, movement, breathwork, role plays, and discussion.

Hours and Days of Operation: Office hours: 9–5, 7 days a week. Courses and workshops offered year-round, usually 2 and 25 days.
Accommodations: Standard and deluxe double and single rooms in seaside resort. Some kitchenettes and fireplaces. Smoking not allowed.
Rates: $31–$80 per night. Courses $220–$3,000.
Credit Cards: MC, V.
Meal Plans: 3 buffet-style meals a day. Vegetarian options available.
Services: Massage, reflexology, workshops, courses.
Recreational Activities: Hiking; nearby golf, tennis, biking, fishing, sailing, kayaking, boat charter tours.
Facilities: Ocean-view dining room, conference and meeting rooms, fully equipped exercise gym, sauna, outdoor hot tub with ocean view, indoor pool with swim jets, outdoor pool.
Staff: All instructors have at least a master's or a PD Seminars diploma in counseling. The minimum practical experience required of all instructors is 5 years.
Special Notes: Smoking allowed in designated areas only.
Nearby Attractions: The island is home to many artists, galleries, and craftspeople. Eagles, deer, seals, heron, and petroglyphs are spotted along forest and beachfront walking trails.
Getting There: 20 minutes by ferry from Nanaimo, B.C., or Vancouver Island.

The Hills Health Ranch

Box 26, 108 Mile Ranch
British Columbia, Canada, V0K 2Z0
(250) 791-5225; fax (250) 791-6384
E-mail: thehills@netshop.net   Web site: http://www.GRT-Net.com/thehills

The Hills Health Ranch combines a down-to-earth rustic ambiance with luxury spa services and wellness programs. In the heart of the Canadian wilderness, this health and fitness resort provides true country charm. An authentic Indian tepee is the gathering site for sing-along parties, and guests can learn new steps at Texas line dancing parties. Swiss-style chalets look out over 20,000 acres of heavily forested hills, mountain lakes, and meadowlands with grazing horses and cattle. Guests who venture out on horseback with knowledgeable cowboys ride past eight different lakes on the Horseback Holiday. An elevation of 3,400 feet, a dry climate, and the clean air of the British Columbian Cariboo region are especially beneficial for people with respiratory disorders.

The Canadian Wellness Centre at Hills Health offers more than 20 homeopathic and aesthetic treatments as well as indoor and outdoor fitness programming, daily wellness workshops, and low-fat gourmet spa cuisine. Programs range from weekend refreshers to 11-day retreats that adhere to an extensive daily agenda. For people committed to serious weight or lifestyle changes, 30-day intensives are available. Programs address a wide range of lifestyle issues such as a wellness kick start, smoking cessation, stress reduction, successful aging, and injury rehabilitation. The six-night Men's Cardio Improvement Workshop is designed to give men a jump start on significant lifestyle changes and to learn the latest home approaches for improving heart health. The program includes lodging, low-fat meals, daily hiking and skiing in season, medical consultations, a complete fitness test and lifestyle assessment, daily wellness workshops, and daily indoor and outdoor fitness activities. Optional treatments include massage, clay packs, and reflexology.

Hours and Days of Operation: 2-night weekend to 11-day programs offered year-round.
Accommodations: 26 deluxe rooms and 20 individual Swiss-style chalets.
Rates: Space must be confirmed by a deposit of $100 or 25% of program fee at least 2 weeks in advance. Cancellations must be received in writing 30 days in advance for a full refund.
Credit Cards: AE, MC, V.
Meal Plans: 3 low-fat, calorie-controlled meals a day.
Services: Massage, full-body mud packs, herbal wraps, aromatherapy, loofah scrubs, reflexology, facials, manicures, pedicures, aerobics, wellness workshops.
Recreational Activities: Horseback riding, swimming, lake fishing, ice-skating, cross-country skiing, tobogganing, sleigh rides, Texas line dancing, hayrides, campfires.
Facilities: Indoor pool, 2 hydrotherapy pools, 2 saunas, aerobic studio, 12 spa treatments rooms, dining room, 3 meeting rooms, 5 lakes.
Staff: 55 total staff, including 4 massage therapists, 5 aestheticians. All licensed and certified.
Special Notes: Smoking not allowed in spa or dining room. Guests should bring warm clothes and all-terrain shoes.
Nearby Attractions: Barker Village, Helmicken Falls, Gibraltar Gold Mine.
Getting There: 2 hours northeast of Vancouver. 3 times a week, B.C. Rail's Cariboo Daytimer serves 100 Mile House.

Hollyhock

Box 127
Mansons Landing, British Columbia, Canada V0P 1K0
(800) 933-6339 or (250) 935-6576; fax (250) 935-6424
E-mail: Hollyhock@oberon.ark.com   Web site: www.hollyhock.bc.ca

A fire circle, tent space, a coastal wilderness, and days left open and unplanned—just like camp except more refined. This holistic learning center on tiny Cortes Island, just 90 miles north of Vancouver, British Columbia, draws internationally acclaimed authors, healers, and artists as guest speakers for its 70 or so workshops each year. Free classes allow guests who have come for a little quiet and a hot soak in the whirlpool a chance to meet other guests and learn new skills. Hollyhock allows plenty of time for quiet introspection, though evidence of the communal atmosphere shows through in the invitation to guests to bring musical instruments and art materials.

Visitors come to Hollyhock for everything from meditating on a moss-covered rock for hours on end to gathering plants in the surrounding woods for a five-day workshop on herbal medicine. Weekends are an easy getaway for Vancouver and Seattle urbanites and provide the opportunity for guests to test the waters of a personal growth workshop. The weekend begins with guests gathering at the two-story cedar lodge on Friday evening for an informal welcome. Saturday starts with a 7 a.m. yoga class followed by meditation, and at 10 a Hollyhock naturalist leads an excursion through the surrounding evergreens. A mini-workshop on either natural healing or the creative arts begins at 3, and a presentation by a workshop leader or Cortes Island instructor begins at 8. Before catching the ferry or seaplane home on Sunday, guests can take a bird walk with an experienced naturalist or hop in the Harlequin for a group canoe over the choppy swells leading to Georgia Strait.

Hours and Days of Operation: Weeklong seasonal packages and 3- to 9-day seminars and workshops offered year-round. Elderhostel and work-study programs also available.

Accommodations: Lodging for up to 70 in private single rooms with private baths on the beach; private single rooms with shared bath on the beach or forest or in the orchard cabin; double-occupancy cabins; shared rooms for 3–6 with choice of ocean or forest views. Men and women assigned to separate rooms. Tent space available; campground has bathhouse. Guests must bring own tents and bedding.

Rates: Vary according to lodging, program, and season. 7-day package in early spring $309–$659 for lodging, meals, one bodywork or skin care session, plus access to community events.

Credit Cards: MC, V.

Meal Plans: 3 gourmet vegetarian meals a day served buffet style. Seafood served twice a week; evening barbecues held once a week.

Services: Personal growth and spiritual workshops and seminars, virtual workshops, massage, aromatherapy, acupressure, Hellerwork, therapeutic bodywork, Breema massage, natural skin care, yoga, meditation.

Recreational Activities: Wilderness tours, walking, hiking, kayaking, sailing.

Facilities: Outdoor hot tub overlooking the ocean, orchard with sanctuary, sailboats, trails.

Staff: 65 total staff, including reiki master, aromatherapist, jin shin do therapist, acupuncturist, craniosacral therapist. All licensed and certified.

Special Notes: Smoking not allowed indoors. Guests must bring flashlights and warm rural clothing. A beach towel, rain gear, and all-terrain shoes recommended. Wheelchair access extremely limited.

Nearby Attractions: Hot Springs Cove; Easter Bluff; shopping, restaurants, and museums of Victoria; petroglyphs; waterfalls; lakes; old-growth forests.

Getting There: 175 miles north of Seattle, 150 kilometers north of Vancouver. Seaplanes fly directly to Cortes Island in summer.

Innsight Center for Wellness and Vision

RR 5, Site 26, Comp 39
Gibsons Landing, British Columbia, Canada V0N 1U0
(604) 885-7118; fax (604) 885-0608
E-mail: Beyond_20/20@Sunshine.net

In the early 1970s, Dr. Robert-Michael Kaplan suffered from double vision. As a result, he began to gather information on complementary methods to improve. Drawing on 25 disciplines from around the world, he discovered the exact formula to achieve his goal. While serving a 10-year tenure at Pacific University College of Optometry in Oregon, he clinically demonstrated that a 30 percent improvement in eyesight is possible in only 21 days. Kaplan and his partner, Lise, created the Beyond 20/20 Vision Fitness Programs to educate and assist individuals and health professionals through residential wellness programs, workshops, 10-day intensives, one-on-one sessions, and phone, fax, and e-mail consultations. The program uses natural methods for improving vision and developing healthy eyesight based on the theory that 90 percent of vision occurs in the brain. Kaplan himself is his own best advertising, as he no longer wears glasses and today his program provides services to 12 countries.

Innsight, the personal home of the Kaplans, is located on the sunshine coast in western Canada, about two hours northwest of Vancouver. Trees surround the three-quarter-acre lot where eagles are often spotted and the ocean is a one-kilometer walk down the road. The center provides a sanctuary in nature where personal growth and improved vision can occur. Healthy vegetarian food is served, and guests receive hands-on learning about food preparation. All rooms have full-spectrum lighting, natural untreated pine furniture, and down comforters. Guests meet daily with Dr. Kaplan for deep-healing sessions for the eyes and inner vision, and special eye-to-eye practices are taught. A reading of the iris is available, as are shiatsu eye massages, sauna, massage, bodywork, and detoxification programs.

Hours and Days of Operation: Office hours: Mon–Sat, 9–9, by appointment only. Weekend workshops and 10-day intensives offered year-round.
Accommodations: 2 double or 4 single rooms in the spacious 2-story home of Dr. Robert-Michael Kaplan.
Rates: $200 a day for lodging, meals, and 2 hours of personal consultations with Dr. Kaplan.
Credit Cards: MC, V.
Meal Plans: 3 meals a day, either vegetarian, macrobiotic, or Ayurvedic.
Services: Therapeutic bodywork, detoxification programs, cooking classes, personal healing sessions, iris readings.
Recreational Activities: Hiking, canoeing, kayaking.
Facilities: Sauna, fireplace, 5-foot trampoline.
Staff: Dr. Kaplan and wife, Lise Doiron-Kaplan.
Special Notes: Smoking not allowed.
Nearby Attractions: Pacific Rim National Forest, beaches, native museums.
Getting There: About 2 hours by car from Vancouver Airport. Transportation available to and from Langdale ferry.

Institute for Embodiment Training

RR 2
Cobble Hill, British Columbia, Canada V0R 1L0
(250) 743-5971 (phone/fax)
E-mail: embodtr@islandnet.com

Will Johnson, founder of the ten-year-old Institute for Embodiment Training, believes that through creating an awareness of the body, we can attain a state of being referred to in ancient spiritual literature. Johnson has practiced Buddhism since 1972 and studied with Ida Rolf and Emmett Hutchins at the Rolf Institute in 1976. He has also authored the books *Balance of Body, Balance of Mind* and *The Posture of Meditation*.

At a retreat center just 40 minutes north of Victoria, Johnson offers five-day programs, seminars, and workshops based on his belief that the body is a doorway, not an obstacle, to personal growth and spiritual transformation. The programs emphasize a body-oriented form of spiritual teaching and meditation practice. Each day, guests spend five hours with a private instructor learning to cultivate an awareness of the body as a united field of tactile sensations. Workshops typically include a combination of breathwork, meditation, Rolfing, aerobic exercise, gentle stretching, and improvisational dance.

The embodied state is best described as a condition of profound physical comfort, mental clarity, and inner calm. Training draws on several orientations of bodywork, psychotherapy, and spiritual practice. Based on the idea that the body "remembers" all experiences, when people are removed from the awareness of their bodies, they hold physical and emotional pain. Through patient observation, guests recognize what types of "holding patterns" they have created. Once they have attained embodiment—better described as the melding of the physical body with the universal divine—sounds, tastes, smells, tactile sensations, and thoughts are transformed into a state of total well-being.

What, then, is the disembodied state? Johnson prescribes a simple exercise of holding out the hand in a comfortable position to simply experience the subtle change of tactile sensations—cool air passing over the fingers or a certain tingling within the muscle fiber. Myofascial holding, or storing systematic patterns of tension in the fibers between the muscles to block out sensation, is one way people hold in, so to speak, the disembodied state. Another sign is the presence of a negative internal dialogue that speculates entirely about the past or the future. During the Embodiment Program, Johnson works to brings guests into the present, both physically and spiritually.

Hours and Days of Operation: Office hours: Mon–Fri, 10–5. Weekend workshops, 5-day programs, and 10-day professional training offered year-round.
Accommodations: Campsites available during professional training, weather permitting; otherwise, guests referred to a nearby bed-and-breakfast.
Rates: Vary according to program. Average $100 per day.
Credit Cards: None accepted.
Meal Plans: 3 vegetarian meals a day offered during professional training.
Services: Breathwork, meditation, Rolfing, mild aerobic exercise, gentle stretching, improvisational dance.
Facilities: Retreat center, workshop, meditation rooms.
Staff: In addition to Will Johnson, staff includes a licensed massage therapist and a psychotherapist.
Special Notes: Certification available in Embodiment Training. Smoking not allowed.
Nearby Attractions: Pacific Rim National Park, Gulf Islands.
Getting There: 45 minutes by car from Victoria International Airport.

Kootenay Tai Chi Summer Retreat

c/o Kootenay Tai Chi Centre
Box 566
Nelson, British Columbia, Canada V1L 5R3
(250) 352-3714 (phone/fax)

Set amid towering mountains and a pristine lake is Camp Koolaree, located in the southeast corner of British Columbia. Once a year, the camp hosts a Tai Chi Summer Retreat. For one week in August, campers learn the slow, graceful system of body-mind exercise that harmonize the body's functions, relaxes the mind, and improves health and vitality. Guests can camp under the brilliant stars or share a rustic cabin. Koolaree has access to a private beach, and the facilities include a kitchen, dining room, and large wooden lodge for fireside socializing and indoor classes. Rex Eastman, the lead instructor, has studied internal arts since 1969 and taught them since 1975. Eastman is recognized by the Chinese Tai Chi Chuan Association of Canada.

A typical day begins at 7 a.m. with qigong, intended to promote flexibility, breath control, and internal energy. Guests enjoy a well-balanced vegetarian breakfast at 8, followed by a weapons demonstration using a sword or a staff for intermediate and advanced groups. A forms demonstration at 10 teaches guests the principles and techniques of movement. The push-hands course at 11 is a two-person exercise teaching agility, self-defense, and sensitivity. The activities pause at noon for lunch and free time, providing the perfect chance to explore remote Canadian forests, canoe across serene inlets, or trek to the nearby hot springs for a relaxing soak. A second weapons class begins at 3, followed by a forms class for beginners. The applications class at 4 is designed to teach self-defense at intermediate and advanced levels. Guided meditation and philosophy is held before dinner, and afterward guests share experiences in a group discussion. Visiting instructors also host evening healing sessions and provide therapeutic bodywork.

Hours and Days of Operation: Camp offered once a year in August. The Kootenay Tai Chi Centre open year-round.
Accommodations: Shared rustic cabins and campsites. Guests supply own sleeping bag and air mattress.
Rates: 7-day camp $360.
Credit Cards: None accepted.
Meal Plans: 3 nutritionally balanced vegetarian meals a day.
Services: Daily tai chi lessons, qigong, meditation, group discussion, healing and bodywork sessions.
Recreational Activities: Swimming, canoeing.
Facilities: Lodge with fireplace, kitchen and dining area, private beach, hiking trails, nearby natural hot springs.
Staff: Rex Eastman and guest facilitators; licensed massage therapists.
Nearby Attractions: Big White Ski Area.
Getting There: Halfway between Vancouver and Calgary, Alberta, on Highway 3A.

Mountain Trek Fitness Retreat and Health Spa

Box 1352
Ainsworth Hot Springs, British Columbia, Canada V0G 1A0
(800) 661-5161 or (250) 229-5636 (phone/fax)
Web site: www.hiking.com

In Canada's Kootenay Mountains, 160 miles north of Spokane, 10,000-foot peaks are named after characters in Norse mythology. Experienced Mountain Trek guides take guests into the cracks and shadows of this alluring terrain and safely return them to a warm, crackling fire and the hands of a professional masseuse. Clear Alpine lakes, powerful jutting peaks, remote mineral springs, and dense evergreens add to the supernatural beauty of this remote mountain retreat. Programs provide healthy adventure, spiritual exploration, and alternative health vacations. This year's vacation schedule includes a Mountain Hiking Spa Vacation; a nature photography workshop; personal coaching for the body, mind, and spirit; and yogakinetics with Nateshvar.

The NaturesPath Center Natural Health Vacation is a facet of Mountain Trek providing supervised fasting, cleansing, and natural hygiene programs. The focus of the vacation is prevention and education, and fasting is emphasized as a nontoxic, natural healing technique that strengthens the systematic health of the whole body. The Basic Water Fasting Program includes round-the-clock supervision by a government-licensed naturopathic physician specializing in fasting and detoxification. A professional board of doctors and public interest members closely regulates the physician's performance in addition to regular inspections by the public health department. The program includes a private room and bath, use of all facilities, a daily self-health program, daily vital signs checkups by the naturopathic physician, health lectures, exercise and stretch classes, and food reintroduction at the end of the fast. Other cleanse programs include a juice fast, a five-day colonic cleanse, and a natural hygiene food program consisting of raw, whole foods.

Hours and Days of Operation: 3- to 7-night vacations offered year-round.

Accommodations: Up to 14 in single and double rooms in 2-story cedar lodge, with private bath, twin and queen-size beds.

Rates: Vary according to program. 7-night Natural Health Vacation $725 and includes lodging, meals, services.

Credit Cards: MC, V.

Meal Plans: 3 low-fat, high-carbohydrate meals a day, served buffet style. Vegetarian and vegan options available.

Services: Health examinations, massage, yoga, guided fasting, colonics, weight training, nature photography.

Recreational Activities: Guided hiking, snowshoeing, kayaking, biking.

Facilities: 34-acre estate with lodge, exercise equipment, full-service laundry room, sauna, outdoor hot tub, nearby hot springs.

Staff: 18 total staff, including 1 naturopathic doctor, 4 certified hiking guides, 5 registered massage therapists, 2 certified yoga instructors.

Special Notes: Guests must bring hiking boots.

Nearby Attractions: Hot springs, spelunking, fishing on 90-mile Kootenay Lake, 6 golf courses, horseback riding, kayaking.

Getting There: Halfway between Vancouver and Calgary, about 160 miles north of Spokane, Washington.

Salt Spring Centre

355 Blackburn Road
Salt Spring Island, British Columbia, Canada V8K 2B8
(250) 537-2326; fax (250) 537-2311
E-mail: ssc@raven.bc.ca

Since 1981, Salt Spring Centre has provided rest and rejuvenation weekends for women in addition to renting its facilities out to various organizations for seminars and retreats. This nonprofit center was inspired by the Indian monk Baba Hari Dass and operates on the philosophy of selfless service. Residents of the Salt Spring community, mostly women, aim to provide a nurturing environment for the pursuit of the creative arts and healing sciences—all within a context of spiritual growth. The Dharmasara Satsan Society, a group that adheres to the principles of ashtanga yoga, manages and maintains the center throughout the year.

On 69 acres of organic garden, orchards, yurt, and greenhouse, guests have a view of cedar forests, mountains, and wild meadows. A fully restored 80-year-old farmhouse houses about 20 guests who have access to a wood-fired sauna and hiking trails throughout the remote Pacific Northwest island. Occasionally, orcas are spotted migrating through the cold waters.

Therapeutic body treatments add to the appeal of Salt Spring. All therapists are trained in swedan, an Ayurvedic rejuvenating steam and bodywork session. Facials use ingredients from the organic garden and steams are scented with balsam. Ongoing yoga and tai chi classes are offered, as are retreats focusing on craniosacral therapy, zero balancing, therapeutic touch, and more. Women's weekends are scheduled throughout the year, as are two- and five-day "health holidays." The weekends typically consist of a choice of Ayurvedic swedan, massage or reflexology, two yoga classes, saunas, an herb walk, three nutrition sessions with hands-on cooking classes, five organic vegetarian meals, a slide show, videos, recipes, and educational handouts.

Hours and Days of Operation: Office hours: Mon–Fri, 10–4. Weekend and weeklong programs offered year-round.

Accommodations: Fully restored heritage 3-story farmhouse sleeps up to 20. Smaller cabin can sleep up to 5. During summer months, campsites with heated showers in a woodland campground. Limited number of private rooms available at an additional cost.

Rates: Vary according to program. 3-day Wellness Weekend, including lodging, meals, swedan or massage, reflexology, and facial, $300.

Credit Cards: MC, V.

Meal Plans: 3 organic vegetarian meals served buffet style. Vegan options available.

Services: Workshops on craniosacral therapy, zero balancing, therapeutic touch, Ayurvedic steam and bodywork, massage, reflexology, acupuncture, facials, yoga, tai chi, meditation, summer solstice celebration including art, drumming, song, dance.

Facilities: 69 acres with 3 seminar rooms, wood-fired saunas, greenhouse, organic gardens, orchard.

Staff: Licensed massage therapists, acupuncturists, aromatherapists, reflexologists, certified Ayurvedic swedan practitioners.

Special Notes: The national best-seller *Salt Spring Island Cooking: Vegetarian Recipes from the Salt Spring Centre* available through mail order. Smoking and alcohol not allowed on the premises.

Nearby Attractions: Artist's market in town on Saturday mornings, Butchart Gardens, shopping, dining and theater in Vancouver and Victoria, rain forests.

Getting There: Convenient ferry access available from Vancouver (Tsawwassen), Vancouver Island (Swartz Bay and Crofton), and Anacortes, Washington.

Self-Realization Meditation Healing Centre

736 Creekside Crescent, RR1 - S4 - C5
Gibsons Landing, British Columbia, Canada V0N 1V0
(604) 886-0898 (phone/fax)

Self-Realization Meditation Healing Centres can be found all over the world. Mata Yogananda and Peter Sevonanda founded the original center in Somerset, England, over 30 years ago with the goal of helping everyone overcome illness and stress in a supportive and loving environment. The centers were established to teach meditation as a means of tapping into the universal consciousness and consequently empowering individuals to create a life of health and happiness.

Workshops, courses, and several types of retreats are offered at the center and are particularly beneficial for people experiencing life changes, burn-out, and chronic physical illness. Natural spiritual healing and progressive counseling are used to bring the whole person into a state of balance, which results in a progressive improvement of the individual's ailment. Relaxation, healing, meditation, personal development, and silent retreats are among program choices.

All healing retreats are individually designed to meet the unique needs of each guest. Mornings usually start with meditation at 7 and a whole-foods vegetarian breakfast at 9. Healing treatments, personal counseling, or yoga begins at 10, followed by free time—considered essential for absorbing the healing treatments. Guests can walk along one of the many ocean and forest trails, read in a sitting room with a woodstove, or listen to music quietly. A light lunch is served at 1, and afterward guests learn relaxation techniques or participate in hatha yoga. Late afternoon is open for more free time, which could mean exploring the library or meditation room or relaxing in the garden overlooking the ocean. Guests gather for dinner at 6, and evening activities include yoga and meditation.

Hours and Days of Operation: 1- and 2-day and weeklong courses, workshops, and retreats, including meditation and professional healing training.

Accommodations: Warm, comfortable single and double rooms.

Rates: Prices vary. Typical healing or counseling session $40; full room and board can be $62.50 per night.

Credit Cards: None accepted.

Meal Plans: Home-cooked whole and vegetarian foods. All diets can be accommodated.

Services: Natural spiritual healing, counseling, hatha yoga, meditation, stress management, workshops, courses, healing and spiritual retreats.

Facilities: Library, meditation room, yoga room, guest sitting room with woodstove, organic garden, sundeck.

Staff: In addition to Mark and Alexandria Nunn (both Progressive Counselors), staff includes natural spiritual healers, workshop facilitators, holistic health therapists. Meditation teachers and professional healing instructors regularly visit from United Kingdom.

Special Notes: The center does not have special facilities for disabled people, nor can it care for patients requiring medical and nursing assistance.

Nearby Attractions: Ocean beaches, forest trails, Gulf Islands, mountains, small fishing village of Gibsons Landing.

Getting There: 45 minutes by ferry from Vancouver from Horseshoe Bay. Guests can arrange to be met at ferry.

Serenity by the Sea

225 Serenity Lane, Galiano Island, RR2 42-14
British Columbia, Canada V0N 1P0
(250) 539-2655 (phone/fax)
E-mail: serenity@gulfislands.com   Web site: www. serenitybythesea.com

Serenity by the Sea is more an effect than a name for this year-round haven perched on Galiano Island, located midway between Vancouver and Victoria in the Canadian Gulf Islands. In the surrounding woodlands and on remote beaches, guests can spot otters, mink, seals, and eagles. The goal of owners Shera Street and her husband, Amrit Chidakash, is to provide a casual and holistic approach in an intimate setting so guests can quickly feel "at home" and safe. Street and Chidakash, both artists and healers, facilitate most workshops. Both have experience in reiki, yoga, meditation, life transitions counseling, journal writing, Gestalt therapy, and mask making.

Though primarily a retreat specializing in stress release, emotional balancing, and creative self-discovery, individual programs are tailored to balance the mind, body, and spirit. Reiki, breathing awareness for stress management, daily yoga, and meditation are also offered. A network of healers is available on call to offer a variety of treatments, including craniosacral therapy, neurolinguistic programming, and psychic counseling.

A unique style of massage is available that focuses on the body, breath, and energy. Known as Expansive Body Integration, the technique was developed by Chidakash on the basis of his belief that stress and trauma result in contraction throughout the body. By creating space in the joints, where contractions tend to focus, the body can shed stress and begin the healing process. The massage focuses on using subtle stretches and pulsing rhythms to open joints and release energy blockages. The result is an expansive feeling of energy flowing throughout the whole body.

In addition to personal healing retreats, several programs are offered throughout the year at Serenity that aim mainly to foster creative self-discovery. Health, however, is often a fundamental aspect of the programs, as in the workshop For the Love of Touch, which explores the idea that touch and healing are as natural as breath. "We want to provide a space where contracted bodies, pressured emotions, and withdrawn spirits will expand naturally and heal themselves," says Chidakash. If space is what he wants to provide, he has certainly managed it with a cliffside hot tub; airy, light-filled rooms with ocean and garden views; and access to tremendous natural Northwest beauty through kayaking, sailing, and hiking.

Hours and Days of Operation: Personal retreats and 2- to 4-day workshops offered year-round.
Accommodations: 2 large rooms and 1 self-contained chalet.
Credit Cards: MC, V.
Meal Plans: Vegetarian breakfast, except in self-contained chalet.
Services: Bodywork, reiki, toning bowls, yoga, meditation, creative therapies.
Facilities: Multilevel lodge with cascading spiral steps down to the ocean, hot tub on cliff terrace overlooking ocean, hammocks.
Staff: Sheri Street, Amrit Chidakash, guest facilitators, including psychic counselors, craniosacral therapist, specialists in neurolinguistic programming.
Special Notes: Smoking allowed only in designated areas.
Nearby Attractions: Forest, creek, waterfall, shopping, dining, museum, theater in Victoria and Vancouver, rain forests.
Getting There: 1 hour by ferry from Swartz Bay (Victoria) or Tsawwassen (Vancouver). Retreat also accessible by public transportation and shuttle.

Sah Naji Kwe Wilderness Spa

Box 98
Rae, Northwest Territories, Canada X0E 0Y0
(867) 371-3144; fax (867) 371-3155
E-mail: xrabesca@ssimicro.com

There is something unusual about the Northwest Territories, as though the place were so cold and remote that no romantic name, like Belize or Indonesia, could be given to it. It's a land where indigenous tribes still have a strong sense of their own cultures and where survival depends on how well you've prepared for winter. Into this secluded climate comes Sah Naji Kwe Wilderness Spa, 600 miles above Edmonton, Alberta, beside Great Slave Lake. Though the area is between the boreal forest and the mixed taiga and tundra to the northeast, summers are still warm enough for guests to pack mud on their skin and sit drying in the sun.

Sah Naji Kwe is Dene for "Bear Healing Rock." The name refers to an ancient Precambrian Shield rock site located on the northern shore of the lake. The story goes that a spiritual offering given by a bear blessed the area with the power to heal. Whether it's the cleansing sweat lodge and spa environment sans alcohol and cigarettes or the fine white clay used in healing rituals, there's something good for the body and soul at this luxury camp.

Holistic living is emphasized during a stay at Sah Naji Kwe. Guests sleep under large sturdy tent frames covered by white canvas, each one heated by a woodstove. Days are left largely open for quiet introspection, hiking the boreal forest, picking berries, observing bald eagles and the aurora borealis, or canoeing through the many islands and shoals with an experienced guide. Planned options include women's retreats with traditional sweat lodge ceremonies and group discussions regarding the philosophies, knowledge, and traditions of indigenous peoples of the North.

Hours and Days of Operation: Workshops, women's retreats, personal retreats offered Jun–mid-Sep. Winter adventure groups available on request.

Accommodations: Tent-frame cabins covered by white canvas tents, heated by wood stoves.
Rates: In Canadian currency, $90–$180 per night; group packages $600–$2,800.
Credit Cards: JCB, MC, V.
Meal Plans: All meals included and include conventional chicken, pork, and beef dishes, and unusual specialties such as steamed whitefish, lake trout, marinated buffalo, moose roast, or caribou stew. Vegetarians can be accommodated; options include cranberry bannock, high-fiber rice and legume dishes, and homegrown herbs and root vegetables.
Services: Clay baths, sweat lodge ceremonies, therapeutic touch, group discussion, survival skills.
Recreational Activities: Swimming, snowshoeing, cross-country skiing, fishing.
Facilities: 9 tent frames with woodstoves, tables and chairs, showers, sauna, kitchen tent, several boats, canoes.
Staff: In addition to group facilitator, licensed and certified bodyworkers and massage therapists, as well as a breath integration specialist, booked on request.
Special Notes: Sheets, towels, and blankets provided, but winter adventure guests should bring sleeping bags during colder months. Guests who are sensitive to insect bites should bring bug spray.
Nearby Attractions: Boreal forest of the Mackenzie Lowland, Shield country and wildlife.
Getting There: 900 miles north of Edmonton; about 1 hour by car from Yellowknife.

Macrobiotics Canada Health and Healing Center

RR 3
Almonte, Ontario, Canada K0A 1A0
(613) 256-2665 or (613) 256-4985

For those who may be wondering exactly what are macrobiotics, Wayne Diotte, founder of Macrobiotics Canada Health and Healing Centers, has this reply: "It is a way of approaching life. Simply translated from the Greek, macrobiotics means 'great life.' Understanding and balancing the energy of our daily food relationships, environment, and activities is an enjoyable and rewarding focus of macrobiotics." Diotte's philosophy is to offer a larger view, a way of perceiving, pursuing, creating, and experiencing the best possible life full of energy, good humor, and adventure. "The spirit and essence of macrobiotic philosophy," adds Diotte, "is to use unifying principles to harmonize and unify the body, mind and spirit in order to create health, freedom and peace—first within our own being, then within our family, our society, and finally within our world community."

Over a day, a week, or longer, individually designed residential programs are offered at the center to facilitate natural healing and awaken participants to the richness of life. Programs can contain any combination of educational consultations, macrobiotic shiatsu, cooking classes, breathwork, issue-focused counseling, ginger compresses, do-ins, yoga, meditation, and pampering facials. Many physical health benefits are derived from the program. For example, in macrobiotic shiatsu, meridians are massaged by thumb, hand, elbow, or foot pressure with the resulting benefit of regulating and balancing the capacity of the organ systems. Ginger compresses—which consist of a topical application of fresh, hot ginger water—dispel cold, stimulate circulation, and assist in the breakdown of fat deposits. Do-In is a self-massage technique said to increase circulation and digestion and strengthen muscles, organs, and nerves. Breathwork involves one-on-one sessions that teach breathing techniques, aiding in the release of accumulated toxins within the tissues.

Evenings include group discussions, videos on the macrobiotic lifestyle by Michio Kushi, and entertainment provided by the more musical and theatrical guests. A picnic on the banks of a river is scheduled at least once during the conference, and a farewell brunch winds up the week's activities.

Hours and Days of Operation: Programs averaging 1 week offered year-round. All services by appointment.
Accommodations: Up to 40 guests in either shared rooms at a nearby conference center or an on-site 3-bedroom cottage or a 5-bedroom house. Limited number of campsites available.
Rates: $95–$395 per person, per day. Rates vary according to services.
Credit Cards: MC, V.
Meal Plans: 3 macrobiotic meals included with residential program.
Services: Health and dietary consultations, shiatsu, compresses, breathwork, palm healing, facials, yoga, meditation, counseling, cooking classes.
Facilities: 5-acre rural village with 3 hand-built wood-frame buildings, treatment and seminar rooms, 4 kitchens, organic gardens, walking trails, river.
Staff: 5 permanent staff; 3–7 student staff, depending on season.
Special Notes: Clients from around the world accommodated after the program through telephone, follow-up. Collaboration done on clients' behalf with medical professionals, chiropractors, naturopaths, various healers.
Nearby Attractions: Clear lakes and rivers, skiing, recreation areas. Downtown Ottawa's world-class museums and galleries.
Getting There: Pickup available from Ottawa's international airport.

Aqua Mer Centre de Thalassotherapie

868, Boulevard Perron
Carleton, Quebec, Canada G0C 1J0
(418) 364-7055; fax (418) 364-7351

Thalassotherapy was developed in the late 1800s by French biologist Rene Quinton, who initially demonstrated its therapeutic curative and preventive qualities. The Aqua Mer Centre, located in the heart of la Baie des Chaleurs, about five hours northeast of Montreal, is the closest thing to authentic French thalassotherapy on the North American continent. In addition to an indoor pool filled with warm seawater, all thalassotherapy treatments use water pumped directly from the Atlantic Ocean. The water is never stored; rather, it travels through a purifier and is warmed to 37 degrees Celsius before being splashed over guests. Algae, mud, and sand used in treatments are also gathered from the shore at low tide. Their rich biological and mineral elements help relieve arthritic and rheumatic aches and pain.

Various "cures" are offered at this 14-year-old restoration center, targeting specific health concerns such as backache, rheumatic pain, heavy legs, stress, and smoking cessation. Cures typically involve a prescribed regime of seawater hydrotherapy; rain, affusion, and Swiss showers; mud and algae wraps; and lymphatic drainage massage. Packages include lodging, meals, an activity program, a Monday-to-Friday thalassotherapy program, and five daily treatments, including those in the heated seawater pool.

Daily activities are designed to promote a gentle muscular awakening. As sea air is part of the cure, guests walk along the shore every morning and participate in guided stretches. For more exposure to seawater, sessions in the Aqua-Gym are available three times a day. Twice throughout the program, guests hike along mountain paths. A large part of the day is left open for fun or quiet rest. Bicycles and pedal boats are at the disposal of all guests, as

are excursions for golf, cruises, guided fishing tours, and regional summer theater.

Hours and Days of Operation: 6- and 7-night programs offered year-round. Day visitors allowed; 5-day "external" package includes meals.

Accommodations: 27 rooms in 3-story inn with private bath or shower, 2 single beds, bathrobe. Overflow lodging available in nearby Thermotel.

Rates: Vary according to lodging and program. Midsummer, 1-week residential cure $1,258.50–$1,521, depending on single or double occupancy and choice of room.

Credit Cards: AE, MC, V.

Meal Plans: 3 low-fat spa meals a day.

Services: Personal health and nutritional consultations, underwater shower, affusion shower, shiatsu, dry or rain massage, hydromassage, lymphatic drainage, localized mud applications, algotherapy, negative ionization, toning and moisturizing treatments, heavy legs treatment, oxygenation walks, guided mountain tours.

Facilities: Seawater hydrotherapy tub, aqua gym, thermal ball, sensibiliss, silent sun room, 3 tennis courts, pedal boats.

Staff: About 50 staff, including registered nurse, massage therapist, nutritional counselors, cosmetologists.

Special Notes: Sportswear and rain gear recommended. Guests should bring 2 swimsuits, beach towel, bathing cap, slippers.

Nearby Attractions: Shopping, churches, golf, tennis, snorkeling, sailboarding, guided mountain and deep-sea fishing tours, summer theater in Carleton, Mont Saint-Joseph, Miguasha fossil site.

Getting There: 5 hours by chartered coach from Montreal.

Ayurvedic Spa

196 Mountain Road
St. Etienne de Bolton, Quebec, Canada J0E 1P0
(888) 252-9642 or (514) 297-0258; fax (514) 297-3957
E-mail: Babaji@Generation.net

The five-year-old Ayurvedic Spa, just one hour and 15 minutes from Montreal's Dorval Airport, offers holistic health programs through the ancient Indian practice of Ayurveda. In Canada's secluded northeastern countryside, guests of the 40-acre Ayurvedic Spa have access to a private lake and panoramic mountaintop views.

The spa's founder, Gaetane Annai Govindan, is a therapist whose background includes training in polarity, therapeutic touch, energetic osteopathy, Chinese auriculotherapy, and focusing. After a near-death experience during a relatively minor surgical operation in 1983, Govindan was diagnosed with cancer. These dramatic experiences inspired her to pursue Tantrism, metaphysics, and Taoist yoga, a method of journeying within the body. Through these efforts, Govindan's cancer was cured, and she later studied at the Aluva Ayurvedic Hospital in Kerela, India.

An underlying emphasis is placed on rejuvenation, healing chronic illnesses, and reinforcing the immune system. The unique constitution of each guest is considered, and a well-rounded method of addressing the physical, emotional, mental, and spiritual is applied. Programs last from one to seven days and include traditional detoxification methods and instruction in diet, exercise, breathing, and meditation. Based on a personalized approach, the initial evaluation includes an examination of the pulse, eyes, and tongue. Depending on an individual's needs, detoxification, herbal oil massage, sauna, therapeutic whirlpool bathing, herbal supplements, and diet recommendations are prescribed. In addition to traditional Ayurveda, Govindan offers some of the healing modalities that underlie her professional background, such as energetic osteopathy and Chinese auriculotherapy.

Hours and Days of Operation: Office hours: 9–6, 7 days a week. 1- to 7-day personalized residential cures offered year-round.

Accommodations: Up to 32 can be accommodated in 11 rooms with private and shared bathrooms.

Rates: $300 per day, including lodging, meals, treatments.

Credit Cards: V.

Meal Plans: All meals consist of a diet designed to support the therapeutic regimen.

Services: Initial evaluation of pulse, eyes, and tongue; detoxification treatments; Ayurvedic oil massage; herbal steam baths; polarity therapy; energetic osteopathy; hands-on harmonization and Chinese auriculotherapy; herbal supplements.

Facilities: 40 acres with private lake, 2-story lodge, treatment center, whirlpool, sauna.

Staff: Dr. Gaetane Annai Govindan and assistant Pierre Audet, trained and certified at the Maharishi Ayurvedic Spa.

Special Notes: Smoking not allowed indoors. Facilities accessible for people with disabilities.

Nearby Attractions: Mount Orford; Lake Memphramagog; dining, theater, and nightlife in Montreal.

Getting There: 1 hour and 15 minutes by car from Montreal's Dorval Airport. Round-trip transportation can be arranged with advance notice.

Centre d'Sante d'Eastman

895, Chemin des Diligences
Eastman, Quebec, Canada J0E 1P0
(514) 297-3009; fax (514) 297-3370
Web site: www.spa-eastman.com

Since 1977, Centre d'Sante d'Eastman has offered award-winning antistress vacations. The center is located about one hour southeast of Montreal in the rolling countryside of the Eastern Townships. The bucolic estate provides guests with a stunning view of Mount Orford, and only 10 of its 300 acres are used for lodging and facilities. No more than 35 guests at a time stay at this former Quebecois farm in seven buildings spread out a couple of hundred feet apart. Despite its location in the heart of French-speaking Canada, all staff speak English. Horseback riding is offered year-round, and guests plunge into the swimming hole in the summer season. Although a terry cloth robe and comfortable rooms with private bath are an option, guests wanting complete seclusion can opt for a stay in l'Ermitage, a room with only running water, a woodstove, and an oil lamp.

Spa treatments are broken into categories, such as the Bodily Approach sessions, which include Feldenkrais, reflexology, and polarity therapy. Take Stock and Stock Up workshops are held every morning, and topics range from applied kinesiology to an introduction to focusing, self-healing techniques, and self-awareness through writing. The seven-night Health Relaxation Stay includes lodging, three gourmet vegetarian meals a day, a body peel with marine sediments, a full body wrap with essential oils, a full body wrap with algae, lymphatic draining, two hydromassage baths with algae or essential oils, two massages, a hydrotherapy massage, two oxygen and steam baths with essential oils, a facial, a pressotherapy session, two Take Stock and Stock Up sessions, three Bodily Approach sessions, three antistress walks, daily fitness walks, and six evening activities, such as sleigh rides, healthy diet secrets, or tai chi.

Hours and Days of Operation: 1- to 15-day packages offered year-round. Day spa services available.

Accommodations: Standard single and double rooms in main house and small hamlets. Some rooms have fireplaces and sitting rooms.

Rates: Vary according to room and package. À la carte treatments range between $18 and $70. Health getaways range between $540 and $1,180 including lodging, meals, and services.

Credit Cards: AE, MC, V.

Meal Plans: All meals included with residential programs and consist of 3 nutritionally balanced gourmet meals a day.

Services: Massage therapy, hydrotherapy, aromatherapy, reflexology, reiki, lymphatic manual drainage, algotherapy, fangotherapy, body exfoliation and wraps, pressotherapy, colonics, anticellulite treatments, salon services, fitness training, health consultations, psychological counseling.

Recreational Activities: Guided and solo nature walks, cross-country and downhill skiing, horseback riding, swimming, golf.

Facilities: 276-acre estate with 19 private rooms and 14 independent enclosures for spa treatments, vibromassage table, 2 oxygen baths, 2 professional bath units, 2 gazebos for outdoor massage.

Staff: 10 massage therapists, 6 aestheticians, naturopathic physician, psychologist, specialist in alignment education.

Special Notes: Smoking allowed only outside.

Nearby Attractions: Mount Orford; Theatre de la Marjolaine; theater, shopping, dining, and nightlife in Quebec City.

Getting There: About 1 hour by car south of Montreal.

Euro-Spa Centre Sante

455, de l'Eglise
St. Ignace de Stanbridge, Quebec, Canada J0J 1Y0
(800) 416-0666 or (514) 248-0666; fax (514) 248-0668

On the border of Quebec's Eastern Township lies Euro-Spa Centre Sante, a European-style health center. One of the largest of its kind in Canada, the center specializes in the three Rs: relaxation, rest, and regeneration. Guests relax in hydrotherapy baths scented with pine, melisse, rosemary, or wildflowers; rest at the country estate between cornfields and a dairy farm; and regenerate with mud, seaweed, or clay body wraps and therapeutic massage.

A typical day at the spa starts with a sumptuous breakfast. Since Euro-Spa is not a weight-loss clinic, guests can expect a plate heaped with pastries, fruits, cheeses, and fresh-baked bread. A hydrotherapy oxygen, mud, or herbal bath might follow a relaxing whirlpool and thermal tub soak. The package also includes access to the Turkish steam bath and Finnish dry sauna, exercise room, and relaxation room. Guests can then either explore the many walking paths through the woods or schedule a therapeutic massage. A health buffet is scheduled for noon, and dinner is served around the intimate Table d'Hotel.

Euro-Spa also offers Kneipp therapy, which combines healthy eating, exercise, sunlight, and adequate rest to combat the effects of an unhealthy lifestyle. Kneipp treatments also involve the practice of warm bathing with aromatic natural herbs. One treatment even entails coating the body with quark cheese to control inflammation.

Hours and Days of Operation: 2- to 7-day packages offered year-round.
Accommodations: 11 rooms with private bath and twin, double, queen, or king beds in modern wooden residential spa.
Rates: Vary according to package. 4-day package with 2 therapeutic treatments $585 and includes lodging, meals, use of spa.
Credit Cards: MC, V.

Meal Plans: All meals included. Choices include salads, seafood, pastries, cheeses, wild boar, venison, sirloin steak, mussel chowder, snails in puffed pastry. Breakfast and lunch buffet style, and dinner served at an evening table d'hote. Lighter choices include salmon, mahi-mahi, chicken.
Services: Various types of massage, including Swedish, lymphatic drainage, Californian, Tragger, and shiatsu; hydrotherapy with herbs, mud, or oxygen; seaweed, mud, and clay body wraps; reflexology; reiki; body peels; Kneipp treatments; salon services.
Recreational Activities: Nature walks, biking.
Facilities: Relaxation room, exercise room, dining room, 10 treatment rooms, Turkish steam room, Finnish dry sauna, indoor pool, outdoor pool with reflexology jets, tanning bed, tennis court, conference center.
Staff: About 20 total spa staff, including 10 massage therapists, 6 body wrap specialists, 2 aestheticians, Kneipp therapist. All licensed, experienced, certified.
Special Notes: Persons with topical skin conditions may be denied spa access. Guests are asked to bring 2 large towels, bathing suit, bathrobe, beach sandals.
Nearby Attractions: Antiquing at Au Fil du Temps in nearby Dunham; l'Orpailleur winery; Dietrich-Joss winery; Mississquoi Museum; sightseeing in Mystic, Frelighsburg, and Stanbridge East; annual duck festival; tennis.
Getting There: 1 hour by car from Montreal, on the border of Quebec's Eastern Townships.

Spa Concept Bromont

90, rue Stanstead
Bromont, Quebec, Canada J2L 1K6
(514) 534-2717; fax (514) 534-0599

Spa Concept Bromont is a health center located in the Chateau Bromont, just one hour from Montreal in the heart of Canada's Eastern Townships. Invigorating mountain air and halcyon countryside await guests at this center dedicated to revitalization. The chateau is equipped with an aerobics studio, gymnasium, indoor pool, and spa.

In addition to the standard spa services, Spa Concept offers some unique health treatments, like the chromotherapy session combined with chakra balancing. Chromotherapy involves the use of colored lights to cleanse, relax, and improve certain pathologies. It works well with chakra balancing, which targets seven specific energy centers throughout the body that receive, transmit, and distribute energy. Guests can also take a reenergizing nap on a natural futon composed of magnets that balance the yin and yang energies, as described in Eastern philosophy. Another unique treatment is the vibrosaun, a minimassage with heat, essential oils, and music therapy. The treatment works particularly well with people experiencing a high level of stress.

Packages begin with a lifestyle evaluation and energy-level test. On the basis of the results, the spa director will recommend a package appropriately balanced with exercise and health treatments. The five-night Total Well-Being Package includes a welcome reception; lodging; meals; four Finnish sauna and shower treatments; three hydrotherapy baths with either sea salt, algae, clay, mud, or essential oils; a vibrosaun treatment; a hydromassage; three massage therapy sessions; a facial with foot massage; an acupressure session; a hand and foot paraffin treatment; a body peel with sea salt; a body wrap; a reenergizing sleep; and five herbal tea pauses. Daily exercise classes are squeezed in between treatments. Choices include low-impact aerobics, aquafitness Jazzercise, and stretch-and-tone.

Hours and Days of Operation: Packages ranging from half a day to 5 days offered year-round. Spa hours Mon–Fri, 7 a.m.–9 p.m., Sat and Sun, 9–5.

Accommodations: 154 single and double standard rooms with queen-size beds in a country chateau. Option of smoking or nonsmoking room.

Rates: 5-night package including meals $1,449.

Credit Cards: AE, MC, V.

Meal Plans: 3 meals a day. Nutritionally balanced breakfast served buffet style; lunch is healthy spa cuisine; a low-calorie dinner served at the table d'hote.

Services: Lifestyle evaluations, energy testing, various types of massage, aromatherapy, reflexology, acupressure, polarity therapy, lymphatic drainage, colonics, algotherapy, balneotherapy, salt glow, herbal wrap, fango packs, body peel, facials, salon services, aquacise.

Recreational Activities: Volleyball, mountain biking, nearby downhill and cross-country skiing, horseback riding, hiking.

Facilities: Lodge with atrium, swimming pool, indoor and outdoor hot tub, men's and women's saunas, squash and racquetball courts, pool table, shuffleboard, horseshoes.

Staff: 35 spa employees, including 15 massotherapists, 8 aestheticians, 3 nurses. All certified with the Quebec Federation.

Special Notes: Some insurance receipts accepted for massage services.

Nearby Attractions: Water slide, golf courses, equestrian center, boutiques, and sightseeing tours in town of Bromont; nearby golf courses; aquatic park; bike trails.

Getting There: 1 hour by car from Dorval Airport in Montreal.

Other Healing Centers

Like all the centers in this book, the following centers offer various alternative healing modalities for a range of health concerns. However, most of these centers are outpatient clinics; as such, they do not provide accomodations, though some refer patients to nearby hotels. Also, while most of the other centers in the book focus on overall well-being, many of the below centers specialize in treating life-threatening illnesses, like cancer, AIDS, and heart disease, and other debilitating conditions, like arthritis, chronic fatigue, and environmental illness.

Abintra Wellness Center

438 NE 72nd
Seattle, WA 98115
(206) 522-9384

At the Abintra Wellness Center, patients can receive massage therapy, relaxation guidance, Trager psychophysical integration, or rebirthing treatments, or they can sweat out impurities in a sauna. The center also offers classes in touch for health, massage, reflexology, yoga, and self-healing through hypnosis.

Accent on Health

2290 10th Avenue
Lake Worth, FL 33461
(561) 547-2770

A variety of chronic illnesses are treated at Accent on Health, including various types of cancer, chronic fatigue, multiple sclerosis, and Parkinson's disease. Chelation therapy, nutritional counseling, and stress management techniques are among the methods used.

Advanced Integrative Medical Center

108-112 South Fourth Street
Darby, PA 19023
(610) 461-6225; fax (610) 583-3356

Dr. Lance Wright, medical director of the Advanced Integrative Medical Center, views the physician's role as teacher, healer, and catalyst to the patient's own inner healing system. At the center, services and programs promote detoxification and a healthy lifestyle through nutrition, exercise, and a healthy balance between mind, body, and spirit. Dr. Wright is also a professor of medicine and psychiatry at nearby Capitol University and a founding member of the American Holistic Medical Association. He treats degenerative diseases in addition to offering group discussion, meditation, health lectures, and educational programs.

Alegent Heart Health Institute

Immanuel Professional Center
6828 North 72nd Street, Suite 6100
Omaha, NE 68122-1799
(402) 572-2198; fax (402) 572-3281

The Alegent Heart Health Institute offers the Dean Ornish Program for Heart Disease Reversal. The three-year program starts with 12 weeks of cardiac care and education that provide the groundwork for lifestyle change and heart disease reversal. The program combines moderate aerobic exercise, stress management, nutritional education, and group support.

Alternative Medicine Center of Colorado
7601 East Burning Tree Drive, Suite 100
Franktown, CO 80016
(303) 688-1111; fax (303) 688-3706
Web site: www.naturesdoctors.com
Several chronic and life-threatening illnesses are treated at Alternative Medicine Center of Colorado, including cancer, multiple sclerosis, coronary vascular disease, arteriosclerosis, and rheumatoid arthritis. A stay of two to five days is recommended; because the center is an outpatient facility, the patient must make hotel arrangements.

American Metabolic Laboratories
1818 Sheridan Street, Suite 203
Hollywood, FL 33020
(954) 929-4895; fax (954) 929-4896
E-mail: apollo9@juno.com
AML specializes in the early diagnosis of cancer and other metabolic disorders. Treatments are based on the belief that the body is equipped with the divine knowledge of healing and repairing itself. Anti-aging treatments are also available.

Arizona Center for Health and Medicine
5055 North 32nd Street, Suite 200
Phoenix, AZ 85018
(602) 508-6850; fax (602) 406-0900
A sea-colored wall mural blends with desert pottery and sand tones to create a calming atmosphere at the Arizona Center for Health and Medicine. The center is part of the Mercy Healthcare Arizona's network of care and a subsidiary of Catholic Healthcare West, which has over 40 locations in California, Arizona, and Nevada. Health and medicine services treat the whole person using an integrated approach. Internal medicine, homeopathy, acupuncture, therapeutic massage, guided imagery, and tai chi are just a few of the complementary services offered. The center also maintains a close relationship with several national academic health institutions.

Ash Center for Comprehensive Medicine
800-A Fifth Avenue
New York, NY 10021-1216
(212) 758-3200; fax (212) 249-3805
Dr. Richard Ash is a leader in the field of environmental medicine, integrating the best of his alternative medical background with the most advanced technology. Treatments are designed to detoxify while replacing vitamin and mineral deficiencies and getting at the source of the problem rather than just treating symptoms. Dr. Ash has made numerous radio and television appearances, most recently on ABC's *World News Tonight*.

Atkins Center for Complementary Medicine
152 East 55th Street
New York, NY 10022
(212) 758-2110; fax (212) 754-4284
Dr. Robert Atkins is the author of *Dr. Atkins' Diet Revolution* and president of the Foundation for the Advancement of Innovative Medicine. He offers nutritionally based treatments for chronic degenerative diseases, including cancer of all types, chronic fatigue, asthma, allergies, and blood sugar disorders. Dr. Atkins also hosts *Design for Living*, a health-related talk radio show.

ATMA Group
185 North Redwood Drive, Suite 220
San Rafael, CA 94903
(415) 499-3319
A group of health care professionals trained in a broad spectrum of healing traditions, this family practice draws on the disciplines of alternative and conventional medicine, including internal medicine, psychotherapy, acupuncture, therapeutic bodywork, gynecology, and herbal medicine. Prevention and self-care are emphasized at the ATMA Group, and each patient is encouraged to attend group classes on a wide variety of health care topics in an effort to learn how to promote their own well-being.

Bastyr University
14500 Juanita Drive NE
Bothell, WA 98011
(425) 823-1300
Bastyr is one of the nation's leading naturopathic universities, offering professional, graduate, and undergraduate degree programs in naturopathic medicine, nutrition, acupuncture, oriental medicine, and applied behavioral science. The Bastyr acupuncture and health clinic is open to the public by appointment. Patients are seen by a team of upper-level students who are overseen by a senior staff doctor. Massage and therapeutic bodywork are also available.

Bio Medical Health Center
McCarran Quail Park
6490 South McCarran Boulevard, Suite C-24
Reno, NV 89509-6118
(702) 827-1444; fax (702) 827-2424
The Bio Medical Health Center provides a combination of nontoxic, biological medicine and traditional and natural health care. A variety of chronic degenerative diseases are treated, as are vascular and heart disease. Treatments include homeopathy, acupuncture, herbal medicine, chelation therapy, human growth hormone therapy, saline or saltwater injections, and others. Special lodging rates are available for chelation therapy patients at certain hotels in the area. Inquire for details.

Block Medical Center
1800 Sherman Avenue
Evanston, IL 60201
(847) 492-3040; fax (847) 492-3045

Dr. Block treats a wide range of health concerns, from prevention and lifestyle enhancement to life-threatening illnesses, including cancer. A wide variety of treatments are applied, depending on the patient's needs, including stress management techniques, massage therapy, acupuncture, and on-site chemotherapy with nutritional, botanical, and detoxification interventions to reduce side effects.

Buchholz Medical Group
1174 Castro Street, Suite 275
Mountain View, CA 94040
(415) 988-8011; fax (415) 988-8012
E-mail: drwnnb@pacbell.net
Bucholz offers comprehensive care for patients and families affected by cancer and blood disease. Dr. Bucholz is trained in internal medicine, hematology, and oncology. His staff includes a clinical psychologist, a medical doctor trained in traditional Chinese medicine, and an oncology nurse. The principles of Prajna (wisdom), Karuna (compassion), and Seva (service) underlie all treatments at Bucholz. Because education is an essential element of all treatments, classes addressing a variety of health concerns are offered throughout the year on topics like stress reduction, exercise, nutrition, understanding medications, and enhancing the immune system.

Burzynski Clinic
12000 Richmond Avenue
Houston, TX 77082
(713) 597-0111
Dr. Stanislaw Burzynski is dedicated to the Hippocratic ideal of "first do no harm." In his treatment of cancer and other disorders, Dr. Burzynski uses nontoxic and naturally occurring peptides and amino acid derivatives to restore cells instead of destroying them.

Carolina Center for Alternative and Nutritional Medicine
4505 Fair Meadow Lane, Suite 111
Raleigh, NC 27607
(800) 473-9812 or (919) 571-4391; fax (919) 571-8968
When the state of North Carolina added a statute allowing for holistic health care by a medical physician to include the right to explore all types of treatments, the Carolina Center was made possible. Treatments include oxidative therapies for the treatment of chronic immune disorders as well as herbal detoxification, vitamin therapy, lifestyle and nutritional counseling, herbal body wraps, and lymphatic massage. Though operating as an outpatient facility, the center accommodates long-distance patients through a temporary residential facility or through referrals to local hotels.

Center for Advanced Medicine
4403 Manchester Avenue, Suite 107
Encinitas, CA 92024
(760) 632-9042; fax (760) 632-0574
Dr. William Kellas, founder of the Center for Advanced Medicine, has authored *Thriving in a Toxic World* and *Surviving the Toxic Crisis*. Both books are based on the healing principles used at this southern California center, which opened nine years ago. The center's goal is to help patients

discover the root of their illness, and an integrated team of practitioners helps educate and advise each patient in the healing process. A medical "road map," known as the Five Steps to Illness, is used to trace the cause of illness and ascertain the best treatment plan.

Center for the Improvement of Human Functioning

3100 North Hillside Avenue
Wichita, KS 67219
(316) 682-3100; fax (316) 682-5054
Web site: www.brightspot.org
The center exists for people whose illnesses are not responding to standard medical approaches. In every case of chronic illness, multiple factors are examined to determine the cause of the illness. The center has evaluated and made treatment recommendations for people from all 50 states as well as 26 foreign countries.

Center for Natural Medicine, Inc.

1330 SE 39th Avenue
Portland, OR 97214
(503) 232-1100
The Center for Natural Medicine takes health care a step further into the realm of luxury. The center's HealthQuest Day Spa Menu provides a variety of therapeutic bodywork, aromatherapy soaks, cleansing herbal steam, and hydrotherapy. Staff include a naturopathic and a medical doctor, chiropractor, nurse practitioner, acupuncturist, colonic therapist, and licensed massage therapist. Health-related seminars, classes, and workshops are offered throughout the year, and the center boasts a full in-house kitchen for classes and demonstrations.

Center for Optimal Health

Bellegrove Professional Park
1545 116th Avenue NE, Suite 100
Bellevue, WA 98004-3813
(425) 451-9116 (call for fax number and e-mail address)
Dr. Ann McCombs is a board member of the American Holistic Medical Association who applies the pioneering approach of "nonprotocol" medicine in the treatment of a wide variety of chronic and degenerative diseases. "Nonprotocol" means that no two patients will receive the same treatment, as no two people are alike. Each patient receives a careful and in-depth evaluation to determine the best and most specific treatment to fit his or her needs. Treatments include preventive dentistry, detoxification, allergy elimination, neural therapy, intestinal hydrotherapy, psychokinesiology, hypnosis, body memory therapy, hands-on energy healing, medical intuitive readings, homeopathy, osteopathy, nutritional counseling, and naturopathy.

Center for Preventive Medicine and Dentistry

109-111 Bala Avenue
Bala Cynwid, PA 19004
(610) 667-2927; fax (610) 660-0616
Just a five-minute drive out of Philadelphia, the Center for Preventive Medicine and Dentistry has been treating patients for 25 years. Classical homeopathy, Ayurveda, and natural healing are the

methods used to treat a variety of chronic illnesses, including cancer, heart disease, arthritis, chronic fatigue, candida, and hypertension. Dr. Howard Posner is a medical doctor and certified homeopath.

Clinic in Integrative Medicine

University Medical Center, 6th Floor
Tucson, AZ 85821
(520) 694-6555

This is the famous Dr. Andrew Weil's training clinic. Though Dr. Weil no longer sees patients himself, he trains the staff of this clinic, which offers outpatient treatments for a variety of conditions, from chronic headaches to cancer. Treatments include acupuncture, osteopathy, and mind-body work. There is a three-year waiting list for new patients.

Commonweal

P.O. Box 316
Bolinas, CA 94924
(415) 868-0970; fax (415) 868-2230

The Commonweal Cancer Help Program is the nation's leader in helping people seek physical, emotional, and spiritual healing in the face of cancer. The Commonweal center is located on a 60-acre oceanside estate at the south entrance to the Point Reyes National Seashore, an hour north of San Francisco. The retreat is not intended to be cancer therapy or treatment. During the program, participants critically review a wide range of choices in established and complementary therapies. Commonweal also helps at-risk children, young people, and the professionals who work with them and supports the evolution of a global citizen awareness for an ecologically sustainable and socially just future.

Connecticut Center for Health

87 Bernie O'Rourke Drive
Middletown, CT 06457
(203) 347-8600; fax (860) 347-8434

A 12-page new patient questionnaire is the first indication that the Connecticut Center for Health provides an in-depth analysis of the root of illness. The center is a family practice offering natural solutions to a wide variety of health concerns, including mood swings, indigestion, chronic fatigue, stomach pain, and liver disease. Initial consultations are free.

Environmental Health Center–Dallas

8345 Walnut Hill Lane, Suite 205
Dallas, TX 75231
(214) 368-4132; fax (214) 691-8432

Since 1974, the Environmental Health Center–Dallas has been treating illness resulting from the various substances people are exposed to in the home and in the workplace. Symptoms of environmental illness include headaches, sinusitis, eczema, fatigue, asthma, bronchitis, arthritis, depression, and learning disorders; in children, it may include attention-deficit disorder. The center treats its patients in rooms constructed using advanced standards of indoor air quality and basic, natural materials. Services and treatments include lab testing, vaccine therapy, nutritional counseling, detoxification programs, saunas, osteopathic manipulation, acupuncture, and immune therapies.

Environmental and Preventive Health Center of Atlanta

3833 Rosewell Road, Suite 110
Atlanta, GA 30342-4432
(404) 841-0088; fax (404) 841-6416
Web site: www.ephca.com
The center specializes in the prevention of cancer and treats all forms of it, as well as other chronic diseases, including chronic fatigue, autism, Alzheimer's disease, multiple sclerosis, environmental illness, and others.

Florida Preventive Health Services, Inc.

4908-A Creekside Drive
Clearwater, FL 34620
(813) 573-3775; fax (813) 572-4489
Florida Preventive Health Services, Inc., specializes in alternative therapies for cancer, heart disease, and chronic pain as well as well women's care and the treatment and prevention of nutritionally related illness. An integrated approach is combined with medicine, nutrition, and alternative therapies such as acupuncture, herbal therapies, homeopathy, orthomolecular supplementation, and massage. Affiliated with the center is the Florida Institute of Health, which sponsors the talk radio show *Here's to Your Health.*

GenesisWest Research for Biological Medicine

P.O. Box 3460
Chula Vista, CA 91909-0004
(619) 429-7002; fax (619) 424-7593
Web site: www.cancertherapies.com
GenesisWest offers natural biological medicine in the treatment of cancer and other degenerative diseases. Technology is used to reveal the source of the problem, followed by an individually tailored program designed to correct imbalances. The motivating philosophy behind treatments is that disease has many causes and must be treated accordingly. Free weekend workshops are available to health care professionals, with last year's theme centering around the causes, prevention, and treatment of illness and disease.

Gerson Institute

P.O. Box 430
Bonita, CA 91908-0430
(619) 585-7600
E-mail: info@gerson.org
Web site: www.gerson.org
Dr. Max Gerson suffered from severe migraines and consequently experimented with diet to prevent them. His "migraine diet" cured his skin tuberculosis, which led him to further study of the healing power of diet. At the Gerson Institute, holistic and natural treatments are used to reactivate the immune system to help the body heal itself. The Gerson diet involves flooding the body with nutrients from almost 20 pounds a day of organic fruits and vegetables. Detoxification methods are also used to eliminate waste and regenerate the liver. Dr. Gerson successfully treated hundreds of patients before his death in 1959. His most famous patient was Dr. Albert Schweitzer, who was cured of diabetes at the age of 75 and went on to win the Nobel Peace Prize for his work in an African hospital.

Heart Disease Reversal Program of UCSF/CPMC
2330 Post Street, Suite 500
San Francisco, CA 94115
(415) 353-HART; fax (415) 885-3766
The Medical Center at the University of California, San Francisco and California Pacific Medical Center are collaborating with the renowned Dr. Dean Ornish to offer a program that can slow and sometimes reverse the progression of coronary heart disease. A select group of health care organizations around the country offers the three-year program, which starts with 12 weeks of cardiac care and education, providing the groundwork for lifestyle change and heart disease reversal. The program combines moderate aerobic exercise, stress management, nutritional education, and group support.

Heart Health Center
Mercy Hospital Medical Center
411 Laurel Street, Suite 1250
Des Moines, IA 50314
(515) 247-3145; fax (515) 248-8909
The Heart Health Center offers the Dean Ornish Program for Heart Disease Reversal. The three-year program starts with 12 weeks of cardiac care and education that provide the groundwork for lifestyle change and heart disease reversal. The program combines moderate aerobic exercise, stress management, nutritional education, and group support.

Hoffman Center
40 East 30th Street, 10th Floor
New York, NY 10016
(212) 779-1744; fax (212) 779-0891
Dr. Ronald Hoffman and staff offer a variety of complementary treatments for cancer, chronic fatigue, heart conditions, HIV, and other diseases at this Manhattan health care center. Chelation therapy, neural therapy, traditional Chinese medicine, and nutritional counseling are among a few of the healing methods used.

Holistic Medical Center
8264 Santa Monica Boulevard
Los Angeles, CA 90046
(213) 650-1789
The Holistic Medical Center offers a natural approach to health, drawing on a variety of complementary services such as chelation therapy, homeopathy, allergy desensitization, acupuncture, chiropractic, reflexology, colonic therapy, and massage.

Institute of Complementary Medicine
715 Route 10 East
Randolph, NJ 07869-2055
(973) 442-2320; fax (973) 442-2330
In affiliation with the Northwest Covenant Medical Center, the Institute of Complementary Medicine offers a variety of healing modalities to enhance and complement traditional medicine.

Courses in therapeutic touch and the health benefits of stress reduction are offered, as are various seminars. Seminar topics include yoga for all levels, introduction to meditation, working with healing energy, strengthening your health, stress management for cancer patients, and introduction to reflexology.

Livingston Foundation Medical Center

3232 Duke Street
San Diego, CA 92110
(619) 224-35156; fax (619) 224-6253
web: www.livingstonmedcentr.com

Dr. Virginia Livingston, founder of the medical center, is the author of *The Conquest of Cancer* and *Cancer: A New Breakthrough*. Established for people who are seeking alternative approaches for their health care needs, the center provides a ten-day comprehensive program designed for those suffering from an advanced, debilitating illness, such as lupus, arthritis, or cancer. In addition to the program, hundreds of patients are treated annually at the center on an outpatient basis.

Lost Horizon Health Awareness Center

P.O. Box 620550
Oviedo, FL 32762-0550
(407) 365-6681; fax (407) 365-1834

Dr. Roy Kupsinel uses a holistic approach to treat the whole person at the Lost Horizon Health Awareness Center. Treatments include chelation therapy, herbal supplements, exercise, and preventive medicine.

Magaziner Medical Center

1907 Greentree Road
Cherry Hill, NJ 08003
(609) 424-8222; fax (609) 424-2599

The Magaziner Medical Center provides comprehensive medical care for the prevention and treatment of chronic degenerative disease, including cancer, heart disease, arthritis, and multiple sclerosis. Dr. Allan Magaziner and staff strive to use safe, nontoxic therapies that emphasize lifestyle modification, healthy diet, and the use of vitamins, minerals, and herbs. Each patient undergoes a comprehensive evaluation to determine individual biochemistry to provide the recovery program most suited to his or her unique needs.

Marino Center for Progressive Health

2500 Massachusetts Avenue
Cambridge, MA 02140
(617) 661-6225; fax (617) 492-2002

The Marino Center offers a multidisciplinary blend of modern medicine, complementary therapies, health education, and prevention programs to promote health and inspire patients to pursue a healthy lifestyle. Healing modalities include the Progressive Stress Reduction Program, yoga therapy, traditional Chinese medicine, chelation therapy, massage, a dietary cleansing program, separate centers for men's and women's health, and more. Free health lectures are held every other Wednesday. Call to pre-register, as seating is limited. *Take Charge of Your Health*, a call-in talk radio show hosted by Dr. Alan Xenakis and Angela Bonin, can be heard Saturday from 4 to 6 p.m. on WRKO 680 AM.

Metabolic Associates

195 Columbia Turnpike
Florham, NJ 07932
(973) 377-7300

Dr. Michael Rothkopf and Dr. Kenneth Storch offer a nutritional approach to healing a variety of diseases. Both doctors are board-certified nutritionists and emphasize that the diet modification and nutritional support they recommend works in conjunction with—not in place of—the care a patient may be receiving from his or her doctor.

Natural Alternative Center, Inc.

310 West 72nd Street, 1G
New York, NY 10023
(212) 580-3333

The Natural Alternative Center, Inc., can claim Marla Maples as one of its satisfied patients. The center specializes in candida remedies, Epstein Barr protocols, parasite and worm removal, and malabsorption readings. Treatments include colonic therapy, oriental coneing, nutritional counseling, herbology consultations, detoxification programs, supervised juice fasting, acupuncture, iridology, shiatsu and Swedish massage, reflexology, and vitamin drips. Referrals for doctors, blood work, and lab reports available.

Natural Health Center

475 Los Coches Street
Milpitas, CA 95035
(408) 946-9332; fax (408) 946-9303

The Natural Health Center provides drug-free treatments for disease, injuries, and imbalances through acupuncture and herbal medicine. Dr. Sebastian Reyes studied in China for five years and has practiced acupuncture for over 20. He combines deep-tissue acupressure and massage with nutritional counseling, acupuncture, and herbal remedies. Dr. Robin Hayes is a licensed acupuncturist and was vice president of the California Acupuncture Association in 1995. She has been practicing in Milpitas since 1985.

Natural Medicine Clinic

213 Hywood Lane
Bolingbrook, IL 60440
(630) 378-0610

The Natural Medicine Clinic treats any illness, including cancer, with natural medicine. Treatments include nutritional and herbal medicine, qigong, and acupuncture.

The Nevada Clinic

3663 Pecos Mcleod
Las Vegas, NV 89121
(702) 732-1400; fax (702) 732-9661

The goal of the Nevada Clinic is to allow patients to regain good health and prevent future problems from occurring. A holistic approach is taken to evaluate each individual's condition. An initial examination includes an orientation film; electrodermal, blood, and urine tests; Kirlian photography; and in some cases a dental evaluation. Treatments include chelation therapy, acupuncture, chiropractic, noncognitive biofeedback, environmental medicine, and nutritional counseling.

New Center Clinic and Wholistic Health Center

The New Center for Health Education and Research
6801 Jericho Turnpike
Syosset, New York 11791-4413
(516) 364-0808
E-mail: newcenter@aol.com
Web site: www.newcenter.edu
The New Center Clinic and Wholistic Health Center, both facets of the New Center College, are well known for their work with arthritis, various forms of cancer, pediatrics, infertility, and muscular/skeletal problems. Over 3,500 people are treated per month at this 20-year-old integrated health care facility. Visits to the New Center Clinic are arranged by appointment, and patients are attended to by both a student and a clinic supervisor. Patients who wish to be treated by a licensed practitioner are referred to the Wholistic Health Center.

New Health Medical Center

23700 Edmonds Way
Edmonds, WA 98026
(206) 783-CURE; fax (206) 776-7119
Dr. Richard Kitaeff, a graduate from Meiji University of Oriental Medicine in Japan and founding member of the Northwest Institute of Acupuncture and Oriental Medicine, has been treating patients since 1975. The New Health Medical Center, which opened in 1981, provides a variety of healing modalities, including naturopathic medicine, acupuncture, massage, hydrotherapy, colonic irrigation, craniosacral therapy, homeopathy, Hellerwork, and spinal adjustments. The center is one of the oldest and largest in the Northwest and helped to introduce techniques and programs of acupuncture and European medical spas to the area.

Nirovi Pain Optimal Health Associates and the Whole Person Fertility Program

100 Remsen Street
Brooklyn, NY 11201
(800) 666-HEALTH or (718) 625-4802; fax (718) 875-3011
E-mail: niravi@aol.com
Nirovi Pain is a psychotherapist, biofeedback specialist, and author of the book *The Language of Fertility*. People interested in the Whole Person Fertility Program can obtain a referral roster of certified therapists.

Ojai Life Enhancement Center

537 East Ojai Avenue
Ojai, CA 93023
(805) 640-8080
The center offers a variety of complementary treatments, including a parasite elimination program, chelation therapy, colonic hydrotherapy, and massage.

Pain Rehabilitation Center

St. Helena Hospital
P.O. Box 399
Deer Park, CA 94575
(800) 358-9195 or (707) 963-6200; fax (707) 983-7239
This center was established in 1983 to help people with chronic pain learn to manage it more effectively and bring some quality back into their lives. A four-week multidisciplinary rehabilitation program involves a preliminary outpatient evaluation, a comprehensive medical evaluation, and a guided diagnostic test, when necessary. The preliminary evaluation determines whether it is right for each individual to go through the program as an inpatient or as a residential outpatient. Patients focus on how well they can be instead of how sick they have become.

Perlmutter Health Center

800 Goodlette Road North, Suite 270
Naples, FL 34102
(941) 649-7400; fax (941) 649-6370
The center deals with a variety of medical problems, including cancer, arthritis, high cholesterol, digestive disorders, asthma, chronic fatigue syndrome, allergies, fibromyalgia, environmental sensitivity, headaches, epilepsy, Parkinson's disease, Alzheimer's disease, multiple sclerosis, and others. Dr. Perlmutter is a board-certified neurologist with over 16 years of experience in his field. Acupuncture, Chinese herbal therapy, classical homeopathy, osteopathy, pain management, massage, craniosacral therapy, chelation therapy, and nutritional counseling are among the healing modalities used at the center.

Preventive Medical Center of Marin

25 Mitchell Boulevard, Suite 8
San Rafael, CA 94903
(415) 472-2343; fax (415) 472-7636
One of the only medical facilities offering a multidisciplinary approach to health problems in the Bay Area, Preventive Medical Center of Marin is run by founder Dr. Elson Haas, author of several books, including *The Detox Diet* and *Staying Healthy with the Seasons*. Created in 1984, the center offers nutritional and herbal therapies, detoxification practices, osteopathy and manipulation, acupuncture and Chinese herbal therapy, bodywork, and psychotherapy. Many types of medical problems are addressed—both acute and chronic illnesses—with a wide range of therapies. A key focus is to help individuals understand the origins of their concerns and to educate and inform them about the various treatment modalities.

Primary Prevention

5589 Greenwich Drive, Suite 175
Virginia Beach, VA 23462
(757) 490-9311; fax (757) 490-9266
Dr. Robert Nash, recently highlighted on the Christian Broadcasting Network for his work at Primary Prevention, blends both traditional and nontraditional medicine in treating a wide variety of chronic and degenerative diseases. Dr. Nash is a licensed acupuncturist and is board certified in neurology, pain medicine, and chelation therapy. "We take the time to get to know each patient, to know their goals and work with them to achieve that," says Nash. Chelation therapy, healing

touch, nutritional counseling, herbal medicine, acupuncture, and stress management are among the healing modalities used at the center.

Quan Yin Healing Arts Center
1748 Market Street, Suite 202
San Francisco, CA 94102
(415) 861-4964; fax (415) 861-0579
This downtown San Francisco nonprofit healing arts centers is dedicated to treatment, education, and research. Quan Yin is committed to offering high-quality, affordable Chinese medicine to the general public. The center promotes its healing philosophy on the local, national, and international levels. To encourage a woman-supportive environment, women-only space is available, and treatments are offered to HIV-positive women and those suffering from PMS or menopausal syndrome.

Reiki Healing Arts Center
7556 Roosevelt Way NE
Seattle, WA 98115
(206) 524-9277
Barbara McDaniel is a reiki master and co-founder of the Reiki/AIDS Project. Lynn Gebetsberger is a reiki master trained in clinical and administrative health care. Together, the two have 20-plus years of experience in the practice of the Usui system of reiki. Both were trained and initiated by the Grand Master Phyllis Furumoto, and both teach throughout the United States and Canada as active members of the Reiki Alliance, an international organization of reiki masters in the Usui system. Treatments and training are available through the center.

Revici Life Science Center, Inc.
200 West 57th Street, Suite 1205
New York, NY 10019
(212) 246-5122; fax (212) 246-1535
Dr. Emanuel Revici, author of *Research in Physiopathology as Basis of Guided Chemotherapy with Special Application to Cancer,* specializes in a nontoxic form of chemotherapy for cancer and other diseases, including AIDS.

Richland Memorial Hospital
Cardiac Ancillary Services
5 Richland Medical Park
Columbia, SC 29203
(803) 434-3852; fax (803) 434-2713
The Richland Memorial Hospital offers the Dean Ornish Program for Heart Disease Reversal. The three-year program starts with 12 weeks of cardiac care and education that provide the groundwork for lifestyle change and heart disease reversal. The program combines moderate aerobic exercise, stress management, nutritional education, and group support.

Ruscombe Mansion Community Health Center

4801 and 4803 Yellowwood Avenue
Baltimore, MD 21209
(410) 367-7300; fax (410) 367-1961
Ruscombe, which means "enclosed field," is a community health center founded in 1984 by Zoe and Bob Hieronimus, both of whom have talk radio shows exploring various aspects of holistic health and current phenomena. Over 30 health practitioners maintain private practices in the center. Services combine modern and ancient therapies, and clients are encouraged to try a number of therapeutic options. Classes, workshops, and occasional retreats are arranged by the practitioners, and a kitchen is occasionally open to serve vegetarian lunches.

Schachter Center for Complementary Medicine

Two Executive Boulevard, Suite 202
Suffern, New York 10901-4164
(914) 368-4700; fax (914) 368-4727
E-mail: office@mbschachter.com
Web site: www.mbschachter.com
The Schachter Center for Complementary Medicine uses a complementary approach to health care, emphasizing nutrition and preventive medicine. The center has been in business for over 20 years and maintains a full staff of doctors, nurses, lifestyle counselors, a homeopathic doctor, and an acupuncturist. Treatments include nutritional education, supplements, chelation therapy, bio-oxidative therapy, vitamin and mineral drips, and neural therapy.

Scripps

Shiley Sports and Center FC2
10820 North Torrey Pines Road
La Jolla, CA 92037
(619) 554-9282; fax (619) 554-4065
Scripps offers the Dean Ornish Program for Heart Disease Reversal. The three-year program starts with 12 weeks of cardiac care and education that provide the groundwork for lifestyle change and heart disease reversal. The program combines moderate aerobic exercise, stress management, nutritional education, and group support.

Shealy Institute for Comprehensive Health Care

1328 East Evergreen Street
Springfield, MO 65803-4400
(417) 865-5940; fax (417) 865-6111
The Shealy Institute is a nationally recognized rehabilitation facility that offers comprehensive outpatient and inpatient programs for pain, depression, and stress management. After working with thousands of patients since 1971, the institute has demonstrated that 85 percent of medical expenses go down after treatment in its multidisciplinary program. Treatments offered include individual counseling, massage, nutritional counseling, acupuncture, drug detoxification, Sarapin injections, smoking control, and musical vibration for deep relaxation.

Victoria Pain Clinic

365 Hector Road, RR 3
Victoria, British Columbia, Canada V8X 3X1
(250) 727-6250
(250) 656-4079
E-mail: vicpain@islandnet.com
Web site: www.vicpain.com

The Victoria Pain Clinic is a residential treatment center designed for people suffering from chronic pain and stress who have unsuccessfully attempted conventional therapies or who wish to explore alternatives to drugs or surgery. Started as an outpatient facility in 1980, the clinic encountered increasingly more severe cases that required intensive forms of treatment. In 1986, five residential accommodations were added, and the clinic now provides in-depth therapies and receives patients throughout Canada and the United States. Therapies offered include biofeedback/relaxation, postural reeducation, acupuncture, group and private counseling, remedial exercise and hydrotherapy, massage and deep-muscle work, visualization, and lectures.

Wellness Center

Broward General Medical Center
1625 Southeast Third Avenue
Fort Lauderdale, FL 33316
(954) 355-4888; fax (954) 355-4347

The Wellness Center offers the Dean Ornish Program for Heart Disease Reversal. The three-year program starts with 12 weeks of cardiac care and education that provide the groundwork for lifestyle change and heart disease reversal. The program combines moderate aerobic exercise, stress management, nutritional education, and group support.

Women to Women

3 Marina Road
Yarmouth, ME 04096
(207) 846-6163; fax (207) 846-6167
Web site: www.womentowomen.com

Located in a large and beautiful Victorian house, Women to Women has an integrated team of qualified and experienced physicians, nurse practitioners, and office staff. The focus is primarily on gynecology, obstetrics, internal medicine, surgery, and related women's issues as well as the 12-step model for recovery. It's so common for people to come in from out of town to this center that it provides a travel resources brochure for anyone interested. Dr. Christiane Northrup is a well-known lecturer and author whose most recent book is *Women's Bodies, Women's Wisdom.*

Resources

Alternative Health Benefit Services

P.O. Box 6279
Thousand Oaks, CA 91359
(805) 374-6003, ext. 515; fax (805) 379-1580
This company provides insurance coverage for alternative health services.

American Association of Naturopathic Physicians

601 Valley Street, Suite 105
Seattle, WA 98109
(206) 298-0126; fax (206) 298-0129
The association provides a list of naturopathic physicians throughout the United States.

American Holistic Medical Association–Headquarters

6728 Old McLean Village Drive
McLean, VA 22101
(703) 556-9245; fax (703) 556-8729
The association provides a list of holistic medical practitioners throughout the United States.

American Holistic Nurses' Association

P.O. Box 2130
Flagstaff, AZ 86003
(520) 526-2196; fax (520) 526-2752
Web site: www.ahna-membership@flaglink.com
The association provides a list of holistic nursing practitioners throughout the United States.

American Massage Therapy Association

820 Davis Street, Suite 100
Evanston, IL 60201-4444
(847) 864-0123; fax (847) 864-1178
Web site: www.amtamassage.org
The association provides referrals to state offices, which have lists of member practitioners.

Desert Institute of Healing Arts

639 North 6th Avenue
Tucson, AZ 85705
(800) 733-0898 or (520) 822-0899;
fax (520) 624-2996
Web site: www.fcinet.com/diha
The institute is a state-licensed educational facility offering training in massotherapy and Zen shiatsu. Introductory classes are available at no charge.

EverGreen Rooms by Hartford, Inc.

432 Landmark Drive
Wilmington, NC 28412
(800) 929-2626
EverGreen offers hotel rooms with fresh air, purified water, and invigorating showers with adjustable shower heads. Rooms, which are free of odors, dust, pollen, chlorine, and iron, are serviced on a regular basis. EverGreen is endorsed by Best Western International, Hampton Inns, and Embassy Suites. A list of "green" hotel rooms throughout the country is available on request.

Institute of Noetic Sciences

475 Gate Five Road, Suite 300
Sausalito, CA 94965
(415) 331-5650; fax (415) 331-5673
This nonprofit research, education, and membership organization is dedicated to the scientific study of consciousness, the mind, and human potential. Grants and global travel-study programs are available.

National Association for Holistic Aromatherapy

P.O. Box 17622
Boulder, CO 80308-7622
(888) ASK-NAHA or (314) 963-2071
fax (314) 963-4454
E-mail: info@naha.org

This nonprofit educational organization is devoted to aromatherapy. The association is a clearinghouse for information on aromatherapy and is not affiliated with any business interests. NAHA is dedicated to promoting aromatherapy as a healing modality throughout the United States through educational institutions, media, universities, and businesses.

National Center for Homeopathy

801 North Fairfax Street, Suite 306
Alexandria, VA 22314
703/548-7790
Web site: homeopathic.org
This organization provides a list of homeopathic practitioners throughout the United States and Canada.

National Women's Health Network

514 10th Street NW, Suite 400
Washington, DC 20004
(202) 347-1140; fax (202) 347-1168
For 20 years, the NWHN has been involved with women's health activism and education, addressing issues such as breast cancer, menopause, osteoporosis, health care and welfare reform, AIDS, and reproductive health. The network also serves as a clearinghouse, and information packets on a variety of health concerns are available for a fee.

Office of Alternative Medicine

National Institute of Health
P.O. Box 8218
Silver Spring, MD 20907-8218
(888) 644-6226
Web site: http://altmed.od.nih.gov
The OAM is a division of the National Institutes of Health. A clearinghouse was established by the OAM to collect and disseminate information on complementary, alternative, and unconventional medicine. Information is available on a variety of health concerns upon request.

Pacific Northwest Center for the Hawaiian Healing Arts and Massage

219 First Avenue South, Suite 405
Seattle, WA 98104
(206) 447-1895
The institute offers certification in a variety of traditional Hawaiian healing methods. A seven-day intensive is offered on the Big Island of Hawaii and includes instruction in Huna principles, LomiLomi, Hawaiian bodywork, and other traditional Hawaiian modalities.

Glossary

acupressure—An ancient Chinese system of healing that involves applying pressure to various meridians, or energy points, located throughout the body. Older than acupuncture, the technique is very similar to the natural response to hold a place in the body that may be aching, wounded, or tense. Acupressure is used to relieve tension-related ailments in preventive health care.

acupuncture—An ancient Chinese system of healing, very similar to acupressure, that involves pressing small needles into various meridians, or energy points, located throughout the body. These energy points can be compared to rivers that flow through the body to irrigate and nourish tissues. Obstructions in the flow of the "rivers" have the effect of a dam, restricting energy in one part of the body and causing backups in others. Through stimulating the meridians with needles, the obstructions are dissolved. Consequently, acupuncture can help the body's internal organs correct imbalances in energy production, digestion, and nutrient absorption.

Alexander technique—A system of bodywork developed in the late 1800s by Shakespearean actor F. M. Alexander, who discovered he could use his breath to change muscular responses. The technique is based on the practical study of the relationship between mind and body and is used to correct imbalances between the head and back. During sessions, a therapist uses gentle, noninvasive touch to increase the client's awareness, observation, and attention. Clients are also encouraged to observe the thought processes and tensions found within their daily lives.

applied kinesiology—The practice of determining health imbalances in organs and muscles through stimulating or relaxing specific muscle groups.

aromatherapy—Flower oil essences used to treat physical and emotional imbalances. The essences are either inhaled or used in massage oil, body wraps, and baths.

Ayurveda—An ancient Indian system of healing that involves determining the specific body type of an individual and then eliminating toxins and prescribing a balanced health regimen. Translated, "Ayurveda" means "science of life."

Bach flower essences—A system of healing developed by Dr. Edward Bach, a homeopath and physician. Dr. Bach created a system of 38 flower remedies designed to treat the person, not the ailment. The remedies address emotional imbalances that may block a positive state of mind, considered essential by Dr. Bach for healing.

balneotherapy—Any healing treatment that specifically involves immersion in baths, whether in ozonated whirlpools, geothermal and mineral springs, or ocean water.

bioenergetics—A form of psychotherapy developed by psychologist Alexander Lowen, author of *Language of the Body*. The technique places emphasis on grounding oneself, breathing properly, and understanding individual character structure. Deep breathing, massage, and bioenergetic (life energy) movements are used to help the patient develop self-awareness and restore vibrancy in body and life.

biofeedback—A system of healing that trains a person to change and control physical reactions to pain and stress. The technique involves using a computer monitor to display tension levels, through which patients learn muscle awareness and control. During sessions, clients learn postural training and techniques for muscle control. Biofeedback is used to treat a variety of chronic ailments, including stress, headaches, and asthma.

body wraps—A treatment that involves lathering the body with algae, clay, mud, or a botanical mixture and sealing in the mixture with heated towels or plastic sheets. The relaxing treatment is used to pull toxins from the body. In the case of herbal wraps, herb-soaked heated linens may be used.

boxercise—A physical exercise that combines a full-body aerobic workout with boxing techniques. Sessions usually involve stretching, punching and footwork, skipping rope, body toning, and abdominal work. Some forms emphasize particular movements, such as Savate-Boxe Française, which emphasizes striking with the toe of the shoe during a kick.

Breema massage—A method of bodywork imported from the small Kurdish village of Breemava, used to restore vitality through a standardized set of movements that express a connection with the Earth. During a Breema massage, the client lies fully clothed on a padded floor while a therapist performs a series of rhythmic movements. The technique is also used to increase physical health, balance energy, and release tension.

centropic integration—A body-focused approach to psychotherapy. The technique is based on the theory that unhealthy life experiences are stored in the body's tissues, often contributing to dysfunctional life patterns and disease. Each CI session lasts two hours and is broken into two phases. Phase 1 can include reviewing the patient's medical history, taking personal histories and histories of how the patient is facing current life situations, examining aspects of the individual's life that have the most meaning and depth of feeling, choosing a desired outcome of current situations, and understanding what the body is "telling" the mind. Phase 2 can involve sustained acupressure, listening to evocative music, breathwork, and verbal emotional facilitation.

chakras—Seven major energy points throughout the human body. The Root Chakra found at the base of the spine is white in color and represents the highest spiritual level. The Sex or Hara Chakra is purple and based in emotions and sexuality. The Solar Plexus Chakra is blue-violet or gold and based in personal power and metabolic energy. The Heart Chakra, considered to be the most important, is rose-pink and based in love, associations, relations, and compassion. The Throat Chakra is blue and based in communication and creativity. The Third Eye, or Brow Chakra, is green and based in intuition and imagination. The Crown Chakra is yellow and based in knowledge, information, and understanding.

chelation therapy—The injection of a solution containing ethylenediaminetetraacetic acid (EDTA), vitamins, and minerals to relieve the body of heavy metals picked up through the normal course of everyday living. EDTA is approved by the FDA to treat lead and heavy-metal toxicity, as evidenced by the U.S. Navy's use of chelation to treat lead poisoning.

chi nei tsang—A holistic approach to massage therapy developed by Chinese Taoist monks who used it to detoxify, strengthen, and refine their bodies. The technique integrates physical, mental, spiritual, and emotional aspects and addresses all the main vital systems—digestion, respiration, lymph, nervous, endocrine, urinary, reproductive, integumentary, muscular, and the acupuncture meridian system. Today, the practice is used to stimulate the immune system, provide deep detoxification of the body, and help overcome addictions. Practitioners focus mainly on the abdomen with deep and gentle touch to train internal organs to work more efficiently.

Chinese auriculotherapy—An acupuncture-related system of diagnosis and treatment that utilizes the outer ear, also known as the auricle. This modern technique saw a renewal in France in the 1950s, when Dr. Paul Nogier founded the French method. The Chinese then studied the French system and greatly expanded the technique. Auriculotherapy is used to determine food, drug, and other sensitivities as well as to treat addiction. It is also used to determine the need for vitamins, supplements, herbs, and medications.

Chinese medicine—An ancient system of healing dating back some 4,000 years that combines the use of herbs, diet, massage, therapeutic exercise, meditation, and acupuncture. The practitioner looks for patterns to indicate the source of an imbalance and considers the effects of personal and environmental factors on the individual's health. The Chinese system emphasizes prevention and the maintenance of optimal health, defined as the proper flow of chi, or qi, along the body's internal energy meridians.

chiropractic—A system of bodywork based on the idea that disease results from a lack of normal nerve function. The chiropractor tries to relieve stress and pressure on the nervous system by manually manipulating the spinal segments or individual vertebra. The technique is used to treat back pain, headaches, and general pain caused by injury or chronic disorders.

colonic therapy—An ancient method of healing based on the theory that a congested colon contains stagnant wastes that pollute the entire body. In most cases, a diet of whole foods is combined with a series of warm-water or herbal enemas to remove fecal waste.

craniosacral therapy—A system of bodywork used to treat mental and physical imbalances that is based on the idea that the body "remembers" emotional or physical trauma. Breathing exercises are combined with the gentle manipulation of skull and pelvic bones. The technique is ideal for injuries, traumas, and chronic pain but may also be used to enhance the body's general state of health.

cupping—Also known as "the horn method" in ancient China. The technique is used to draw blood to the surface to produce a counterirritant and stimulate chi. One or more small cups made of glass, metal, or wood are placed on a relatively flat body surface after a partial vacuum has been created in them through heat. The cups are left on the body for five to ten minutes.

Do-In—A self-help method of healing, otherwise known as self-acupressure massage, that incorporates body awareness, stretching, and breathing. Do-In focuses on vigorous techniques that stimulate the body's energy channels, or meridians.

electro-acuscope—A computer-controlled device designed to operate either as an independent unit or in conjunction with a personal computer. The machine, which has both diagnostic and treatment capabilities, is used in physical therapy, rehabilitation, and preventive medicine.

energy medicine—A diagnostic system of healing that employs a screening device to determine imbalances in the body's energy levels.

Enneagram—A nine-pointed, starlike figure believed to have originated with the ancient Sarmoun Brotherhood of Sufis, who used it as part of their mystical training. The figure represents the relationships among interacting elements of various personality patterns. Each pattern possesses a character that perceives the world and self in a fundamentally unique way and that has both a positive and a negative side. The points are as follows: (1) serenity or anger, (2) humility or pride, (3) truth or deceit, (4) equanimity or envy, (5) detachment or avarice, (6) courage or fear, (7) temperance or gluttony, (8) forbearance or lust, and (9) action or sloth.

ethnoherbology—A term coined by Lynne Ihlstrom, holistic psychotherapist and founder of Peaceways. Ethnoherbology involves the study of the edible and medicinal plants of a specific region, combined with a study of the cultures that used them and in which ways.

fango—A type of clay mud from the hot springs at Battaglio, Italy, used in body wraps and other external therapeutic applications.

fasting—Allows the body to rest from the digestion process and eliminate toxins. Fasting is recommended for a variety of symptoms, including colds and headaches. Anyone considering a fast should conduct extensive research or consult a physician.

Feldenkrais—A system of bodywork developed by Russian physicist Moshe Feldenkrais in the 1940s. The technique is based on the theory that the way an individual perceives him- or herself is central to the way he or she physically carries herself. Through gentle movement and directed attention, the client improves movement and enhances the overall function of body, spirit, and mind. Clients are encouraged to expand their self-image through movement sequences that bring attention to parts of the self that may ordinarily be left unnoticed.

fomentation (sometimes spelled "foomentation")—Involves applying hot moist substances, as with an herb-soaked linen cloth, to specific areas of the body to ease pain.

Gestalt—A therapy used by psychologists and counselors that emphasizes the inner experience of being and heightened sensory awareness through stimulus, perception, and response. "Now" is emphasized in Gestalt therapy, as evidenced by the fact that therapists do not focus on the client's past. Rather, the therapist deals directly with elements that comprise the "here and now." The client is encouraged to develop a more focused awareness and to fully experience and appreciate his or her complete self.

guided imagery—A process that involves relaxing the body muscle by muscle, concentrated breathing, and visualizing positive scenarios. Guided imagery is particularly useful for people prone to stress and anxiety.

harmonics—The study of the physical properties and characteristics of musical sound. Also, a curative method of chanting, developed and practiced by Tibetan monks, in which particular sounds are associated with specific physical energy centers.

Hellerwork—A system of bodywork developed by Joseph Heller, a student of the late Ida Rolf. The technique is designed to realign the body and release chronic tension and stress. It consists of a series of one-hour sessions of deep-tissue bodywork and movement re-education.

Verbal dialogue is used in addition to hands-on therapy to help the client become more aware of emotional stress and how it relates to physical tension. For example, a physical manifestation of depression may be a sunken chest.

holoenergetics—A psychotherapeutic form of energy healing that, literally translated, means "to heal with energy of the whole." The technique, developed by Dr. Leonard Laskow, author of *Healing with Love*, is based on five premises: (1) separation is an illusion, (2) to maintain this illusion requires energy, (3) physical or mental illness can result from consuming this energy, (4) release from illusion liberates energy, and (5) healing is the gradual result of eliminating the illusion of separation. Throughout the session, clients are encouraged to recognize the source of their illness, come to terms with the truth of this source, release it, replace dysfunctional patterns with healthy ones, and align their bodies with the positive life force within the universe.

holotropic breathwork—A self-exploration and healing technique developed by psychiatrist Dr. Stanislov Grof and his wife, Christina Grof, a transpersonal teacher. The word "holotropic" literally means "moving towards wholeness." The method is intended to activate a "nonordinary" state of consciousness in order to activate the psyche's innate healing potential. The technique involves sustained breathing and relaxation exercises, evocative music, focused energy work, and mandala drawing.

hydrotherapy—A system of bodywork that involves the external use of water, such as showers or mineral soaks. Treatments typically take place in a specially designed hydrotherapy tub equipped with 16 or more jets aimed at targeting the body's pressure points. It can also involve an underwater massage with a therapist manipulating a high-pressure hose. The treatment is particularly beneficial for people experiencing arthritis.

iridology—A diagnostic tool that involves close scrutiny of the iris to determine the patient's health, either through a special camera or through face-to-face examination.

jin shin jyutsu—A system of bodywork developed in Japan by Jiro Murai and based on the flow of qi, or life energy, throughout the body. Combinations of energy points are held for a minute or longer. Jin shin do and jin shin acupressure are slight variations of the original jin shin jyutsu.

journaling—The habit of regularly maintaining a journal, often recommended by counselors as a therapeutic tool. The benefits of journaling include increased creativity and the clarity to reflect on and grow from experiences.

kiatsu massage—An acupressure massage that utilizes life energy, or ki, also known as chi or qi.

Kneipp—Developed in Austria during the 1800s by Father Sebastian Kneipp, whose remedies recognize a natural lifestyle and emphasize the five basic elements of hydrotherapy, medicinal plants, diet, exercise, and lifestyle as a means to health. Father Kneipps's healing methods have evolved into the term "kneippism," which also indicates cold-warm-cold water stimulation.

kur—A series of spa treatments involving the use of natural ingredients and thermal baths received in combination with regenerating activities, which can include cultural history and the fine arts as well as health and wellness lectures.

LomiLomi—A system of bodywork based on ancient Hawaiian healing traditions. The therapist uses long broad strokes and rhythmical rocking techniques.

macrobiotics—The study of the natural laws of change for the purpose of life extension. Macrobiotic principles are thousands of years old, but George Ohsawa is the father of the modern-day practice. Ohsawa's teachings promote nutrition and healing based on the fundamental belief that humans are designed to be healthy. Through eating and living in as natural a way as possible, one becomes and remains well. "Natural" includes a diet based on grains and fresh vegetables that is free of over-processed foods.

marma point therapy—An Ayurvedic healing technique that involves applying medicated warm oil to specific points on the face that are key areas of circulation, otherwise known as marma points. The points are similar to the acupuncture points described in Chinese traditional medicine, but they are juncture points rather than points along a meridian. The facial points are massaged, then oil is spread across the entire face in broad strokes. Afterward, a heated towel is placed over the face. The technique is intended to release bodily toxins.

meditation—Literally hundreds of forms of meditation exist that cross all religious boundaries. In general, meditation involves focusing on a specific spoken or written idea for the purpose of bringing the mind's attention acutely into the present.

Moor mud—Mud taken from a 2,000-year-old Neydhardting Moor in Austria that contains more than 700 herbs and plants. The mud is used in baths, masks, soaps, and even in special mud drinks. The health spa adjacent to the Moor has a three-year waiting list.

moxabustion—A technique used to stimulate chi and characterized by the burning of a counterirritant, usually from dried leaves of the common mugwort or the wormwood tree. Moxas are attached to an acupuncture needle, then placed directly on the skin in the form of small cones. The cones can also be placed on a thin layer of ginger.

myotherapy—A technique used to relax muscle spasms, improve circulation, and alleviate pain. The method was developed by Bonnie Prudden, internationally recognized fitness and health pioneer and author of *Pain Erasure the Bonnie Prudden Way*. In myotherapy, pain is viewed as a valuable warning tool, particularly acute and chronic pain that is closely tied to emotional stress. Clients learn to seek out and diffuse trigger points within the muscles that are responsible for a variety of aches, pains, and disabilities. Exercises designed to re-educate the muscles are also a part of the therapy.

nature therapy—Relaxing activities in nature, including walking, swimming, mineral soaks, viewing wildlife, and gardening.

naturopathic medicine—A system of healing disease that emphasizes natural remedies and treating the whole person—physical, emotional, spiritual, and social. Naturopathic physicians look for the root cause of disease rather than treating symptoms. Nontoxic remedies are prescribed on the basis of the theory that "like treats like."

neural therapy—A system of healing that involves the injection of anesthetics to relieve short circuits in the body's electrical network. Neural therapy is used to treat a wide variety of chronic ailments.

neurolinguistic programming (NLP)—A system of healing that helps people recognize and change unconscious thought patterns and behavior to aid the overall healing process. It has been successful with a variety of chronic illnesses, including AIDS, cancer, migraines, and arthritis.

neuromuscular therapy—See trigger-point therapy.

Ohashiatsu—A method of centering touch developed by Ohashi, founder of the Ohashi Institute and author of several books, including *The Ohashi Bodywork Book*. The technique involves touch, exercise, meditation, and Eastern methods of healing that integrate mind, body, and spirit. Rather than focusing on specific acupuncture points, the therapist tries to sense and work with the overall flow of energy throughout the body and consequently balance it in order to activate the body's natural impulse to heal itself.

osteopathy—A system of healing based on the idea that disease is a result of structural imbalances in the tissues and that balance can be restored through the manipulation of specific areas of the body. Osteopathy treatments are supported by medicine, proper diet, and other therapies, which may include surgery.

par course—A walking trail equipped with several stations for exercise at various points.

permaculture—The term is a result of combining the words "permanent" and "agriculture." A Tasmanian by the name of Bill Mollison coined the phrase in 1972 as a result of having no other word to describe a system of agriculture that does not deplete the land or endure without constant human interaction. The goal of permaculture is to create sustainable human settlements. Permaculture principles are explained in Mollison's book *An Introduction to Permaculture.*

Pilates—A series of controlled movements that engage both body and mind, developed by physical trainer Joseph Pilates in the 1920s. The method focuses on improved flexibility and strength without building bulk.

polarity therapy—A system of bodywork develop by Dr. Randolph Stone, who believed that illness resulted from energy blockages. Polarity combines the manipulations of pressure points, massage, hydrotherapy, breathing exercises, and reflexology.

pre- and perinatal psychology—Counseling that involves the examination of time spent in the womb, during labor, in delivery, and up to a few days afterward. Regressive techniques, such as hypnosis or breathwork, are used to look at the emotions, behavior, defense mechanisms, and attitudes, both positive and negative, that may result from these experiences.

pressotherapy—A system of bodywork generally used in rehabilitation therapy designed to gradually and progressively drain metabolic waste and facilitate cell regeneration. The technique involves the use of hand massage and the application of varying degrees of pressure.

psychosynthesis—Developed by Italian psychiatrist Roberto Assagioli in 1910. The term implies the process of growth and the integration of previously separate elements into a more unified whole. The technique is based on the belief that every human being has an enormous potential that largely goes unrecognized or unused. Psychosynthesis also maintains that the individual possesses the inner wisdom and knowledge of what is necessary for life processes at any given time. During sessions, a guide helps the individual identify inner resources, supports the process, and is attentive to what is happening.

qigong—An ancient Chinese system of healing that combines the use of breathing, meditation, and movement exercises to increase vital energy, boost immune functions, and improve circulation. Qigong has a variety of spellings, including *chi kung.*

rebirthing—Through a combination of breath exercises, meditation, and in some cases therapeutic bodywork, a counselor guides the patient back to a deep unconscious level to relive the experience of birth. During a rebirthing session, many people remember details about their birth. From these details, they learn how decisions made at birth and in early childhood have affected their life and relationships. The technique is intended to dissolve tension and stress in the body while integrating the body and mind into a rejuvenated sense of awareness.

reflexology—A system of bodywork based on the idea that the feet and hands are maps of the entire body. Pressure is applied to nerve endings in the feet and hands to relieve chronic pain and stress.

reiki—Literally translated from the Japanese, *reiki* means "universal life energy," which is similar to that of the Chinese *chi* and the Indian *prana* or *kundalini.* Reiki is a hands-on method of healing that involves a practitioner laying hands on the body to realign energies.

Rolfing—A system of bodywork, also known as structural integration, developed by the late Ida Rolf. Rolf was inspired by the method her osteopathic doctor used to successfully treat her for a kick from a horse. Rolf was also heavily influenced by hatha yoga and developed the Rolfing technique based on the idea that the body structure influences mental and physical processes. The method is a process of re-educating the body through movement and touch. It is intended to release patterns of stress and impaired function through lengthening and opening the patterns in the body's connective tissue, otherwise known as the myofascial system.

Rubenfeld synergy—A method of healing designed to integrate body, mind, emotions, and spirit developed by Ilana Rubenfeld, eminent healer and pioneer in the field of mind-body medicine. The technique is based on the theory that memories, emotions, and deep yearnings are stored in the body and can result in psychospiritual imbalances. Rubenfeld integrated the techniques of F. M. Alexander and Moshe Feldenkrais with Gestalt practice and Ericksonian hypnotherapy to create a method of compassionate and "listening" touch that opens doors to recognizing and expressing feelings. The method includes body-mind exercises to relax, stretch, and enhance awareness.

salt glow—An exfoliation and cleansing treatment that involves lathering the body with moist salt grains.

shamanism—A religious practice found in many indigenous cultures that can involve attributing conscious life to natural objects, a belief in spirits separate from our bodies, and the idea that immaterial forces inhabit the universe. A shaman mediates between the visible and spirit worlds for divination, healing, and controlling events.

shiatsu—A Japanese system of bodywork that involves applying finger pressure to specific points throughout the body for a period of three to ten seconds. The technique is used to "awaken" energy meridians throughout the body to relieve pain and prevent illness.

somatoemotional release—Physical, energetic, and verbal support used in conjunction with craniosacral therapy to help empower the client to identify emotional or physical trauma and find a positive solution.

tai chi—An ancient Chinese method of movement, sometimes described as the physical expression of the principles of Taoism. Movements are intended to connect body and mind.

Thai massage—A 2,500-year-old system of bodywork that implements the techniques of stimulating pressure points, joint movement, and muscle stretching. The client lies fully clothed on a floor mat as a therapist increases the range of motion and flexibility through gently rocking the body and applying rhythmic acupressure combined with yogalike stretching.

thalassotherapy—Developed in the late 1800s by French biologist Rene Quinton, who initially demonstrated its therapeutic curative and preventive qualities. Authentic thalassotherapy treatments use water pumped directly from the ocean. Algae, mud, and sand used in treatments are also gathered from the shore at low tide. Fresh sea air is also a part of the cure.

therapeutic massage—A system of bodywork useful in controlling pain that targets specific areas of the body to correct posture, release toxins, and eliminate headaches and stress.

therapeutic touch—A system of bodywork developed in 1972 by Dora Kunz, past president of the Theosophical Society in America. Hands rarely touch the body during the treatment, with practitioners using slow, rhythmic hand movements between two and six inches away from the body to locate and release energy blockages.

Trager—A system of bodywork developed in the late 1920s by a medical doctor. Trager involves gentle and rhythmic manipulation, movement exercises, and movement re-education.

trigger-point therapy—Also known as neuromuscular therapy. A method of deep-tissue massage therapy developed by Togi Kinnaman, president and founder of the Colorado Institute of Massage Therapy. The technique is intended to release stress through specific and sensitive hand movements and relaxation and self-care techniques. Through the use of a charting system, the therapist recognizes and locates stress/trigger points in the muscular system. The points are tender spots or bands of excess muscle tension located within muscle groups.

tui na Chinese bodywork therapy—A 2,000-year-old system of bodywork that uses traditional Chinese medical theory concerning the flow of qi through the body's meridians as its basic therapeutic orientation. The method includes hand techniques to massage the muscles and tendons, acupressure techniques to directly affect the flow of qi, and manipulation techniques to realign the musculoskeletal and ligament relationships. Herbal poultices, compresses, liniments, and salves are also used to enhance the therapeutic effects.

vibrational healing—Also known as energy healing. A healing technique that utilizes the vibrations of gemstones and crystals to heal injuries or wounds, improve stress, and balance the body's natural energy systems (meridians and chakras). Gems and minerals can be taken orally or applied externally. Flower essences, color healing, and affirmations may also be used in vibrational healing.

Vichy shower—A large rectangular showerhead situated above a massage table equipped with several jets aimed at specific areas of the body.

Watsu—An in-water form of massage developed by Harold Dull, director of Harbin Hot Springs in Middletown, California. The treatment involves cradling, pulling, stretching, and applying pressure to "energy centers," described in the Taoist creation myth.

yoga—A system of exercises based on Hindu philosophy rooted in the idea that the progressive discipline of the body will lead to a connection with the universal spirit, self-liberation, and well-being.

zero balancing—A form of bodywork developed by Dr. Fritz Frederick Smith that includes both structural and energetic balancing. Gentle holding and applied traction are used to stimulate energy flow through the body's structure to balance and relax the client and to make him or her feel more alert, open, and centered.

zero-point process—A psychospiritual development course offered through the Tree of Life Rejuvenation Center that examines methods for dissolving dysfunctional habits, beliefs, and identities. The process blends ancient and modern Eastern and Western philosophies of mind and spirit.

Index by Healing Center

Index by State and Province

United States

Alabama

Arizona

California

Colorado

Connecticut

Florida

Canada

Index by Therapy Type

This index is organized first by general services and then by state or province. Certain specific services do not appear because they are considered part of a broader category of services; for example, yoga and tai chi are both classified under Movement Therapy. Keep in mind that some of the centers listed may offer an in-depth approach to the method while others may offer only a partial aspect of it. For example, the Maharishi Ayur-Veda Health Center provides a thorough immersion in Ayurvedic treatments, whereas the Grand Wailea simply offers Ayurvedic massage. The therapies offered by these centers do change from time to time, so it is a good idea to ask about current offerings. For definitions of the various therapies covered, see the glossary on page 190.

Ayurveda

This category includes any combination of ancient Indian healing practices, including pulse diagnosis, marma point therapy, panchakarma detoxification treatments, diet recommendations, meditation, herbal steams, body scrubs, and oil massage.

Bioenergetics

California
Vega Study Center, 33

Wyoming
Antelope Retreat and Education Center, 152

Biofeedback

Arizona
Association for Research and Enlightenment (A.R.E.), 4
Canyon Ranch, 5
Phoenix Program, 9

Colorado
Peaks at Telluride, The, 45

Indiana
Lomax Wellness Center and Retreat, 72

Maine
Healing of Persons Exceptional (H.O.P.E.) and
    Interface Integrative Health Services, 75

Massachusetts
Canyon Ranch in the Berkshires, 78

Ohio
Beechwold Natural Clinic, 116

Pennsylvania
Himalayan Institute, 121

Breathwork

California
Chopra Center for Well-Being, 14
Quantum Shift, 30
STAR Foundation, 32
Vega Study Center, 33

Florida
Hippocrates Health Institute, 50

Hawaii
Angel's Nest of Mother Maui, 57

Kalani Oceanside Retreat, 66

Maine
Northern Pines Health Resort, 76

Michigan
Song of the Morning, 85

New Hampshire
HealthQuest Clinics and Resorts, 92

New York
Abode of the Message, 100
Healing Tao USA, 104
New York Open Center, Inc., 106
Omega Institute for Holistic Studies, 107
Omega in the Caribbean, 108

North Carolina
Pavillon International Retreat and Renewal Center, 114
Spirit Journeys, 115

Pennsylvania
Kirkridge Retreat and Study Center, 122

Puerto Rico
Ann Wigmore Institute, 123

Texas
Eupsychia, Inc., 130

Washington
Camp Indralaya, 142
Sacred Healing, Sacred Retreats, 145
Trillium Retreat Center, 146

Wisconsin
Christine Center, 150

British Columbia
Haven by the Sea, 156
Institute for Embodiment Training, 160

Ontario
Macrobiotics Canada Health and Healing Center, 167

Chinese Medicine

This category includes any combination of acupressure, acupuncture, Chinese auriculotherapy, the use of herbs, diet, massage, therapeutic exercise, meditation, and other techniques as practiced by the ancient Chinese healers.

Chiropractic

Colonic Therapy

Craniosacral Therapy

Arizona
Association for Research and Enlightenment (A.R.E.), 4
Canyon Ranch, 5
Centre for Well-Being at the Phoenician, 6
Merritt Center, 7
Miraval, Life in Balance Resort and Spa, 8

California
Esalen Institute, 15

Hawaii
Hale Akua Shangri-La Bed and Breakfast Health
     Retreat, 62

Massachusetts
Canyon Ranch in the Berkshires, 78

Michigan
Song of the Morning, 85

Missouri
Wholistic Life Center, 89

New Mexico
Light Institute of Galisteo, 95
Vista Clara Ranch, 99

Oregon
Breitenbush Hot Springs and Retreat, 118

Washington
Annapurna Inn and Retreat Center, 140
Pacific Center for Naturopathic Medicine, 144

West Virginia
Coolfont Resort and Wellness Spa, 147

British Columbia
Salt Spring Centre, 163

Quebec
Centre d'Sante d'Eastman, 170

Detoxification
*This category includes any combination of fasting, juic-
ing, colonics, body treatments, and herbal remedies.*

Arizona
Association for Research and Enlightenment (A.R.E.), 4
Centre for Well-Being at the Phoenician, 6
Tree of Life Rejuvenation Center, 12

California
Maharishi Ayur-Veda Medical Center, 25
Optimum Health Institute of San Diego, 28
We Care Holistic Health Center, 35
Weimar Institute, 36

Colorado
Earth Rites, Inc., 39
Eden Valley Lifestyle Center, 40
Global Fitness Adventures, 41
HealthQuarters Lodge, 42
Peaceways, 44
Rocky Mountain Ayurveda Health Retreat, 46

Florida
Fit for Life Health Resort and Spa, 49
Hippocrates Health Institute, 50

Georgia
Atlanta Center for Chronic Disorders, 53

Hawaii
Anuhea Health Retreat, 58
Hawaiian Wellness Holiday, 63
Kalani Oceanside Retreat, 66

Illinois
Chicago Center for Chronic Disorders, 70

Indiana
Lomax Wellness Center and Retreat, 72

Iowa
Raj, The, 73

Kentucky
Foxhollow Life Enrichment and Healing Center, 74

Maine
Northern Pines Health Resort, 76
Poland Spring Health Institute, 77

Massachusetts
Maharishi Ayur-Veda Health Center, 25

Guided Imagery

Homeopathic Medicine, Naturopathic Medicine, and Herbal Remedies

Jin Shin

This category includes Jin Shin Do, Jin Shin Jyutsu, and Jin Shin acupressure.

Arizona
Canyon Ranch, 5
Miraval, Life in Balance Resort and Spa, 8
Centre for Well-Being at the Phoenician, 6
Phoenix Program, 9
Reevis Mountain School and Sanctuary, 10

California
Heartwood Institute, 20
Mendocino Summer Camp, 26

Maine
Healing of Persons Exceptional (H.O.P.E.) and
    Interface Integrative Health Services, 75

Massachusetts
Canyon Ranch in the Berkshires, 78

New York
Abode of the Message, 100

Wisconsin
Christine Center, 150

Macrobiotics

California
George Ohsawa Macrobiotic Foundation, 16
Health Classic, 19
Mendocino Summer Camp, 26
Vega Study Center, 33

Massachusetts
Kushi Institute of the Berkshires, 79

Massage

This category includes general therapeutic massage as well as reflexology, aromatherapy, acupressure, Alexander technique, Ayurvedic, Feldenkrais, kiatsu, LomiLomi, myotherapy, Rolfing, shiatsu, sports, Swedish, Trager, Hellerwork, and Watsu.

Alabama
Uchee Pines Institute, 3

Arizona
Association for Research and Enlightenment (A.R.E.), 4
Canyon Ranch, 5
Centre for Well-Being at the Phoenician, 6
Merritt Center, 7
Miraval, Life in Balance Resort and Spa, 8
Phoenix Program, 9
Tree of Life Rejuvenation Center, 12
Sound Listening and Learning Center, 11

California
Chopra Center for Well-Being, 14
Esalen Institute, 15
George Ohsawa Macrobiotic Foundation, 16
Harbin Hot Springs, 17
Health Action—Institute for Self-Initiated Healing at
    the Maes Center for Natural Health Care, 18
Health Classic, 19
Heartwood Institute, 20
Land of Medicine Buddha, 24
Maharishi Ayur-Veda Medical Center, 25
Mendocino Summer Camp, 26
Mount Madonna Center, 27
Optimum Health Institute of San Diego, 28
Preventive Medicine Research Institute, 29
Redwood River Lodge, 31
STAR Foundation, 32
Vega Study Center, 33
Vichy Springs Resort, 34
Wilbur Hot Springs, 38
We Care Holistic Health Center, 35
Weimar Institute, 36
Well Within, 37

Colorado
Eden Valley Lifestyle Center, 40
Global Fitness Adventures, 41
HealthQuarters Lodge, 42
Lodge and Spa at Cordillera, The, 43
Peaceways, 44
Peaks at Telluride, The, 45
Rocky Mountain Ayurveda Health Retreat, 46

Connecticut
Norwich Inn and Spa, 47

Medical Profile

Meditation

Movement Therapy

This category includes any combination of movement therapies, such as yoga, tai chi, and gentle therapeutic exercise combining stretches and breathwork.

Nature Therapy
This category includes walking, hiking, boating, skiing, and outdoor adventures in invigorating natural environments.

Neuro-Linguistic Programming

Nutritional Counseling

Polarity Therapy

Relaxation Skills and Stress Management Techniques

Qigong

Shamanic Practices and Native American Ceremonies

Spa Services

This category includes any combination of body wraps, fango packs, salt glows, aromatherapy, facials, manicures, pedicures, waxing, and other salon services.

Vibrational Healing

Alabama
Hawkwind Earth Renewal Cooperative, 2

Arizona
Canyon Ranch, 5
Tree of Life Rejuvenation Center, 12

California
Health Classic, 19
We Care Holistic Health Center, 35
Well Within, 37

Colorado
Peaks at Telluride, The, 45

Florida
Dreamtime Cruises, 48

Hawaii
Hale Akua Shangri-La Bed and Breakfast Health
    Retreat, 62
Hawaiian Wellness Holiday, 63

Maine
Healing of Persons Exceptional (H.O.P.E.) and
    Interface Integrative Health Services, 75

Massachusetts
Canyon Ranch in the Berkshires, 78

Michigan
Song of the Morning, 85

New York
Abode of the Message, 100

North Carolina
Spirit Journeys, 115

Oregon
Breitenbush Hot Springs and Retreat, 118

Washington
Sacred Healing, Sacred Retreats, 145

Quebec
Spa Concept Bromont

Water Therapies

Alabama
Uchee Pines Institute, 3

Arizona
Association for Research and Enlightenment (A.R.E.), 4
Canyon Ranch, 5
Centre for Well-Being at the Phoenician, 6
Miraval, Life in Balance Resort and Spa, 8
Tree of Life Rejuvenation Center, 12

California
Harbin Hot Springs, 17
Preventive Medicine Research Institute, 29
Redwood River Lodge, 31
Vega Study Center, 33
Vichy Springs Resort, 34
We Care Holistic Health Center, 35
Weimar Institute, 36
Wilbur Hot Springs, 38

Colorado
Eden Valley Lifestyle Center, 40
Lodge and Spa at Cordillera, The, 43
Peaks at Telluride, The, 45
Rocky Mountain Ayurveda Health Retreat, 46

Connecticut
Norwich Inn and Spa, 47

Florida
Fit for Life Health Resort and Spa, 49
Hippocrates Health Institute, 50
PGA National Resort and Spa, 51

Georgia
Spa at Chateau Elan, The, 55
Wildwood Lifestyle Center and Hospital, 56

Hawaii
Anuhea Health Retreat, 58
Grand Wailea Resort Hotel and Spa, 61
Hale Akua Shangri-La Bed and Breakfast Health
    Retreat, 62
Hono Hu'Aka Tropical Plantation, 64
Kalani Oceanside Retreat, 66
Mana Le'a Gardens, 68